REGIONAL
INTEGRATION AND COOPERATION
IN WEST AFRICA

REGIONAL INTEGRATION AND COOPERATION IN WEST AFRICA

A Multidimensional Perspective

Edited by
Réal Lavergne

Africa World Press, Inc.

P.O. Box 1892
Trenton, NJ 08607

P.O. Box 48
Asmara, ERITREA

INTERNATIONAL DEVELOPMENT RESEARCH CENTRE
Ottawa • Cairo • Dakar • Johannesburg • Montevideo • Nairobi • New Delhi • Singapore

Africa World Press, Inc.

P.O. Box 1892
Trenton, NJ 08607

P.O. Box 48
Asmara, ERITREA

 IDRC INTERNATIONAL
DEVELOPMENT
RESEARCH CENTRE
PO Box 8500
Ottawa, Canada
CANADA K1G 3H9

Cover Design: Jonathan Gullery

Library of Congress Cataloging-in-Publication Data

Regional integration and cooperation in West Africa : a
    multidimensional perspective / edited by Réal Lavergne.
        p. cm.
    Includes bibliographical references and index.
    ISBN 0-86543-566-9 (cloth). -- ISBN 0-86543-567-7 (paper : alk.
paper)
       1. Africa. West-- Economic integration. 2. African cooperation.
I. Lavergne, Réal P.
HC1000.R427   1997
337. 1'66--dc21   97-4957
                                         CIP

CONTENTS

PREFACE

Most West African countries are very small, not only in population, but also in terms of economic output. Only three countries (Nigeria, Ghana, and Côte d'Ivoire) have populations over 10 million; the others have national products equal to that of small cities or medium-sized towns in industrial countries. Nigeria stands out among the rest, with a population of over 100 million, but low income levels make even Nigeria a fairly small country in economic terms.

Development requires the organization of social and economic activity on a much larger scale than this. Increased scale brings with it opportunities for a wide range of benefits associated with lower unit costs of production, increased specialization and competition, access to a wider range of technology, and greater sharing of ideas and experience in all areas of endeavour. Country size is not the sole consideration, however. A large country that is weakly integrated internally due to poor infrastructure, ethnic rivalries, or sociopolitical factors may provide fewer opportunities for development than a smaller country that is well integrated. Size may be a secondary consideration for countries able to maintain close links to other countries at the regional or international level.

West African countries today are weakly integrated nationally, regionally, and internationally. Ethnic and sociopolitical divisions are particularly significant in certain countries, like Liberia, Sierra Leone, and Nigeria, and all countries in the region suffer from weak transport and communications infrastructure and other impediments to socio-economic integration at the national level. Regionally, West African countries are divided by a wide range of institutional, legal, and infrastructural barriers. At the international level, Africa is increasingly marginalized from world markets, from technology and communications networks, and from the world community in general.

Efforts are required on all these fronts. The sense of disconnectedness in Africa is strong, and Africans are searching for new forms of community able to overcome some of the development challenges of today's fast-changing world. Disillusionment with the nation-state as an agent of development at the national level in African countries, combined with Africans' fear of being absorbed into a world outside its control, lead to regional integration and cooperation as an important focus of attention in this search for community.

Prospects for integration into world markets under better conditions seem limited in many respects due to the weakness of world markets for traditional West African exports and the underdeveloped industrial base of these countries. Regional integration and cooperation afford an intermediate solution. Although regional integration is sometimes advocated, even today, as a substitute for links with the rest of the world, increased openness to world markets and regional integration are increasingly being seen as complementary aspects of a multipronged development strategy of reduced isolation.

The first half of the 1990s witnessed a remarkable growth of interest in regional integration and cooperation everywhere in Africa. There have been numerous conferences and seminars on the topic, and substantial efforts have been made on several fronts. The adoption of a revised treaty for the Economic Community of West African States in 1993 and the creation of the Union économique et monétaire ouest-africaine in 1994 were major events in West Africa. Other favourable changes have included substantial progress in the reduction of trade barriers through generalized trade policy reform, currency devaluation, including that of the CFA franc and the increased commitment of donors to promoting regional cooperation and integration.

This volume is a contribution of the International Development Research Centre (IDRC) toward sustaining the momentum. It represents the last installment of a program of activities launched in 1991. The aim was to mobilize scholars from a wide range of disciplines to share their reflections on issues of regional integration and cooperation in West Africa, by critically reviewing the experience of the past and exploring alternatives for the future. The program began with a series of national seminars held in Abidjan, Accra, Dakar, Lagos, and Ouagadougou and was followed by the organization of the International Conference on Regional Integration in West Africa, in Dakar in January 1993. Proceedings from that conference were published separately, while work proceeded on the papers represented in this volume.

Regional integration is not just an economic issue; the approach adopted in this volume is a multidimensional one in which integration is seen as a process of community-building or social construction, not limited to the expansion of regional trade. Also noteworthy is the relatively broad approach taken by most of the authors in treating various aspects of the problem. Their papers are not lacking in disciplinary focus, because the authors focus on topics of interest from their particular perspective, but each has viewed the problem on its own merits, in uncloistered fashion. The authors have attempted to bridge disciplinary divides by making each paper as accessible as possible to decision-makers and professionals from other disciplines. The overall perspective on regional integration which results is a relatively holistic one, accessible to a wide audience.

ACKNOWLEDGMENTS

Producing this volume was a collective endeavour involving numerous institutions and individuals. I thank each one of them for their contribution. Special mention must be made of IDRC's regional director of the time, Pierre Sané, and Professor Boubacar Barry, of Cheikh Anta Diop University in Dakar, who launched the initiative. The key collaborating institutions included those who hosted the national seminars and others who contributed financially or materially to the organization of the international conference.

The national seminars were hosted by the Centre Ivoirien de Recherches Économiques et Sociales, the University of Ghana, IDRC's regional office in Dakar, the Nigerian Institute of International Affairs, and the Centre d'Études, de Documentation, de Recherches Économiques et Sociales in Ouagadougou. Contributing institutions for the International Conference included the Canadian International Development Agency, the Ford Foundation, the Regional Integration Promotion Unit for West and Central Africa (CINERGIE), the Council for the Development of Social and Economic Research in Africa (CODESRIA), and the Banque centrale des États de l'Afrique de l'Ouest.

Other institutions collaborated through their participation in the Scientific Committee. These included the Association of African Women for Research on Development, the African Centre for Monetary Studies, CODESRIA, the African Institute for Economic Development and Planning, the African Regional Centre of Technology, the Institut sénégalais de recherches agricoles, and Cheikh Anta Diop University.

Collaborators in the production of this volume included Ousmane Badiane, Jean Coussy, Amady Dieng, and Jeggan Senghor, who provided advice and comments on the papers to be included in the volume; Robert Showman and Emmanuel Mensah, who contributed to the translation into English of the papers by Adotevi, Bach, Bourenane, and Debailleul et al.; Momar-Coumba Diop, Catherine Daffé, Magatte Guèye, Penda Guèye, and Amy Barboza, who assisted in the editing, indexing and layout; Sandra Garland, who did the copy editing; and Esther Beaudry, Bill Carman, and Michèle Wilson, who helped to marshal the necessary resources.

Heartfelt thanks are due to all, including the many unnamed individuals who made institutional collaboration on the project a reality.

CHAPTER 1

INTRODUCTION: REFLECTIONS ON AN AGENDA FOR REGIONAL INTEGRATION AND COOPERATION IN WEST AFRICA

– Réal Lavergne –

WORK ON THIS VOLUME began with the Dakar Conference on Regional Integration in West Africa, of January 1993, whose proceedings are summarized by Diop and Lavergne (1994). Of the 40 papers presented at that conference, 11 are included here in revised form. Four new papers have been added,[1] in addition to this introductory chapter, to fill gaps and provide a rounded picture of what regional integration is and could be in West Africa. Some gaps inevitably remain, and attention will be drawn to them in this chapter by referring the reader to work available elsewhere or in progress in specific fields such as agriculture, health, education, communications, and regional security.

We begin this chapter by reviewing the major "strategic visions" or perspectives represented in the first part of the volume. The rest of the chapter provides an overview of specific issues and options. We look at two broad areas: issues having to do predominantly with economic integration, including trade policy, monetary integration and sectoral policy issues; and those having to do with the role of the public sector, including the provision of regional infrastructure, regional cooperation in the provision of public services, and selected issues of a governmental character (protection of human rights, regional security and natural resource management). We then address the sovereignty issue, looking at alternative approaches for achieving regional objectives through shared sovereignty, regional cooperation, or unilateral action, before offering some suggestions for future research and some concluding comments.

Some conceptual clarification may be useful before going on to better appreciate the differences between four major concepts: those of

---

[1] Bourenane, Mytelka, Stryker *et al.*, and Lavergne and Daddieh (chapters 3, 6, 7 and 10).

regionalism, regional integration, regional cooperation and economic integration. The concept of "regionalism" does not require much elaboration. We take it to represent a regional approach to problem solving including regional integration, regional cooperation or both. The terms "regional integration" and "regional cooperation" have in common the involvement of neighbouring countries in collaborative ventures. However, regional cooperation implies that this is organized on an ad hoc and temporary basis through contractual arrangements of some sort, around projects of mutual interest, while regional integration involves something more permanent (Bourenane*).[2]

Most of the discussion in this volume bears on regional integration, characterized by the establishment of joint institutional mechanisms, and a degree of shared sovereignty. As many of the authors in this volume point out, existing regional integration schemes in Africa function in an "intergovernmental" rather than "supranational" mode, and the actual sharing of sovereignty is minimal (Ntumba*). However, member states do accept certain obligations, such as the payment of dues, the reduction of trade barriers, the reduction of barriers to the free movement of people, etc.

The concept of regional integration takes on a predominantly economic slant in the literature, to the point of confusion with that of "economic" integration. However, it should not be viewed exclusively in such terms. Regional integration can cover the full range of public-sector activity, including not only the coordination of economic policies, but also regional security, human rights, education, health, research and technology, and natural resource management. The concept of regional integration is thus a broader one than that of economic integration. The expression "economic integration" can be used in different ways. As Bourenane* points out, it can be used generically in reference to growing economic ties among countries which may or may not be geographically contiguous — linkages between Africa and Europe, for example. However, the authors in this volume usually use the term more restrictively to refer to increased trade and factor flows between neighboring countries, as a result of trade liberalization or the coordination of economic policies.

---

[2] Starred items (*) refer to chapters in this volume.

Visions and priorities

The revival of interest in regional integration and cooperation is a world-wide phenomenon, inspired by the success of the European experience. It also reflects a growing appreciation of the benefits to be derived from regional unity and cooperation in meeting the challenges posed by increasingly competitive world markets (Mytelka*). One often speaks of the "new regionalism" (De Melo and Panagariya 1992; CEC 1992). In Africa, regional unity is seen as a possible solution to the continent's deep and prolonged economic and social crisis, at a time when private energies are being released thanks to the strengthening of civil society and the deregulation and privatization of national economies, while the continuing decline of state-imposed barriers to intercountry flows is paving the way for increased regional trade (World Bank 1994, pp. 62–76, 230–231).

Regional aspirations as shared by West African statesmen, intellectuals, and citizens alike reflect a general desire to break the confines of the nation-state, and a denial of all that divides the region, including the multiple barriers to the free movement of goods and services, people, and capital among countries, and differences in legal, governmental, and educational structures. West Africans are aware that the kingdoms and cultures of West Africa were relatively well integrated in precolonial times, as accounts of the region amply attest (Oliver and Atmore 1981a,b), and the quest for regional unity is in many respects a search for one's roots (Adotevi*). These regional aspirations also constitute a response to the manifest incapacity of the state to generate development. They thus include a search for solutions extending beyond what existing nation-states appear capable of providing, including better regional infrastructure, better management of the region's resources (Olomola 1993; Debailleul et al.*), and even a broader range of freedoms (Quashigah*; Adewoye*).

This search for new solutions also has its centripetal side, not only in Africa, but worldwide, in the growing demands of communities and private citizens for greater control over their own affairs. The manifestation of this is clear in calls for greater decentralization of government and public services, greater community participation in decision-making, and withdrawal of the state from certain types of intervention in the economy. The state in West Africa is thus being assailed from both directions: it is called upon to share power with lower levels of government and other social entities *and* with regional bodies. These pressures are not contradictory, and do not amount to a negation of the state, but clearly the day has passed when the nation-state is expected to be all things to all people, from policeman to ultimate provider. The objective is for each level of government to provide such services and functions as it can supply most efficiently and effectively, and it is for the better application of such a principle that the peoples of West Africa seem to be striving.

Because of its holistic and multidimensional coverage of the issues, the Dakar conference provided a useful gauge of evolving views on regional integration and cooperation, while confirming the attachment of African intellectuals to the regional ideal (Diop and Lavergne 1994).[3] However conference participants noted the failures of past efforts, and some of the key papers analyzing the reasons for such failures are represented in this volume (Bundu*; Bach*; and Ntumba*). Bourenane* and Lavergne and Daddieh* help to complete the picture by reviewing the theoretical literature and the often critical points of view of donors on this subject.

Former executive secretary of the Economic Community of West African States (ECOWAS), Abass Bundu,* presents a vision of all that ECOWAS could be, and calls for renewed leadership and commitment from the member states. He assesses the impediments to regional integration in West Africa, but points to some of the factors increasing the odds of success in the present conjuncture, in particular the more liberal economic policies recently being adopted in most countries, the advance of democracy in the region, and the approval of the revised ECOWAS Treaty by the Authority of Heads of State and Government in 1993.

However, as some of the other authors in this volume point out (Bourenane*; Adotevi*; and Bach*), one cannot simply wish regional integration into existence, as the current institutional approach would have it. Bourenane* provides a survey of the theoretical models and approaches to regional integration that have been proposed. He and Bach* critically describe the current view as "voluntaristic," "institutionalist," "state-led," and "functionalist". More simply put, the approach is one whereby heads of state assemble on a regular basis and pronounce ambitious declarations of what they are going to do, as a prelude to actually doing very little.

According to Adotevi,* regional integration cannot properly succeed in the absence of a sense of belonging and identity of the general population with the proposed community of countries. He reminds us of the

---

[3] The interest of African intellectuals in regional integration was indicated by the large number of abstracts and papers received in response to the call for papers for the conference: over 300 submissions of abstracts and over 100 papers, from all parts of the subregion.

complex cultural identities inherited from the precolonial era, with its fluid and shifting borders, and suggests the need to draw upon those cultural identities if modern states and regional schemes are to acquire the legitimacy they currently lack. This suggests a model of regional integration based on a fairly radical restructuring of political authority of some sort. It also signifies the need to adopt a multilayered approach to community-building in which no particular community, such as the state, can lay claim to exclusive loyalty. Bourenane* develops the same point. In his view, regional integration must be built up brick by brick, and what is required is a dynamic strategy for moving forward along realistic lines, on the basis of achievable targets. Such an approach would involve a shift in emphasis, toward community-building, as against institution building or the pronouncement of empty treaty declarations.

Bach,* who is critical of the Abuja Treaty and holds out little hope for the success of ECOWAS, is nonetheless extremely concerned about the need to reconcile economic policies between the francophone union and its anglophone neighbours, Nigeria in particular. He considers the discrepancies in the exchange rate and trade policies of those two groups of countries to be fundamentally disruptive. Misalignments of real exchange rates such as we have seen between the franc zone and Nigeria, the franc zone and Ghana, and other pairs of countries, generate enormous rent-seeking opportunities through smuggling, thus crowding out legitimate trade as an entrepreneurial activity, while contributing to the gradual collapse of the state in the region.

The result is not regional integration, but disintegration all around. The 50% devaluation of the CFA franc in January 1994 will help to redress the situation, but the region would have been better served had Nigeria not complicated things by officially revaluing the naira, by an equally substantial proportion, at virtually the same time. The reconciliation of macroeconomic and trade policies between the franc zone and its anglophone neighbours is no doubt *the* priority issue for regional integration in West Africa.

Many of the ideas and criticisms expressed by other authors are to be found also in the review of donor viewpoints provided by Lavergne and Daddieh*. Drawing lessons from the failure of past schemes, the donor community advocates a pragmatic and flexible approach constructed around the concept of "variable geometry" which allows for the choice of countries participating in different schemes to change over time or from one project to another. They also share a liberal view of economic policy, considering that economic integration will most rapidly be achieved through the structural adjustment process. Worth noting is the current support of several donors for the West African Economic and Monetary Union (UEMOA). This support is viewed with mixed or sometimes hostile feelings by advocates of ECOWAS, who feel that the UEMOA project is the perfect example of how the "pragmatic" and "flexible" approach of the donors can be used to undermine the more ambitious plans of the Abuja Treaty, with its emphasis on ECOWAS as the preferred instrument for regional integration in West Africa. Although advocates of the UEMOA project deny the antithetic relationship of the two schemes, the marriage is certainly not an obvious one, and substantial effort will be required to ensure the complementarity as against the opposition of these two schemes.

Mytelka's paper, which constitutes the last chapter in the "Strategic Visions and Prospects" part of the volume, provides a fresh viewpoint on regional integration. She notes the changing character of regional integration efforts in recent years, away from the protectionist bent of the past, in favour of a new approach involving integration in world markets based on strength through regional unity. Mytelka* considers regional cooperation and coordination in the field of technology to be essential if Africa is to compete and survive in the international markets of the 21st century. Stressing cooperation in the application of knowledge to all sectors, she proposes an approach to regional integration described as "innovation-driven," as opposed to earlier "exchange-driven" or "production-specialization" models.

ECONOMIC INTEGRATION

REGIONAL TRADE

Not long ago, regional integration was identified essentially with economic matters — regional trade in particular. Most people still think predominantly in those terms. Yet, there is widespread consensus that preference schemes to stimulate regional trade have not worked as intended in the region and probably cannot be made to work without some major rethinking about the costs and difficulties of implementing such schemes (Robson 1987; Foroutan 1993). There are two aspects to this argument. One has to do with the wisdom of import-substituting industrialization as a development strategy. This is an age-old debate, to which justice cannot be done in this short chapter. However, the empirical evidence does support some version of neoliberal thinking in this regard. The prevailing consensus among development economists does not oppose protectionism in all forms and circumstances. However, it does oppose excessively high levels of protection accompanied by over-valued exchange rates, which end up penalizing exports and stifling economic growth (Badiane*). It also requires that protection be accompanied by certain performance criteria, as in Southeast Asia (World Bank 1993). Finally, it requires a degree of strategic thinking that has not been present in West Africa, where a rentier mentality of "protectionism at all costs" has been the rule. Protectionism of this sort long ago exhausted its potential in West Africa, and there should be no question about the need for alternative strategies at this time.

The second part of the argument concerns the fiscal implications of preference schemes and the unequal impact of those measures on different countries. Lavergne and Daddieh* summarize some of that thinking as reflected in the World Bank's position on regional integration. In the absence of workable compensation schemes, the less-industrialized countries in an economic union come out losers in two respects: they lose revenue by purchasing imports from partner countries that pay lower tariffs; and they may lose what little industry they have to competitors in more industrialized neighbouring countries. Compensation schemes such as that of the CEAO are meant to rectify this, but merely shift the fiscal burden onto the exporting country.[4]

The solution advocated by the donor community is for liberalization to proceed along fairly general lines, with only limited preference margins for member countries of any particular scheme (Lavergne and Daddieh*). Such a solution does not solve the fiscal problem resulting from the loss of tariff revenue — although actual collection might improve due to the decline of informal trade — but it does benefit consumers, through a decline in prices, in a way that trade preferences usually do not. It also increases competitive pressures on local industry. The Achilles' heel of this approach remains the fiscal problem to which other solutions need to be found, in the form of increased donor support, increased taxation of selected products or activities, or the reduction of certain government expenditures.

Competitiveness under this approach is maintained through currency devaluation, as currently practised in every country of the region

---

[4] In the case of the former CEAO (dissolved in March 1994), the principal exporting country was Côte d'Ivoire. With fiscal problems becoming ever more acute as it struggled through the economic crisis of the 1980s and early 1990s, Côte d'Ivoire was unable to sustain its obligations to the community, and a scheme that might have worked ended up grinding to a halt.

now that the CFA franc has been devalued. The combination of trade liberalization with collective devaluation in real terms is a remarkable one in terms of its likely impact on regional trade. Liberalization should stimulate trade in general, while collective devaluation should keep more of that increased trade within the region (Lavergne and Daddieh*). Devaluation can also help resolve the fiscal crisis, by permitting higher taxation of traditional exports.

With trade liberalization and currency devaluation figuring prominently in ongoing economic reform programs, the potential importance of preferential trading arrangements pales in comparison. Trade barriers of the tariff and non-tariff varieties remain excessively high in West Africa, but tend to come down too little and too slowly when this is done as part of preferential trade schemes. Macroeconomic policy reforms are without a doubt more important. Yet macroeconomic policies have been a neglected dimension in regional integration schemes over the last 20 years (Badiane*). A particularly noteworthy aberration was the substantial overvaluation of the CFA franc, for over a decade, cheapening imports from the rest of the world and discouraging exports. The devaluation of the CFA franc should stimulate trade in regional products, and the impact of this single move will probably be greater than all the preference schemes one could develop over a decade of painstaking negotiations. Better coordination of ongoing trade policy reforms could similarly boost regional trade.

One question frequently being posed concerns the extent to which economic integration may already be taking place through informal channels capable of bypassing intercountry trade barriers. In one view, informal trade becomes a form of popular resistance to excessive taxation and interference by the state. Meagher* joins Bach* in taking issue with this notion, arguing that parallel trade as it currently exists is mainly a re-exporting trade based on arbitrage activities that contribute little to the development of regional industry or agriculture. Such trade is organized in networks of large traders with government collaboration to take advantage of disparities in economic policies among neighbouring countries, in the extraction of economic rents from parallel trade. Those who are involved in such trade have little interest in the rationalization of economic policies through the establishment of viable regional integration schemes.

The only solution is not more informal trade, but the coordination and liberalization of economic policies to eliminate the rationale for such trade in the first place, while freeing up the energies of the informal sector for more productive activities. However, because of conflicts of interest at the level of powerful actors involved in parallel trade, it may be difficult to achieve policy reform without recourse to external intervention, through some sort of regionally-focused structural adjustment program.

There is also some question about the extent to which the entrepreneurial energies of the informal trade sector can, in fact, be directed to other ends. According to Bach, the rent-seeking behaviour of the informal sector is fundamentally inconsistent with normal commercial activity, with its more modest profit margins. In his view, any reduction in opportunities for profiteering in cross-border trade will force the participants into more criminal types of activity, like the international drug trade or arms smuggling.

Stryker et al.* take a relatively detailed look at some of the possibilities for trade promotion in the West African subregion. Although their starting point is the development of a general trade strategy for West Africa, with no particular reference to regional integration, the greatest opportunities they identify are at the regional level. It could hardly be otherwise. West Africa cannot continue to flourish based on the current range of primary exports whose markets are limited, and does not have the industrial base which would readily allow it to penetrate manufactured export markets in the North. In comparison, there is substantial room for expansion of regional agricultural trade in cereals, livestock, and horticultural products. In the industrial sector, increased trade will depend on the implementation of major policy reforms away from the heavily distorted structure of incentives currently existing in the region, but there is no reason why substantial trade could not develop around basic manufactures.

MONETARY INTEGRATION

The West African Monetary Union (UMOA, now UEMOA) continues to be one of the major assets of the region in matters of integration, and Medhora* points out the various benefits of this scheme. Most notably, the UMOA countries have managed to maintain stable, noninflationary monetary policies, thanks to the insulation of the BCEAO from political interference. The major deficiency of the union was for many years the inability to devalue the CFA, but now that this has been resolved, the benefits of monetary integration, such as the reduction of risk and the decline of transaction costs, could help stimulate regional trade and promote investment in the region.

Cobham and Robson* extend this discussion further to ask whether the experience could not be enlarged to the whole of West Africa, with the European Union playing the support role currently provided by the French under UMOA. Like Medhora, Cobham and Robson stress the advantages of increased macroeconomic stability that an extended monetary union could bring. Of course, the issue is not just one of stability, but also one of policy harmonization between countries to avoid the sort of rent-creating situations currently plaguing trade relations between French-speaking and English-speaking countries of the zone.

The topic covered by these two papers acquires increased importance with the recent emergence of UEMOA. UMOA's success is largely attributable to the outside support provided by the French, and the supranational features of the UMOA framework. There are lessons in this for other schemes, and if UEMOA is the best way of implementing those lessons, by building upon the UMOA experience, it may constitute the best instrument for moving forward with regional integration in West Africa at this time. This assumes that the member states are willing to pursue the UEMOA initiative aggressively in action as well as words. The most tantalizing image at this point would involve the extension of UEMOA to other countries (as envisaged in the UEMOA Treaty itself), and its gradual expansion over time to the whole of West Africa. The parallel with the European experience, where the original six countries progressively took on new members on the basis of their initial success, is all too obvious.

SECTORAL APPROACHES

Most current research in the area of regional integration is being done at a sectoral level of analysis, on the agricultural, livestock and industrial sectors. Much more of this kind of down-to-earth strategic thinking and attention to detail is required to stimulate trade in the region along paths consistent with long-term economic viability as discussed in Stryker et al.* (see also Stryker et al. 1994).

The agricultural sector has been the object of substantial research, including work on regional food security and cereals markets undertaken under the sponsorship of the Club du Sahel and the Permanent Interstate Committee to Combat Drought in the Sahel (CILSS).[5] Pradelle and

[5] See also some of the work of the International Food Policy Research Institute, USAID-funded research on the livestock sector, the activities of the Réseau sur les stratégies alimentaires, and recent work by the Dutch-funded network, Sécurité alimentaire durable en Afrique de l'Ouest centrale (SADAOC). For a summary of recent work on the livestock sector specifically, see Josserand and Sidibé (1993) or the briefing notes produced by the Réseau sur les stratégies alimentaires (1994).

Snrech (1993) and Brah et al. (1993) have summarized the results of several years of research since plans were first put forward for regional food
security in the Sahel at the Mindelo conference in 1986. This sort of
research has contributed greatly to our knowledge of trade patterns in the
region, and has highlighted the need for greater coordination of food policy to avoid the sort of counterproductive trade in imported cereals
resulting from different pricing policies. Also worth emphasizing is the
progressive shift of emphasis of such research away from its exclusive
focus on the Sahel. This is a logical response, because most trading
opportunities in agricultural products involve trade between the Sahelian
countries and the Coast, with livestock, cereals, chea butter, and horticultural products moving southward, and tropical fruits, poultry products,
kola nuts, and tropical agroindustrial products moving the other way.

Comparatively little has been published on the industrial sector,
despite the high priority that national governments place on industrial
development. The industrial policy research network (Réseau sur les
politiques industrielles), managed by the Council for the Development of
Economic and Social Research in Africa (CODESRIA), is dealing with
issues of industrial incentives in francophone Africa, but even in that
case, virtually no attention has been paid to regional integration matters
until now. There is in fact little intra-African trade in industrial products. Industrial structures are similar in most countries of the subregion,
and there is a perception by governments that one cannot have greater
regional trade without destroying major parts of national industries. This
fear is exaggerated because intraindustrial trade (i.e., trade within a single industry) represents a major phenomenon everywhere else in the
world, where it has stimulated growth through increased competition
and economies of scale due to specialization.

As Lavergne and Daddieh* point out, there is an urgent need for
greater efforts at policy coordination in matters of trade policy reform
such as are being carried out under structural adjustment programs. Substantial trade liberalization has already taken place in the region, but
there seems to have been virtually no effort to tap this systematically for
the reinforcement of regional trade by focusing on products with particular regional trade potential, such as those identified by Stryker et al.* —
for example, textiles, footwear, cooking utensils, or processed foods and
beverages.

The service sector has traditionally been ignored in development
theory, and somewhat forgotten in development practice. It is finally
receiving more of the attention it deserves. Services were thus brought

into the General Agreement on Tariffs and Trade (GATT) talks during the Uruguay Round, and constituted a major part of that agreement. Further work on the topic is being carried out in Africa under the Coordinated Action Programme of Assistance on Services sponsored by the United Nations Conference on Trade and Development. In the financial sector specifically, there has been some work on increased resource mobilization through the development of regional and subregional capital markets by both the BCEAO and the African Centre for Monetary Studies (ACMS). In West Africa, much of what is to be done under the UEMOA agreements involves the reinforcement of key service functions, including the rationalization of the insurance subsector, the development of regional capital markets, and the harmonization of business law.

Services include a wide range of activities, such as trade, finance, insurance, law, consulting and engineering, transport, health, education, communications, and research. Many of these functions are provided in the form of basic public services in areas such as education, health, and law enforcement, but most services remain in the private sector. The underdevelopment of the service sector is part of Africa's problem, and Badiane's contribution to this volume* points to the importance of improved policies in the marketing and transport sectors as a stimulus to increased regional trade. Major gains could probably be realized through productivity growth in the service sector generally, through greater regional collaboration and policy harmonization of the kind mentioned above under the UEMOA scheme.

PUBLIC SECTOR ISSUES

The public sector offers a wide range of opportunities for greater regional collaboration. Prevailing orthodoxy here has evolved in step with neoliberal approaches now dominant in development thinking, and shies away from large public-sector investments in joint industrial facilities (Lavergne and Daddieh*). However, there is plenty of scope for inter-country cooperation in the provision of infrastructure, public services, and government.

INFRASTRUCTURE

The need for improved regional infrastructure for communications, transport, and energy systems is widely recognized in the literature on regional integration and cooperation, and provides an opportunity for collaboration to proceed along project-driven lines that are less likely to encounter political difficulties than other schemes — provided that funding can be found. The experience of the Southern African Development Community (SADC, formely SADCC, the Southern African Development Coordination Conference) is often cited as a model of regional cooperation centred around the development of infrastructure, but comparable achievements in West Africa can be found in the transportation and communications sectors (Bundu*).

Transport and communications have been given the highest priority in both SADCC and ECOWAS because of their importance in achieving goals in other areas such as food security, industrial production, and trade. Much certainly remains to be done, particularly in the communications field, and particularly between francophone and anglophone countries of West Africa, where telecommunications links remain woefully inadequate (in no small part because of the weak domestic telecommunications systems within those countries, Nigeria in particular). In an increasingly information-driven world, international competitiveness, regional trade, and interfirm competition cannot be expected to develop until these barriers are eliminated.

There may also be untapped potential in the energy sphere. According to Sarfoh (1993), the gross potential hydroelectricity that can be generated by Africa's large water resources has been estimated at about 300 gigawatts, of which less than 4% is currently exploited. Although Sarfoh does not provide the corresponding figures for West Africa (where the potential is surely much less due to the flatness of the terrain), he identifies hydropower as the natural energy base offering the best prospects for satisfying West Africa's future electricity needs and advocates interconnecting the region through hydroelectric schemes as a catalyst for political and economic unification.

PUBLIC SERVICES

Regional cooperation could probably be increased in various public-service sectors as well, including health, education, and information services. Numerous health programs are currently operating on a regional basis within the scope of activity of international organizations such as the World Health Organization or projects such as the African AIDS Research Network, which involve multidonor support. In francophone countries, the Organization for Coordination and Cooperation Against Major Endemic Diseases (OCCGE) involves eight countries and nine specialized health research institutes. The equivalent organization for the five countries of anglophone West Africa is the West African Health

Community (WAHC). OCCGE and WAHC are currently undergoing a merger, scheduled to be completed by April 1995.

Avocksouma (1994) takes an innovative theoretical approach to regional cooperation in the health sector by focusing on interorganizational links forged independently of conventional regional integration schemes. He scrutinizes the theoretical reasons behind the emergence of such links, in terms of the advantages to the organizations themselves through extended market reach and improved service to clients, improved opportunities for professional development, and enhanced possibilities for the mobilization of outside resources. According to Avocksouma, such interorganizational linkages constitute an important mechanism for the growth of regional cooperation. Such a mechanism has parallels in all types of private enterprise or public-sector activity with a regional dimension, and it is precisely this sort of autonomously driven initiative that authors such as Bourenane* see as essential building blocks in the creation of a true West African "community" with substance beyond the institutional fabric of existing intergovernmental organizations.

Much has been attempted with outside donor support in the fields of higher education, training, research, and technology, with varying degrees of success. Here too, there are possibilities for economies of scale, mutual learning, and information sharing, which can justify the pursuit of regional initiatives (Ekane 1993). Higher education can be a difficult field for donors to support, because of the large recurring costs entailed or the difficulty of finding workable formulas for governing regional institutions. Regional schools such as the former CEAO's African Centre for Management Studies (CESAG) have encountered difficulties of both types, and institutions with pan-African mandates such as ACMS or the Institute for Economic Development and Planning (IDEP) have been forced to scale back the level of their activities in the face of continuing financial difficulties.

However, there exist other formulas than the creation of new regional institutions of higher learning. The alternatives do not resolve all the recurrent cost problems, but they can facilitate the mobilization of national resources or simplify some of the governance issues. One formula which seems to have worked in certain cases is the attachment of regional programs to national institutions. A case in point is the regional graduate-training program in agricultural economics run by the Ivoirian Centre for Social and Economic Research (CIRES), which is attached to the University of Abidjan. However, programs such as these may have to be sustained through high student fees, paid for in CIRES's case through scholarships supported by outside donors. The sustainability of programs such as these requires that scholarships be funded at least in part by national sources. One solution would be to create a regional scholarship program funded by donors, national governments and the private sector, aimed at students interested in the pursuit of studies outside their country of origin in the region. By pooling support for all disciplines in a single program, this formula would encourage universities in each country to define areas of specialisation in which to excel in order to attract a regional base of students.

Regional initiatives can build upon national programs in other ways. One way is to set regional standards, as do the West African Examinations Council and the African and Malagasy Council of Higher Learning. An interesting program whose success will be worth watching is the Inter-University Graduate Training Program in Economics for Francophone Africa (PTCI), which builds upon national training programs, but offers regional support for improved facilities and higher standards under the umbrella of the Conference of Economics Research and Training Institutions in Francophone Africa (CIEREA). Other interuniversity collaboration programs of various sorts are also being developed under the Association of African Universities based in Accra. One can thus point to a wide range of formulas for the reinforcement of higher learning through regional cooperation. The key is to let the principle of "subsidiarity" be the guide to interventions where regional cooperation can increase the efficiency and effectiveness of national programs without duplicating what is being done at lower levels.

Research and information constitute a final area worthy of special mention because of the economies of scale that can be achieved through the centralization of such activities. It is significant that successful research in the region is often undertaken through regional networks of one sort or another, under the aegis of institutions such as the Institute du Sahel, CODESRIA, IDRC and others. Regional information systems, such as the French-supported Afristat being established in Niamey for the collection and coordination of basic statistical information can also fill an important gap.

HUMAN RIGHTS

Several papers presented at the Dakar conference inquired into the possible role and mandate of regional institutions in areas of government activity such as human rights, regional security, and natural resource management.

Quashigah* considers the possible role of regional institutions in the promotion of human rights, arguing that collective values could be mobilized through regional fora as a way of pressuring individual countries in matters of human rights and fundamental liberties. Quashigah sees the world evolving toward a redefinition of national sovereignty — from the absolutist notions of the monarchical era, toward one supportive of the rights of all human beings, including those in foreign countries. In Africa, he points to the gradual recognition of such principles in various charters and treaties and argues that new instruments, such as the proposed regional and subregional parliaments and courts or recourse to humanitarian intervention, could be used for the collective promotion of human rights.

REGIONAL SECURITY

Another area worthy of further investigation is regional security, touched upon by Bundu.* Two papers on this topic were presented at the Dakar conference (Danfulani 1993; Osadolor 1993), and they raised a great deal of controversy about the feasibility of such measures and the dangers of a regional approach in this area of activity given the lack of true democracy in much of the West African subregion. However, the regional impact of the Liberian conflict on neighbouring countries, due to the spill over of violence into Sierra Leone, the exodus of hundreds of thousands of refugees into Côte d'Ivoire and Guinea, and the spread to all of West Africa of arms and drugs originating in the war zone is a clear illustration of the regional interest in managing this sort of conflict (see *Jeune Afrique*, 23 February 1995, pp. 30–33).

NATURAL RESOURCE MANAGEMENT

Finally, certain issues of resource management would benefit from a regional approach due to the lack of correspondence between political boundaries and ecological zones. The need for regional collaboration in river basin management is an obvious case in point, and a number of regional programs designed for this purpose already exist, including the Senegal River Valley Development Organization (OMVS) and the Gambia River Valley Development Organization (OMVG).

Debailleul et al.* address the issue of desertification, which is of concern to the whole of West Africa. The regional scope of this issue has two principal dimensions. First is the shared nature of the problem, because desertification affects all countries in West Africa to some extent. The second aspect is the interdependence of various countries with regard to this issue, as desertification is a major cause of migration from the Sahel to the coast, while deforestation in coastal areas is a likely factor contributing to declining rainfall in northern parts of the region. Desertification control is being pursued at the international, regional, and local levels. Debailleul and colleagues propose a geopolitical approach as a frame of reference for sorting out the actors involved at different levels and thinking strategically about desertification control on a regional scale.

A third example worth noting is in the fisheries sector. Olomola (1993) provides a rationale for better management of Africa's abundant fisheries through intraregional cooperation, joint efforts at stock management, regional cooperation in fisheries research, and a range of other activities for drawing greater value from the region's fisheries.

THE SOVEREIGNTY ISSUE

The last two papers in this volume deal with political issues having to do with the sharing of power at the regional level. Ntumba* reviews the three largest integration schemes in Africa and points to the lack of supranationality in these arrangements, which he qualifies as "interstatal" in their approach. Malam-Kandine (1993) makes the same argument in somewhat less detail in a comparison of ECOWAS and CEAO, and both authors contrast this state of affairs with the experience of the European Union, which involved the partial cession of sovereignty by member states at an early stage, in the design of regional institutions. The absence of this condition in the African communities is seen to explain their relative failure compared with the European Union. This argument is bolstered by Medhora* who attributes the relative success of UMOA to the supranationality of the BCEAO over monetary policy.

According to Adewoye,* the problem begins with the political philosophy of nations, which he argues is fundamentally different in Africa than in Europe where a long tradition of "constitutionalism" makes it easier to accept limits upon the exercise of power. This in turn has made it easier to engineer the sharing of sovereignty with regional levels of government and justice in Europe than in Africa. Supranationality in Africa is therefore unlikely to materialize in a significant way until constitutionalism itself becomes more strongly entrenched at the national level. However, this may not prevent advances from being made in piecemeal and possibly iterative fashion. Adewoye advocates using the ECOWAS framework itself as a tool for promoting constitutionalism, through the operation of a tribunal, as foreseen in the revised ECOWAS Treaty, which might become increasingly capable of enforcing human rights and checking abuses of power by national governments.

It is widely recognized that existing regional institutions will not succeed until the principle of supranationality is firmly established, as increasingly seems to be the intent with the signature of the Abuja Treaty, the revised ECOWAS Treaty, and the UEMOA Treaty (see Bundu* and Ntumba* for comments on the revised ECOWAS Treaty). Each of these projects involves movement in the direction of increased supranationality through the creation of a regional parliament, the strengthening of a regional tribunal or court of justice, and some move away from rule by consensus, toward qualified majority rule.

THE UEMOA TREATY

The most recent and most significant advances to be made on this front involve the UEMOA Treaty, which was ratified by the Heads of State and Government on 11 January 1994 and ratified by the member states over the following 6 months. The papers in this volume do not dwell extensively on UEMOA, whose Commission and Court of Justice were created in February 1995 (however, see Bach* and Lavergne and Daddieh*). We thus permit ourselves some pause to review the contents of the treaty itself, with regard to the supranationality issue. Of all the regional integration schemes in Africa, UEMOA incorporates the largest measure of supranationality. This is manifested first in UEMOA's objectives in terms of policy harmonization, which are more far reaching than those of other regional integration schemes. Article 4 of the treaty lists five broad objectives:

- ◆ greater economic competitiveness, through open and competitive markets along with the rationalization and harmonization of the legal environment;
- ◆ the convergence of macroeconomic policies and indicators;
- ◆ creation of a common market;
- ◆ coordination of sectoral policies; and
- ◆ harmonization of fiscal policies.

Articles 5 and 6 then define UEMOA's basis principles in the matter of supranationality. Article 5 implicitly recognizes the principle of subsidiarity,[6] while Article 6 affirms the supranationality of UEMOA's statutes over those of national governments. The institutional structure proposed for UEMOA incorporates several important innovations in support of this intended supranationality. In addition to features common to the Abuja Treaty and the revised ECOWAS Treaty as mentioned in the previous section, these innovations include: the creation of an UEMOA commission, analogous to the Commission of European Communities, responsible for representing the interests of the Union (Articles 26-33); the creation of an independent budget authority (cour des comptes); and provision for an independent tax base (Articles 38 and 54). With regard to parliamentary representation, the UEMOA Treaty provides for the creation of an interparliamentary committee as the first step toward the establishment of a regional parliament (Articles 35-37). More gradual in its approach to parliamentary representation than the Abuja and ECOWAS Treaties, the UEMOA may have a greater chance of actually being implemented.

Finally, the legal instruments available to UEMOA are of four types:

◆ the UMOA Treaty, which remains in force and accords total supranationality to UEMOA in matters of monetary policy;

◆ the UEMOA Treaty, which defines the union's institutional framework, but also includes some specific strictures, such as those in Article 77, which prohibit the application of new protectionist measures against member states;

◆ the statutes of UEMOA's constituent organs, particularly those emitted in the form of regulations, directives, and decisions, which have obligatory force (Article 43); and

◆ the surveillance mechanisms and sanctions foreseen in the area of economic policy harmonization (Articles 64, 65 and 72-75).

Taken together, these various arrangements should translate into a substantial degree of supranationality for UEMOA, assuming successful implementation.[7]

---

[6] This is our interpretation of the reference to the power of UEMOA's organs to edict "minimal prescriptions and regulatory frameworks, which the Member States will themselves complete as required according to their own constitutional rules" [our translation].

[7] For a more detailed analysis of the UEMOA Treaty, see Ghymers 1994.

REGIONAL COOPERATION AND UNILATERAL ACTIONS

However, development along regional lines can take different paths, and regional cooperation, based on the identification of positive-sum opportunities involving more than one country, may sometimes be the fastest way forward. As Lavergne and Daddieh* point out, donors have a special interest in promoting regional cooperation, as this allows them to avoid having to deal with sovereignty issues. Donors have no control over the sharing of sovereignty which is implied by regional integration schemes, and are sometimes impotent to promote progress if "political will" is lacking at the level of participating countries. At the same time, donors do have a special role to play in the financing of infrastructural or other regional cooperation projects.

Economic integration can also proceed through unilateral policy reforms of the kind emphasized by Badiane.* This option has been much ignored by African governments and intergovernmental institutions. However, this is essentially what the neoliberal approach advocated by the World Bank and other donor institutions entails, in calling for unilateral trade liberalization and currency devaluation. Although economic liberalization as pursued under structural adjustment programs is not designed to promote regional trade in particular, its intent is certainly to promote trade, and the fact that it can be pursued unilaterally makes it potentially a powerful and immediately available instrument for the stimulation of regional trade.

The major preoccupation of certain scholars, such as Meagher,* or of institutions such as the Economic Commission for Africa (ECA) is that this will encourage the overconcentration of regional economies on the export of primary products. This is a legitimate concern, and particular attention should be given to resolving the rift between the World Bank and the ECA and other advocates of protection on matters of trade liberalization, by searching out appropriate combinations of liberalization, protection and supply-side measures capable of encouraging the development of the industrial sector and the growth of alternative exports in Africa.

RESEARCH PRIORITIES

It is conventional to complete reviews such as this one with a discussion of priority areas for research. It is not immediately obvious to what extent research is the key missing ingredient in this field, because the problems and needs are common knowledge. Furthermore, research is unlikely to

materialize unless there is a "market" for it. As long as all policy decisions are national in orientation due to the weakness of regional institutions, most research is likely to address national issues.

However, one of the principal obstacles to research to date has been
the tendency of researchers to identify with specific models of regional
integration. Researchers limiting themselves to the conventional trade-
preferences model find they have little new to say. Researchers identifying the Abuja Treaty as the sole model for regional integration may find
themselves complaining about the lack of political will of member states
or engaging in broad strategic discussions at an abstract level, but will
probably not advance very far in operational terms.

The options for research are greatly increased when one recognizes
the many options for regional action identified in this volume.
Researchers able and willing to broaden their horizons will discover a
richness of opportunities open to them at more operational levels of
investigation. The so-called "variable geometry" concept is particularly
interesting, because it permits problems to be attacked on the basis of
available opportunities, as understanding develops and solutions are
found, in a variable geographic framework. Researchers would then be
able to identify specific problems and solutions at a relatively microre-
gional level and be in a position to influence constituencies that are more
proximate and manageable than is the case under the current grand
schemes. The notion of variable geometry thus provides an answer of
sorts to the "market" problem for research, by narrowing the geographic
field of intervention. Without listing all the options for research here,
one might mention two types of research that would fit this sort of
micro- or mesoregional framework of analysis. One would be to pursue
fine-tuning of current mechanisms for trade liberalization, to identify
mechanisms for liberalizing trade in key industries without necessarily
"deindustrializing" individual countries or the region as a whole. The
other would be to undertake further sectoral studies to identify the complementary policies required to increase trade between neighbouring
countries or to pinpoint required areas for increased collaboration in various sectors of public activity.

CONCLUSION

An attempt has been made in this volume, and in this introductory chapter in particular, to survey the limits and possibilities of regional integration and cooperation in West Africa. We have discussed some of the

key concepts involved, and the reasons why the subject is considered so important by African decision-makers, intellectuals, and citizens. Whatever discrepancies in points of view there may be about immediate priorities or preferred strategies, neither Africans nor outside parties are ready to abandon regional integration as a major strategic objective. The need is too obvious in a region as arbitrarily fragmented as West Africa, and the advantages of greater integration altogether too clear. Much of the rethinking about regional integration is thus not so much about whether it is necessary or desirable, as about the choice of priorities and operational strategies. A major aspect of this rethinking is a reconceptualization of the subject matter itself, to make room for subjects other than economic ones, while allowing for a more holistic view of regional integration aimed at community-building over the long term.

We have reviewed various areas of endeavour lending themselves to regional integration and cooperation, distinguishing between economic matters and various opportunities for public-sector collaboration or integration. Clearly, the regional integration and cooperation "menu" is a rich one, and the failure of conventional approaches to regional integration through the creation of regional institutions, the establishment of trade preference schemes or large public-sector investments in industry should not be cause for discouragement. The way forward can be pursued along three different paths: 1) the creation of truly supranational mechanisms, 2) regional cooperation, or 3) unilateral action. What may have gone unnoticed due to the great deal of attention paid to the failure of existing regional integration schemes is that some progress is apparent on each of these fronts. One can point respectively to the adoption of the revised ECOWAS and the UEMOA treaties, both of which involve commitments to increase supranationality (Bundu*; Bach*; Ntumba*); to the promise of increased donor support for regional cooperation (Lavergne and Daddieh*); and to the continuing liberalization of economic policies on a unilateral basis throughout the region (Lavergne and Daddieh*).

A major priority at this time should be the coordination of economic policies, particularly in the monetary and trade policy spheres (Bach*; Meagher*; Badiane*; Cobham and Robson*). This is already being done in UEMOA, but UEMOA represents only about one third of the combined population and economic product of West Africa. Much more clearly needs to be done to improve policy coordination between the UEMOA countries and such important neighbours such as Nigeria and Ghana, as well as other ECOWAS partner countries. The donor community could be an important catalyst in this process, by increasing its support and encouraging recalcitrant parties along.

The coexistence of multiple and sometimes competing strategic options, such as we observe in West Africa, is not, in my view, an unhealthy one. In the context of uncertainty, which is inevitable in all innovative endeavours, it is often not possible to predict what will work until some effort is actually made. Although it is too soon to tell which of the many initiatives currently being pursued will bear fruit, it would seem foolish to dismiss progress on any one front on the basis of institutional jealousies or ideological blockages and suspicion.

The wisest course would seem to be to adopt a flexible, pragmatic and multipronged strategy, based on available opportunities for common advantage in different fields. As Bourenane* suggests, we should be engaging in a long-term process of community-building, recognizing that certain targets may be out of reach for the time being, but channeling efforts into those initiatives with positive long-term impacts on regional aspirations. Although priorities will have to be set, the opportunities for progress in specific areas of endeavour should be obvious for all whose interest extends beyond the limiting confines of the existing nation-states in the West African subregion.

REFERENCES

Asiwaju, A.I. 1990. Artificial boundaries: Les frontières artificielles. Civiletis International, New York, NY, USA.

Avocksouma, D.A. 1994. "Les alliances multi-institutionnelles des organisations de santé dans la perspective de l'intégration économique en Afrique Noire." Université de Montréal, Montreal, Canada, 1994 unpublished manuscript.

Brah, M.; Pradelle, J.M.; d'Agostino, V. 1993. Regional cooperation and integration in West Africa: a contribution to the corpus of knowledge from the collaborative research of the CILSS, the Club du Sahel and the Cinergie Unit. Club du Sahel, Paris, France. SAH/D93,

CEC (Commission of the European Communities) 1992. "European Community perspectives on regional integration among developing countries." Background note for consideration at the DAC informal meeting of 27-28 April.

Danfulani, S.A. 1993. West African regional security framework: a diplomatic instrument of peace, stability, democracy and development. Presented at the International conference on regional integration in West Africa, 11–15 January, Dakar. International Development Research Centre, Dakar, Senegal.

de Benoist, R. 1993. L'intégration de l'Afrique occidentale française aurait-elle pu être irréverstible? Institut fondamental d'Afrique noire, Université Cheikh Anta Diop, Dakar, Senegal. Unpublished manuscript.

De Melo, J.; Panagariya, A. 1992. "The New Regionalism." Finance & Development, (Dec.):37-40.

Diop, M.C.; Lavergne, R. 1994. Regional integration in West Africa: proceedings of the international conference organized by IDRC in Dakar Senegal, 11–15 January 1993. International Development Research Centre, Ottawa, Canada.

Ekane, W.N. 1993. Regional cooperation and higher education. Presented at the International conference on regional integration in West Africa, 11–15 January, Dakar. International Development Research Centre, Dakar, Senegal.

Foroutan, F. 1993. Regional integration in sub-Saharan Africa: past experience and future prospects. In de Melo, J.; Panagariya, A., ed., New dimensions in regional integration. Cambridge University Press, Cambridge, MA, USA.

Ghymers, C. 1994. Note de présentation du Traité de l'Union économique et monétaire ouest africaine. European Commission, Directorate-General for Economic and Financial Affairs, Economic Evaluation of Community Policies Directorate. (Document II 1103/94-FR, 7 February). Brussels, Belgium.

Josserand, H.; Sidibé, S. 1993. Échanges de produits de l'élevage : problématique et contribution de plusieurs initiatives actuelles à l'intégration régionale. Presented at the International conference on regional integration in West Africa, 11–15 January, Dakar. International Development Research Centre, Dakar, Senegal.

Malam-Kandine, A. 1993. Les faiblesses des structures institutionnelles comme frein au processus d'intégration régionale en Afrique de l'Ouest. Presented at the International conference on regional integration in West Africa, 11–15 January, Dakar. International Development Research Centre, Dakar, Senegal.

Oliver, R.; Atmore, A. 1981a. The African middle ages, 1400–1800. Cambridge University Press, London, UK.

———— 1981b. Africa since 1800. Cambridge University Press, London, UK.

Olomola, A. 1993. A framework for regional cooperation to enhance African fisheries research and development. Presented at the International conference on regional integration in West Africa, 11–15 January, Dakar. International Development Research Centre, Dakar, Senegal.

Osadolor, B. 1993. Regional security and integration: a study of ECOWAS initiatives in military cooperation. Presented at the International conference on regional integration in West Africa, 11–15 January, Dakar. International Development Research Centre, Dakar, Senegal.

Pradelle, J.M.; Snrech, S. 1993. Sécurité alimentaire et développement agricole en Afrique de l'Ouest : qu'attendre de l'intégration régionale? Presented at the International conference on regional integration in West Africa, 11–15 January, Dakar. International Development Research Centre, Dakar, Senegal.

Réseau sur les stratégies alimentaires. 1994. Bétail et viandes en Afrique de l'Ouest et du Centre : enjeux et perspectives. Solagral, Paris, France. 180/94.

Robson, P. 1987. Variable geometry and automaticity: strategies for experience of regional integration in West Africa. In El-Agraa, A.M., ed., Protection, cooperation, integration and development: essays in honour of Professor Hiroshi Kitamura. Macmillan Press, New York, NY, USA. Pp. 159–173.

Sarfoh, J.A. 1993. Energy production and use as a strategy for regional integration: the case for hydro substitution in West Africa. Presented at the International conference on regional integration in West Africa, 11–15 January, Dakar. International Development Research Centre, Dakar, Senegal.

Stryker, J.D.; Salinger, B.L.; Metzel, J.C. 1994. A regional strategy for trade and growth in West Africa: sectoral analyses and action plan. Associates for International Resources and Development, Cambridge, MA, USA.

World Bank. 1993. The East Asian miracle: economic growth and public policy. World Bank, Washington, DC, USA.
———— 1994. Adjustment in Africa: reforms, results and the road ahead. World Bank, Washington, DC, USA.

PART I

STRATEGIC VISIONS
AND
PROSPECTS

CHAPTER 2

ECOWAS AND THE FUTURE OF REGIONAL INTEGRATION IN WEST AFRICA

– Abass Bundu –

This chapter by the former executive secretary of ECOWAS provides a review of regional integration in West Africa over the last two decades. There are about 40 major intergovernmental organizations (IGOs) in the region, and Bundu considers that this is in itself an achievement and testimony to the community spirit and solidarity that have developed among West African states. However, these IGOs have not had any significant development impact, because of difficulties in securing the effective implementation of integration programs in the member countries.

Some of the factors impeding regional integration in West Africa are identified. These include: 1) the absence of an integration culture and, indeed, a development culture generally, in the countries of the region; 2) the priority accorded to nation-building in the years following independence; 3) differences in ideology and approach; 4) the fear of domination by Nigeria; 5) the burden of certain institutional and economic structures inherited from the colonial era; 6) the economic crisis that has plagued the region since the early 1980s; and 7) political instability.

Progress toward regional integration will require stronger institutional arrangements at the national level, a degree of external support, and renewed leadership from all quarters. The chapter ends with a review of some of the features and potential of the revised ECOWAS Treaty approved in July 1993 and calls for renewed effort and ambition in favour of regional integration.

THE SIGNING OF THE African Economic Community (AEC) Treaty in Abuja in June 1991 provides a renewed and ambitious blueprint for economic integration and development in Africa. However, one of the remarkable features of this historic event was the relative lack of analysis of the major issues and problems of regional cooperation and integration before the Treaty was drafted. Although some studies were undertaken, a thorough and critical examination of the West African integration experience remains necessary to prepare for the subregion's participation in the continental experiment, while enhancing the role of regional integration in the development process.

The 20th century stands out in history as a period of rapid and dramatic change. Revolutionary changes have been sustained since the turn of the century through a series of technological innovations, resulting from continuous research and experimentation in all fields of human endeavour. The climax of this process is occurring in this last decade of the century with a whirlwind of change sweeping the world.

West Africa has not been spared. Everywhere one turns in this part of the world, one is confronted with so much turmoil and change that West Africa can be said to be undergoing a societal upheaval. Every aspect of life — religious, political, social, and economic — is in a state of flux and the changes are so overwhelming that they are undermining the cultural values of our peoples and threatening the very existence of some countries (ECOWAS 1993a). Social change elsewhere in the world tends to be just as fundamental but generally positive and desirable, whereas in this region the changes appear to be initiated and sustained by economic decline and decay. The challenge thus facing the governments and people of West Africa is how to halt the disintegration of the economic base and arrest the deterioration of societal norms and values.

The economic performance of sub-Saharan Africa, as measured by the growth in per capita income, has been declining since political independence. The modest annual growth rate of 1.5% achieved during the 1960s fell to an average of only 0.7% in the 1970s, and turned negative in the 1980s (−1.2%), as a combination of external and endogenous factors conspired to derail the development process launched after political independence (ECA various issues). The legitimate aspirations of African people for a higher standard of living have been frustrated, and our national economies retain the characteristics of a colonial economy. If anything, economic problems appear to have accumulated over time as policymakers battle with chronic food shortages, high population growth rates, deforestation and desertification, excessive dependence on commodity exports, deteriorating terms of trade, huge balance-of-payments deficits, government deficit financing, and increasing indebtedness (both domestic and external). Nowhere in West Africa have development strategies been successful in reversing the structural imbalances of our economies.

After a decade of economic regression and the traumas of structural adjustment, West African countries are in search of viable development strategies and looking increasingly to the role that regional integration and cooperation could play in revitalizing and redirecting the development process.

WEST AFRICAN EXPERIENCE
WITH REGIONAL INTEGRATION

Although the concepts and practice of regional integration and cooperation as they have come to be known in the international community are
of relatively recent vintage, West Africa should be counted among the
regions of the world with a certain experience in this area. There are some
40 IGOs in this region, some of which have their origins in the colonial
past. Most of them are subject-specific or represent loose forms of
regional cooperation, but there are also three economic communities,
each pursuing the economic integration of its member countries.

The first of these to be established was the West African Economic
Community (CEAO) in 1972, through the conversion of the much older
customs and economic grouping, the Union douanière et économique de
l'Afrique de l'Ouest (UDEAO). Disbanded on 14 March 1994, CEAO
has been supplanted by the West African Monetary and Economic Union
(UEMOA). The other economic communities are the Mano River Union
(MRU), established in 1973, and the Economic Community of West
African States (ECOWAS), formed in 1975. Membership in these com-
munities just prior to CEAO's disbandment consisted respectively of
Benin, Burkina Faso, Côte d'Ivoire, Mali, Mauritania, Niger, and Sene-
gal for CEAO;[1] Guinea, Liberia and Sierra Leone for MRU; and all 16
West African countries, from Cape Verde to Nigeria for ECOWAS.

The major emphasis in creating each of the three communities was
the liberalization of intracommunity trade and related forms of cooperation, such as the regional roads and telecommunications networks supported by ECOWAS. Other areas of ECOWAS activity have included
measures to facilitate the free flow of people, through the introduction of
visa-free travel for citizens of West African countries throughout the
region, and recognition of people's right to reside and settle in any country of the region. ECOWAS has also adopted agricultural and industrial
cooperation programs designed to expand the regional production base
and foster greater complementarity among the various national production systems.

The three communities have also promoted some specific projects.
CEAO has established a management institute in Dakar (CESAG), a fish-
eries institute in Nouadhibou, Mauritania, and the Regional Centre for
Solar Energy (CRES) in Bamako. MRU has similarly created a number of

---

[1] Membership in UEMOA also includes Togo, but not Mauritania. Togo's status in CEAO
was that of an observer country.

institutes at the service of the union: telecommunications in Freetown, maritime training in Monrovia, and forestry training in Bomi Hills, Liberia. Financial institutions responsible for funding regional integration projects and programs have been part of both the CEAO and ECOWAS initiatives (FOSIDEC and the ECOWAS Fund, respectively).

Unlike the three economic communities, other West African IGOs have more specialized ambitions. Each of them was established to help its member countries solve a common problem or promote the development of shared resources (see ECA/MULPOC 1993).

In the area of monetary cooperation, the West African Monetary Union (UMOA) has now become UEMOA, as of January 1994. It groups seven francophone countries under the Central Bank of West African States (BCEAO), which is the issuing authority of the Union's common currency, the CFA franc. Relatively successful, thanks to the supranational nature of the institution and external support from France, the Union has now expanded its functions beyond that of monetary cooperation, into the economic sphere. For West Africa as a whole, the central banks of the region established the West African Clearing House (WACH) to facilitate intraregional transactions and economize on the use of foreign convertible currencies. The scope of WACH is now being enlarged, and it is being transformed into the West African Monetary Agency. This Agency will be a specialized ECOWAS institution responsible for the ECOWAS monetary program, whose objective is the creation of a single monetary zone, with a single common currency replacing the ten existing ones (the CFA franc and nine inconvertible currencies).

Several IGOs are active in the fields of agriculture and natural resource management. These include:

- the Permanent Interstate Committee for Drought Control in the Sahel (CILSS), created in 1973 to address the growing menace of drought and desertification; this organization has been the focal point for both external and local efforts at controlling ecological degradation and promoting sustainable development in the Sahel;

- the Communauté économique du bétail et de la viande (CEBV) set up in 1970 to strengthen the livestock industry (a major economic sector in the savannah zone) and better organise the cattle trade between the producing and consuming countries of the region;

- ◆ the West African Rice Development Association (WARDA), established in 1970 to improve the production of rice, a staple in West Africa;

- ◆ two major pest-management organizations, the Organisation internationale de lutte contre le criquet migrateur africain (OICMA) and the Organisation commune de lutte anti-acridienne et de lutte anti-aviaire (OCLALAV), created to address the widespread destruction of crops by locusts and other migratory pests, in the Sahelian region especially;

- ◆ river and lake basin organizations, such as the Niger Basin Authority, the Senegal River Development Organization (OMVS), the Gambia River Development Organization (OMVG), and the Lake Chad Basin Commission (LCBC); and

- ◆ the Liptako Gourma Authority, an organization for the coordinated and accelerated development of the resources of a region shared by Niger, Mali, and Burkina Faso.

In the area of human resource development, there are two West African organisations in the health sector: the West African Health Community (WAHC) and the Coordination and Cooperation Organization for the Control for the Major Endemic Disease (OCCGE). They are being merged into the West African Health Organization, a specialized agency of ECOWAS. In the field of education, there are the West African Examinations Council (WAEC) and its francophone equivalent, the African and Malagasy Council on Higher Education (CAMES).

Finally, ECOWAS has encouraged the formation of a number of associations to involve the citizens of West Africa in the integration process; these include the West African Youth Union, the West African Women's Association, and the West African Workers' Union. There are also regional business associations like the Federation of West African Chambers of Commerce, the Federation of West African Manufacturers Associations, the West African Banks' Association, and the Union of West African Road Transporters.

This is an impressive array of regional organizations, and the policies and programs initiated by these various IGOs provide a ready foundation on which to build the integration process. It is an achievement for 16 developing countries to have agreed on schemes for a free-trade area, the free movement of people, monetary union, regional defence cooperation, and the joint development of regional transport and communications networks, as ECOWAS member states have done. This is a mark of the solidarity and the community spirit that have evolved over the years among West African countries, despite the different colonial experiences, linguistic and cultural backgrounds, and legal and administrative systems that have divided the region.

A question frequently asked is how the coexistence of so many different IGOs affects the regional integration process. Although the multiplicity of IGOs may be indicative of the desire of West African countries to cooperate, the resultant duplication and financial burden must also be kept in mind. The ECOWAS Authority of Heads of State and Government first addressed this issue in 1983, and proposed the rationalization of these IGOs. A joint ECA-ECOWAS study on rationalization was completed in 1987 (ECA and ECOWAS 1987) and its proposals for institutional reform were adopted by the ECOWAS Authority in 1991. It was decided that there should be a single regional economic community whose responsibility it would be to set integration policies and monitor the general process of regional integration. Specialized institutions of ECOWAS were to evolve out of certain existing sector-specific IGOs to manage regional programs in such areas as monetary integration, the mobilization of development finance, environmental protection (particularly drought and desertification control), regional food security (cereal production, livestock development, and pest control), development of river basins, human health, and human resource development.

The rationalization issue is of particular relevance for the three economic communities, ECOWAS, CEAO/UEMOA, and MRU, which overlap and compete with each other, each with a different scheme for the elimination of tariff and non-tariff barriers. These three schemes were conceived to operate with different rules of origin, customs documents and compensation schemes, so it should come as no surprise that the operation of three trade liberalization schemes in the same region has created certain difficulties and impeded the development of trade between member countries. Some efforts at coordination have been made, and the secretariats of the three economic communities developed a single regional scheme that was adopted by the 16 ECOWAS countries in 1983. The scheme was reviewed in June 1992, and certain modifications were adopted by the member countries. However, there has been little progress since then.

Resolutions such as the 1991 decision to designate ECOWAS as the sole economic community in West Africa and to rationalize the other IGOs under its umbrella, accomplish little if they are not actually implemented, and efforts should be made to deepen our understanding of the politics behind this and similar decisions. As Bourenane argues elsewhere in this volume (chapter 3), such analysis is fundamental to the definition of a realistic set of objectives and strategies for regional integration and cooperation in West Africa. Why was the relationship between ECOWAS and the other two communities not defined in 1975 and incorporated into the ECOWAS Treaty from the start? Why, less than 3 years after the 1991 decision to make ECOWAS the sole economic community in West Africa, did the francophone countries decide to establish the competing UEMOA?[2] Issues such as these, relating to the motivations and expectations of countries involved in regional cooperation and integration schemes, cannot properly be addressed in this short paper but do merit further attention, because they condition the realistic expectations that one may have of the possibilities for closer cooperation or the acceleration of the integration process.

That the current trade liberalization schemes have had little impact on trade flows within the region is readily acknowledged. Trade liberalization has been largely insignificant under MRU, negligible under ECOWAS, and somewhat limited even under CEAO, which has had the most success in this area. Intra-ECOWAS trade has stagnated since the creation of the Community. It finally increased as a proportion of total trade during the recessionary years of the late 1980s, rising from about 7% to 10% (Hess 1991, vol. II, p. 8), but this cannot be attributed to ECOWAS, in the absence of effective implementation of the trade-liberalization program under that regional body. Intra-CEAO trade increased rapidly in the early years, but then stabilized. At the end of the 1980s, it stood at about 10% of officially recorded trade among those countries (Hess 1991, vol. II, p. 11).

Progress on other ECOWAS initiatives has been mixed. Highlights include the impressive progress in the transport and communications sector thanks to external funding of the coastal highway (now 82% complete), the trans-Sahelian highway (76% complete), and the West African portion of the Pan African Telecommunications Network that now links all the countries in the region.

Much has also been achieved under the first two phases of the ECOWAS protocol on the free movement of people. Visa-free travel has been achieved since 1986, and the right of residence is now fairly widely applied. The third and last phase, the right of establishment, is yet to be widely applied in the region.

---

[2] This change of heart is reflected in the amendment to the revised ECOWAS Treaty of July 1993 (art. II), which now specifies only that ECOWAS will "ultimately" become the sole economic community of the subregion.

A development that augurs well for the future of regional integration is the establishment of regular dialogue among West African economic and financial policymakers since 1987. ECOWAS ministers of planning and finance have been involved in discussions aimed at greater harmonization of national approaches to macroeconomic issues, such as external indebtedness and the effects of the European Common Market on West African countries. They have also attempted to reassess national structural adjustment programs from a regional perspective with a view to developing a regional program for economic recovery. The governors of central banks also meet regularly to evaluate and reorient the ECOWAS monetary integration program, whose objective is to establish a single West African monetary zone by the year 2000. A Consultative Forum was finally established in 1992 to formalize meetings between central bank governors and ministers of planning and finance as a mechanism for the harmonization of economic and financial policies of ECOWAS member states. The Forum met for the first time during the Council of Ministers' session of July 1993, thus launching the regional process of economic harmonization to ensure that future structural adjustment or economic reform programs are better suited to the development and integration needs of member states.

In the monetary sphere, UMOA stands as an example of successful cooperation that has remained intact from the colonial era, but for West Africa as a whole, the record is dismal. So far, WACH has accomplished little of substance and has been described as "practically defunct" (Hess 1991, vol. II). One can only hope for better results from the new West African Monetary Agency, which has set itself the role of greater coordination of monetary policy as a first task, in preparation for eventual monetary union in the region.

ECOWAS, CEAO, and other regional institutions have been involved in such a wide range of activities that one can hardly hope to do justice to their achievements in an overview such as this one. However, there is general consensus that the various regional cooperation and integration schemes in West Africa have not had a significant impact on development in the region. For the most part, it would appear that IGOs have succeeded in getting their member countries to adopt their various programs and schemes while falling short of actual implementation. Among the problems encountered within ECOWAS have been the slow rate of ratification of Community conventions and protocols, the low rate of implementation of Community acts and decisions, delays in reacting to requests for information from member states, poor attendance at

ECOWAS meetings, and delays in payment of contributions. Obviously, not all West African countries have come to terms with what regional integration entails and what contributions and sacrifices are expected of the partner states.

Some observers have tried to attribute such apparent indifference and apathy to the economic crisis, which emptied government and interrupted national long-term development programs. However the problem is not so simple. The rest of this chapter discusses some of the other factors that have affected the process and how these problems are being addressed in the revised ECOWAS Treaty.

FACTORS AFFECTING THE INTEGRATION PROCESS

Like the economic development that it is meant to promote, the regional integration process cannot be understood without careful consideration of the basic factors that shape and influence West African society — its ideological, socio-cultural, political, economic, institutional, and administrative dimensions — studied with regard to their impact on the regional integration process. Several issue-areas emerge as particularly relevant to an understanding of the limited progress of regional integration to date or the conditions of renewed dialogue in defining new approaches for the future. The present section systematically addresses each of these issue-areas.

THE ABSENCE OF A DEVELOPMENT AND INTEGRATION CULTURE

For economic integration in West Africa to succeed in its role as an instrument for fostering the development of the partner states requires that these countries have a clear sense of their own development objectives and strategies and be fully committed to the pursuit of these goals. A development culture must be fostered, both within government and among the people, so that concern for a better future replaces preoccupation with the satisfaction of immediate needs. With development objectives placed high on the national agenda, well thought-out development strategies would not be so easily replaced with ad hoc economic management decisions, and regional integration would more easily come to the fore as a necessary component of such strategies.

Since 1975, when the countries of West Africa committed themselves to forming an economic community, how many member states have drawn up national development plans or programs with regional considerations or the regional market as their point of reference? What measures have been introduced by governments as incentives for their business communities to venture into cross-border investments and transactions, and what encouragement are ordinary people offered to think in West African terms? An integration culture is not yet conspicuous in the region nor is integration accorded the high priority it deserves on national economic agendas.

The required level of regional solidarity and community spirit can be expected to develop by itself, over time, through the accumulation of shared experiences, growing awareness of the advantages of belonging to the Community, or a clearer perception of common interests. However, this process could be actively reinforced through national mechanisms to promote the virtues of regional integration while propagating knowledge and understanding of how regional cooperation can be used in support of national development goals.

THE POLITICAL DIMENSION

It was the rise of nationalism that inspired the peoples of the colonies to seek political independence. Subsequently, the creation of a national identity and the exercise of national sovereignty have been prominent features of the post-independence political agenda. Today, that legacy of national sovereignty and the jealousy with which it is guarded have become obstacles to progress on the road to regional integration, which requires a certain sharing of sovereignty among members of the community. Exacerbating this tendency are other aspects of the colonial heritage that continue to influence national institutions and attitudes in the political as in other fields, including differences in legal and educational systems or administrative structures or the North-South orientation of national economic structures.

Differences in political ideology have also influenced attitudes and approaches to regional integration. For example, during the negotiation of the ECOWAS rules of origin and the Protocol on Community Enterprises, socialist governments and national administrations that were pursuing strong indigenization policies fought for a regional policy that encouraged greater state or indigenous participation. Against this were member states wedded to the laissez-faire ideology, who advocated a more liberal approach to the issue of third country participation in Community projects. The latter ideological school eventually won the day, since the rules have recently been revised, by lowering to 25% the share of indigenous equity participation required for goods to qualify as originating from the Community.

Always lurking in the political shadows is the unexpressed fear of domination by Nigeria: the "big country" issue. Nigeria overshadows every other country in the region several times over in terms of population, gross domestic product, and natural resource endowment. An effort has been made to counterbalance this by placing ECOWAS member states on an equal footing in all things except their financial contributions to the Community (which are prorated), but the concern remains. The French tend to provoke and sustain this fear of domination, as they strive to maintain their sphere of influence in the region. It is in the interests of the Community that this issue be carefully dealt with to dispel any remaining fears and promote greater commitment to the regional integration process.

The wave of reforms currently sweeping the region in favour of political pluralism and economic liberalism should help to narrow political and ideological differences among member states. This tendency may be reinforced by the Community's adoption in 1991 of the Abuja Declaration of Political Principles, which enshrines a minimum set of democratic principles as guidance to member states in their quest for a well-established democratic society. This is a modest beginning of political cooperation, but constitutes a vital step nonetheless. The revised Treaty also envisages the establishment of a West African parliament to promote grassroots involvement and popular participation in regional integration and cooperation. More democratic rule should bring about a more stable and congenial political atmosphere, which is a sine qua non for regional integration. The establishment of liberal democracy throughout the region would also enhance free enterprise, freedom of association, and the free flow of information and ideas, all of which are fundamental to the viability of an economic community.

The revised ECOWAS Treaty also postulates a degree of supranationality for the Community, and member states must attune themselves to this new perspective. The wranglings that accompanied the ratification of the Maastricht Treaty in Denmark, Britain, Germany, and France are indicative of the difficulty of selling the idea of supranationality to national governments and their electorates. However, this should not blind ECOWAS countries to the precedent set by the European Union (EU) in according important supranational powers to the European Commission and other EU institutions in economic matters.

THE ECONOMIC DIMENSION

The poor economic health of member states since the early 1980s has been a major impediment to integration efforts. Severe economic recession has obliged member states to abandon all plans for long-term economic development, including regional integration, in the pursuit of short-term stabilization. The economic crisis has also emptied government coffers. The limited revenue that has been available to the public sector has thus had to be rationed in accordance with short-term priorities that excluded regional integration or gave it only token recognition. After the deep decline of the early 1980s, national economies are only now barely achieving a measure of stabilization. Unfortunately, there is little evidence that the reforms have had the desired effect of restructuring the region's economies, and the need to transform and diversify the regional economic base is more acute than ever. The establishment of a more stable economic environment, capable of encouraging long-term investment and development, should be one of the preoccupations of the ECOWAS Consultative Forum mentioned earlier.

REGIONAL PEACE AND SECURITY

No provision was made in the ECOWAS Treaty for regional cooperation in political and defence matters. However, the need to create an atmosphere of confidence and trust throughout the region as a precondition for regional integration was felt soon after the Community became operational. This led to the adoption of the 1978 Protocol on Non-Aggression and the 1981 Protocol on Mutual Assistance in Defence. Unfortunately, neither protocol was ever implemented, while political tensions within and among member states continued to mount.

The climax of these developments was the outbreak of civil war in Liberia and the establishment of an ECOWAS mediation mechanism for regional disputes. The usefulness of concerted action by member states in the Liberian conflict can be gauged by the contribution that the ECOWAS peace initiative has made: arrest of the carnage, restoration of peace, and initiation of the electoral process in Liberia. However, the ECOWAS peace initiative is only an ad hoc arrangement designed to address a specific problem. It was not meant as a recipe to meet the future needs of the Community.

The disruption of regional integration programs by political tensions is apparent. Regional instability also retards the economic growth and development of member states and acts as a disincentive to investment. What is needed, therefore, is some sort of common security arrangement that would safeguard and guarantee the long-term peace and security of the region and meet the needs of all member states. The two protocols mentioned above address conflicts between member states as well as aggression by external forces, and could form the basis for the establishment of such a system. With the limited resources at their disposal, member states could extend on-going public expenditure reforms to cover national defence spending, in the context of such a regional security system.

INSTITUTIONAL ARRANGEMENTS AT THE NATIONAL LEVEL

Public administration in West Africa was a creation of the colonial powers and an instrument for taxation, coercion, and general administration. Developmental functions were added when Africans took over the reins of government in the 1960s. Despite their limited technical and managerial capabilities, governments of the time were more inclined to keep a tight rein on the economy than to foster a congenial economic environment for the private sector. This could not but hamper the regional integration process. Recent liberalization measures are lowering the profile of government in the economy and encouraging its adoption of a more positive and supportive role in its dealings with the private sector. This should have a positive affect on the regional integration process, through the reduction of administrative barriers and restrictions to international trade, investment, and migration.

Economic liberalization should also influence the character of regional politics. In the past, decision-making for regional integration was carried out by heads of state, with business conducted on a strictly government-to-government basis. As liberalization proceeds, governments can be expected to encourage a more active role for the private sector in the integration process, through the close involvement of regional private-sector organizations, such as the Federation of West African Chambers of Commerce, the Federation of West African Manufacturers Associations, and the West African Banks' Association, in the ECOWAS decision-making process.

For regional integration to flourish as an instrument of economic development also calls for a restructuring of national institutional arrangements. The importance of regional integration requires that a key ministry be established in each country to act as a focal point. It should be mandated to assume the coordination of all forms of regional integration and cooperation and should ensure that national development policies and decisions are cast in a regional perspective. Although attempts of this sort have been made in a number of member states, such arrangements are not effective anywhere in the region. Instead, one finds small coordination units, created in certain ministries as token gestures representative of how peripheral regional integration remains to the national economic agenda. Such deficiencies have a deleterious effect on the attention accorded to regional integration matters and the level of preparation and participation at ECOWAS meetings.

Participation of the sectoral ministries in the integration process should be encouraged through the creation and proper functioning of interministerial coordination committees. Regional development policies and strategies have been adopted at the national level in almost all sectors of economic activity, but these must be pulled together into a national strategy and their implementation must be ensured.

Support should likewise be provided for regional efforts to mobilize and create community awareness among the different strata and socio-professional groups of West African society. This requires that the relevant ministries be involved in the organization of these groups at the national level and that they actively promote their participation in regional integration programs.

EXTERNAL SUPPORT

Since the adoption of the Second United Nations Development Decade in the 1970s, African countries have repeatedly reaffirmed that the main responsibility for the development of their economies rests with them. However, considerable support from the rest of the world remains necessary, especially in the area of regional cooperation, where the lack of an independent tax base reduces access to financial resources.

Donor attitudes regarding regional cooperation among developing countries have been improving. The signing of the AEC Treaty in 1991 gave impetus to this trend, and many international organizations are currently looking for ways to promote economic integration in Africa (see Lavergne and Daddieh, chapter 6). These initiatives should be coordinated to ensure a more positive contribution to the continental economic integration process. Inadequate funding continues to plague regional cooperation efforts, and the growing interest of the donor community in regional integration will hopefully be translated into financial support. What is certain is that external support will be forthcoming only when the donor community is convinced of the strong commitment of member states to the process.

THE NEED FOR RENEWED LEADERSHIP

It has been said that Africa's current political instability, economic decline, and social discontent reflect a leadership crisis on the Continent. If this is true of individual countries, it is equally valid for the regional integration process. The emergence of stronger leadership could supply the vision and necessary direction and demonstrate the sacrifice and commitment that are essential in any cooperative endeavour.

Not all countries have the same appreciation of the need for cooperation; some have to be coaxed and pulled along by others. West Africa has been fortunate in having certain leaders and countries that are strongly committed to the ideal of regional integration. Some member states have always been more assiduous in meeting their financial obligations to the community; and some have taken the lead in initiating important regional cooperation projects and programs. Some community arrangements have required special sacrifices from certain member states (regarding formulas for determining financial contributions, trade liberalization schedules, or compensation formulas for the loss of tariff revenue), and the acceptance of these arrangements is a clear manifestation of solidarity and community spirit.

At this stage in West African integration, when many bold and new initiatives are required to propel the process forward, there is an urgent need for such leadership qualities. Each member country should be able to determine its obligations to the community. Each should define an area where it can make some unique contribution and set an example by assuming a leadership role. Such an attitude would permit member states that have not participated as fully or actively as they are capable of doing to redress the imbalance.

REVISED ECOWAS TREATY

Certain initiatives have been undertaken in the early 1990s to revitalize the regional integration process in West Africa. In 1991, the ECOWAS Summit of Heads of State recognized that the 1975 Treaty was in need of overhaul, and a Committee of Eminent Persons was created to examine most of the issue-areas identified above and make appropriate recommendations in the form of revised Treaty provisions. In carrying out its assignment, the Committee interpreted its mandate to include consideration of institutional matters, regional economic integration, political cooperation, regional peace and security, and the financing of regional integration efforts (ECOWAS 1992).

The revised Treaty was submitted to the Summit of Heads of State held in Cotonou in July 1993, and was adopted at that level. Although there were delays in securing ratification of the Treaty,[3] and ratification in itself does not guarantee implementation, the revised Treaty lays out some clear directions for progress on regional integration in West Africa, and reaffirms in different ways the priority that should be given to regional integration by all 16 West African countries (ECOWAS 1993b).

♦ It defines ECOWAS as ultimately the sole economic community in the region and clearly spells out the relationship between ECOWAS and all other West African IGOs.

♦ A certain change of orientation is evident in the supranational status accorded the Community and the undertaking to pool national sovereignties through measures that would strengthen community institutions and make community decisions directly enforceable in member states.

♦ The powers of the community institutions and the executive secretary are enhanced to reflect the greater priority being placed on regional integration. Instead of a community tribunal, the revised Treaty provides for a court of justice to reflect the important role this body has to play. A West African parliament will be part of the political cooperation program to be developed. Similarly, the expected greater involvement of the professions and interest groups in general has led to the inclusion of an economic and social council in the revised Treaty.

♦ Sector ministers will be more involved in the decision-making process and the technical commissions have been reclassified to ensure better representation at meetings as well as a more efficient organization of the corresponding technical departments of the executive secretariat. Rationalization of IGOs is expected to lead to the creation of specialized agencies to handle specific sectoral programs.

♦ The institutions provided for in the two existing protocols on defence matters will be reviewed and made operational to handle the defence cooperation program and ensure regional peace and security.

---

[3] Ratification of the Treaty came into effect on August 23, 1995, when the ninth instrument of ratification was received by the Secretariat. The countries that had still not ratified the Treaty at the end of 1995 were Cape Verde, Côte d'Ivoire, Gambia, Guinea Bissau, and Mauritania.

- The revised Treaty proposes that the perennial problem of arrears in contributions should be overcome by instituting a system for generating an independent resource base. A community levy, representing a percentage of the value of total imports from third countries, would be imposed to generate sufficient funds for both the operational budget of the Community and the development assistance extended to member countries by the ECOWAS fund.

- In the field of economic integration, the objective is the achievement of a common market and a monetary union. Equal attention is given to all economic sectors and activities, including the service sector. The revised Treaty aims to ensure that not only market integration, but also production and physical integration are achieved.

- Emphasis is placed on private-sector participation. The private sector is to be encouraged to participate actively in community decision-making and is assigned a bigger role in the implementation of community programs. The ECOWAS protocol on community enterprises is expected to be revised to reflect greater reliance on the private sector, and a community investment code is proposed, to favour private-sector involvement in cross-border investments.

- Building on the 1975 ECOWAS Treaty, which recognized the need for regional cooperation in the social and cultural sector, the revised Treaty spells out measures to be adopted in various fields. Important areas of cooperation, such as science and technology, information, and defence, which did not feature in the 1975 Treaty but were included in the community work program are now provided for in the revised Treaty, and the democratic principles contained in the Abuja Declaration of Political Principles form part of the general undertaking by member states in the preamble to the revised Treaty.

PROSPECTS FOR THE FUTURE

With the adoption of the AEC Treaty and the revision of the ECOWAS Treaty, West Africa seems to possess the institutional framework necessary to move forward on regional integration. The future course and success of that process cannot, of course, be taken for granted, if experience to date is any guide.

Some commentators have argued that West Africa's low level of economic development and the indifference of some governments to regional integration under ECOWAS make it necessary for West Africa to adopt only a loose form of regional cooperation conducted on a pragmatic and ad hoc basis. The successes of the Southern African Development Community (SADC, formely SADCC, the Southern African Development Coordination Conference) and the Association of South East Asian Nations (ASEAN), and the loose arrangement within the Latin American Economic System (SELA) have been cited in support of this argument.

I argue for a more ambitious approach, in light of the limitations on economic development imposed by the small size of national markets and the limited resource base. Already, West African countries have slipped far behind in the development race, and unless a more serious attempt at economic development is made, the current sociopolitical crises will continue to threaten the very survival of most West African states. A well-structured approach to regional integration and cooperation holds the promise of accelerated development through the coordinated exploitation of the region's human, natural and capital resources.

Regional economic integration involves more than market liberalization. The ECOWAS experience illustrates the importance of investments in physical infrastructure, and direct interventions of various sorts are required to promote the development and diversification of the regional production base. Monetary integration is also needed in order to harmonize monetary policies, improve macro-economic management, and eventually replace the weak inconvertible domestic currencies of the region with a single regional currency. Regional integration should also embrace cooperation in the social, cultural, defence, and political fields, if only because the absence of stable and compatible policies in these areas militates against the success of regional integration in other respects. Developments in the European Union amply demonstrate the need for serious consideration of these other dimensions of regional integration.

The time has come for the region to embark on a viable development strategy. The functioning of ECOWAS and the problems that regional integration has encountered clearly indicate that member countries have not completely accepted regional integration as a development tool and have yet to accord it the necessary priority. Hopefully, the signing of the revised ECOWAS Treaty will mark an important step in the redynamization and reorientation of ECOWAS. The success of implementation of the new Treaty will depend on many factors, including a change of attitude on the part of all the actors involved in the integration process.

REFERENCES

ECA (United Nations Economic Commission for Africa). Various issues. Survey of economic and social conditions in Africa. ECA Secretariat, Addis Ababa, Ethiopia.

ECA (United Nations Economic Commission for Africa); ECOWAS (Economic Community of West African States). 1987. Proposals for the rationalisation of West African integration efforts. ECA, Addis Ababa, Ethiopia.

ECA/MULPOC (United Nations Economic Commission for Africa, Multinational Programming and Operational Centre). 1993. Directory of West African intergovernmental organisations. UNECA/MULPOC, Niamey, Niger.

ECOWAS (Economic Community of West African States). 1992. Final report of the Committee of Eminent Persons for the Review of the ECOWAS Treaty. ECOWAS Secretariat, Lagos, Nigeria.

———— 1993a. Economic Community of West African States Revised Treaty. ECOWAS Secretariat, Lagos, Nigeria.

———— 1993b. Regional peace and stability: a pre-requisite for integration, 1992/93. Annual report of the executive secretary general. ECOWAS Secretariat, Lagos, Nigeria.

Hess, R. 1991. Report on study on constraints to trade, payments and investment flows in ECOWAS. Report prepared for ECOWAS by Imani Development Ltd, Harare, Zimbabwe.

OAU (Organization of African Unity). 1991. Treaty establishing the African Economic Community. OAU, Abuja, Nigeria.

CHAPTER 3

THEORETICAL AND STRATEGIC APPROACHES

— Naceur Bourenane —

This paper analyzes the theoretical and strategic underpinnings of conventional approaches to regional integration in Africa. The key feature of these conventional approaches is seen to be their voluntarism — the analysis of regional integration as an exercise in economic optimization independent of underlying social and political realities. The issue of implementation is thus reduced to the choice of instruments for achieving one's goals, be it the design of institutional mechanisms or the choice of operational modalities. The lack of attention to socio-political considerations leads to a lack of realism in the definition of objectives and strategic orientations.

Bourenane proposes an alternative approach based on the notion of community-building. Such an approach would more rigorously take into account the sociopolitical impediments to regional integration, while actively promoting those agents of change with a stake in the process. Community-building is conceived as a long-term process requiring attention to national priorities and the evolving interests of stakeholders, and a progressive and flexible approach. Under this strategic approach, the state is no longer perceived as the sole agent and promoter of regional integration, becoming instead a sort of catalyst in a process involving multiple actors.

RECENT ECONOMIC TRANSFORMATIONS, marked by the emergence of the European Union and the North American Free Trade Agreement, have brought into focus the issues of regional integration and regional community. This is reflected in political speeches and has been the subject of numerous studies. Some studies on economic recovery and future global trends have devoted entire chapters to the issue.

However, this renewal of interest in regional integration seems to be occurring without any serious rethinking of regional integration as an exercise in community-building. Existing models and analytical approaches have failed to adapt to changing realities, and have taken little account of the failures and successes of ongoing efforts at regional integration. Operationally, the trend is one of continued reliance on a voluntaristic, instrumentalist and mimetic approach, as opposed to the sort of strategic and realistic approach called for by the complexity of economic, social, and cultural realities. Our way of thinking about regional integration needs to be revisited, and we begin here with a critical examination of the way the problem has been posed in the theoretical literature, before considering how this approach could be improved and better alligned with operational realities to increase its likelihood of success over the long term.

CONVENTIONAL APPROACHES TO REGIONAL INTEGRATION

BASIC CONCEPTS

Let us begin by clarifying some conceptual ambiguities. Regional integration is often perceived as a prelude to unification, understood to represent the existence of homogeneous rules and principles governing behaviour in a given spatial area. Historically speaking, this is false. As the example of the Association of South-East Asian Nations shows, integration does not lead automatically to union. Despite the fact that these countries are economically integrated, they are far from constituting a union. Similarly, a union can exist without integration, as was the case with the colonial unions in Africa. To avoid confusion, the notion of integration refers here to a voluntary pooling of resources for a common purpose by two or more sets of partners belonging to different states. The process aims to reinforce structural interdependencies of a technical and economic sort, with positive effects on economic welfare. According to this definition, it is clear that the unions imposed by the colonial powers in Africa (French West Africa, French Equatorial Africa, the South African Customs Union, etc.) were not the outcome of an integrative process. These unions resulted from the outside imposition of uniform policies on unintegrated partners and geographic areas. Viewed in this way, a union can be the result of either integration or the submission of several contiguous areas to the same authority, with or without recourse to violence.

As revealed in the title of this volume, the notion of integration is often used contiguously with that of cooperation, and the latter is often considered to be the instrument of the former. However, cooperation does not necessarily lead to integration. The rationale behind it can be quite different. Cooperation is a collaborative venture between two or more partners, with common interests in a given issue. It can be limited to a single issue, field of activity, or a particular sector and the contractual nature of cooperative arrangements means that they are time bound, and reversible. These are agreements born of special circumstances, to address particular problems. Furthermore, cooperation does not necessarily imply a relationship of equality among partners, as it may include an element of foreign aid by one partner in favour of the other. It involves specific initiatives, bringing together two or more partners, on a collaborative basis. The notion of integration is more closely related to that of community and community-building. It takes into account the collective nature of the process of building a collective space in a conscious, negotiated, and irreversible manner by partners who have chosen to share a common destiny in a politico-institutional framework pre-established through negotiation, based on a strategic vision of their common future.

A distinction should also be made between regional integration and economic integration. The latter implies the integration of economic activities, sectors, or subsectors in the pursuit of economic advantage. In this, the geographic dimension, notably spatial proximity, is not always fundamental. In contrast, the notion of regional integration cannot be detached from its association with geographic and physical space. Regional affiliation becomes a determining factor around which are defined feelings of cultural and political cohesion and a shared vision of the future for a defined group. The two notions are frequently confused in the literature, although they only partially intersect. Economic integration may even prevent regional integration, if it takes place between regions that are geographically removed at the expense of neighbouring regions.

To summarize, the concept of regional integration can be distinguished from associated concepts along three main lines: it is *voluntary* (unions may or may not be voluntary); it is *collectively undertaken*, bringing into play the concept of community-building (in contrast to the contractual and temporary nature of regional cooperation); and it is *geographically defined* (in contrast to the notion of economic integration in the generic sense of the term).

THEORETICAL FOUNDATIONS

The theoretical foundations of conventional approaches to regional integration date back to three important schools of economic thought in the 1960s: neoclassical economics, marxism, and development economics.

The earliest theoretical work on regional integration emanated from the theory of comparative advantage in international trade, and the interest of liberal economists in promoting the reduction of tariff and nontariff barriers to trade. At issue was the choice of modalities for implementing such policies and the effectiveness of regional integration as a mechanism of trade liberalization.

Viner's classic article on the subject pointed out that regional economic integration could lead to either "trade creation" or "trade diversion" (Viner 1950). By reducing trade barriers between neighbouring countries, customs unions and free trade areas could promote economic efficiency in the allocation of resources by contributing to the gradual strengthening of international trade. However, the emergence of such economic entities could also promote trade "diversion" and become a source of economic inefficiency, if the most competitive producers of a particular product suddenly found themselves excluded from the regional market as a result of the customs union.

This approach continues to inspire the economics profession even today, and the issue of integration seen from the point of view of comparative advantage and the trade creation/diversion dichotomy is still prevalent in the specialized literature, as reflected in contemporary debate on whether the formation of major economic blocs constitutes progress or a hinderance to the liberalization of international trade. However, there are serious analytic limitations to this model, with its focus on static efficiency in the allocation of resources, for countries whose main interest lies in the dynamics of development and industrialization.

Marxist-Leninist thinkers have adopted a different approach (see Inotai 1982; Benallègue 1987). In their view, integration emerges as a reflection of the internationalization of capital and is intrinsic to the evolution of the capitalist economy. For example, the creation of a single European market is seen to reflect the concentration of capital and the internationalization of European firms, rather than the desire of welfare-maximizing governments to rationalize the allocation of resources among the countries concerned. The integration of the European market is thus the consequence, not the precursor, of the transformation of production and trade in favour of larger firms. Regional integration, so conceived, is a source of exclusion and impoverishment of small-scale enterprise and a range of social groups through the usual mechanisms of market displacement. Developing countries intent on actively promoting development through the initiative of the state are urged not to rely on free market forces. Integration among developing countries, in this view, should be geared toward the rational use of available resources according to a planned and centralized approach to production for the satisfaction of the region's own needs.

Although appealing in its dynamic vision of development, this approach is based on some questionable assumptions, notably about the effectiveness of planning in relation to markets. The rapid collapse of the Eastern Bloc's Council for Mutual Economic Assistance (COMECON) after the break up of the Soviet Union has largely relegated to the history books an approach to economic cooperation and integration based on centralized planning and government directives.

The analysis adopted by Marchal (1965) and Perroux (1966) seemed to mark a watershed in thinking about integration. These authors proposed an alternative approach that would take into account the historical dimension of economic and social phenomena. According to Marchal, integration as the *result* of development is distinct from integration as an *instrument* or precondition of development. Economic integration can be perceived as the historical product of evolving technical, economic, and social structures; or it can be the product of conscious efforts on the part of human societies, acting collectively to improve their economic condition as a matter of policy choice. Marchal shows that integration taken as a product of history is first and foremost the result of social transformation. It cannot occur just anywhere or under just any conditions. Perroux (1966) follows a similar approach, centred upon three questions: who integrates? through what process? and to whose advantage?

However, in operational terms, these two authors do not stray very far from the voluntarist approach of their predecessors or from related development thinking prevalent at the time. For Marchal (1965), integration must be based on industrialization as its driving force, and it must be sustained by those social forces capable of supporting and organizing the industrialization process. Similarly, borrowing from development and industrialization thinking of the 1960s, Perroux (1966) builds his model around the concepts of growth poles, strategic investments, and industrialization. Industrialization is presented here as a collective instrument of development, based on import protection. He draws a distinction between three models of integration and industrialization, based respectively on the use of markets, productive investments, or institutional mechanisms.[1]

---

[1] The early thinking of the United Nations Economic Commission for Africa (ECA) on the subject of regional integration was marked by the same orientation in promoting an approach based on productive investments, in which development would spread from its origins in selected growth poles to all regions of the continent (ECA 1988).

This developmentalist and industrializing view of integration ends up assigning a secondary role to the social dimension of the issue, thus abandoning the approach initially adopted and replacing it with a technocratic and geographically focused one. Perroux (1966) thus begins by proposing a socioeconomic and political approach to integration, but allows it to be deformed by the influence of existing development theories.

This brief overview suffices to illustrate the voluntaristic thread of these various approaches. Each of these models is based on the absence, or at least the neutrality, of extra-economic factors in decision-making, thus ignoring the social and political dynamics likely to have an impact on the integration process. Such an approach may be of some use in the design of theoretical constructs, but it is hopelessly inadequate if the aim is to design actual economic policies or strategies for change.

INSTRUMENTS AND MODALITIES

The voluntaristic character of the above models has encouraged scholars and practitioners to focus on the choice of instruments for implementing regional integration, to the detriment of community-building as an issue. Analysis has thus revolved around the kinds of institutions to be set up and the choice of modalities to be promoted, as opposed to the identification of key stakeholders or the definition of the conditioning environment necessary for integration to occur under their impetus.

The institutional approach

The institutions to be established may be of a predominantly multilateral or intergovernmental character. The core institutions in the former case will consist of specific, permanent structures charged with responsibility for designing and proposing integration programs for government approval and pursuing their implementation once they are adopted. Such community organizations have their own headquarters, staff and operating budgets, and their decisions have a binding supranational character for all parties concerned. The intergovernmental approach is more ad hoc in orientation. Emphasis is given to specialized intergovernmental commissions that meet periodically to make decisions or monitor their implementation by participating countries. These commissions are made up of appointed high officials with ministerial responsibilities who are liable to change at any time, and only the structures themselves have a degree of permanence.

Notwithstanding the contrary impression that might be derived from the existence of permanent secretariats and structures in all African IGOs it is the second orientation which prevails in Africa (see Ntumba, this volume). The powers and scope of action of existing IGOs and their secretariats are severely limited, and the real power in each case rests with intergovernmental bodies such as the Authority of Heads of State and Government, the Council of Ministers, or specialized technical commissions composed of government representatives. This corresponds to an approach based on cooperation rather than community-building, and reflects the underlying objective, which is not to transcend, so much as to reaffirm, national sovereignty.

IGOs all over Africa, and ECOWAS in particular, have attempted to imitate the European experience by creating bodies structurally similar to those of the European Union, without giving them the same functions or powers. The lack of a truly African strategy manifests itself in the choice of priorities, which have little impact on integration, because they are too ambitious in view of the resources available to member countries, or simply irrelevant.

The West African experience is probably the most elaborate example of this. Although a degree of progress has certainly been achieved, some of the objectives pursued by ECOWAS were clearly overambitious and unrealistic in terms of the established time-frames. This has been the case in the attempt to liberalize intraregional trade through the establishment of a customs union. A second example was the effort to establish joint air transport facilities. Similar observations could be made with regard to CEAO which was dissolved on 14 March 1994. Examination of the results achieved under CEAO with regard to economic integration and the establishment of a customs union indicates a lack of sustained progress in redefining the structure of trade or increasing its volume, despite member countries' adherence to the same francophone community and the prior existence of the West African Monetary Union (UMOA) (ACP-EEC 1990). Such examples illustrate the difficulty of implementing an integration strategy in the absence of adequate resources and a community-building perspective from the very beginning.

Modalities

The shortage of theories of economic integration to serve as a reference point for empirical work and applied research has encouraged scholars to focus on the definition of operational modalities, their sequencing, and the identification of specific measures to be taken (such as the review of customs duties and nomenclatures or the definition of rules of origin), with little assessment of their likely impact or social ramifications.

Balassa (1961) distinguishes two alternative approaches, one based on individual projects and the other on some form of packaging. The advantage of the latter approach is to offer some benefit to each partner country. This would allow trade liberalization to proceed by concentrating on products that guarantee each country some increase in income. In the case of developing countries whose resources are limited, the package would also include external financing to support the development of infrastructure, the launching of new export products, etc.

Adopting a similar form of analysis, the ECA (1990) examines three alternative approaches, involving comprehensive, sectoral, or project-based perspectives. The comprehensive approach implies comprehensive action involving all sectors of economic activity. It calls for rigorous planning of the integration process, harmonization of economic policies, and coordination of development plans. It also requires the establishment of multilateral bodies with supranational powers capable of managing the process. Although such an approach has obvious appeal due to the intersectoral trade-offs that could be arranged among the partner countries to ensure an equitable distribution of benefits and costs, its implementation would be complex, cumbersome, and costly. The approach also takes for granted a higher degree of economic management at the national level than is currently possible, given the limited capabilities of national planning structures, limited control over national economic realities, and the conditioning effects of structural adjustment programs and overwhelming debt burdens.

The sectoral approach is more progressive, focusing on one sector at a time through the harmonization of development policies and action plans. Though easier to implement, this approach could stumble on the issue of compensation to participants negatively affected by the restructuring of any particular sector, because promises of benefits to come are unlikely to satisfy the parties concerned.

The third approach is limited to the identification and implementation of specific projects. It is the easiest and least burdensome approach for participating countries to adopt, but it is also very limited, involving no significant effort to harmonize global and sectoral economic policies. It also fails to address the distribution issue regarding the indirect costs and positive impacts of the projects to be implemented.

Various international institutions, including those belonging to the UN system, the World Bank, and the European Union have adopted a different approach based on integration through cooperation. An EEC document (1988) defines two preliminary stages in the pursuit of regional integration: thematic or functional cooperation and sectoral policy coordination. The former involves collaboration in the exploitation of shared resources (e.g., river basin development) or joint efforts in fighting a common problem (e.g., locust control). The second stage involves harmonizing sectoral policies (in the textile industry, for example) to avoid the contradictions and problems stemming from the adoption of uncoordinated national policies.

The World Bank appears to favour regional cooperation along three main lines: economic liberalization aimed at market deregulation and increased access to global markets; greater regional coordination of monetary and macroeconomic policies in the context of its structural adjustment programs; and maximum pragmatism in the design of cooperation schemes involving different groups of countries or areas of collaboration (World Bank 1989). However, little has been done to incorporate such measures in World Bank practice in most of Africa, especially in the the Bank's application of structural adjustment programs, which have yet to make the shift from a national approach to a regional one.

LIMITATIONS OF THE INSTRUMENTAL APPROACH AND ELEMENTS OF A NEW APPROACH

The primacy accorded to the instrumental approach in dealing with community issues has severely handicapped past attempts at economic integration. The application of this approach has been characterized by excessive state control in the definition and implementation of regional integration schemes, inordinate voluntarism in the face of operational constraints, and the mimicry of approaches used elsewhere, particularly in Europe (Bach, this volume).

Regional integration has come to be identified with the definition of technical and bureaucratic modalities and institutional mechanisms for enhancing economic cooperation between neighbouring countries. The potential for conflict in the pursuit of different partners' socioeconomic objectives is overlooked or glossed over, along with the need for setting priorities in the timing and geographic impact of various actions. It is only through studies such as those by the Club du Sahel, the Permanent Inter-State Committee for Drought Control in the Sahel (CILSS), or the

Conference of Ministers of Agriculture on problems of food security that new and more realistic ways of thinking are emerging.[2]

From an historical point of view, this instrumental approach can be attributed to two myths carried over from colonial times and the national liberation movements: the idea that certain areas are naturally amenable to integration due to their historical past as colonies of the same foreign power; and the notion of fraternal bonds of solidarity among states and peoples as a result of their struggles for political independence. The first of these two myths continues to influence the thinking of numerous researchers with regard to French-speaking Africa (Diouf 1993). However, the notion of regional integration is misapplied in this context, because the subjugated and pacified areas in question were united by force of the colonial authorities, and not by choice of the original inhabitants. The resulting unity was short-lived in many ways, because the very purpose of the struggle for independence was to abolish the dominant relationships established by the colonial regimes. As for the liberation movements, they covered a wide range of opinions and political philosophies whose only common feature was their opposition to the colonial state and its socially discriminatory and repressive nature. This accounted for the opposing views that surrounded the discussions leading up to the creation of the Organization of African Unity following independence.

The instrumental stance taken in most scholarly treatments of regional integration led to a dearth of analysis regarding the socio-economic, political, cultural, and spatial feasibility of integration projects and helped to reinforce the voluntarism of state-led initiatives. This helps to account for the excessive optimism of government leaders and high officials at summit meetings of intergovernmental organizations. Heads of state were thus reinforced in their apparent belief that it was sufficient to agree among themselves at the highest level for regional integration to magically occur over the short or medium term. Everything was done as though the authority of heads of state was absolute, as though they were the total masters of their respective societies and totally independent of their regional and international environments, and only had to copy the experience of others to succeed.

The idea of indiscriminately copying institutions found in Europe and elsewhere is not only a delusion, but an obstacle to progress in

---

[2] See Brah et al. (1993) and the studies they cite. A summary of the Conference of Agricultural Ministers project, the Sissokho initiative, is outlined by Lavergne and Daddieh, this volume.

building a regional community in West Africa or elsewhere on the continent. The institutional choices made by the European Union resulted from specific historical circumstances based on high growth rates, low income differentials among the various countries, considerable local managerial and technological capability, high levels of economic trade, government structures with a high degree of legitimacy, a strong desire to end generations of war and conflict, and access to massive external support through the Marshall Plan. None of these conditions exist in Africa!

A regional community cannot be constructed without taking into account the specificities of the countries and stakeholders involved, including their own historical experiences, in identifying the errors of the past and new paths for the future. Only in this way will it be possible to overcome the limits of existing models that remain totally divorced from sociohistorical realities, despite all their apparent pragmatism in focusing on concrete modalities and timetables for action. Efforts to develop a general theory of regional integration and community-building should not blind us to the specific problems of each region, in light of its own social and economic reality, history, and culture.

THE BUILDING BLOCKS OF A REALISTIC AND DYNAMIC INTEGRATION STRATEGY

We propose a progressive approach to the construction of regional communities focused on what is strategically useful and possible at the social and technical levels. The choice and design of instruments and modalities so central to conventional approaches become secondary in this context. The type of institution to be established, the specific measures to be applied, and the time-table to be followed will depend on the nature and content of the strategy chosen, the context in which it is to be applied, the nature of the actors involved, and the nature of their interest in the process. They cannot be defined in advance.

Building on national strategies

The approach should be a pragmatic one, based on the adoption of a realistic and dynamic integration strategy. Among the building blocks constituting such a strategy, the first relates to the very notion of community-building, which should reflect a cumulative consensus among the actors concerned at the subnational, national, and international levels. This implies that regional construction should be based on national strategies, defined as part of the democratic process.

Integration should be viewed as a gradual process, in which higher and higher levels of cooperation are achieved, through a process aimed more at the strengthening of emerging national economies than their dissolution into a larger regional body. Regional integration should not be viewed as a panacea in the pursuit of economic recovery and development. It can at best be a complement, not a substitute, for national programs, and it is essential for member countries to have a clear vision of their own development priorities. The objective should be to use the community as a vehicle for the promotion of selected economic sectors or activities, in collaborative fashion. Such an approach requires that participating countries rise above petty national rivalries and ulterior motives that are capable of undermining the integration process to foster long-term understanding, solidarity, and mutual confidence among states and economic actors.

The first priority should be the coordination of economic and social policies to harmonize the economic environments in different countries, in favour of stakeholders whose activities are capable of promoting economic integration in a sustained and irreversible way.

A gradual and flexible approach

The second requirement of a more realistic and pragmatic approach lies in the composition of regional groupings. The idea of carving up the continent into a small number of large and exclusive economic communities should be replaced by an approach which follows the lead of stakeholders in various areas of activity. This implies the need for a highly flexible approach and the organization of countries into groups along variable lines according to the objectives of different stakeholders.

The definition of integration programs and time-frames should also take into account the nature of socioethnic structures in and among the countries concerned, the recent history of social relations, and the geostrategic context within which they operate. Socioethnic ties continue to play an important role in conditioning the behaviour of individuals and economic actors everywhere in Africa, and in West Africa specifically. The animosities that prevailed in the past between various social groups can flare up at any time, especially under difficult or unstable economic conditions. As has often occurred, a simple sporting event involving teams from two neighbouring countries or a theft of cattle can have an incommensurate impact on intercountry relations, seriously jeopardizing cooperative initiatives or joint investment projects, which are sometimes perceived by local populations as a source of resource transfer at their expense to the benefit of neighbouring countries.

The role of the state and IGOs

The regional integration process needs to be revisited in terms of the roles assigned to various actors, the state in particular. The evolving political economic context, in which the state is progressively withdrawing from economic activity, suggests a less interventionist role for the state in the promotion of regional integration. The state's role will increasingly be one of informing and supporting the integrative activities of private traders and economic agents operating under competitive market conditions.

However, the role of the state should not be neglected. As the arbiter of resources and provider of regulatory functions, the public sector plays an important role in the promotion or marginalization of different interest groups. Voluntarism in the choice of overall goals and time-frames can thus translate into support for specific groups of actors considered as potential agents of change. Three groups of economic and social actors should be distinguished: those likely to benefit from integration, those mostly unaffected by it, and those likely to lose from it. An understanding of these actors' strategies and ambitions and their economic, political, social, and geographic base is essential to the design of community-building strategies. Under this approach, decisions such as the creation of a free-trade area or the choice of deadlines for its implementation would take into account the existence or absence of private parties interested in taking advantage of new trading opportunities in the countries concerned. The study of transborder flows, such as Meagher's (in this volume), is an example of the type of study needed to understand better the actors involved and the networks through which they operate. Both governments and IGOs should make it a priority to understand the strategic concerns of different groups, in order to build on appropriate sources of support for regional integration.

The future role of IGOs and their affiliated institutions should be reassessed in this light. IGOs should be restructured to serve a support function for stakeholders, instead of continuing to function as extensions and outgrowths of governments without any prerogatives of their own. Such a shift could offer the dual benefit of freeing these bodies from the emasculating grip of higher authorities, while offering some prospect of self-financing by interested parties involved in the on-going community-building process.

Strengthening the knowledge base

The complexity of the issues and the need to balance competing interests in the various African subregions mean that the general approach being advocated here can only be implemented gradually, as the weaknesses of voluntarist and instrumentalist approaches come to be better appreciated, and there develops a better understanding of the various actors, their projects, and strategies.

The knowledge needed to pursue an optimal community-building strategy is neither easily available nor easily obtained. Such knowledge will come from the act of construction itself, which will confirm or invalidate various hypotheses and strategic options, enrich them, or supersede them, as the case may be, in the quest for alternative solutions.

In view of the uncertainties involved, efforts should be made to encourage the participation of stakeholders in the process through the provision of information regarding the stakes involved, the constraints to be faced and the resources to be made available, the dynamics of the process and its possible repercussions, and the successes and failures of experience to date. It is not sufficient to popularize the content of the treaties and decisions, nor to mobilize the support of stakeholders for decisions already taken by the heads of state.

A participatory approach of this sort calls for a change in the status of IGO staff and associated personnel who have, until now, been the handmaidens of the member states. Their contribution as observers of what is happening in the field is essential to any opening up of the process to stakeholders. This sort of shift will require that the IGOs themselves be restructured, and the status of IGO staff clarified. It requires also that IGO staff be sensitized to the need for a more open approach and that they be encouraged to disseminate knowledge that is available to them but has remained confidential or unavailable in documented form.

Better information and understanding of the process should enable us to transcend the conventional explanation of the failure of regional integration by appealing to insufficient "political will." What appears as such should be seen as the political outcome of a combination of factors, strategies, and constraints that cannot be reduced to the will of heads of state, however powerful they may be.

References

ACP (Africa, Caribbean and Pacific); EEC (European Economic Community). 1990. ACP-EEC joint assembly: intra-ACP trade. Internal Document, 7 July.

Agraa, A. (el) (ed.). 1982. International economic integration. St. Martin's Press, New York, NY, USA.

Balassa, B. 1961. Towards a theory of economic integration. Revue internationale des sciences sociales, 14.

Belaouane-Gherari, S. 1988. Les organisations régionales africaines. La Documentation française, Paris, France.

Benallègue, M. 1987. L'intégration économique internationale, politiques et théories, le cas du Maghreb. Université d'Alger, Algiers, Algeria. Magister's thesis.

Brah, M.; Pradelle, J.M.; d'Agostino, V. 1993. Regional cooperation and integration in West Africa: a contribution to the corpus of knowledge from the collaborative research of the CILSS, the Club du Sahel and the Cinergie Unit. Club du Sahel, Paris, France.

Diouf, M. 1993. Intégration, coopération dans le rapport de la Commission sud : un point de vue africain. Council for the Development of Economic and Social Research in Africa, Abidjan, Côte d'Ivoire.

ECA (United Nations Economic Commission for Africa). 1988. Célébration du 25e anniversaire de la CEA. ECA, Addis Ababa, Ethiopia.

———— 1990. Approche régionale de l'intégration économique en Afrique. ECA, Addis Ababa, Ethiopia.

EEC (European Economic Community). 1988. Coopération régionale en Afrique au sud du Sahara : évolution de l'idée régionale et expériences des Conventions de Lomé I-II-III. EEC, Brussels, Belgium.

Inotai, A. 1982. Regional economic integration and international division of labour. Hungarian Scientific Council for World Economy, Budapest, Hungary.

Marchal, A. 1965. L'intégration territoriale. Presses universitaires françaises, Paris, France.

Perroux, F. 1966. Le walraso-parétianisme de commodités escamote les deux questions : qui intègre ? Au bénéfice de qui s'opère l'intégration ? Revue d'économie appliquée, 19 (3/4).

Van Hoek F.J. 1990. Regional cooperation and integration in Europe: lessons to be learned. European Centre for Development Policy Management, Maastricht, Belgium.

Viner, J. 1950. The customs union issue. Carnegie Endowment for International Peace, New York, NY, USA; Stevens and Sons, London, UK.

World Bank. 1989. Sub-Saharan Africa: from crisis to sustainable growth. World Bank, Washington, DC, USA.

CHAPTER 4

CULTURAL DIMENSIONS OF ECONOMIC AND POLITICAL INTEGRATION IN AFRICA

– *Stanislas Adotevi* –

As an African speaking directly to other Africans, Adotevi urges Africa to ground the regional integration process in its own historical and cultural roots. He considers that the notion of precise geographic boundaries is profoundly alien to Africa's historical and cultural traditions, because the rigid geographic boundaries of the post-colonial state contrast sharply with the fluid areas of sociopolitical and cultural integration that existed in the pre-colonial era.

In his view, the fact that the nation-state tends to look upon alternative historical and cultural identities as a form of rivalry to its own authority has led to a profound crisis of identity among the populace that has weakened the nation-states themselves, while condemning to failure any attempt at regional integration limited to the economic or political spheres. Integration cannot be achieved without enlisting the feelings of community and cultural affinity that are so deeply rooted in Africa's history, and the great challenge in promoting regional integration in Africa is therefore to find ways of fostering these feelings of community, which transcend national borders, without threatening the viability of the state.

Adotevi brings a fresh viewpoint to the issue of ethnicity, wherein ethnic loyalties no longer appear merely as a source of political strife and violence. They also represent a wellspring of social identity that could be tapped in facilitating regional integration while reasserting Africa's historical social and cultural values. In contrast to Meagher and Bach, Adotevi sees the dynamism of informal cross-border trade as proof of the vitality of social and cultural identities transcending national borders. However, their points of view are not mutually exclusive, because Adotevi's intent is not to glorify everything that is traditional or informal, but to ensure due recognition of the need for social and cultural identity. He finds that the regional perspective opens a far richer field of options than existing national structures, which are not only artificial, but actually hostile to alternative forms of social identity.

AFRICA TODAY PRESENTS a sorry spectacle of disintegrating social structures in nation-states that are themselves breaking apart. Our euphoric faith in pan-Africanism in the early years after independence has been sadly disappointed. Africa today is divided and torn from within and increasingly marginalized from the rest of the world. In fact, it has never effectively recovered from the shocks of contact with the rest of the world — the impact of the slave trade, Islam, colonialism, and Christianity. Uprooted, partitioned, and divided, Africa today is on the verge of collapse. Africans everywhere recognize this, because the threat is increasing daily that Africans will once again be the unwitting victims of their own history, and accessories to the history of others. Africa needs to be rebuilt, if not to say reinvented. It must be politically united, on the basis of sound economic underpinnings, as part of a process firmly rooted in its own history.

There is general consensus, loudly proclaimed by economists, political scientists, and journalists, but also by historians, sociologists, and anthropologists, that the many and costly IGOs set up to promote regional integration in Africa have been a failure, both subregionally and Africa-wide.

For 30 years, we have listened to Africans repeating the same litany — as if it were some kind of exorcism against their own impotence — whereby integration is a *sine qua non* for development. This was the message at the summit meeting in Addis Ababa in 1963, in Algiers in 1968, and in Addis again in August 1970 and May 1973. Several declarations of bold intention have been made — the Declaration of Kinshasa calling for the creation of an economic community, the Lagos Plan of Action, the Abuja Treaty establishing the African Economic Community — but these have had no real impact. There has been no follow-up of any consequence, and Africa is as far as ever from being truly integrated.

Africa has repeatedly failed to transcend the confines of the nation-state because the foundation was unsound to begin with. We have been building castles in the air, in a process disconnected from African history and current social realities. It is only by returning to Africa's cultural and historical roots that an African homeland can be created and African people freed from the artificial shackles of today's national borders. Only in those roots can be found the conditions for creating the dynamic and viable institutions that are indispensable to the mastery of African history through regional unity.

An individual in Africa is defined by his or her culture, perhaps more so than anywhere else. Africans cut off from their culture are nothing, like the biblical shoot whose life-giving sap no longer flows when it is pruned from the vine. I am Bamileke, Adja, Fula, Wolof, Haussa, Zulu, Tutsi, Amara, or Hutu. I am the child of my culture. It is the sense of rootedness in the community that makes for great civilizations and therein, despite the ethnic conflicts staining African soils today, should lie our hopes and dreams for the future. If Japan and the "dragons" of Southeast Asia have made such astonishing progress, it is because they have remained true to themselves, to their culture, their history, and traditions.

To plant the seeds of regional integration in Africa, we must plumb the very depths of the African soul. There is a whole archeology of integration in Africa to be written to understand how best to marshall our meagre resources and take our own destiny in hand, in a quest that may prove utopic in the end, but constitutes the only way forward if Africa is to escape the sombre prognosis that its recent history otherwise seems to predict.

FALSE SOLUTIONS

We should start by contemplating our failures, not simply as a way of doing penance for them, but to find in our past some still-live embers capable of throwing some light, however diffuse and weak, to point the way.

Three phenomena stand out most clearly as false solutions that have paralysed our thinking and crippled our actions in terms of African integration. First has been a remarkable degree of reductionism and "purity" in creating new regional entities. Unions are created through sheer political will, along purely geographic or linguistic lines, in pursuit of purely economic goals above all else. In disciplinary terms, our thinking has not been allowed to stray beyond the confines of economics, institutionalism, or jurisprudence. History, anthropology, and even sociology have been left out of the picture entirely.

Our second failing has been our veneration of the nation-state and its institutions and structures, notwithstanding the fact that the nation-state in Africa is a remarkably recent and largely arbitrary phenomenon resulting from partition of colonial empires along geographic lines. Post-independence leaders have attempted to create new nations out of these constructs, by closing themselves off, curtailing people's actions and movements, and attempting to control all the "parallel" relationships that people have maintained, in spite of national borders.

Third, we have nearly always tried to impose regional integration from above, ignoring or denying popular practice and the long-standing relations that already exist between peoples. Built on sand, with no solid foundation, the resulting structures have crumbled, demonstrating the natural limits of a strictly economic approach to integration that failed to consider the cultural foundations prerequisite to any true integration process.

THE ARTIFICIALITY OF THE NATION-STATE IN AFRICA

Everywhere in Africa, precolonial states consisted of multiethnic federations. Central authorities in these states limited their functions to maintaining security and collecting taxes, eschewing any effort to meddle in social relationships. This allowed each group to preserve its own language, laws, and customs, and left in place, instead of cultural disintegration, a mutually enriching patchwork of cultural groups.

The colonial powers paid no attention to these traditions when they partitioned the continent; they relied on geographic features like rivers and mountain ranges or meridians and parallels. Only the existence of empires and federations at the level of each colonial power allowed a degree of continuity for certain communities, which became markets of significant size, through the force of events and the quirks of history.

The colonial powers did not always encourage the survival of the federations at the time of decolonization. They were more interested in the survival of separate territories and were supported in this approach by certain African countries. The federations thus did not survive the withdrawal of the imperial powers; and although colonial authorities had engineered a degree of economic complementarity among territories, interlinked in unequal fashion with the economies of the colonial powers, the newly independent states oversaw the break-up of the federations, throwing the proverbial baby out with the bath water. Once the colonial linchpin had snapped, barriers to social and economic interaction totally lacking in rhyme or reason sprang up everywhere, becoming ever more visible and destructive. Everything that divided Africa was unearthed and systematically given new importance. Everything that united Africa was neglected, denied, or scorned. "Modern" efforts at nation-building in Africa thus ended up promoting form without substance.

Africa's independent states ignored not only their own history, but also the European experience that illustrates that a nation is the product of a complex fabric of cultural, social, and economic interests shared by different communities convinced that they are united by something more important than the regional, tribal, or other differences that divide them. By insisting on building nation-states of equal status with precise geographic borders, the post-colonial states turned their backs on the organic structure of groups and tribes inherent to Africa's cultural and historical traditions.

These grafted states are inherently artificial and unstable. If they are incapable of opening up without disintegrating or fearing for their existence, it is because their foundations are not solidly rooted in popular culture. These new African nations are a sort of legal fiction incapable of coming to terms with the geopolitical structures of an older Africa, that was composed of mixed and sometimes independent tribal groupings held together in pluralistic but symbiotic ways. We should, therefore, not be surprised if these states have largely failed the test of time.

The supposed predisposition of Africans toward tribalism and provincialism, sometimes cited as a threat to sociopolitical integration, did not emerge from the traditions of precolonial societies. As Kohnert (1992, p. 9) so brilliantly put it:

> Pre-colonial modes of production in usually multi-ethnic communities created bonds between their various ethnic components through an economic and social division of labour. Granted, there were attempts, even then, in the Songhai empire, for instance, to use religion and ethnicity as a means to consolidate power over subjugated peoples. But generally speaking, ethnic policy was only promoted on a large scale by colonial administrators to ensure the effective domination of different ethnic groups across the artificial ethnic, religious and regional dividing lines of the new colonial state. This policy has been perfected by national leaders of the post-colonial state, who have done so with all the more zeal when pursuing their own interests.

Africa's tragedy has never been more clearly stated.

The argument about how to apportion the blame for Africa's current divisions is far from settled. This is an important issue, worthy of further investigation, but it is clear that colonization built nothing that had to be destroyed or undone before reconstruction could begin. Colonization came and swept away what had existed before and failed to sustain the subregional federations it had established, but in the end planted nothing that took root to any great depth. The land it left behind was hardly virgin territory, but it was still fertile enough to yield a harvest, if properly cultivated. It is the attempt to integrate Africa by the pure and simple extrapolation of formal state structures, inherited from the colonial era and cordoned off following independence, that has condemned our regional organizations to exist as hollow shells of intentions and pious hopes, with no writ beyond the confines of their own bureaucracies.

THE CULTURAL FOUNDATIONS OF INTEGRATION

THE EXPERIENCE OF THE FRANC ZONE

The economists' analysis of integration, focused on the efficient allocation of resources at a given time, is relatively limited in operational terms, despite the many sophisticated variants this analysis has produced. As a case in point, the franc zone — whose two branches in Africa, the West African Monetary Union and the Bank of Central African States, share a common currency and monetary policy — is not, as the economists would have it, the outcome of gradual evolution toward economic integration among countries satisfying the criteria for an optimum currency zone. It represents rather the political will and solidarity of French-speaking countries and the desire to endow the French empire with its own, single currency.

Whatever its failings, the franc zone has the merit of being fully operational, in contrast to the many overlapping regional integration projects whose existence is largely theoretical. Certainly, these monetary unions have been the object of legitimate criticism, mainly with regard to the exchange rate of the CFA franc, which remained overvalued for many years to the detriment of member countries. Yet, when we look at it closely, we find that the franc zone today represents the only mechanism of regional integration whose grounding in reality goes beyond the magical incantations of summit Declarations. Nothing durable will be achieved if we lose sight of this simple fact.

There are probably many reasons behind the relative success of the franc zone, but one in particular should be highlighted: what makes these monetary unions among the countries of francophone Africa so uniquely successful is their grounding in historical reality and a cultural reality supported by a common language of business, elites cast in the same educational mold, and similar traditions of public administration and fiscal management.

If such recent constructs can take root and bind inter-state groupings together so securely, then what prevents Africans from drawing upon centuries of historical experience for inspiration to build Africa's great economic units for the 21st century? There lies, in our common African heritage, a wellspring of strength upon which we could draw. Our appreciation of this common heritage is perhaps fragmentary and sometimes hypothetical, but we know it exists, in our history as well as in our shared hopes for the future.

A COMMON HERITAGE

African peoples separated by great distances have developed similar institutions and mythological constructs whose homogeneity attests to our commonalities. Legends about creation provide a good example.

For the Dinkas of southern Sudan — distant descendants of Homer's "noble Ethiopians" — there was a golden age long ago when God lived among men. This African Eden was shattered when a woman so coveted a parcel of land that she struck God with her hoe. God retreated to heaven, and sent a little blue bird to cut the cord that had allowed men to climb to heaven and God. The earth has been cursed ever since: men must work to gain their food, and often go hungry despite it all. It was also then, for good measure, that Death first visited the world.

Several thousand miles away, in the forests of Ghana, the Akans recount virtually the same story, although there is no reason to think that they were ever in contact with the ancestors of the Dinkas. According to the Akan legend, long, long ago, God lived on earth, or was at least very close to us. But there was an old woman whose custom it was to pound her fufu (a cassava dish), and she would bump God with her pestle. God then said to the old woman: "Why do you always do that? Thanks to you, I shall retire to heaven." Which is exactly what he did.

Despite the apparent diversity of ethnic and language groups in Africa, there is at the core what Leopold Senghor (1971) and the "négritude" school, as well as Cheikh Anta Diop (1959, 1960) and his disciples, called a "common fund" of experience. When we examine family organization in precolonial Africa, the structure of the state, and prevailing philosophic and moral precepts, we find many similarities and constants, in spite of distances and geographic barriers. Although African cultures are pluralistic and encompass many ways of life, they just as surely express a certain complementarity that could be tapped to mutual advantage.

The "common fund" expresses itself also in the daily use of African languages in penetrating the linguistic barriers erected by the colonial powers (Ki Zerbo, 1986). African languages could be a force for political integration, becoming a source of social regeneration, without necessarily displacing the foreign languages that allow us to deal with the rest of the world.

CONTINUITY IN CHANGE

The precolonial contacts and linkages that were permitted by African geography survived the colonial assault remarkably well, as if to demonstrate that they draw their vitality from the very source of our cultural identity. Although colonial borders forcibly separated and divided our communities, ethnic groups, and families, they could not sever the blood bonds and family ties that centuries of history and shared experience had forged.

Contacts have been sustained as though borders did not exist, as African people continue to mix and travel. Someone living today in Benin may be elevated to the court of the Sultan of Sekoto in Nigeria tomorrow. Another, who resides in Benin, may work his fields in Togo.

Who among us does not have brothers or cousins somewhere in a neighbouring state or elsewhere in the region? Ethnic groups are scattered all across the region's political frontiers. I know families in Ghana who have relatives in Côte d'Ivoire, and perhaps in Togo and Benin. Ancestor worship as practised among some Ivoirians is found in Ghana as well, because these countries share territory belonging to the same Akan kingdom. Parallels can be found straddling the borders of Zaire and Congo, or Zambia and Zimbabwe. Touré, Traoré, Diallo, and Kane families can be found in Guinea, Mali, Sénégal, and Côte d'Ivoire and even in Niger and Cameroon. One could cite any number of such examples.

Those who deny that Africans have much to trade among themselves ignore the history of precolonial trade, which was based on the exchange of good across different ecological zones, in a dynamic regional trading system centred on the entrepot markets that sprang up at the interstices of these zones. Markets such as these could have become commercial centres of regional economic integration. These included, from east to west, Kukuwa, the famous capital of the state of Borno; Kano, the centre of the African caravan trade; Salaga, the major kola market in Dagoumba country, and finally Kong, at the head of one of the main caravan trade routes linking the Middle East and West Africa.

The problems encountered in promoting regional integration at the formal level stand in contrast to the dynamism of African people who have already managed to integrate in many respects, based on extraordinary levels of intercountry migration and the growth of traditional or "informal" trade.

Circumventing every official barrier thrown up against it, this flourishing integration process is supported by two well-known phenomena in West Africa:

- the sustained ethnic and cultural intermingling of peoples through migration, dating back to the great empires of medieval times;

- the legacy of the great political and social groupings of a previous age, represented today by traditions of social unity among the extended families now scattered through various countries across the Sahel.

To promote the free movement of goods and services is simply to recognize the everyday reality of the marketplace. For in spite of all the linguistic, economic, and legal barriers, you will find, at the Sandaga market in Dakar, Guineans buying products from Niger sold by a trader from Mali.

The fact that contemporary African states have failed in their integration efforts, despite all this, should lead us to question the wisdom of policies espoused over the last 30 years. Having set themselves up as the exclusive arbiters of regional integration, these post-colonial states have denied the legitimacy of any independent integration process, rather than relying on local historical and cultural realities.

SEEDS OF HOPE

The creation of independent African states has had as a corollary the notion of national sovereignty as defined and managed by the state, which has sought to suppress all other sources of social identity. Claims of regional or ethnic identity, leading all too often to violence, are really a desperate form of protest against the painful disconnection of sociocultural entities from the state that determines their destiny.

Today's African states are an inescapable reality. However, if these states hope to play an active role in African integration, they will have to restore some of the sovereignty they have wrested from Africa's sociocultural and regional communities. Only then will contemporary states be able to play an effective part in the integration process, taking fully into account Africa's precolonial history with its emphasis on a communal concept of sovereignty as opposed to a purely national one.

Mechanisms must be found to allow ethnic groups to contribute to nation-building, through socially committed and voluntary forms of participation. To do this requires that certain powers and rights be devolved to ethnic groups in ways that avoid the disintegration of the state itself, through greater regional openness. So conceived, nation-building involves the encouragement and promotion of open societies and open economies, despite any erosion of national sovereignty that might result. Africa can draw on the richness of its own history, in which Fulani can move through Africa, from country to country, while remaining true to their own spirit and contributing to the life of each place they visit.

Africa continues to be the object of our own contempt and the arrogance of others. The task of resurrecting it belongs to us, as a people finding themselves in the very pit of social, political, and economic decay. With nowhere to go but up, the opportunity is ripe for daring departures from existing reality.

I am reminded of what Machiavelli wrote in Chapter XXVI of *The Prince*, at a time when Italy was in even more tragic straits:

> And if, as I said, the Israelites had to be enslaved in Egypt for Moses to emerge as their leader; if the Persians had to be oppressed by the Medes so that the greatness of Cyrus could be recognized; if the Athenians had to be scattered to demonstrate the excellence of Theseus: then, at the present time, in order to discover the worth of an Italian spirit, Italy had to be brought to her present extremity. She had to be more enslaved than the Hebrews, more oppressed than the Persians, more widely scattered than the Athenians; leaderless, lawless, crushed, despoiled, torn, overrun; she had to have endured every kind of desolation. [Exhortation on delivering Italy from the Barbarians]

Trapped at the bottom of the abyss, and contemplating his own historical roots, every African should meditate on these words, drawing from them the courage to make the dream come true that one day the people of our continent will join forces, as tributaries feeding into the same river into the same sea, to build a united Africa.

REFERENCES

Abiola, I. 1992. African education and identity. Hans Zell Publishers, London, UK.
Balmond, L. 1989. Rapport du séminaire de sensibilisation des responsables des organisations d'intégration économique régionale sur la dimension culturelle du développement, Abidjan, août. Unesco, Paris, France.
Behnam, D. 1986. L'enjeu culturel du développement. Unesco, Paris, France.
Birindelli, M.H. 1990. Les langues nationales. Le Courrier, 119 (Jan.-Feb.).
Davidson, B. 1971. The African genius: an introduction to social and cultural history. Little, Denver, CO, USA.

Davidson, B. 1992. Black man's burden: Africa and the curse of the nation state. Random, New York, NY, USA.

Diagne, P. 1985. Construction de la nation et évolution des valeurs politiques. Unesco, Paris, France.

Diop, C.A. 1959. L'unité culturelle de l'Afrique noire. Présence Africaine, Paris, France.

———— 1960. Les fondements économiques et culturels d'un état fédéral d'Afrique noire. Présence Africaine, Paris, France.

Dupuis, X. 1988. La prise en compte de la dimension culturelle du développement, un bilan méthodologique. Unesco, Paris, France.

Etounga-Manguelle, D. 1990. L'Afrique a-t-elle besoin d'ajustement culturel? Éditions Nouvelles du Sud, Paris, France.

Fabrizio, C. 1993. Culture et développement : conflits et complémentarités. Séminaire international de Dakar sur la dimension culturelle du développement, organized by the Centre régional de recherche et de documentation pour le développement culturel and the Institut culturel africain, Dakar, Senegal, April.

Gazzo, Y. 1991. Démocratie et développement. Le Courrier, 128 (July-Aug.).

Igué, J. 1992. Situation de la coopération économique en Afrique de l'Ouest : analyse critique. Séminaire international sur l'intégration économique en Afrique de l'Ouest, organized by the Konrad Adenauer Foundation, Cotonou, Benin, 1-3 October.

Ki Zerbo, J. (dir.). 1986. Histoire générale de l'Afrique (vol. 1). Unesco, Paris, France.

Kohnert D. 1992. De l'articulation entre développement socio-culturel et la coopération économique régionale Afrique de l'Ouest : de l'état-commando à l'état gardien. Séminaire international sur l'intégration économique en Afrique de l'Ouest, organized by the Fondation Konrad Adenauer, Cotonou, Benin, Oct. 1st-3.

Laya, D. 1988. Impact de la tradition sur le développement de l'Afrique. Unesco, Paris, France.

Machiavelli, N. 1981 [1513]. The Prince. Penguin, New York, USA.

Maquet, J. 1981. Les civilisations noires. Marabout, Paris, France.

McCarthy, S. 1991. Développement et héritage politique africain. Le Courrier, 128.

Mounier, J.P.; Pruneau, G. 1993. Développement et identités culturelles : pour un programme d'actions réalistes. Séminaire international de Dakar sur la dimension culturelle du développement, organized by the Centre régional de recherche et de documentation pour le développement culturel and the Institut culturel africain, Dakar, Senegal, April.

Mudimbe, V.Y. 1980. La dépendance de l'Afrique et les moyens d'y remédier. Actes du Congrès International des Études Africaines de Kinshasa. Agence de coopération culturelle et technique, Paris, France.

Paulme, D. 1953. Les civilisations africaines. Presses universitaires françaises, Paris, France.

Senghor, L. S. 1971. Liberté 2 : nation et voie africaine du socialisme. Seuil, Paris, France.

Wondji, C. 1990. Construction de la nation et évolution des valeurs politiques. In el Fasi, M. (ed.). Histoire générale de l'Afrique (vol. 3). Unesco, Paris, France.

CHAPTER 5

INSTITUTIONAL CRISIS AND THE
SEARCH FOR NEW MODELS

— Daniel C. Bach —

Bach critically reviews the institutional underpinnings and actual practice of regional integration in West Africa and sets this against the growth of "trans-state" or unofficial forms of regionalism, whose effects on the regional economy have been far more remarkable than those of existing integration schemes. Taking the Treaty of Abuja as his starting point, he emphasizes the voluntarism of the institutional approach represented therein, and the incongruities likely to undermine the feasibility of what is proposed. He then reviews the poor results obtained so far under ECOWAS and CEAO, before commenting on the recent UEMOA initiative. In his view, none of these schemes will succeed until national governments agree to transfer a part of their sovereignty to community institutions.

Bach then points to the growth of "informal" cross-border flows, and the trans-state regionalism represented by such flows. The paradox of such flows is that they escape the control of the state, but involve alliances between traders and government officials, while depending for their profit base on the maintenance of national borders and official barriers to the free flow of commerce. For Bach, as for Meagher, this trans-state regionalism is destructive, insofar as it undermines the state and impedes the integration of production systems. Disparities in monetary policy and tariff and customs regimes provide a ready source of profits for traders engaged in trans-border flows; and the elimination of such policy discordances is a necessary condition for progress toward regional integration.

ALTHOUGH THE STATE remains the key actor in the conduct of international affairs, its capacity for sovereign and independent action is increasingly under pressure from internal and external factors. External constraints resulting from the globalization of trade and financial flows have undermined the state's capacity for independent action much more effectively than the traditional games of power politics, while domestic instability resulting from the revival of ethnic, religious, or regional claims threatens the states of Sub-Saharan Africa and Eastern and Central Europe. The end of the Cold War has allowed new challenges to be raised against the boundaries inherited from European colonialism or Soviet

Russian imperialism, and even where these boundaries are not being challenged, the failure of authoritarian regimes to promote nation-building and economic development nurtures the revival of primordial attachments at the expense of national values.

Such developments lend new meaning and relevance to regional integration in Sub-Saharan Africa. Progress on this front has been limited so far, despite the existence of some 200 intergovernmental organizations (IGOs), some of which date back to the colonial era. The failure of these institutional schemes contrasts with the spectacular development of new forms of regionalism whose effect is to weaken the territorial integrity of the state, while undermining the effectiveness of economic policy. As will be seen later, this "trans-state" regionalism encompasses the so-called informal trading and financial networks whose dynamism attenuates some of the shortcomings of official circuits, but does so at the cost of undermining the regulatory capacity of the state. This new form of regionalism is thus assailing the territorial foundations of the state, at a time when the state is weakened by declining resources and the lost credibility of authoritarian regimes as nation-builders. In many cases, the rise of trans-state regionalism may be signaling the end of an era modeled on the predominance of nation-states whose precisely defined boundaries were introduced by European colonialism.

West Africa was long spared the disruptive impact of trans-state regional flows due to the coexistence of two well structured regimes: the Nigerian Federation and the West African Monetary Union (UMOA). The resulting bipolarization of interstate and trans-state relations should be properly understood and effectively addressed if regional integration is to be successfully revived in West Africa. This chapter first presents a review of the various institutional arrangements for regional integration that coexist in the West African subregion. We then examine the growth of trans-state regionalism and analyze its significance for regional integration in West Africa.

INTERGOVERNMENTAL ORGANIZATIONS

The Abuja Treaty signed by the OAU Heads of State on 3 June 1991 envisages the establishment of an African Economic Community (AEC) by the year 2025. The resulting integration scheme would constitute the largest economic community in the world, with no fewer than 53 member states, representing a combined market of 645 million people, including South Africa.

The Abuja Treaty

The Abuja Treaty succeeds the Lagos Plan of Action (LPA), adopted in 1980, which aimed to establish a pan-African common market by the year 2000. Three stages were identified in the pursuit of this objective: trade liberalization, the establishment of customs unions, and, ultimately, the creation of a single economic community (Onwuka 1985). Four subregional organizations were expected to spearhead the process: ECOWAS, already in existence since 1975; the Economic Community of Central African States (ECCAS), created in 1983; the Preferential Trade Area for Eastern and Southern African States (PTA), established in 1981, which became COMESA, the Common Market for East and Southern Africa, in 1994; and the Arab Maghreb Union (AMU), established in 1989. When the Abuja Treaty was signed in 1991, its chief objective was to consolidate these subregional schemes as a prelude to their harmonization at the continental level (Lancaster 1991). To this end, the Treaty spells out the six following stages (OAU 1991, Article 6):

- Stage 1 (5 years): reinforcement of existing regional economic communities and creation of others where none now exist;
- Stage 2 (8 years): stabilization of tariff and nontariff barriers; reinforcement of sectoral integration; coordination and harmonization of activities among existing economic communities;
- Stage 3 (10 years): establishment of free-trade zones and customs unions;
- Stage 4 (2 years): establishment of a continent-wide customs union, through coordination and harmonization of tariff and nontariff barriers among regional economic communities;
- Stage 5 (4 years): establishment of an African common market (common policies in certain areas, harmonization of monetary policies, free movement of people, establishment of an independent financial base for the Community);
- Stage 6 (5 years): creation of the AEC through consolidation of the African common market, the creation of an African monetary union and the establishment of a pan-African parliament.

Three kinds of objections can be raised regarding the feasibility of this ambitious undertaking. These concern its administrative and institutional features, the choice of development strategy implied by the Treaty, and, more generally, the difficulties encountered when schemes are based on integration through trade liberalization. This last point refers to deficiencies that apply equally well to integration programs developed outside the Abuja framework, such as the West African Economic and Monetary Union (UEMOA).

The first set of problems arises due to the reluctance of member states to forsake any true measure of their national autonomy in designing the ECA's institutional apparatus. The Abuja Treaty envisages the creation of an impressive political and administrative structure. However, it is better suited to intergovernmental cooperation than the establishment of truly supranational decision-making processes. The proposed institutional machinery establishes a tight hierarchical structure enjoying very little autonomy from the Authority of Heads of State. Furthermore, decisions at this level have to be reached by consensus or, failing that, by a two-thirds majority of the member states (Article 10, para. 4). The Authority will be assisted by the Council of Ministers, which is empowered to make recommendations and to exercise any powers that the Authority may delegate to it (Article 11).

The Abuja Treaty stipulates the establishment of an economic and social commission intended to include the ministers of development, planning, and economic integration of each member state. It proposes a court of justice, whose rulings would be binding (Article 18), but it does not provide for any sanction mechanism. The structure will be supported by a number of specialized technical committees and a secretariat resulting from a merger with the Secretariat of the OAU. The Abuja Treaty also envisages the creation of a pan-African parliament, although it does not define its composition, the process to be followed for its implementation, or the extent of its powers. In total, some 30 protocols are being negotiated to harmonize the objectives of the four main IGOs and the pursuit of these objectives in progressing toward the establishment of the AEC.

Unfortunately, there is nothing to indicate that individual African countries will be any more inclined toward a transfer of power than they were after the LPA was adopted in 1980. Ten years later, a status report on the LPA (ECA 1990, p. 8) observed:

> There is no sub-regional integration process under way at this time. Sub-regional economic groupings in Africa... have not been able to make their impact felt. Where they have had an impact, it has been on balance negative: [as a result], member-states are providing financial support to agencies that make no significant contribution in terms of improving Africa's economic situation.

Despite their severity, these criticisms did not lead to any adjustment of the tasks assigned to the IGOs by the Abuja Treaty.

The Treaty also postulates a reorganization or "rationalization" of existing regional IGOs in such a rigid and hierarchical fashion that the chances of such a scheme becoming reality are severely limited. By rejecting the concept of "integration through variable geometry" inspired from the European experience (see Lavergne and Daddieh, this volume), member governments may well have sacrificed realism and effectiveness for the sake of symbolic commitments to pan-Africanism. None of the signatory states to the Abuja Treaty has so far renounced its membership in IGOs that compete with the four large subregional communities and that are, at times, far more effective. Such apparent inconsistencies are not surprising given the prevailing influence of geopolitics and international clientelism on state behaviour when it comes to joining one organization or another. All too often, the facade of unanimity and the nonimplementation of decisions result from overlooking the politics of regional affiliations and treating the rationalization of relations among IGOs as a purely technocratic issue.

A second flaw of the Abuja Treaty is its adoption of a development model increasingly divorced from the policies applied by member states at the national level. Throughout the world, governments have progressively abandoned development strategies based on import-substituting industrialization or delinkage from the international system, in the face of pressure for external trade liberalization and the search for increased competitiveness on international markets. In most parts of the Third World, the revival of regionalism has thus coincided with the abandonment of the earlier generation of autarkic, state-driven approaches to regionalism. As we near the end of the 20th century, integration schemes have to meet the challenge of an international order where transnational linkages develop independently from any precise supranational, territorial, or institutional framework (Badie and Smouts 1992, p. 197).

The much vaunted revival of Latin American regionalism is guided by a view of regional integration conceived as complementary to structural adjustment policies. The spectacular shift in Mexico's macroeconomic management created an enabling environment for its subsequent decisions to join the North American Free Trade Agreement (NAFTA) and engage in a free-trade agreement with Chile. Elsewhere in Latin America, countries are opening their markets to the world as part of their structural adjustment efforts, while also launching new subregional initiatives. Members of the Andean Pact agreed to set up a free-trade zone and a customs union, as of 1 January 1992; Argentina, Basil, Uruguay, and Paraguay have established a customs union of the Southern Cone (MERCOSUR) beginning 1 January 1995. For several years, the countries of Latin America, unlike those of Africa, have demonstrated a readiness to combine regional integration with adjustment on global markets. There has thus emerged an IGO model more in tune with the desire of national governments to consolidate and enhance the gains of competitiveness achieved through the liberalization of domestic policies.

Last but not least, the Abuja Treaty draws much of its inspiration from the highly institutionalized character of the European experience, but ignores some of the European Community's key features. The first of these is the way the construction of Europe has combined the integration process with an increasingly open international stance to which even the Common Agricultural Policy is no longer immune. Europe's economic power has grown due to market liberalization and the increasingly tight coordination of national economic and financial policies. Consider, secondly, the circumstances favouring the progress of the European Community. European construction is often understood to have proceeded according to a succession of institutional steps implemented by strongly motivated member states. What this overlooks is that the steady progress in institution-building that was achieved sanctioned the preexisting intensification of economic, financial, and societal interactions. The dynamics at work in Sub-Saharan Africa are quite different, due in part to structural constraints generated by cross-border trade. As we shall see in the second part of this paper, the Abuja Treaty's emphasis on integration through the liberalization of intracommunity trade underestimates the obstacles posed by the existence of cross-border trade.

The difficulties inherent in the Abuja Treaty suggest that it was too hastily conceived, perhaps in response to the growth of regionalism in international economic relations and the difficulties of the OAU in redefining its role since the end of the Cold War. In signing the Abuja Treaty, African leaders demonstrated their desire to participate in the general trend toward the concentration of trade around regional areas. However, their laudable ambition to prevent the further marginalization of Africa was not matched by the definition of a workable strategy.

THE ECONOMIC COMMUNITY OF WEST AFRICAN STATES

Chapter 2 (Bundu, this volume) shows that the experience of ECOWAS's first 20 years provides little reason to believe that the institutional approach of the Abuja Treaty will promote regional integration in West

Africa. Indeed, ECOWAS seems to have reached a state of paralysis in virtually every area of endeavour:

- Twenty years after the 16 member states of ECOWAS signed the Lagos Charter, official intraregional trade still represents an insignificant portion of total exports, having grown from 3.9% to 4.9% between 1980 and 1988. More recently, the executive secretary of ECOWAS regretted, in his May 1992 report, that "in the two years since ECOWAS's trade liberalization project was launched, there has been no growth to record in community trade."

- The plan, adopted in 1983, to create a single monetary zone by 1994 had made no progress by July 1992, when the target was changed to the year 2000. In the interim, the West African Clearing House has received a mandate as a specialized institution of ECOWAS, and a new title as the West African Monetary Agency. Its task is now defined as the promotion of a limited form of currency convertibility (ECOWAS 1992b, p. 4).

- The protocols on the freedom of movement, residency, and rights of establishment for ECOWAS citizens have also suffered a series of setbacks since their implementation began in 1979. By 1992, the seven ratifications required to implement the final phase had still not been obtained, 2 years after the deadline. In addition, governments had only partly implemented the first two phases of the protocols and had printed or distributed few of the required documents. This accumulation of technical delays reflects a lack of political will on the part of member states to apply the Treaty. By July 1993, not one of the ECOWAS states was using the harmonized immigration and emigration forms; and only five of the 16 members had distributed the ECOWAS travel card.

- When it was adopted for ECOWAS in June 1987, the 4-year Economic Recovery Plan (ERP) contained two parts, one dealing with short-term policy reform, the other with the promotion of investment in regional and national projects under a plan for the rehabilitation of key sectors. Hailed as a success for ECOWAS, the first phase, focusing on national policies, was implemented quite independently of the Community; it came about as part of structural adjustment measures adopted by the member states under the aegis of the IMF and the World Bank in an effort to redress their trade and financial accounts. ECOWAS was expected to play a more direct role in promoting the second phase of the ERP, but for reasons relating to the regional character of the projects and the limited short-term priority attributed to them, results to date have been well below initial expectations. By July 1991, only 31 of the 136 projects originally selected had secured financing, and the amounts involved totaled USD 462 million compared with a planned USD 1.6 billion. ECOWAS's 1990–91 annual report suggested a lack of coordination and follow through on the part of the member states. More than half of the 136 projects failed to meet the selection criteria they had set for themselves and some projects that member states had originally classed as priorities had been withdrawn from national programs, thus making it impossible for ECOWAS to mobilize international financing for them (ECOWAS 1991).

The repeated delays and obstacles encountered by these programs have gone hand in hand with a tendency toward the multiplication of initiatives in an ever-widening range of activities including transportation and telecommunications, drought and desertification, the coordination of agricultural research, livestock, health, youth movements, women's associations, applied science and technology, the harmonization of educational degrees, etc. Even when it was not equipped to do so, ECOWAS seems to have tried to position itself at the sole reference point for all large-scale or multisectoral undertakings. In some cases, this may represent an awkward attempt to make up for the failure to "rationalize" the 30 subregional IGOs that ECOWAS is meant to regroup under its aegis.

In an effort to resolve ECOWAS's problems, an Eminent Persons' Committee conducted a review of the Lagos Treaty in 1991–92. The Committee's proposals led to the adoption of a revised version of the Treaty in Cotonou in January 1993. The revised Treaty reaffirms the ultimate goal of making ECOWAS the only economic community in West Africa. It also introduces the principle of supranationality in that the Authority's decisions will automatically acquire the force of law 90 days after they are signed by the heads of state. The Cotonou Treaty also foresees the establishment of a community parliament and an economic and social council. Merit, rather than national quotas, will be the basis for all senior appointments in Community institutions. The new Treaty also provides for the strengthening of mechanisms for conflict prevention and resolution within or between states. Finally, the Community will be given access to an autonomous source of financing, through the taxation of third-country imports.

These changes were intended to harmonize the ECOWAS Treaty with that of the AEC. Unfortunately, as ECOWAS's executive secretary noted, "The slow pace of regional integration in West Africa has very little to do with any inadequacies of the 1975 ECOWAS Treaty. Even a perfect treaty will make little difference if member states are not willing to consider regional integration as a national priority" (ECOWAS 1992a, p. 8).

The secondary priority accorded to ECOWAS by member states is reflected in the fact that only Burkina Faso, Côte d'Ivoire, Nigeria, and Togo have contributed to the Community budget on a regular basis since 1975. In July 1991, on the eve of the Summit of Heads of State, a decision to adopt automatic sanctions against defaulting countries resulted in a relative improvement in payments. However, 1 year later, the amount of contributions in arrears still equaled the Secretariat's operating budget for 3 years. Meanwhile, subscriptions to the ECOWAS Fund had barely reached USD 12 of the 50 million expected by 31 May 1992, and no state had fully paid its contributions. This situation led the Secretariat to note that, "the repeated imposition of sanctions by the Fund against members in default does not as yet seem to have had any positive effect" (ECOWAS 1992b, p. 26).

FRANCOPHONE IGOs: THE EX-CEAO AND UMOA/UEMOA

In addition to ECOWAS, the francophone West African IGOs merit special attention in light of their multisectoral character. Frequently cited as a reference point, CEAO was finally dissolved on 14 March 1994, following the decision to transform UMOA into UEMOA.

Created in 1973, with the signing of the Abidjan Treaty, CEAO was the most ambitious program for regional economic integration since the East African Community (1967–77). CEAO called for the progressive liberalization of trade by reducing tariffs on imported manufactured products originating within the Community. A "regional cooperation tax" (the TCR) was applied on a product-by-product basis, following government approval of industrial products qualifying for preferential treatment. In practice, the TCR mainly favoured exports from Côte d'Ivoire and Senegal, the two most industrially advanced states. The implied loss of tariff revenues by CEAO's least-developed members was compensated through the Community Development Fund (FCD), which allocated two-thirds of its resources as direct compensation for reduced fiscal revenues; the remaining third was used for regional studies and projects in favour of the less-advantaged states. From 1977 on, the Solidarity and Development Assistance Fund (FOSIDEC) complemented the FCD's role, thanks to funding provided mainly by Côte d'Ivoire (50%) and Senegal (16%).

The redistribution mechanisms established by the CEAO Treaty were accepted by wealthier member states under the pressure of circumstances. In 1971, Nigeria's growing regional influence so concerned the presidents of Senegal and Côte d'Ivoire that they decided to bury 20 years of rivalry and establish a francophone regional grouping capable of acting as a counterweight. The two richest states of the former Customs Union of West African States (UDEAO; Union Douanière des États de l'Afrique de l'Ouest) were determined to come to an agreement at any cost, and Côte d'Ivoire eventually agreed to set up the substantial compensation mechanism demanded by Mali, Niger, Burkina Faso, and Mauritania as a quid pro quo for their participation in a process of trade liberalization primarily beneficial to Côte d'Ivoire and Senegal (Bach 1983). Throughout the 1960s, Côte d'Ivoire had systematically opposed attempts to promote regional economic cooperation among members of the Conseil de l'Entente or the broader UDEAO. It was President Félix Houphouët Boigny's view that the Ivoirian contribution to the Conseil de l'Entente's Solidarity Fund (1959–63) and Fund for Mutual Assistance and Loans Guarantee (from 1966 on) should be limited to enhancing the Council's political cohesion and encouraging the free flow of foreign capital to the subregion's poorest countries. Efforts to intensify regional cooperation were systematically blocked by Côte d'Ivoire in the Council, as in other francophone West African institutions, most notably in 1964, when Senegal attempted to transform the essentially political African and Malagasy Union (UAM) into a more economically oriented IGO, the still-born Union Africaine et Malgache de Coopération Économique (UAMCE).

While breaking new ground as a result of joint efforts undertaken by Côte d'Ivoire and Senegal, the CEAO also benefited from a strong foundation of preexisting linguistic and economic ties. These included the use of French as an official language, shared membership in the former colonial French West African Federation (AOF), high levels of intrazone labour migration, and the use of a common currency by most member countries (Mauritania being the only country in CEAO that is not also a member of UMOA). These foundations encouraged the rapid growth of intracommunity trade following the creation of CEAO. Trade in industrial products registered under the TCR scheme increased sevenfold between 1976 and 1982, by which time intracommunity trade amounted to more than 10% of total exports. This performance led the World Bank to present CEAO as a model. "Of all trade integration schemes, the CEAO has had the greatest success," wrote the authors of the 1989 report on Sub-Saharan Africa (World Bank 1989, p. 178).

However, bottlenecks became apparent from the mid-1980s on, due to the segmentation of regional markets and the limited complementarity of CEAO's economies. As a result, the 400 industrial products registered under the TCR scheme in 1980 had increased to only 428 by 1985. Contrary to the initial expectations of the landlocked countries, intracommunity trade patterns grew increasingly lopsided in favour of Côte d'Ivoire, whose share of products registered under the TCR had grown to 80% in 1986, compared with 51.6% in 1976. The Senegalese share of exports declined over the same period from 46% to 13.5% of TCR products (*Bulletin d'Afrique noire*, 13 March 1986). Tensions created by these trends were exacerbated by the dysfunction of CEAO's compensation mechanisms and fallout from the embezzlement of FOSIDEC resources in the Diawara affair. By 1991, member states' arrears to the Secretariat and the FCD had increased to 45.5 billion CFA francs, approximately four times the combined budgets of those institutions. The CEAO Secretariat tried vainly to secure an independent revenue base to resolve this financial impasse by introducing a Community Solidarity Tax (CST) on third-country imports. However this mechanism, which remained dependent on the willingness of member states to pay, proved ineffective.

Although the TCR system fostered the rapid growth of intracommunity industrial trade, it also contributed to the survival of industries that otherwise could not have withstood the full liberalization of such trade. Seven different customs areas were maintained within the CEAO; and the weak complementarity of member economies eventually crippled any further progress under the TCR. There can be little doubt that a common market in industrial products free of mechanisms to compensate for inequalities in competitiveness would have brought about the disappearance of industry in the poorer countries (Centre du commerce international 1990, 52ff). The institutional cohesion of CEAO would not have survived such a shock, and the status quo thus prevailed. Bottlenecks accumulated, until CEAO was finally dissolved in March 1994 subsequent to the transformation of UMOA into an economic and monetary union (UEMOA).

UEMOA's origins date back to the April 1991 meeting of UMOA finance ministers in Ouagadougou, which launched an ambitious program to promote regional integration through the harmonization of regulatory mechanisms and policies. The original intent was to address the economic crisis in the franc zone, without devaluing the CFA franc, through a combination of regional integration and internal adjustment. To achieve this goal, the finance ministers launched a vast program of budgetary and fiscal policy harmonization involving multilateral surveillance. The first objective was to consolidate the reform of banking systems through the establishment of regional banking commissions for West and Central Africa. Plans were also made to harmonize legislative and regulatory frameworks governing economic and social activities (social insurance, business law, etc). The ultimate ambition of this unprecedented program was to create an economic union with a single financial market, a regional stock market, and a free-trade zone (Guillaumont and Guillaumont 1993).

Three years after the Ouagadougou meeting, UEMOA had achieved substantive progress in terms of functional cooperation, as witness the signing of the Single Treaty on Insurance by member states in 1992 and the creation of an Inter-African Conference on Social Security (CIPRES) — which, however, abandoned the initial idea of harmonizing the franc zone's social security systems in recognition of the broad disparities among the member states. The Dakar Treaty of 10 January 1994 capped these various initiatives and transformed the UMOA into the UEMOA on the eve of a 50% devaluation of the CFA franc.

The devaluation cleared the way for the reopening of negotiations with the Bretton Woods institutions and the resumption of financial aid from both multilateral and bilateral donors. Contrary to the more pessimistic prognoses, the franc zone survived the devaluation. Meanwhile, the return to classical models of structural adjustment also meant a reduction of previously existing opportunities for "escapism," as support from France may no longer be mobilized against the policy prescriptions of the World Bank or the IMF.

The reluctance of francophone governments to engage in any form of shared sovereignty has often constrained efforts to revive integration among the former UMOA countries. If this tendency is maintained,it will condemn UEMOA to the ranks of the many IGOs confined to the pursuit of functional cooperation due to their inability to promote their integration objectives. Although monetary integration in the franc zone involves the sharing of sovereignty, this does not automatically imply further progress along these lines. Monetary integration in UMOA or under the Bank of Central African States (BEAC) is based on the survival of integration schemes established during the colonial period (Coussy 1993), and, except in the cases of Equatorial Guinea and Mali which reintegrated UMOA in 1984, membership in the franc zone was not built on the concession of previously existing sovereign powers. Despite the franc zone reforms of 1973, the internalization of constraints imposed by the sharing of sovereignty remained limited due to the supervision of operations by an extra-African state, as opposed to a subregional, supranational institution.

These antecedents suggest that attempts to revive regional integration in the franc zone call for a radical change of attitude that political leaders may not have fully appreciated in launching the various UEMOA programs. For the first time since independence, countries of the franc zone are expected to implement transfers of sovereignty that will be managed on a subregional basis. Reflected in these reforms are unprecedented pressures for francophone Africa to internalize the structural adjustment imperative, with regional fiscal and budgetary surveillance mechanisms substituting for the conditionalities typically imposed by international financial agencies (Michailof 1993, p. 96).

The CEAO and ECOWAS experience contains important lessons for the advancement of regional integration in West Africa and elsewhere. Within the former CEAO, the innovative character of the TCR mechanism and the existence of a common currency encouraged the rapid growth of trade among member states. However, the stagnation of trade flows from the early 1980s on was a reminder of the limited complementarity among these economies. To overcome these limitations would have required economic restructuring on a regional scale, involving substantial transfers of sovereignty. In ECOWAS, the debate did not even reach this stage, in the face of bottlenecks intrinsic to the adoption of a global approach to trade liberalization. The heterogeneity of monetary regimes further undermined efforts to stimulate intraregional trade, because the juxtaposition of inconvertible currencies with convertible ones greatly complicated the dismantling of tariff and nontariff barriers. Currency overvaluation in many countries was one problem, as countries whose competitiveness was thus weakened could not be expected to make their economies even more vulnerable by liberalizing imports. The existence of large disparities in monetary and customs policies created opportunities for rent-seeking that overshadowed any gains that traders and state agencies could expect to derive from trans-border trade liberalization.

The disruptive effects of
trans-state regionalism

Policies designed to promote integration through trade liberalization should be reassessed in relation to the social effects of cross-border trade flows, commonly referred to as informal, parallel, or black market trade or smuggling. As Meagher (this volume) shows, these flows have a hybrid character. Trade and financial transactions may be legal and openly tolerated on one side of the border, while regarded as black-market activities on the other. Indeed, the term "informal" is at times inappropriate, in the presence of highly structured networks involving close contacts with official circuits and state bureaucracies.

The concept of trans-state regionalism introduced in this paper should be understood in terms of these different features. First, the concept emphasizes the autonomy of trans-state flows from official trade. To be sure, the traders involved maintain close links with the government and may benefit from complicity at the highest levels. Indeed, the states' financial difficulties and their patrimonial nature provide fertile ground for the development of shared interests. However, state administrations are in no position to control trans-state networks (Grégoire and Labazée 1993). Second, the status of trans-state trade and financial flows is unofficial. Here too, the vital role performed by trans-state activities in wealth accumulation may lead to their decriminalization on one side of a boundary, as exemplified by the West African "entrepôt states" (Igué and Soulé 1992). Yet, such strategies cannot be officially acknowledged because doing so would involve the risk of reprisals from neighbouring countries harmed by such trade. Also fundamental, finally, is an understanding of the factors accounting for the dynamism of trans-state regionalism. Contrary to a widely held opinion, trans-state regionalism does not result from traders' ignorance or rejection of national borders. To the contrary, the traders involved are acutely aware of opportunities arising from the existence of national borders. However, the exploitation of these opportunities generates a pattern of trade having little to do with underlying comparative advantage (based on ecological complementarities or production costs) and more to do with disparities in fiscal, customs, and monetary regimes, which first emerged along the interimperial frontiers of the colonial era.

The products exchanged along these circuits include not only commodities that people have exchanged since precolonial times, such as kola nuts, meat, cereals, and natron, but also products like ivory, gold, diamonds, manufactured items, fuel and fertilizers, narcotics, and arms, whose market value is derived from a sophisticated exploitation of cross-border opportunities afforded by differences in tariff structures and fiscal policies, the existence of a parallel exchange rate, or the illegality of the products exchanged. Because the agents of trans-state regionalism owe their living to cross-border disparities, they have an interest in avoiding any sharp deterioration of political relations between neighbouring states. However, they will also oppose any attempt to dismantle the disparities that are the source of their profits. This leads to a fundamental incompatibility between trans-state regionalism and the rationalization of regional trade on more integrated lines. The circumstances surrounding the collapse of the Senegambian Confederation in 1989 offer a vivid illustration of this phenomenon (Sall 1992; Lewis and Hughes 1993).

Over the past two decades, declining state resources, economic deregulation, and the collapse of official trading circuits have combined to convert cross-border disparities into opportunities for an ever-broadening range of people. Trading circuits that were originally confined to the peripheries of colonial blocs have now extended to embrace the entire subregion. Egg and Igué (1993) have rightly highlighted the social regulatory functions of these trans-state activities, but they go too far in their interpretation of trans-state flows as a popular, "grass-roots" form of regionalism. Although small traders are prominently visible at border crossing points, such traders often participate in highly structured networks dominated by powerful merchants or government officials, if not by elements of international mafias. Trans-state regionalism thrives on the mobilization of patron–client relationships reinforced by traditional ties of family, ethnicity, kinship, or religion, for the better exploitation of weaker individuals faced with a dearth of alternatives in official circuits.

The spectacular growth of trans-state regional networks in Sub-Saharan Africa has fueled global trends toward the continentalization and multilateralization of trade flows and the further integration of Africa into the world economy. However, it would be misleading to treat trans-state regionalism as a "market-driven" form of regional integration as Egg and Igué (1993) do. The intensification of trans-state flows since the 1970s has indeed locked the economies of a number of neighbouring states in West Africa into quasi-organic relationships focused around Nigeria, Ghana, and the Senegambia. However, the interpretation of this trend as a form of market-driven integration is semantically confusing. Trans-state trade between Senegal and Gambia or between Nigeria and its neighbours has nothing to do with trade liberalization or the deliberate reduction of national economic barriers. To the contrary, such linkages *depend* on the existence of significant discrepancies in fiscal and customs policies or exchange rate regimes. These discrepancies lead to the development of rent-seeking strategies that have a negative effect on the economy, in contrast to market-driven integration programs. The exploitation of such disparities leads to the disarticulation of smaller economies by weakening the state's capacity for intervention and undermining government institutions. Moreover, networks based on patronage and historic ties lead to a pattern of social interactions based on personal control as opposed to a territorial reference point. Trans-state networks thus curtail the state's ability to control and manage the economy, but do nothing to throw existing borders into question or to promote the emergence of alternative regional arrangements.

The increasing recourse of African countries to structural adjustment programs and the relative erosion of tariff and monetary disparities have inaugurated a new phase in the development of trans-state flows since the mid-1980s. Throughout Africa, the contraction of cross-border discrepancies has reduced opportunities for the growth of trans-state flows. However no substitute has yet emerged to perform the social regulatory functions of such flows. The economic crisis continues, and governments remain unable to address their people's most basic needs in terms of economic survival and personal safety. Meanwhile, the proliferation of conditionalities imposed by international donors has constrained the ability of the authoritarian regimes still in power to manage public resources in a patrimonial fashion. Trans-state networks are adapting to the decline of the state and adjusting to reduced opportunities to profit from intra-African frontier disparities, by seeking out new sources of rent in the global economy, through criminal activities, in particular. Linking with organized crime in Europe, Asia, Latin America, and North America, these networks have become increasingly involved in the drug trade and arms trafficking, in addition to the more traditional smuggling of gold, diamonds, and ivory. As participants in the narcotics trade consolidate their activities and become more professional, Africa is becoming a key region for transshipment or money laundering operations. In some rural areas of West Africa, the cultivation of cannabis and poppies is already supplementing the low incomes derived from traditional crops. In other parts of West Africa, such as Liberia and Casamance, smoldering conflicts encourage the close association of drug trafficking and arms procurement. The decline of Nigeria's oil revenues and the drastic reduction in standard of living over the last 10 years have made Nigeria a hub for the transit of drugs to Europe, the rest of Africa, and the United States

(Newswatch 1990, 1994; Southern African Economist 1992; Observa-toire géopolitique des drogues 1993, pp. 204–207). In response to cur-tailment of opportunities along Africa's intracontinental borders, the prosperity of trans-state networks thus depends increasingly on opportu-nities across Africa's external frontiers.

To control the deleterious effects of trans-state regionalism means coming to grips with the currency and tariff disparities at the root of such flows. Efforts to do this will nevertheless be doomed to failure if they do not address the socioeconomic functions that these networks currently perform. The development of trans-state trade beyond the African conti-nent illustrates the limitations of attempts to dismantle tariff and cus-toms barriers while ignoring the income-generating opportunities represented by these barriers.

THE DISINTEGRATION OF A SPECIFICALLY
WEST AFRICAN MODEL

The disruptive effects of trans-state regionalism were kept within rea-sonable bounds in West Africa until the mid-80s, due to a unique com-bination of circumstances. This included the cushioning effect of Nigeria's oil windfall and the implementation of sociopolitical reforms in Nigeria at a time when the integration of the francophone West African states in the franc zone helped to compensate for the weakness of their economies. This combination of factors had the paradoxical effect of favouring the development of trans-state flows while limiting their adverse effects on state policies, thus helping to perpetuate the myth that trans-state flows could somehow counterbalance the limitations of inte-gration according to the IGO model.

Nigeria's civil war and the spectacular increase in the country's oil revenues coincided with dramatic socioeconomic and political reforms. In 1967, the military administration of General Gowon carved several new states out of the existing ones to take into account "minority" claims for autonomy and for improved access to federal resources. Successive military regimes also adopted a series of measures to ensure a shift of party politics away from the zero-sum games of the three federal regions, which plagued the first Republic. This was accompanied by more sys-tematic use of federalist principles as a reference point and the introduc-tion of minimal guarantees of geo-ethnic representation in candidacies for election or appointment at the federal level. Finally and most impor-tantly, a new revenue allocation formula was introduced, away from one based on the constituent states' own resources to one based on principles of equity and demographic balance. This was a decisive move in ensuring a more even distribution of resources in the Federation and contributed to an improvement of territorial control and cohesion (Bach 1989). Although Nigeria's swelling oil revenues made the country a pole of attraction for trans-state trade flows, this did not trigger any major territorial destabilization, thanks to transformations in Nigeria's domestic regulatory mechanisms, which reinforced its capacity to resist the weakening of territorial control usually associated with the development of trans-state networks.

Nigeria's oil wealth and the division of West Africa into convertible currency areas (franc zone, Liberia) and nonconvertible currency areas (Ghana and Nigeria, in particular) resulted in an unprecedented intensification of trans-state flows. Until the early 1980s, these flows benefited both the population and the governments of countries belonging to the franc zone. The resulting polarization and the growing economic dependence of Nigeria's francophone neighbours on trans-state trade were reinforced by the frequent involvement of national authorities in those networks. In Benin, Togo, and, to a lesser extent, Niger, governments adjusted tariff regimes, customs policies, and sometimes even infrastructure programs to support the interests of the reexport sector. For these countries, trans-state trade functioned as a low-profile but effective mechanism for poaching on Nigeria's oil revenues. The purchase of consumer goods from around the world for reexport to Nigeria significantly improved public-sector finances and generated unprecedented wealth in banking and merchant circles. Although competition from imports of subsidized fertilizers and petroleum products and low-priced cereals from Nigeria meant some loss of government revenues, consumers clearly benefited. More generally, Nigeria's prosperity spurred all concerned to overlook the risks inherent in this growing dependence on rent-seeking activities and the consequent downgrading of productive ventures in favour of trade and financial operations based on the exploitation of very unstable cross-border opportunities.

Although this went unnoticed at the time, the positive effects of trans-state regionalism were closely linked to the integration of the francophone "entrepôt states" in a single monetary zone. Membership in a common and convertible currency area considerably reduced the disruptive effects of trans-state networks by removing opportunities to profit from exchange rate differentials and restricting the range of possibilities for destructive competition between member states. The limitation of opportunities for rent-seeking along UMOA member states' boundaries thus reduced the disruptive effect of trans-border flows, while encouraging their development along the Union's external boundaries where the destructuring impact of trans-state networks was at its strongest.

The dramatic fall in oil prices that plunged Nigeria into recession from 1982 on challenged a system based on the converging interests of government officials, consumers, and traders. The system of political regulation and territorial organization in Nigeria began to unravel as the federal government's distributive capacities receded, thus undermining the Federation's very foundations and revealing the weaknesses of the sociopolitical model prevailing since the end of the civil war (Bach 1989). Far from promoting the rationalization of public spending, the adjustment policies introduced in 1986 by the military regime became synonymous with the "deinstitutionalization" of resource allocation and the exacerbation of nepotistic and authoritarian practices (Olukoshi 1993).

The collapse of Nigeria's oil revenues also led to sharp changes in its foreign relations with neighbouring states. By 1983, Nigerian leaders were growing impatient with the tenuous progress of regional integration under ECOWAS. The results were negligible or even negative, as far as Nigeria was concerned, while Nigeria's laissez-faire attitude toward trans-state networks had in no way advanced the objective of regional integration. Ever since the adoption of the ECOWAS charter, such countries as Benin and Togo (who had both actively supported the charter against the exclusively francophone CEAO), had been anxious to maintain good relations with Nigeria, but remained equally reluctant to implement ECOWAS protocols to reduce tariff and currency disparities in the Community. As a result, many Nigerian decision-makers considered the cost of trans-state flows of goods, currency, and migrants unacceptably high in light of the country's own recession and the absence of any tangible compensation.

Nigeria's rulers were initially tempted to become isolationist, attempting to eradicate trans-state flows through coercive measures (Bach 1988). They successively ordered the departure of foreigners residing in the country "illegally" (1983 and 1985), demonetized the naira and tightened exchange controls (April 1984). Finally and most importantly, the army sealed the country's borders for almost 2 years (April 1984 to February 1986). The macroeconomic measures of the Babangida regime's structural adjustment program took over from there, and were dramatically more effective. The devaluation of the naira, the selective liberalization of Nigeria's external trade, and the collapse of domestic demand forced trans-state operators to readjust drastically their trading networks and product strategies. Neighbouring francophone consumers continued to enjoy the social and wealth-generating effects of the trans-state networks, but it was quite a different matter for the national administrations of these countries. For them, the adjustment of trans-state activity meant that UMOA countries were becoming an outlet for Nigeria exports (or reexports) and a source of foreign exchange for the crisis-stricken Federation of Nigeria (Club du Sahel 1994).

From 1986 until 1993, the repeated devaluation of the naira and successive reforms of the foreign currency allocation system brought the naira's official exchange rate increasingly close to that on the parallel market (Herrera 1992, pp. 31–33; Meagher, this volume). These monetary policies sharply reduced opportunities to profit from the exchange-rate differential of the naira. However, the devaluation and instability of the naira created a strong demand for CFA francs, and monetary factors thus continued to be of primary importance in determining the direction and composition of trans-state flows. This was accompanied by export pressures from Nigeria in response to the collapse of internal demand and the improved competitiveness of Nigerian products following the devaluation of naira, which cut Nigerian prices by three-quarters between 1985 and 1991 (Herrera 1992). There ensued a scramble for CFA francs in exchange for Nigerian exports. Products made in Nigeria or imported cheaply from world markets (Southeast Asia, in particular) thus competed directly with industrial and agricultural facilities in francophone countries (Egg and Igué 1993). With Nigeria continuing to subsidize gasoline and fertilizer prices, the massive outflow of these products was also stimulated.

The francophone economies were thus destabilized through the loss of customs revenue and the competition of illegal imports with local or legally imported items. The impossibility of any real economic policy dialogue with Nigeria due to the illegality of the offending trans-state flows aggravated the situation. The franc-zone countries thus paid a price for the imbalances that state policies had tolerated, or even encouraged, during the heady years of the oil boom. From the mid-1980s, the franc zone also encountered its own difficulties stemming from the loss of budgetary discipline, commercial bank failures, massive state indebtedness and falling export earnings. Finally, the financial regulations that had long provided the underpinnings of better economic performance in the franc zone (the fixed exchange rate against the French franc, full convertibility, the operations account with the French treasury) had instead become a source of rigidity following the adoption of structural adjustment programs by Ghana and Nigeria (1986). The CFA franc devaluation of 12 January 1994 was an attempt to escape a vicious circle of uncompetiveness and estrangement from international funding agencies. However, the union's future remains fraught with uncertainty given the slow pace of the UEMOA negotiations, the previously mentioned reluctance of member states to consent to transfers of sovereignty in a subregional context, and the need for structural reforms to consolidate the expected gains of the devaluation.

CONCLUSIONS AND PRIORITIES

The conventional implementation of structural adjustment programs on a strictly national basis introduces opportunities for plunder-thy-neighbour policies that contribute to the vitality of trans-state flows. The recent evolution of trade linkages between the Gambian "entrepôt state" and Senegal is a telling illustration of the issues at stake. Adopting a policy package similar to that of some of Nigeria's francophone neighbours in the 1970s, the Gambian government aided and abetted the development of the reexport trade into Senegal and other francophone states. By the early 1990s, 85% of Banjul's imports were reexported, mostly "illegally." Such trans-state trade produced a degree of economic prosperity for Gambia that was portrayed both in and outside the country as a triumph for neoliberalism. The link between this prosperity and the adoption of a rent-seeking strategy based on the exploitation of tariff and currency discrepancies with Senegal was conveniently ignored. This strategy ceased to be viable when Senegal adopted economic adjustment reforms that reduced the disparities and opportunities. A first measure was taken in August 1993, with the suspension of convertibility for CFA banknotes circulating outside the franc zone banking system. Then came the devaluation of the CFA franc in January 1994 and the alignment of Senegal's custom duties against those prevailing in Gambia. Stricter border controls were also introduced, officially to check the destination of products purportedly "in transit" through Senegal. These measures were particularly effective; the reexport business collapsed in the Gambia, while trans-state trade flows between Senegal and the Gambia fell more nearly into balance (Fall and Abron 1994). Gambia's government and its merchant lobby complained bitterly, and unashamedly accused Senegal of violating GATT and ECOWAS provisions on the free circulation of goods (Le Soleil, 5–6 March 1994).

Regional integration in Africa, and West Africa more specifically, is currently blocked in two ways. The first bottleneck stems from the current institutional approach to regional integration, which has proved to be ineffective and is condemned to remain so until decision-making mechanisms of a supranational nature are agreed upon and adhered to. The voluntarism enshrined in the Abuja, ECOWAS, and UEMOA treaties fails to compensate for the absence of this fundamental prerequisite.

The second bottleneck is attributable to the vitality of trans-state regionalism that blocks the progress of conventional approaches, while remaining incapable of offering any alternative. The agents of trans-state regionalism are eager to avoid tensions between neighbouring states, but they are equally anxious to prevent real trade liberalization that would eliminate the cross-border disparities they find so profitable. The spread of trans-state networks thus undermines the states' territorial and institutional bases, while supporting the maintenance of existing frontiers.

Current attempts to revive the regional integration process are taking place in a context that is profoundly different from that of 30 years ago. In many parts of the continent, the post-colonial state's tenuous claims to legitimacy and the threat of increasing market segmentation call for a comprehensive reappraisal of the linkages between structural adjustment, the social regulatory functions of the state, and the creation of regional economies. In rethinking our approaches to integration, the cost of nonintegration has become a secondary issue compared with the threat of disintegration through formal means or the corrosive impact of trans-state networks (Bach 1993). The sanctity of colonial borders, protected by the OAU charter since its adoption in 1963, is increasingly being questioned since the end of the Cold War; several West African states are confronted by demands for regional autonomy or even independence; and civil peace is being threatened, when it has not already broken down.

A two-pronged approach, involving regional trade liberalization and the consolidation of supranational institutions, on one hand, and a reduction of regional inequalities, on the other hand, could help meet the demands for autonomy of some groups, while avoiding the further fragmentation of the subregion. This strategy would require partial transfer of sovereignty to a supranational institution, in a spatial framework better adapted to the realities and pressures of competition in world markets.

The stabilizing effect of French influence allowed the franc zone to survive the shock of independence. However, three decades later, the weaknesses of this "vertical" integration model have become all too clear.

The international clientelism that it nurtures has gone hand in hand with the inward-looking orientation of the franc zone and the lack of motivation to join forces with non-French-speaking neighbouring countries. It has been suggested on a number of occasions that anchoring the CFA franc to the ECU might provide an opportunity for opening up the franc zone to West Africa's English- and Portuguese-speaking countries (Guillaumont and Guillaumont 1989; L'Hériteau 1993; Cobham and Robson, this volume), and something along these lines could conceivably be done in the context of the revision and regionalization of the Lomé convention (Kappel 1993). Non-francophone countries have so far been conspicuously absent from attempts to renew the drive toward integration in UEMOA, although their involvement has never been formally excluded. Nothing better illustrates the need for coordination than the announcement on the very eve of the CFA franc devaluation in January 1994, that the naira was returning to a fixed peg, at an official exchange rate revalued by 100%. It is disturbing indeed that such decisions and associated measures can still be made in isolation.

Is it possible to envisage the type of supranational mechanism necessary to the success of regional integration in West Africa, in light of current sociopolitical realities and the region's place in the global economy? The UEMOA project is a move in the right direction, and the implication of external actors in that project as part of the structural adjustment process paradoxically increases the likelihood of success. It is, of course, much too soon to predict the failure or success of that endeavour given the reluctance with which member states are likely to share their national sovereignties. Either way, the success of UEMOA will not suffice to eliminate the destructuring effects of trans-state regionalism. For that to happen would require the establishment of policy dialogue between Nigeria and the franc zone in particular, and among all countries of the subregion more generally.

References

Bach, D. 1983. The politics of West African regional cooperation: CEAO and ECOWAS. Journal of Modern African Studies, 21 (4), 601–621.

———— 1988. Les frontières du régionalisme : le Nigéria en Afrique de l'Ouest. In Bach, D.; Egg, J.; Philippe, J. (ed.). Le Nigeria, un pouvoir en puissance. Karthala, Paris, France. Pp. 195–218.

———— 1989. Managing a plural society: the boomerang effects of Nigerian federalism. Journal of Commonwealth and Comparative Politics, 27 (2), 218–245.

———— 1993. Afrique subsaharienne : appréhender les coûts de la désintégration. *In* M'Bokolo, E. (ed.). Développement : de l'aide au partenariat. Commissariat général au Plan, La Documentation française, Paris, France. Pp. 119–137.

Badie, B.; Smouts, M.C. 1992. Le retournement du monde, sociologie de la scène internationale. Dalloz-FNSP, Paris, France.

Centre du commerce international. 1990. CEAO : les stratégies de promotion du commerce extérieur. United Nations Conference on Trade and Development/ General Agreement on Tariffs and Trade, Geneva, Switzerland. Unpublished manuscript.

Club du Sahel. 1994. Le Nigéria et les perspectives d'intégration régionale en Afrique de l'Ouest. Permanent Interstate Committee for Drought Control in the Sahel, Club du Sahel, Organisation for Economic Co-operation and Development, and African Development Bank, Paris, France.

Coussy, J. 1993. La zone franc : logique initiale, infléchissements ultérieurs et crise actuelle. *In* Bach, D.; Kirk-Greene, A. (ed.). États et sociétés en Afrique francophone. Economica, Paris, France. Pp. 177–200.

ECA (United Nations Economic Commission for Africa). 1990. Progress report on the strengthening of subregional economic integration: establishment of the African Economic Community. ECA, Addis Ababa, Ethiopia. Document ECA/ECO/90/2/4.3(1).

ECOWAS (Economic Community of West African States). 1991. West African development in the continental context: need for greater regional cohesion, 1990–1991. ECOWAS Secretariat, Lagos, Nigeria.

———— 1992a. Rapport annuel 1991/1992 du Secrétaire exécutif Abass Bundu. ECOWAS Secretariat, Lagos, Nigeria.

———— 1992b. Rapport intérimaire du Secrétaire exécutif Abass Bundu. ECOWAS Secretariat, Lagos, Nigeria.

Egg, J.; Igué, J. 1993. L'intégration par les marchés dans le sous-espace Est : l'impact du Nigeria sur ses voisins immédiats. Organisation for Economic Co-operation and Development, Permanent Interstate Committee for Drought Control in the Sahel, Club du Sahel, Paris, France. OECD synthesis report.

Fall, A., 1994. Différend commercial entre le Sénégal et la Gambie : un livre blanc pour faire la lumière. Le Soleil, Dakar, Sénégal, 5-6 March, 13.

Fall, A.; Abron, K. 1994. La Gambie dans l'oeil du cyclone. Le Soleil, Dakar, Sénégal, 24 February, 6–7.

Grégoire, E.; Labazée, P. (ed.). 1993. Grands commerçants de l'Afrique de l'Ouest. Karthala, Paris, France.

Guillaumont, P.; Guillaumont, S. 1989. The implications of the European Monetary Union for African countries. Journal of Common Market Studies, 139–153.

———— 1993. La zone franc à un tournant vers l'intégration régionale. *In* Michailof, ·S. (ed.). La France et l'Afrique : vade mecum pour un nouveau voyage. Karthala, Paris, France. Pp. 411–422.

Herrera, J. 1992. Impact des politiques différentielles et échanges transfrontaliers Cameroun-Nigeria. Observatoire OCISCA, ORSTOM, August. Unpublished document.

Igué, J.; Soulé, B. 1992. L'état entrepôt au Bénin : commerce informel ou solution à la crise? Karthala, Paris, France.

Kappel, R. 1993. Future prospects for the CFA franc zone. Intereconomics, Nov.-Dec., 269–278.

Lancaster, C. 1991. The Lagos Three: economic regionalism in Sub-Saharan Africa. *In* Harbeson, J.; Rothschild, D. (ed.). Africa in world politics. Westview, Boulder, CO, USA. Pp. 249–267.

Le Soleil. 1994. 5–6 March.

Lewis, J.; Hughes, A. 1993. L'expérience de la confédération sénégambienne (1982–1989). *In* Bach, D.; Kirk-Greene, A. (ed.). États et sociétés en Afrique francophone. Economica, Paris, France. Pp. 253–265.

L'Hériteau, M.F. 1993. Intégration régionale en Afrique et coopération monétaire euro-africaine. *In* Michailof, S. (ed.). La France et l'Afrique : vade mecum pour un nouveau voyage. Karthala, Paris, France. Pp. 15–35.

Michailof, S. 1993. Faut-il brûler la coopération française? *In* Michailof, S. (ed.). La France et l'Afrique : vade mecum pour un nouveau voyage. Karthala, Paris, France. Pp. 63–100.

Newswatch. 1990. 20 August, 10–18.

———— 1994. 21 February, 18–19.

OAU (Organization of African Unity). 1991. Traité instituant la Communauté économique africaine. OAU, Addis Ababa, Ethiopia.

Olukoshi, B. (ed.). 1993. The politics of structural adjustment in Nigeria. James Currey, London, UK.

Onwuka, R.I.; Abegunrin, D.G. (ed.). 1985. African development: the OAU/ECA, Lagos Plan of Action and Beyond. Brunswick Publishing Company, Lawrenceville.

Observatoire géopolitique des drogues. 1993. La drogue, nouveau désordre mondial : rapport 1991/92. Observatoire géopolitique des drogues, Paris, France.

Sall, E. 1992. Sénégambie : territoires, frontières, espaces et réseaux sociaux. Travaux et Document du CEAN, 36, 1–28.

Southern African Economist. 1992. The drug trade. September, 3–12.

World Bank. 1989. L'Afrique subsaharienne : de la crise à une croissance durable. World Bank, Washington, DC, USA.

CHAPTER 6

DONOR PERSPECTIVES

— Réal Lavergne and *Cyril Kofie Daddieh —*

This paper reviews the perspectives and activities of five of the major donors operating in West Africa. The European Union, France, the Bretton Woods institutions, the United States Agency for International Development, and Canada account for the bulk of the aid going to West Africa and are most involved in policy dialogue with African countries on the subject of regional integration. These donors are also the most active in the ongoing process of structural adjustment involving policy changes such as trade liberalization and currency devaluation, which carry major implications for regional economic integration, by virtue of their impact on the competitiveness of exports in regional markets.

The arrival of foreign donors as advocates of regional integration in Africa is a new phenomenon that provides a fresh view of how regional integration should be pursued if it is to succeed. This vision includes the possibility of outside support, to be sure, but also a more liberal trade agenda, advocacy of greater participation on the part of civil society, and a pragmatic, step-by-step approach to regional integration, baptized "variable geometry" by the European Union.

Many of the ideas put forward by these donors are now quite generally held not only in the donor community but also increasingly by African institutions, despite remaining doubts about trade liberalization or appeals to variable geometry. Meanwhile, experience clearly shows the importance of external support for the success of regional integration schemes. Under the circumstances, conditions seem ripe for increased dialogue between donors and African institutions in the pursuit of shared objectives and strategies.

AFRICA'S ASPIRATIONS FOR greater regional unity are not new. On the threshold of independence in the late 1950s, Kwame Nkrumah of Ghana, the torchbearer of African independence, implored African leaders to work toward continental unity. Bringing his enormous charisma and the power of his ideas to bear, he continued to animate debate about the political economy of Africa's future in the early 1960s. These debates argued pan-Africanism versus nationalism or regionalism, central planning versus the free play of market forces, and self-reliance versus the continued extraversion of African economies. These competing political and economic visions were manifested in the interactions and tensions of three camps — the radical pan-Africanist "Casablanca" group; its conservative antithesis, the nationalist "Monrovia" group; and the Franco-African "Brazzaville" group — during the period before the formation of the Organization of African Unity (OAU) in May 1963 (Zartman 1987).

Nkrumah and his radical colleagues staked their reputations on continental union as the most effective vehicle for the structural transformation of Africa. However, their efforts were derailed or deferred by the combined opposition of the numerically stronger nationalist and EurAfrican factions. In the end, Nkrumah and his Casablanca colleagues had to accept major revisions to their pan-African political and economic vision to prevent a total collapse of their dream of African unity. The OAU which emerged from this process provides a structure, as well as the necessary legitimation, for the promotion of regional integration through the creation of regional organizations. What it did *not* do was to construct a continental political kingdom capable of planning economic development and harnessing African energies and resources for that purpose. Instead, and virtually to the contrary, the African leaders established a club of heads of state that sought to protect the sovereign equality and territorial integrity of each state and its inalienable right to independent existence.

From these tentative beginnings, the search for new definitions and processes of continental integration continued, culminating in the adoption of the Lagos Plan of Action (LPA) by the African heads of state in 1980. African leaders hoped that the agenda for action espoused in the LPA would "lead to the creation at the national, sub-regional and regional levels, of a dynamic and interdependent African economy and... thereby pave the way for the eventual establishment of an African Common Market leading to an African Economic Community" (OAU 1981, p. 2). As Ayele (1985, p. 53) points out, the shadow of Nkrumah's ideas is clearly felt in the LPA.

The climate of discussion and debate about the desirability and feasibility of economic and political integration has changed over the years. In the first decade after independence, when the mood was still optimistic, African leaders could initiate discussions about integration, create the necessary institutional infrastructure, and adopt programs of action for integration in an atmosphere of confidence. There was no shortage of leadership whose personality and ideas about Africa's future could command attention and reaction, both favourable and unfavourable. In contrast, recent discussions and debates are occurring in a crisis atmosphere, and there is considerable scepticism about the pious declarations of the Abuja Treaty signed by the heads of state in 1991 for the creation of a Panafrican Economic Community (Bach, this volume). The old confidence has vanished, along with exit from the political stage of leaders such as Kwame Nkrumah, Julius Nyerere, Leopold Senghor, and Houphouet Boigny. Although rhetorical support for integration exists, there is no dominant personality to articulate a vision and turn it into a crusade the way Nkrumah once did.

The cast of characters participating in discussions about African integration has also changed in recent years. It has expanded outward, and the voices extolling the virtues of regional integration today are just as likely to be European or North American as African. For instance, in late 1989, Jacques Pelletier, then French minister of cooperation and development urged African officials to intensify their own efforts toward regional cooperation, based on the European model. In his words,

> Without a regional market, Sub-Saharan Africa will not be organised on a sufficient scale to become an arena of economic growth. Without political co-ordination in all areas — fiscal, social and legal — it will remain too weak in the face of the large groupings which are being established everywhere in the world (Pelletier, cited in Callaghy 1991, p. 64).

These sentiments were later echoed by former commissioner for development of the European Community, Edgard Pisani, who asserted confidently that "Africa will be regional or not at all" (CEC 1991, p. 1). World Bank vice-president, Edward Jaycox (1992, p. 65) expressed similar views when he suggested that the two urgent imperatives that face the countries of sub-Saharan Africa are:

> for governments of the region to adjust their policy frameworks, get their economies back on track, make them as efficient and productive as possible, and liberate the vast entrepreneurial potential of their people; [and] for increased economic cooperation and, eventually, integration of African economies.

The increased interest of the international community in African regional cooperation and integration is demonstrated by the recent flurry of conferences on the subject and numerous position papers by international aid agencies; similarities among these position papers reflect the wide range of consultation and coordination that has taken place among development and donor agencies within the Global Coalition for Africa (GCA) and the Donor Advisory Committee of the Organization for Economic Cooperation and Development.

The highly visible and active participation of extra-continental actors in the debate about regional integration in Africa is a marked departure from the strong African leadership manifested earlier. It has been welcomed partly because it fills a gap, due to the current lack of internal leadership in defining alternative goals, objectives, and agendas for regional action or in providing sustained financial commitment to regional organizations (Daddieh 1994). Nonetheless, questions arise about the degree of compatibility, complementarity, or competition among different visions of regional integration at this juncture. Furthermore, the activism of the donors contrasts with the self-reliance that was emphasized in the LPA, and may raise issues of "ownership" of the African integration process somewhere down the line as has happened with structural adjustment. Donors should be sensitive to this, and there is much to be said for the ongoing process of dialogue among African decision-makers and donor institutions currently organized on a regular basis under the aegis of the GCA, on regional integration and other issues.

In this chapter, we attempt to identify the common elements and differences in the core orientations and professed visions of international donors with regard to regional integration focusing on the European Union (EU), France, the World Bank, the International Monetary Fund (IMF), the United States Agency for International Development (USAID), and the Canadian International Development Agency (CIDA). The second part of the chapter deals with the role of the donor community as a whole in the regional integration process and reviews some of the differences and possibilities for convergence between the strategic vision of the donors and of their African partners. The study draws principally on official documents and papers presented at recent conferences in Florence (February 1992), Dakar (January 1993) and Cotonou (June 1993), supplemented by the work of independent scholars, and interviews conducted in Washington, Ottawa, and Brussels. Use was also made of a similar, and in some respects more detailed, study by Brah et al. (1993, pp. 25–53).[1]

---

[1] Note that donor agencies are never monolithic. Policy debates in these agencies are conditioned by individual personalities, perceptions, experiences, and ideologies, with the result that there may be no single overarching strategy or blueprint for promoting regional integration in an agency. Even when an official position exists, the strategy so implied may or may not be fully implemented or it may change over time. Such considerations complicate the task of defining the particular perspective of different donors. However, dominant perspectives can generally be found, and that is what we try to do here.

THE MAJOR DONORS

THE EUROPEAN UNION

The EU is a long-standing advocate of regional integration in Africa and an important source of financing for regional schemes. Intellectual leadership has been provided by the Commission of European Communities (CEC), which has been instrumental in stimulating new ways of thinking and debate and has sponsored numerous studies and policy statements. Working in conjunction with other donors through the GCA, the CEC has recently drawn up an action plan to promote regional cooperation and integration in sub-Saharan Africa (CEC 1991).

Recent thinking at the European Commission has resulted in "the new regionalism." Drawing lessons from the failure of regional institutions in Africa and elsewhere in the Third World and from the EU's experience in support of regional integration in developing areas, this new regionalism argues in favour of modest initiatives and a focus on realistic, limited objectives. Lessons are also drawn from the European experience. Aspects considered to have been important to success include strong but flexible institutional arrangements, the full convertibility of national currencies, the existence of economic and social policies to reduce regional disparities, and the opportunity for subgroups to proceed at different speeds (CEC 1992, 1993).

An important principle has been that of "subsidiarity", which calls for the responsibility of dealing with an issue to be kept as close as possible to the population concerned; responsibilities should shift to a higher level such as the national or regional one only if the issue can be more effectively handled at that level. In this way only problems that are truly transnational and cannot be resolved at the national or subnational level reach the regional bodies.

The EU contends that regional integration can proceed at different speeds for different subgroups within a given community. The proposed approach, called "variable geometry," allows for the implementation of community policies to vary by subgroups of states. The continued existence of the Belgium–Luxembourg Economic Union and Benelux is one example of the tolerance for flexible arrangements within the EU. The EU considers it normal that some groups should proceed at different speeds in integration schemes involving large numbers of participants; variable geometry allows integration to proceed at an accelerated pace where the strong and sustained political commitment is present. The approach is illustrated by the progressive growth of the EU itself from the original core of six countries to the current 12, and the special arrangements that have been made with surrounding countries.

Such an approach is currently being applied in Eastern and Southern Africa, where the EU and the World Bank are sponsoring a regional integration initiative in association with the IMF and the African Development Bank (ADB). This is a concerted donor initiative to assist national governments in projects consistent with the pursuit of regional integration, through trade policy reform and other measures consistent with a Common Program of Action (CPA) adopted in Sept. 1993 by 14 countries in eastern and southern Africa. What is remarkable about the scheme, labelled the Cross-Border Initiative, is its flexibility in providing support to any country wishing to undertake reforms consistent with the CPA, in conformity with the variable-geometry perspective (d'Agostino 1993).

For West Africa, the CEC action plan considered parallel movement in both ECOWAS and the West African Economic Community (CEAO) as a possible approach in the context of variable geometry (CEC 1991, p. 10). The EU is now one of the donors supporting the West African Economic and Monetary Union (UEMOA), which has effectively supplanted the CEAO since the latter's dissolution in March 1994.

However, the action plan is careful not to condone unnecessary duplication. It recommends the streamlining of regional integration institutions to mitigate the problems and associated costs of overlapping functions, competition for funding, and multiple membership (CEC 1991).

The EU has taken a leading role in trying to influence the attitude of the donor community as a whole in favour of regional integration. It has challenged the donor community to provide greater financial and technical assistance and to demonstrate a regional cooperation "reflex," whereby all their assistance is programmed and evaluated on the basis of its contribution to regional cooperation and integration. It also suggests the need for an enabling international trading environment that complements rather than detracts from the integration efforts of African countries.

The EU has called on the donor community to be more aware of the link between regional economic integration and policy reforms carried out under structural adjustment or similar programs, in the interests of overall policy coherence and compatibility. In that regard, the EU has shown a greater willingness than the IMF or the World Bank to entertain a degree of regional protectionism against third countries in favour of infant industries. Policy reforms advocated by the EU nonetheless emphasize the removal of tariff and nontariff barriers to trade and factor mobility and improved monetary cooperation.

The EU has provided funding for regional transport and communications infrastructure and has supported regional organizations, such as the Permanent Interstate Committee for Drought control in the Sahel (CILSS) and the Regional Centre for Agrometeorology and Operational Hydrology (AGRHYMET), and regional research and health projects. It has also made significant contributions to ECOWAS and the former CEAO. The Lomé IV agreement (1991–95) allocates 10% of the European Development Fund to regional activities, and ECU 228 million for regional cooperation and integration activities in West Africa (Hugon 1991a, p. 12; Brah et al. 1993, p. 33) .

FRANCE

French policy toward regional integration in Africa is revealed directly, in French foreign policy, and indirectly, through the EU, since the signing of the Treaty of Rome in 1957. French policy with regard to its then colonial interests was extended through Title IV of the Treaty of Rome, which was inserted as a condition for French participation in the European Economic Community (Schreurs 1993). Title IV accorded special status to the French and Belgian colonies at the time and was the precursor to the Yaoundé and Lomé agreements which have since defined EU policies toward ACP countries (Africa, the Caribbean, and the Pacific).

Regional links among countries of the franc zone were actually strongest in the colonial era (de Benoist 1993). These links deteriorated under the weight of competing interests and nationalist pressures on the eve of independence with the effective dissolution of the French West African Federation in 1959, but survived in some form through institutions such as the West African Monetary Union (UMOA) and CEAO. UMOA was made possible thanks to French support and was an outgrowth of the colonial era. CEAO succeeded the Customs Union of West African States, whose antecedents go back to the Federation of French West Africa, established under French colonial rule in 1895. Thanks to continuing French support, the franc zone countries currently have the densest network of regional cooperation arrangements in sub-Saharan Africa (Bach 1993).

French policy in West Africa today remains focused principally on the UEMOA countries (formerly UMOA), which have established a certain tradition of shared sovereignty and collaboration in monetary matters. Interest in regional integration across linguistic boundaries in West Africa is limited, although it may grow as a result of increasing French investments in Nigeria.

Current emphasis is on the adoption of a pragmatic and progressive approach, which seeks to impose a limited financial burden on partici-pating countries while building on the strengths of the franc zone (France 1993, p. 4). This approach is reflected in a number of concrete initiatives aimed at improving the economic environment in franc zone countries. These include the reform of the insurance industry, business law, social security, and banking and finance, through the harmonization of legal and institutional structures and the creation of regulatory mech-anisms at the regional level. Also receiving immediate attention are the creation of regional training centres and the Afristat project aimed at the development of a reliable economic database for the franc zone (France 1993; Brah et al. 1993).

French support was also provided during the metamorphosis of UMOA into UEMOA.[2] The UEMOA initiative is an all-embracing one that envisages the creation of an economic union among the members, including the eventual establishment of a customs union (UEMOA 1994, art. IV, par. 2). Substantial emphasis is being placed on the need for economic policy reform and coordination, and the harmonization of fiscal and sectoral policies. This emphasis is consistent with recent French policy and conforms to the views of other participants, including the BCEAO, which is responsible for the implementation of UEMOA (see Brah et al. 1993, pp. 38–39; France 1993, p. 9; Wilson 1993; BCEAO 1993; and the interview with the governor of the BCEAO reported in Groupe Jeune Afrique 1994, p. 6). Increased French concern with economic policy reform was manifested most dramatically through France's crucial role in securing the 50% devaluation of the CFA franc in January 1994, a measure likely to provide a major boost to regional trade within the CFA zone. This emphasis on macroeconomic policy reform and coordination is different from the focus on regional trade preferences that characterized previous endeavours, such as CEAO.

There is a marriage of interests in all this. Measures to improve the economic environment in UEMOA countries are desirable in their own right, but also benefit French enterprise, which is strongly established in the industrial and service sectors everywhere in the region. French eco-nomic interests in trade liberalization are less obvious, as French firms

---

[2] Feasibility studies were financed by France, the World Bank, BCEAO, and the West African Development Bank.

and subsidiaries are often the main beneficiaries of import restrictions, and this may explain the relative lack of enthusiasm of the French for trade liberalization measures as reported in Berg (1991) or Brah et al. (1993). However there has been a shift in French policy, described as part of the "modernization of French capitalism," in favour of reduced protectionism in the zone and the promotion of greater competitiveness by French firms established there (Daniel Bach, personal communication). France is thus collaborating closely with the World Bank in the design of a common external tariff for the franc zone, as part of the UEMOA initiative.

A second area of support from the French is the Cissokho initiative, named after the Senegalese minister of rural development who launched it in 1991. It focuses on the agricultural and livestock sectors specifically, and involves the ministers of agriculture and rural development from 15 West and central African countries. The initiative was launched in March 1991 at an agriculture ministers' conference to discuss the establishment of a regional free-trade zone for grain, meat, and oilseeds. Using an approach pioneered under the Southern African Development Coordination Conference (SADCC, now the Southern African Development Community, SADC), agriculture ministries in various countries have each taken the lead in specific subsectors or activities: Mali in regional cereals markets; Cameroon in livestock and meat; Togo in vegetable oils and oilseeds; Côte d'Ivoire in commodity exports; Guinea in other products; Nigeria in applied research; Burkina Faso in support mechanisms and cross-cutting issues; and Senegal in overall coordination and broad economic policy issues. The initiative takes a pragmatic approach, aimed at the progressive integration of agricultural markets through policy coordination on a product-by-product and sectoral basis, with a view to increasing the competitiveness of the region in world markets (Diop and Lavergne 1994).

Another aspect of France's recent views on regional integration is a reexamination of its support to regional institutions in favour of ones that permit the collective management of infrastructure or key services, the development of common sectoral policies, or the achievement of significant economies of scale, for example, the Senegal River Development Organization, CILSS, and the Agency for the Safety of Aerial Navigation in Africa (Brah et al. 1993, p. 41). Special attention is being given to the development of a regional cereals market (Brah et al. 1993, pp. 41–42).

THE BRETTON WOODS INSTITUTIONS:
THE WORLD BANK AND THE IMF

The viewpoints of the Bretton Woods institutions are relatively homogeneous and probably the most familiar as a result of World Bank publications.[3] Although the Bretton Woods institutions are not as actively involved in supporting regional integration schemes as the EU or France, they can strongly influence the process through the structural adjustment programs they support in the region and their effect in promoting more liberal trade and investment policies. They also have substantial influence on conventional ways of thinking about economic development.

Although the World Bank has expressed support for regional economic integration and cooperation in some form (World Bank 1989a; Conable 1991; Jaycox 1992), the dominant view in the Bretton Woods institutions is that the preconditions for successful economic integration using the traditional approach do not exist in Africa. Foroutan (1993) identifies three reasons for the failure of intraregional trade liberalization in Africa:

- heavy reliance on import-substitution policies, resulting in an uncompetitive industrial structure and overvalued currencies;
- dependence on tariff revenues as a major source of government income; and
- unequal distribution of the costs and benefits of regional integration likely to accrue to participating countries.

Foroutan argues that for the theoretical gains from integration to be realized, partners must be more similar than dissimilar, so that each has something to gain from integration; failing that, an efficient and equitable compensation mechanism from the gainers to losers must be instituted. As IMF officials pointed out in interviews, the limited complementarities to be found in West Africa and the large disparities in population, resources, industrial capacity, and per capita incomes tend to skew the benefits of regional integration, in the form of increased exports, in favour of certain countries. The data bear this out: in 1990, Côte d'Ivoire accounted for 75% of intra-CEAO exports, but only 13% of imports; Côte d'Ivoire and Nigeria together accounted for 72% of ECOWAS exports, but only 22% of ECOWAS imports (Foroutan 1993). Because compensation mechanisms are costly and difficult to implement,

---

[3] On regional integration specifically, see World Bank 1989a, 1989b; Langhammer and Hiemenenz 1991; Mansoor and Inotai 1991; Jaycox 1992; Foroutan 1993.

the World Bank and the IMF are generally sceptical about the capacity of regional economic integration along traditional lines to improve intra-African trade.

Scepticism has also been expressed regarding support for capital-intensive multinational industrial projects, following bad experiences with large projects such as the West African Cement Mill (CIMAO) in Togo and the joint-venture oil refinery of the Central African Customs and Economic Union in Port Gentil. The CIMAO project was established with financing from the World Bank and Germany to provide its three partners (Ghana, Côte d'Ivoire and Togo) with clinker for cement production in the early 1980s, and had to be closed down after only a few months of operation. Demand proved to be far lower than anticipated and its clinker was about double the world price. Two smaller joint industrial projects (sugar and cement) between Benin and Nigeria also failed following the 1984 decision by Nigeria to close its borders (World Bank 1989a, p. 150; Berg 1991). As the World Bank (1989a, p. 152) concludes, "all past experience shows... that public sector management combined with protected markets results in costly and unviable projects; this is an unsound basis for integration."

The alternative strategy proposed by the World Bank (1989a, p. 152) involves three major thrusts: "incremental but comprehensive approaches to regional cooperation and integration, strengthening specific functional forms of cooperation, and creating an enabling environment for the free movement of goods, services, labour and capital."

The Bank and the IMF's concern over short-term viability leads them to advocate partial agreements among smaller groups of countries or a project approach to regional integration. One Bank official criticized ECA's LPA approach as an all or nothing proposition. He accepted the desirability of working toward the formation of large-scale communities, but argued that nothing should prevent middle-range or small-scale projects in the interim. The incremental approach to economic integration advocated by the Bank encourages two or more countries to pursue integration in whatever ways they can at an accelerated pace whenever they perceive mutual benefits to be achievable.

The Bank advocates donor support for such efforts. Consistent with this approach, it is one of the institutions that strongly supports the UEMOA initiative. It is also involved in multicountry sectoral initiatives, such as the livestock action plan, which seeks to liberalize trade in livestock products among Mali, Burkina Faso, and Côte d'Ivoire.

A major role for donors is also conceived in support of specific projects or initiatives in many areas of development activity of regional importance including: regional transport, communications, and energy; banking and insurance; education and research; and natural resource management (World Bank 1989a, pp. 153–157). People that we interviewed (Samen and Foroutan at the World Bank; Corsepiuz and Kimaro at the IMF) believed that initiatives based on cooperation, policy coordination, and harmonization hold greater promise than preferential schemes for the integration of trade and factor markets. It was proposed that project-based support could be used in combination with trade liberalization to compensate for loss of tariff revenue in a more sustainable way than has been the case in traditional tariff-revenue-compensation schemes in West Africa.

However the main influence of both the World Bank and IMF on regional integration is likely to come through policy reforms similar to those embodied in existing structural adjustment programs. Structural adjustment programs almost invariably include trade liberalization and currency devaluation as part of the package. When this is done in a single country, the effect is increased openness of that country to the rest of the world, including neighbouring countries, as trade liberalization makes imports from neighbouring countries more competitive and currency devaluation increases the attractiveness of the adjusting country's own exports. The implementation of structural adjustment programs simultaneously in virtually every West African country, as has been the case in the 1980s and 1990s, produces a cumulative effect strongly favourable to regional integration. Following the devaluation of the CFA franc in early 1994, the region has now devalued virtually all of its currencies in real terms with regard to the rest of the world, making regional products substantially more competitive today than they have been in a very long time (for data on devaluation outside the franc zone, see World Bank 1994, p. 242.).

The World Bank report on Africa's long-term prospects is rather circumspect regarding the role of structural adjustment in regional economic integration. Its discussion of the "enabling environment" for economic integration deals with trade liberalization, financial instruments for regional trade, labour and capital mobility, and the reduction of regulatory barriers to trade, with only passing reference to structural adjustment (World Bank 1989a, p. 159). Actual practice is much more conventional, however, and recent papers by World Bank economists more clearly reflect World Bank and IMF orthodoxy (Mansoor and Inotai

1991, pp. 226–228). The practice of the Bretton Woods institutions regarding regional economic integration is inspired by the principles of free trade, competition, and liberal economic policies that one normally associates with those institutions. Although regional trade liberalization may be supported as a first step to general liberalization, the view is that this should not be accompanied by increased protectionism toward the rest of the world. Trade preferences and overall trade liberalization are seen as initiatives to be undertaken in parallel, the formula allowing for small preference margins to minimize trade diversion and associated losses of economic efficiency, combined with low external tariffs (World Bank 1989a; Mansoor and Inotai 1991). Economic integration in this context is seen less as a way of protecting regional markets and more as a vehicle for improved trade with the rest of the world, through increased competitiveness in external markets.[4]

USAID

Although USAID engages in both bilateral (country-to-country) and regional activities in Africa, the bulk of its programming is done on a bilateral basis, from country desks in the countries of operation. Regional activities for West Africa are managed by a relatively small group based in the Africa Bureau in Washington.

USAID's activities in Africa are supported through the Development Fund for Africa (DFA), and one can get a good sense of the organization's strategic orientation from its presentation to Congress regarding the DFA for fiscal year 1993 (USAID 1993). The document describes four "strategic objectives": better management of African economies, the reinforcement of competitive markets, long-term growth in productivity, and improved food security. An important new dimension since the introduction of the DFA is flexibility to integrate sector assistance with traditional project and food-aid activities, which has permitted USAID to become more closely involved in sectoral policy reform, much as the World Bank has done at the macroeconomic level (USAID 1993). The omission of any reference to regional integration in the DFA document reflects the limited priority USAID places on the subject.

Officials interviewed at the Africa Bureau were sceptical about regional integration schemes based on preferential trading arrangements. Like their counterparts at the World Bank and the IMF, they argued that

---

[4] This position was eloquently expressed by the World Bank resident representative for Senegal, Elkyn Chaparro, in his speech to the International conference on regional integration in West Africa, 11–15 January 1993.

greater returns could be derived from trading internationally. They emphasized that USAID would not support protectionist schemes, as opposed to a more general approach to trade liberalization, and were suspicious of the "training ground argument" for protecting infant industries as advanced by the EU. They were unconvinced that African governments were very serious about liberalizing regional markets. However, faced with budget cutbacks, USAID is going through a period of transition and is seeking to determine the most effective use of available resources. This seems to have created greater interest in regional initiatives.

Although USAID does not have a large program focused on regional integration, it has supported a substantial number of projects and initiatives of a regional nature. These include regional organizations and programs with relatively narrow, technical objectives and a wide range of regional activities designed to give practical expression to the four "strategic objectives" listed above. Examples are support for the USAID–World Bank Livestock Action Plan and for various regional organizations engaged in resource management, drought and desertification control, population control, and disease control, such as CILSS, AGRHYMET, the Sahel Institute (INSAH), the Development Centre for Study and Research on Population (CERPOD), and the Regional Integration Promotion Unit for West and Central Africa (CINERGIE).

USAID also supports regional capacity-building and research in economic analysis through various mechanisms. Support for capacity-building includes the African Economic Research Consortium, the Network on Industrial Policy (Réseau sur les politiques industrielles), and the establishment of collaborative graduate training programs in economics at the master's level. Research initiatives include work on monetary reform, research on comparative advantage in West Africa (see Stryker et al., this volume), work on formal and parallel trade flows between certain countries, and a search for ways to support and eliminate trade barriers or create new trading opportunities. USAID is also supporting the development of a business network in West Africa as a vehicle for building the private sector.

CANADA

Canada's bilateral aid program has traditionally focused on country-to-country forms of collaboration, but seemed ready for a change in focus following the publication of its vision for Africa for the 21st century, *Africa 21*, in October 1991. *Africa 21* identified a number of priorities for Africa, on which there exists a consensus within the international community, and selected regional integration as a main area of strategic intervention in which Canada could play a "catalytic role" (CIDA 1991, p. 2). *Africa 21* was officially approved, and this led to a flurry of activity and reflection and the preparation of regional strategies for southern Africa, North Africa and the Middle East, and West Africa. Strategic thinking about West Africa led to the production of a series of background papers, including one on regional integration (CIDA 1992).

Institutional restructuring within CIDA increased its ability to plan regionally. An important move in this direction was made in 1991, when the francophone and anglophone African branches were merged into a single Africa and the Middle East Branch, divided along geographic lines, including a single directorate for the 16 countries of West Africa. Restructuring of the West African Directorate along regional lines has also been implemented. This provides for a strategic analysis unit at the regional level and allocation of regional program staff in four divisions including one for regional projects and three others covering the Sahelian countries, a second group consisting primarily of anglophone countries along the coast (Ghana, Nigeria, Togo, Liberia and Sierra Leone), and a third group including Côte d'Ivoire, Guinea, and Benin.

The regional strategy for West Africa, approved in principle in June 1994, will provide a regional framework for the development of country-level programming, and should encourage greater focus on regional issues than in the past. However the strong strategic thrust of *Africa 21* around regional integration has been diluted since its publication, particularly with reference to West Africa. The election of a new government in September 1993, associated changes at senior levels of CIDA, and general discussion in the Agency have led to a de-emphasis on regional integration, the future status of which is now uncertain.

This is evident in the regional strategy for West Africa, which is articulated around four themes: economic growth based on the dynamism of the export sector; social change and human resource development; good governance and democracy; and natural resource management. Regional integration is not included and is identified only as an underlying and omnipresent consideration in all program areas. Mention of regional integration is actually quite reserved, and the strategy considers it to be too ill-focused and difficult to operationalize at this time (CIDA 1994, section 6.3.3).

CIDA's views on this subject are similar to Bourenane's (this volume), when he calls for a long-term view in developing a sense of regional community and achievement. According to an earlier CIDA document, "formal and substantive regional integration is almost certainly years away, and is likely only to come when governments have come to know each other better and developed a basis of mutual trust and confidence which comes from joint effort and accomplishment in a variety of smaller areas" (CIDA 1993, p. 16). CIDA's approach will thus include the promotion of regional dialogue on policy matters, support of activities providing tangible benefits for participating countries, and the involvement of national institutions most open to dialogue with regional partners (CIDA 1994, section 6.3.3). In accord with its current conception of regionalism for West Africa, CIDA advocates cooperation and integration among small groups of countries on a product-by-product or country-by-country basis in projects designed for mutual advantage, along the lines of the Common Program of Action of the Cross-Border Initiative advocated by the ADB and the World Bank for Southern Africa.

How far CIDA will go in its support of regionalism is a matter for conjecture. Much of the thinking at CIDA, as applied to West Africa in particular, has been around notions of economic integration (see in particular CIDA 1992), as opposed to the more general concepts of regional integration and cooperation envisaged in this volume. This limited view of the regional agenda may explain some of the reticence to be found in the Agency. However, CIDA is currently reexamining the concept of regional integration, and one could easily envisage a strategy that retained a broadly defined role for regionalism, despite the relative downgrading of support for economic integration as traditionally understood. A careful review of the regional strategy for West Africa confirms an abundance of opportunities for regional initiatives, not only under the first theme, which focuses on trade, but also in the areas of human development (through regional initiatives), and natural resource management (in the area of fisheries management, in particular).

CIDA's greater emphasis on regional programming and cooperation may bring it to collaborate more closely with its sister organization, IDRC, which has identified regional integration and cooperation as a priority. Although IDRC is relatively small, it is one of the few donor agencies to operate on a strictly regional basis, and one of the few to support research by African scholars and institutions. This has allowed it to innovate in various areas of regional collaboration in the field of research, through networking and institutional support.

CIDA can also be expected to cooperate with other donors. Its views with respect to economic integration as expressed in a key working paper (CIDA 1992) do not differ radically from those of the World Bank or other donors. Like others, CIDA supports the liberalization of regional trade and factor movements, while expressing the usual caveat about the importance of liberal trade policies more generally. There is also considerable emphasis on the need for policy harmonization; in this, CIDA accords top priority to the need for stable monetary arrangements between UEMOA and Nigeria, as advocated by Bach (this volume). CIDA joins other donors, finally, in advocating a pragmatic, step-by-step approach. Favour is expressed for the UEMOA and Cissokho initiatives being supported by the French and other donors.

WHAT ROLE FOR DONORS IN REGIONAL INTEGRATION?

Donors have a special and perhaps indispensable role to play in regional integration for several reasons. The first is obviously their access to financial resources. External funding is particularly important for initiatives that are regional in scope, because of the lack of a regional tax base for funding such projects. This contrasts with the situation at the national level, where the tax base may be inadequate, but at least covers the highest priority needs. External funding is practically the only viable source of funding at the regional level.

Donors also distinguish themselves by the operational bent of their approach. Run by technocrats with budgets to spend, and relatively disconnected from political considerations in the region due to their external status, donors tend toward the sort of pragmatic and concrete approach that we observed in the previous section.

The strong market orientation and liberal economic convictions of the donors, which reflect the economic philosophy currently prevalent in industrial countries and within the economics profession in particular, constitute the third feature worth mentioning. Through their pursuit of such an economic development philosophy, the donors have become an important force for regional integration by supporting trade liberalization and the free movement of factors in Africa.

Certain forms of intervention lend themselves more readily to donor involvement than others, and the distinction between regional cooperation and regional integration that donors frequently make deserves some pause. Regional cooperation constitutes a relatively flexible approach, involving voluntary efforts at collaboration among neighbouring countries, in an ad hoc and often temporary fashion, in areas of common interest to two or more participating countries (Berg 1991; Brah et. al. 1993, pp. 27–28; Bourenane, this volume). In contrast, regional integration is both more demanding and more constraining, involving not only cooperation among countries, but also the sharing of sovereignty. It thus demands an important degree of commitment from all participating countries from the beginning.

This is a useful distinction in understanding what donors can or cannot do in support of regional integration and cooperation in Africa. Although donors can supply the financial wherewithal to promote cooperative ventures, they cannot generally oblige countries to cede sovereignty over their affairs, as implied by regional integration. One might thus expect a certain reluctance to support regional integration schemes, as opposed to cooperative types of endeavour, in the absence of sufficient political will from African governments themselves. To a large extent, this is what has happened, and one should not expect otherwise, unless and until African states show the political will to resolve the sovereignty issue.

The external character of donors as development agents does not necessarily suggest an unwillingness to engage in policy matters. Donors' access to financial resources provides a substantial lever for influencing behaviour that donors do not hesitate to apply in the context of structural adjustment programs. The question thus arises whether this sort of policy reform could not be similarly applied at the regional level. Greater coordination of structural adjustment programs along regional lines and greater attention to policy changes favourable to regional integration have been suggested (Berg 1991; Hugon 1991b; ADB 1993; Larbi 1992; Daddieh 1994), and this option is attracting more interest as an area of donor involvement in favour of regional integration. Indeed, the ADB dedicated a major section of its 1993 *African Development Report* to this topic (ADB 1993).

The close collaboration between donors and the BCEAO under the UEMOA initiative can also be understood largely in these terms, and the introduction of multilateral surveillance and sanctions aimed at coordinating economic policy, which one might associate with structural adjustment programs, is a defining feature of the UEMOA project (Ghymers 1994). The major limitation of that initiative from a West African perspective is its organization along linguistic lines, although it is the diverging policies of francophone and anglophone countries in the region that most need harmonization (see Bach, this volume). There is clearly a role for donors to extend policy harmonization beyond the UEMOA initiative to include other countries of West Africa.

DIFFERENT BUT CONVERGING APPROACHES

Donors are called upon to work as partners with African governments and institutions, whose views may differ on the choice of strategic orientation. African views on regional integration include those of regional institutions such as ECA, the OAU, and the ADB, for Africa as a whole, and those of ECOWAS and the BCEAO, for West Africa specifically. They also include the views of government leaders and officials and various parts of civil society. Regional institutions tend to be more ambitious about regional integration than either national governments or the donor institutions, for reasons naturally having to do with their responsibilities as its advocates; comparing the views of donors and regional institutions alone may tend to overstate any apparent gap between African and donor positions. In emphasizing regional cooperation, as they often do, donors tend to work more closely with national governments and specialized regional cooperation agencies than with institutions such as ECOWAS or ECA. However, the regional institutions play an important role in setting the agenda for regional integration, and it is important to appreciate the extent to which the donors and regional institutions might be working at cross purposes.

THE ABUJA TREATY OR VARIABLE GEOMETRY?

The principal difference between donors and most African regional institutions concerns the implementation of the Abuja Treaty as an umbrella scheme for all others, and the ability of schemes currently covered by the Abuja Treaty to lead the way. The donors are unanimous in their scepticism regarding the Abuja Treaty, which remains the key reference point for African institutions.

This difference is reflected in the reaction of African institutions to the notion of variable geometry, which all the donors espouse in one form or another. Although African institutions generally welcome the new-found support of the donor community for regional integration and cooperation, they have had some misgivings about the emphasis on loose forms of regional cooperation conducted on a pragmatic and ad hoc basis (ECA 1993; London 1993). The ECA regards the variable-geometry approach as a distraction from African efforts to create integrated regional spaces and effective institutions, as it would complicate attempts by African heads of state to consolidate the many integration schemes into a small number of large but cohesive communities.

Differences between donors and regional institutions on this issue have been debated in the context of the GCA, as illustrated in the following citation from the report of its co-chairpersons at the June 1993 meeting in Cotonou (GCA 1993):

> The contrasting views and areas of debate were between those who emphasized (these included the ADB, OAU, ECA) that since the Abuja Treaty is an expression of the will and intentions of African countries, the Treaty and its implementation should be the chosen path, and donors should accordingly take into account Africa's chosen path in their approach to supporting integration in Africa; and other groups (including many donor countries and institutions) who believed that integration has to be carried out pragmatically from the bottom up, with countries that share common goals and interests moving faster and further along with integration while allowing others to catch up later on.

African institutions have been particularly suspicious of the UEMOA initiative and its equivalent in central Africa, the Central African Economic and Monetary Union (CEMAC), as highlighted in ADB's *Report on Development in Africa*, which referred to expressions of "grave concern" about the implications of these initiatives for the future of the Abuja Treaty or existing economic communities in those regions (ADB 1993, p. 166 in the French edition). As London (1993, p. 9) puts it in a paper for the ADB:

> If the more advanced Member States of an economic community proceed along decisions in which the remaining Member States of an economic community have not taken part, the variable geometry strategy can become a disintegrative strategy, splitting the community in two, as the remaining Member States of the Community have only two options: implementing the decisions taken by the "core community" or taking a direction more consistent with their joint interests. The variable geometry strategy becomes an especially important concern when the pace of progress of the core countries depends on the impetus carried into the community from outside the region. Indeed, an integrative strategy is unlikely to succeed if the steam for the locomotive is not generated by the Member States forming the very community.

However, such concerns have not prevented African institutions from initiating or supporting new initiatives in line with the variable geometry approach, as evidenced by the central role of the BCEAO in the UEMOA initiative, or the support of the ADB for the Cross-Border Initiative in Eastern and Southern Africa, mentioned earlier. Remarkably, even the OAU has expressed support for the Cross-Border Initiative. Caution on the part of the African institutions should, therefore, not be interpreted as blind resistance, provided appropriate efforts are made to meet the long-term concerns of the various parties involved.

DIFFERING VIEWS OF INTERNATIONAL TRADE AND DEVELOPMENT

A second area of differentiation among various parties is in their trade orientation. African institutions tend to be more protectionist than the donors. It is fair to say that the first priority for the IMF, the World Bank, and USAID is sustained structural adjustment favouring across-the-board liberalization as the most effective way to promote global and regional trade. The tendency is to support schemes or projects that encourage trade creation rather than trade diversion. In contrast, the ECA sees the liberal economic orientation of the major donors as tending to reinforce Africa's traditional role in the international market as a supplier of primary products and an excessive level of economic extroversion. It criticizes the structural adjustment programs of the IMF and World Bank, partly because they do not really restructure the foundations of Africa's national economies (ECA 1991). As Berg (1991) points out, the ECA approach to regional integration continues to advocate a strong measure of economic planning, with special emphasis on heavy industry (see also ECA 1993).

However, there are some points over which it now seems redundant to be arguing. In particular, trade liberalization, under structural adjustment programs or otherwise, is already taking place, and will continue. What must be discussed is not whether to liberalize or revert to preferential models of regional integration, but how to liberalize so that regional markets are best served, and how to ensure the diversification of national economies and increased competitiveness in the context of market liberalization. As noted earlier, much could be achieved through better coordination and some redirection of structural adjustment programs, and regional institutions might do well to encourage that process.

LESSONS OF EXPERIENCE

A consideration that might facilitate the coexistence of different visions is the realization that different approaches have worked, to some extent, in Africa. These include: two market-oriented schemes, CEAO and PTA (which became COMESA, the Common Market for East and Southern Africa, in 1994); the monetary integration schemes of the franc zone in

West and central Africa; and the project-based approach used by SADC. The successes of these schemes are relative, to be sure, but they include CEAO's expansion of regional trade among its members, the PTA's institution of a multilateral clearing house for the settlement of payments (Lipumba and Kasekende 1991, p. 240; London 1993, p. 3), the franc zone's main0tenance of economic stability (Medhora, this volume), and SADC's well-known mobilization of support for infrastructure projects.

These schemes were inspired by quite different interests and actors. CEAO was inspired by political calculations associated with the survival of the francophonie as a sociopolitical and economic entity and the interests of various parties (such as France and Côte d'Ivoire) in maintaining their own spheres of interest. The monetary unions of the franc zone are outgrowths of the colonial period, amended to suit the post-independence period while retaining the benefits of convertibility. The PTA was the brainchild of the ECA and is one of the four regional integration schemes advocated by that institution for Africa. Finally, SADC's origins date back to the years of consultation among the front-line states in their struggle with South Africa's apartheid system. It is encouraging that these different schemes, with different origins and instigators, espousing varying perspectives and priorities, and with different internal and external sponsors should each have achieved a measure of success.

However, these success stories do have one obvious thing in common: the substantial support of outside donors — the Europeans and France for CEAO and the franc zone, the World Bank and others for the PTA clearinghouse, and the whole community of donors acting in unison in the case of SADC. African countries acting on their own have unfortunately failed to marshall the financial resources needed for regional integration and cooperation to work. Increased donor support thus seems to be a necessary condition for substantial further progress.

THE COMPATIBILITY ISSUE

The significance of differences in vision among the various parties depends on the extent of their compatibility and the extent to which it might be increased over time. Certain ways of thinking about regional integration and cooperation and how to achieve it may help reinforce such compatibility, and we offer a few suggestions in this section. A useful starting point is the realization that the pragmatic approach being proposed by the donors for the short-term is not necessarily incompatible with the long-term ambitions contained in the Abuja Treaty, provided an effort is made to avoid conflicts in its actual implementation.

Improved dialogue between the donors and the regional institutions could, in our view, increase the compatibility of these short- and long-term objectives, while offering a degree of reassurance to all concerned. Meanwhile, the growing consensus in favour of market liberalization and economic reform should facilitate dialogue between actors more likely to be in tune with each other than they were in the past, despite continuing differences in emphasis.

All parties recognize the need for donor support in favour of regional infrastructure and related projects. The SADC experience is often held up as a successful example, as are some of the achievements in the fields of transport and telecommunications in ECOWAS. However, the actual proportion of aid going to regional projects remains fairly small. Probably no donor exceeds the share of 10% projected for regional projects in 1991–95 from the EU's European Development Fund under Lomé IV, and it is doubtful that even that figure will be reached, due to the usually slow disbursement of funds for regional projects. Comparable figures under Lomé II and III were only 7% and 1.5% respectively (Hugon 1991a, p. 12). For other donors, the share of loans going to regional projects in the 1980s was in the order of 2.3% for the ADB, 3% for the Caisse Centrale de Coopération Économique (CCCE), and less than 1% for the World Bank (Hugon 1991b, pp. 205–207).

Regional institutions might thus be more aggressive in encouraging donor support for regional cooperation projects. As Brah et al. (1993) point out, this can include a wide range of initiatives, for example,

> The creation of regional centres of excellence, regional programs to fight river blindness, regional transportation infrastructure, regional pest management initiatives, regional management of a natural resource such as a river, the exploitation of oil and natural gas reserves on a regional scale, the regional sharing of hydroelectricity, etc.

African governments and regional institutions alike would do well to recognize the special needs of regional projects for external financing, to urge the donor community to make such projects a priority, and to promote a larger degree of aid programming on a regional, rather than country or project, basis.

There is not much disagreement between the donor community and African institutions regarding the diagnosis of problems confronting existing integration schemes.[5] All agree that regional integration has

---

[5] This consensus can be appreciated in position papers by donor agencies or African institutions and the work of scholars working on regional integration in Africa (World Bank 1989a, p. 149; Ndiaye 1990, p. 36; Okolo and Wright 1990; Ravenhill 1990; OECD 1992a, p. 2; Camara 1993; London 1993; Daddieh 1994).

been a failure in Africa, and in West Africa in particular, as described by Bundu (this volume) and the ECA (1993).

There also seems to be general agreement on the need to bring various elements of civil society more fully into the regional integration process. The donors are in favour of this, while ECOWAS, which is a regional institution of the traditional kind, created and governed by the heads of state, has been active in promoting and supporting various sorts of regional associations (Bundu, this volume). The consensus is that more must be done in this sphere if regional integration is to succeed in the long term.

As Bourenane argues elsewhere in this volume, the strategic imperative is to surpass the volontaristic approach, which has dominated thinking and discourse to date, to develop an alternative, dynamic approach capable of building political momentum for regional integration over time. In this, the donor community may be on the right track in its pragmatic pursuit of regional cooperation and variable geometry, as well as more liberal economic policies, capable of stimulating growth of the private sector and its interest in regional integration. However, this should be accompanied by a strong strategic thrust, ensuring that such mechanisms effectively lay the foundations for the long-term, more ambitious schemes of the ECA and other African institutions. Donors should ensure the coherence of short-term pragmatic solutions with the long-term visions of their African partners, and should be *seen* to be doing so, rather than merely bypassing African ambitions.

Some of the tools now being used by the EU are useful in this regard: these include the concepts of widening, deepening, and broadening. *Widening* is defined as adding more member states to the regional initiative. *Deepening* relates to the level or intensity of cooperation; in government policy, for example, deepening could run the gamut from simple exchange of information, through harmonization of policies, to the formulation of common policies. *Broadening* refers to increasing the number of areas that are covered: trade policy, monetary policy, environmental management, etc. (CEC 1993, p. 15). A gradual approach to regional integration could thus proceed along any of all of these various lines.

The regional integration process requires nurturing through carefully calibrated steps, proceeding from a low to a higher order of interaction, commitment, emotional attachment, and loyalty transfer among leaders, elites, and citizens to arrive at an increasing willingness to share national sovereignty. A focus on strategic approaches to achieving this could help to resolve the differences between various parties involved in the integration debate by raising the discussion to a higher plane.

CONCLUSION

What is needed now is dialogue between donors and African leaders — such as that being promoted by the GCA — to ensure greater convergence of the aspirations of African institutions and leaders with the projects being pursued by the donor community. African institutions have to meet the challenge posed by the new thinking of the donor community and its preference for flexible, multi-pronged cooperative approaches involving several contiguous member states as opposed to the macroregional spaces advocated by the ECA. Although some at the ECA are clearly frustrated by this latest external challenge, other African institutions seem to be taking the different approaches in stride. In the end, coexistence of different perspectives is inevitable and probably quite healthy, given Africa's own diversity, until one approach or combination of approaches emerges as the most effective means of achieving an integrated continental economic space.

REFERENCES

ADB (African Development Bank). 1993. Report on development in Africa. ADB, Abidjan, Côte d'Ivoire.

Ayele, N. 1985. Kwame Nkrumah and the Lagos Plan of Action. In Adedeji, A.; Shaw, T.M. (ed.). Economic crisis in Africa: African perspectives on development problems and potential. Lynne Rienner Publishers, Boulder, CO, USA. Pp. 47–58.

Bach, D. 1993. Régionalisme francophone ou régionalisme franco-Africain? In Bach, D.; Kirk-Green, A. (ed.). État et société en Afrique francophone. Economica, Paris, France.

BCEAO (Central Bank of West African States). 1993. L'expérience et le rôle de la BCEAO en matière d'intégration sous-régionale : perspectives d'union économique envisagée au sein de l'UMOA. Presented at the International conference on regional integration in West Africa, 11–15 January, Dakar. International Development Research Centre, Dakar, Senegal.

Berg, E. 1991. Strategies for West African economic integration: issues and approaches. Club du Sahel, Organization for Economic Co-operation and Development, Paris, France.

Brah, M.; Pradelle, J.M.; d'Agostino, V. 1993. Regional cooperation and integration in West Africa: a contribution to the corpus of knowledge from the collaborative research of the CILSS, the Club du Sahel and the Cinergie Unit. Club du Sahel, Paris, France.

Callaghy, T.M. 1991. Africa and the world economy: caught between a rock and a hard place. *In* Harbeson J.W.; Rothchild D. (ed.). Africa in world politics. Westview press, Boulder, CO, USA. Pp. 39-68.

Camara, L. 1993. La contribution du groupe de la Banque africaine de développement dans la réalisation de l'intégration économique et son rôle dans la mise en oeuvre du Traité d'Abuja instituant le Marché Commun Africain. Presented at the International conference on regional integration in West Africa, 11–15 January, Dakar. International Development Research Centre, Dakar, Senegal.

CEC (Commission of the European Communities). 1991. Regional cooperation and integration in sub-Saharan Africa: basic issues for an action programme. CEC, Brussels, Belgium.

———— 1992. Promoting regional cooperation and integration in sub-Saharan Africa. Prepared for the Second advisory committee meeting of the Global Coalition for Africa, Kampala, 8–9 May 1992. Global Coalition for Africa, Washington, DC, USA.

———— 1993. Outline of a programme of action to promote regional integration and cooperation in sub-Saharan Africa. Prepared for the Global Coalition for Africa ministerial meeting, Cotonou, Benin, 9–11 June. Global Coalition for Africa, Washington, DC, USA. Document GCA/AC.3/NO.9/06/1993.

CIDA (Canadian International Development Agency). 1991. Africa 21: a vision of Africa for the 21st century. Africa and the Middle East Branch, CIDA, Hull, Canada.

———— 1992. Intégration régionale. Chapter E in the series of background papers produced for the meeting of May 22, 26, and 27, 1992, in preparation of the West Africa Strategic Framework. Africa and the Middle East Branch, CIDA, Hull, Canada.

———— 1993. Africa 21: into year two. Africa and the Middle East Branch, CIDA, Hull, Canada.

———— 1994. Proposition d'un cadre stratégique régional pour l'Afrique de l'Ouest. Africa and the Middle East Branch, CIDA, Hull, Canada.

Conable, B.B. 1991. Reflections on Africa: the priority of sub-Saharan Africa in economic development. World Bank, Washington, DC, USA.

Daddieh, C.K. 1994. Structural adjustment programmes (SAPs) and regional integration: are they compatible or mutually exclusive? *In* Mengisteab, K.; Logan, B. (ed.). Beyond economic liberalization in Africa: structural adjustment and the alternatives. Zed Press, London, UK.

d'Agostino, V. 1993. The regional integration initiative underway in eastern and southern Africa. Club du Sahel, Paris, France. Briefing note, Nov. 17.

de Benoist, R. 1993. L'intégration de l'Afrique occidentale française aurait-elle pu être irréverstible? Presented at the International conference on regional integration in West Africa, 11–15 January, Dakar. International Development Research Centre, Dakar, Senegal.

Diop, M.C.; Lavergne, R. 1994. Regional integration in West Africa: proceedings of the International conference organized by IDRC in Dakar, Sénégal, 11–15 January 1993. International Development Research Centre, Ottawa, Canada.

ECA (Economic Commission for Africa). 1991. African alternative framework to structural adjustment programs for socio-economic recovery and transformation: a popular version. ECA, Addis Ababa, Ethiopia.

———— 1993. L'intégration économique en Afrique, situation et perspectives: le point de vue de la Commission économique des Nations Unies pour l'Afrique. Presented at the International conference on regional integration in West

Africa, 11–15 January, Dakar. Economic Commission for Africa, Addis Ababa, Ethiopia. Document E/ECA/CM.17/2.

Foroutan, F. 1993. Regional integration in sub-Saharan Africa: past experience and future prospects. In de Melo, J.; Panagariya, A. (ed.). New dimensions in regional integration. Cambridge University Press, New York, NY, USA..

France, Mission de Coopération et d'Action Culturelle. 1993. L'intégration régionale à travers les espaces économiques et financiers. Presented at the International conference on regional integration in West Africa, 11–15 January, Dakar. International Development Research Centre, Dakar, Senegal.

GCA (Global Coalition for Africa). 1993. Co-chairmen's report. Presented at GCA meetings, 9–11 June 1993, Cotonou, Benin. GCA, Washington, DC, USA. Document GCA/AC.3/CCR No.003/06/1993.

Ghymers, C. 1994. Note de présentation de Traité de l'Union économique et monétaire ouest-africaine. Directorate-General for Economic and Financial Affairs, Economic Evaluation of Community Policies Directorate, European Commission, Brussels, Belgium. Document II 1103/94-FR.

Groupe Jeune Afrique, 1994. UEMOA : l'intégration sur les rails. Groupe Jeune Afrique, Paris, France. Information brief, July.

Hugon, P. 1991a. Introduction. In Hugon, P.; Coussy, J. (ed.). Intégration régionale et ajustement structurel en Afrique sub-saharienne. Ministère de la Coopération et du Développement, Paris, France. Pp. 9–15.

————— 1991b. Les programmes d'ajustement structurel et les différentes formes d'intégration régionale. In Hugon, P.; Coussy, J. (ed.). Intégration régionale et ajustement structurel en Afrique sub-saharienne. Ministère de la Coopération et du Développement, Paris, France. Pp. 195-227.

Jaycox, E.V.K. 1992. The challenges of African development. World Bank, Washington, DC, USA.

Langhammer, R.J.; Hiemenenz, U. 1991. Regional integration among developing countries: survey of past performance and agenda for future policy action. Trade Policy Division, World Bank, Washington, DC, USA.

Larbi, G. 1992. Structural adjustment programmes in subsaharan Africa: prospects ans problems for economic integration in West Africa. Prepared for the International conference on West African integration, 11-15 January 1993, organized by IDRC and ECOWAS.

Lipumba, N.H.I.; Kasekende, L. 1991. The record and prospects of the preferential trade area for eastern and southern African states. In Chhibber, A.; Fischer, S. (ed.). Economic reform in sub-Saharan Africa: a World Bank symposium. World Bank, Washington, DC, USA. Pp. 217–232 .

London, A. 1993. Promoting regional economic cooperation and integration in Africa. Prepared for the GCA ministerial meeting, 9–11 June, Cotonou, Benin. Global Coalition for Africa, Washington, DC, USA. Document GCA/AC.3/No.8/06/1993.

Mansoor, A.; Inotai, A. 1991. Integration efforts in sub-Saharan Africa: failures, results and prospects: a suggested strategy for achieving efficient integration. In Chhibber, A.; Fischer, S. (ed.). Economic reform in sub-Saharan Africa, a World Bank symposium. World Bank, Washington, DC, USA. Pp. 217–232.

Ndiaye, B. 1990. Prospects for economic integration in Africa. In P. Anyang Nyong'o (ed.). Regional integration in Africa: unfinished agenda. Academy Science Publishers, Nairobi, Kenya. Pp. 35-41.

OAU (Organization of African Unity). 1981. Lagos plan of action for the economic development of Africa, 1980–2000. International Institute for Labour Studies, Geneva, Switzerland.

OECD (Organization for Economic Co-operation and Development). 1992a. Regional co-operation in developing countries. Background paper for informal preparatory meeting, 27–28 April. OECD, Paris, France.

———— 1992b. The new regional initiatives and roles for development co-operation. Note submitted by the Secretariat for consideration by the Development Assistance Committee at its meeting, 15–16 September. OECD, Paris, France.

Okolo, J.E.; Wright, S. (ed.). 1990. West African regional cooperation and development. Westview Press, Boulder, CO, USA.

Ravenhill, J. 1990. Overcoming constraints to regional cooperation in Africa: coordination rather than integration? In Background papers: the long-term perspective study of sub-Saharan Africa (vol. 4). World Bank, Washington, DC, USA. Pp. 81–85.

Schreurs, R. 1993. L'Eurafrique dans les négotiations du Traité de Rome, 1956–1957. Politique Africaine, 49 (March), 82–92.

UEMOA (Union Économique et Monétaire Ouest-Africaine). 1994. Traité de l'Union économique et monétaire ouest-africaine. Central Bank of West African States, Dakar, Sénégal.

USAID (United States Agency for International Development). 1993. Congressional presentation overview development fund for Africa, fiscal year 1993. USAID, Washington, DC, USA. Mimeo.

Wilson, E.J. 1993. French support for structural adjustment programs in Africa. World Development, 21 (3), 331–347.

World Bank. 1989a. Regional integration and cooperation: from words to deeds. In Sub-Saharan Africa: from crisis to sustainable growth (chapter 7). World Bank, Washington, DC, USA.

———— 1989b. Intra-regional trade in sub-Saharan Africa (vol. I). Africa Region Technical Department, World Bank, Washington, DC, USA.

———— 1994. Adjustment in Africa: reforms, results and the road ahead. Oxford University Press, New York, NY, USA.

Zartman, I.W. 1987. International relations in the new Africa. University of America Press, Lanham, MD, USA.

CHAPTER 7

BUILDING PARTNERSHIPS FOR INNOVATION: A NEW ROLE FOR SOUTH–SOUTH COOPERATION

– Lynn K. Mytelka –

Lynn Mytelka takes a global view of developing-country experience with regional integration. In her view, "market-driven" and "specialization-driven" models have failed, due to the zero-sum nature of the game and the lack of a constituency at the firm level. However, beginning in the late 1970s and early 1980s, developing countries began to turn away from the import-substitution policies of the past. This was accompanied by a shift in strategic orientation at the firm level that included greater attention to technological advancement, greater use of information systems and networks in gaining access to technology, and the transformation of subsidiaries into independent profit centres.

Such changes provide the basis for a new approach to South–South cooperation around notions of dynamic competitiveness and innovation. Most developing countries in Africa and elsewhere lack the critical mass and technological infrastructure necessary to meet the challenges of a rapidly changing and increasingly competitive world market. Regional cooperation could help overcome these constraints by providing a framework for the adoption of new formulas for stimulating innovation. The author provides examples of the sorts of activities that could be pursued and calls for the establishment of a "Fund for Innovation and Development" in Africa.

DURING THE 1970s and 1980s, several important changes took place in the world economy. The most salient of these, for the purposes of this paper, were the heightened pace of global competition and the accelerated rate of technological innovation and diffusion. Even in traditional industries such as textiles and clothing (Mytelka 1987, 1991a), the need to strengthen competitiveness has led to a rapid increase in the knowledge-intensity of production, where knowledge is understood to include research and development (R&D), design, engineering, maintenance, management, and marketing.

As the knowledge-intensity of production increased, both governments and firms came to regard technology as one of the key components
in a strategy for building competitiveness. As one recent report (OECD
1992) pointed out,

> Technology and other innovation-related phenomena, along with cor-
> porate organization and the proper use of human capital in all the
> phases of the production process, now represent one of the main pillars
> of competitiveness.... These features are not simply the attributes of
> individual firms, but also, to a large extent, those of national or local
> environments where organisational and institutional developments
> have produced conditions conducive to the growth of the interactive
> mechanisms on which innovation and the diffusion of technology are
> based.

Innovation has thus become a vital link in the relation between trade
and development, and development itself can be seen as a continuous
process of transformation, adaptation, and adjustment in advanced industrial and developing countries alike.

However, most African and many Latin American and Caribbean
countries are singularly unprepared to meet the challenges of a changing
technological and competitive environment. They lack the strong knowledge base, integrated physical infrastructure, and diversified economy
required to weather shocks and to innovate by recombining existing
resources in new ways or by introducing new products, processes, and
organizational practices. The ability of their institutions to perceive
opportunities and constraints and to translate them into effective policies
for change is limited. The financing and skills needed to innovate, adapt,
and diversify are also rare in these countries.

Although regional integration among developing countries might
have compensated for some of these weaknesses, the application of such
schemes, whether of the "exchange-driven" or "production-specialization" variety, has historically not focused on innovation and change.
Their underlying conception was based on the replication of imports and
reliance on intraregional trade as the agent of change.

Exchange-driven models of regional integration were based on a mix
of considerations combining notions of comparative advantage and
allocative efficiency derived from traditional neoclassical economics, with
infant-industry arguments for protectionism. Typical example are the
Latin American Free Trade Area (LAFTA) established in 1960, the Customs and Economic Union of Central Africa (UDEAC) as it was initially
set up in 1964, the Caribbean Free Trade Areas (CARIFTA) of 1967 and

the Preferential Trade Area for Eastern and Southern African States (PTA) formed in 1982. Each involved the adoption of comprehensive external protection and, to achieve balance, a step-by-step negotiated reduction of tariffs and other barriers to trade among the member countries. Advancement of the integration process thus depended on the constant renewal of government initiative in response to expected pressures for trade liberalization on the part of local firms. As we will see below, however, such pressures did not materialize.

Production-specialization models of regional integration adopted by the Central American Common Market (CACM), UDEAC after 1974, the Caribbean Community (CARICOM) which replaced CARIFTA in 1973, ECOWAS established in 1975, and the Andean Group created in 1969, were somewhat more dynamic. Taking as their point of departure the low level of existing industrial capacity and the tendency for production to be concentrated in the manufacture of similar finished goods, these integration schemes sought to enhance complementarity, prevent the intraregional imbalances that were likely to emerge in the course of trade liberalization (Myrdal 1957; Dell 1966), stimulate economies of scale, and create an internal dynamic based on increased domestic linkages, through regional planning and regulatory mechanisms. Yet only in the Andean Group were efforts made to stimulate the development of technological capabilities. Sustained efforts of this type were limited to the mining sector, although initial designs for regional industrial programs in the metalworking and petrochemical sectors stressed the development of technological capabilities in addition to productive capacities (Mytelka 1979; Warhurst 1985). Top-down decision-making in all these integration schemes limited the involvement of precisely those economic actors whose cooperation was needed to give effect to investment and trade policies.

By the late 1970s, integration groupings of both the exchange-driven and the production-specialization types were stagnating or had collapsed. Trade liberalization had ceased or been postponed in LAFTA, CARICOM, UDEAC, and the Andean Group. Members had withdrawn — Chad from UDEAC, Chile from the Andean Group — or failed to honour regional commitments — Honduras in the CACM, Nigeria in ECOWAS. The motive force of the integration process had, for all practical purposes, ground to a halt.

THE FAILURE OF TRADITIONAL REGIONAL INTEGRATION SCHEMES[1]

Much of the conventional literature lays the failure of traditional regional integration schemes squarely at government's doorstep (UNCTAD 1973; Robson 1983; Berg 1988; Mansoor and Inotai 1990). Two variants of this approach can be found. The first emphasizes conflicts over the costs and benefits of integration that bedevil these organizations and the lack of political will to resolve them. Yet this deals only with the most proximate cause of the crisis in regional integration and fails to explain why regional integration generated distributional conflicts that proved so intractable.

The second stresses the economic inefficiencies generated by government policy, particularly those associated with "attempts at regional industrial planning... [and] the politically motivated allocation of investment" (Mansoor and Inotai 1990, p. 2). Although efforts to extend import substitution strategies to the regional level have clearly failed, such arguments cannot explain the exceedingly low level of intraregional trade in "exchange-driven" integration schemes, where little or no effort at industrial planning was undertaken and a movement towards trade liberalisation was under way, as in the case of LAFTA and of UDEAC before 1974.

As these examples suggest, there is a need to surpass the narrow confines of government policy by setting those policies in a broader context. The following analysis does this by stressing the strategic orientation that states and firms brought to the integration process and points to changes in the international context that reinforced the negative dynamics flowing from this relationship.

GOVERNMENT POLICIES

During the 1950s, development theorists and practitioners embraced both the notion of industrialization as progress and the characterization of industrialization as the mass production of standardized manufactured goods with all that this implied for the organization of labour — the regrouping of workers into factories, Taylorization, increased mechanization — and with its particular requirements for capital, mass markets, and sophisticated managerial know-how. Although smaller scale,

---

[1] In this and the following section, I draw heavily upon Mytelka (1993), in which a range of regional integration initiatives is examined.

network-based forms of industrial organization catering to local income levels and tastes were already common in Japan, northern Italy, and parts of Germany in the 1960s, little attention was paid to them (Brusco 1982; Priore and Sabel 1984). The choice of products for local manufacture in developing countries was largely determined by the existing range of imports, itself sustained by an urban-biased pattern of income distribution. Mass production of an import-reproducing kind went hand in hand with what Arthur Lewis called "industrialization by invitation" based on efforts to induce capital, engineering, management, and marketing skills to flow from the North to the South. Tariff, exchange rate, wage, price, tax, and credit policies were combined to create a profitable environment for foreign capital.

Regional integration was intended to extend these national policies of import-substituting industrialization to the regional market, reproducing a development strategy that paid little heed to those sectors of the economy in which the vast bulk of the population was employed — agriculture, services, and mining. It thus did little to improve the pattern of income distribution or the structure of demand. Moreover, by insulating the regional market from the world economy, a disincentive to extraregional exports of manufactured goods was created. By their very design, traditional models of regional integration thus narrowed the payoff matrix of gains and losses for individual member countries to those associated with intraregional trade. When a lack of complementarity limited the gains from trade, and inequalities in levels of wealth and industrialization among member countries led to their uneven distribution, most integration schemes involving developing countries took on the form of zero-sum games (Mytelka 1973a, 1984).

FIRMS' STRATEGIES

Pressures to pursue national import-substitution policies within the regional system were exacerbated by the interests and inward-looking orientation of the business elite during this period. Few local entrepreneurs had large enough businesses or the credibility to penetrate neighbouring markets, and the high-cost, import-intensive nature of their manufacturing activities was itself an impediment to market integration. These actors, therefore, could not provide the support base needed for trade liberalization.

Foreign-owned firms that might have been the first to engage in intraregional trade, by virtue of their size and reach, failed to rationalize to take advantage of the larger market, whether in UDEAC, LAFTA, the

Andean Group, or CARICOM. A number of factors explain this. For the most part, multinational corporations (MNCs) engaged in manufacturing were purveyors of mature technologies and standardized goods to the developing world, in this period. Their principal objective was market penetration rather than overseas production for export (Caves 1982, pp. 253–257). In the areas covered by regional integration schemes, market segmentation was the rule, and the same firm, present in several neighbouring markets, would produce similar, if not identical, products. In Africa, this was particularly true for products such as cigarettes, shoes, textiles, and beer which were among the first industries to develop an export capacity (Mytelka 1984).

Exports were generally prohibited by licensing agreements between parent firms and their subsidiaries or between licensors and nationally-owned local firms. On the import side, regional markets were also of limited importance to these firms, because the bulk of their imports came from their parent firm or from other firms in the industrialized countries. Parallel production by these MNCs in heavily protected national markets was thus a powerful disincentive to intraregional trade, because intrafirm transfer pricing and higher retail prices compensated for production inefficiencies resulting from continued market segmentation. The point was well put by the top manager of a large foreign automobile subsidiary in Mexico, when he said,

> It might make a lot of economic sense in the long run to merge our operations in the region and to introduce some degree of intra-firm specialisation in respect to final products, parts and accessories, instead of working for a dozen individual markets absorbing annually from 10 000 to 130 000 finished cars each. But such operations would involve a complete overhaul of our productive or assembling facilities within the area with the outlay of perhaps several hundred million dollars.... There is little reason for us to engage in such gigantic financial and technological operations as long as we can get fairly satisfactory profits from actual investments with small additional capital outlays and technological adjustments geared to the slow growth of individual domestic markets and the demands of both consumer and individual governments. [Vaitsos 1978, pp. 732–733]

AID, INVESTMENT, AND REGIONAL INTEGRATION

Toward the mid-1970s, the share of global foreign direct investment (FDI) going to the developing countries stagnated or began to decline. In 1980–84, if we exclude offshore tax havens in the Caribbean, that share was roughly 20%. By 1985–89, it had fallen to barely 10% (Oman 1990,

p. 4). Although in current dollars, FDI flows to the developing countries rose toward the end of the decade, total amounts expressed in constant 1988 prices and exchange rates declined from $11 517 million in 1980–84 to $10 211 million in 1985–89 (Mytelka 1993, Table 2). The Asian share of FDI in developing countries rose over this period from 43.6% to 59.1%, whereas the Latin American and African shares declined from 41.3 to 30.1% and from 15.4 to 7.9%, respectively. The regions most engaged in regional integration were thus receiving a decreasing share of an ever smaller pool of FDI.

Flows of foreign aid did not solve the problem because they rarely supported joint ventures between integration partners (Mytelka 1973b). The bilateral bias that characterizes most aid relations strengthened the predilection of governments to view aid as something distinct from the regional effort, and the tendency in the industrial sector was to use it in support of national import-substitution projects.

Structural adjustment programs further contributed to a reduction in intraregional trade in CACM, UDEAC, ECOWAS, and the Andean Group. This resulted partly from the imposition of austerity measures that weakened domestic markets in the South. But it was also due to the attempt to restore debt-servicing capacity as quickly as possible by cutting imports and refocusing exports on northern markets (UNCTAD 1989, pp. 5–7). Declining terms of trade for commodity exports further worsened the situation in most developing countries. The dramatic decline in intraregional trade in CARICOM and CACM during the 1980s can largely be explained in these terms (INTAL 1990, pp. 160–182).

CONCLUSION

In sum, exchange-driven and production-specialization models of regional integration both failed, not because of government policies or lack of political will but because their very design did not take into account the interests, capabilities, and strategies of key actors in the integration process. Neither model anticipated the potentially negative dynamics that flowed from the interaction between development strategies based on national import substitution and the market-penetration strategies of foreign manufacturing firms in developing countries. Combined, these strategies favoured market segmentation over integration and protectionism over liberalization. In conjunction with the limited possibilities for rapid gains in trade from integration resulting from a lack of complementarity and an absence of additional resources in the form of foreign aid and investment, this generated a zero-sum situation marked by protectionist pressures and conflicts over the costs and benefits of regional integration. What mainstream theorists identify as the causes of failure in traditional regional integration schemes are thus reflections of a deeper structural relationship, the evolving nature of which is central to the future viability of regional integration among developing countries.

INNOVATION DRIVEN MODELS OF SOUTH–SOUTH COOPERATION

During the 1980s, government policies and private-sector strategies in Latin America, and to a lesser extent in Africa, both underwent major transformations away from traditional forms of import substitution toward policies promoting competitiveness. This shift was influenced by two factors: the negative impact of indebtedness and austerity on the capacity to import and to undertake new capital investments needed for industrial rehabilitation; and the marginalization from major flows of finance, trade, and technology that had sustained national import-substitution strategies in these countries during the 1960s and 1970s. One consequence of the new focus on innovation and competitiveness has been a rethinking of regional integration and the role of trade and innovation in that process.

At their Galapagos summit in December 1989, for example, the Andean Heads of State endorsed a new approach to South–South cooperation in which regional integration was no longer to be viewed as an alternative to North–South ties, but rather as a means to change production patterns in Latin American and Caribbean countries by "strengthening the countries' insertion into the international economy" (ECLAC 1990, p. 158; INTAL 1990, p. 107). Abandoning traditional import-substitution strategies, the Andean Group thus embraced a new "openness to the world, based fundamentally upon its own enlarged market and an increased capacity for technological research, product development and negotiation" (INTAL 1990, p. 107). This redefinition of the function of regional trade, from one of stimulating national import substitution to one of promoting international trade competitiveness, transformed a closed regional market, within which gains for some were losses for others, into a lightly protected economic space within which firms can hone their ability to compete in the world economy. It thus lifts the zero-sum conditions that characterized earlier models of integration.

This, in turn, precipitated a rapid reversal in trade policy within the region. After more than a decade of increasing protectionism, less than 3 years after the elaboration of its new *Diseño Estratégico para la Orientación del Grupo Andino*, the Andean Group had moved toward complete liberalization of intraregional trade.

During the 1970s and 80s, a number of factors also altered the strategic options available to economic and other actors whose participation is essential if an innovation-driven process of South–South cooperation is to be launched and sustained. Three changes bear mentioning: the increased cost of nonmaterial investments, such as R&D, process engineering, design, training, and marketing, that resulted from the growing knowledge intensity of production; the growing uncertainty resulting from continuous innovation and from intensified international competition that has complicated planning at the firm level; and the need for flexibility arising from these changes (Mytelka 1991a, 1991b).

To achieve the critical mass required for technological innovation, while reducing uncertainty without adding to the inertia of the firm, companies in industrialized countries have developed new competitive strategies to complement more traditional practices, such as mergers and acquisitions. Three of these have direct consequences for innovation in the South and for North–South partnerships as a complement to South–South cooperation.

First, these strategies involve a shift away from competition solely or even primarily based on price, toward the development of value-based competitive advantages through innovation, quality, and close ties to clients and suppliers. To take advantage of these trends, developing countries will need to revive markets in the South and create a denser network of user–producer linkages within and across those markets than existed in the past. Because of the continuous shifts in comparative advantage of countries in all products and the rapidity with which such changes are taking place, the need to strengthen the knowledge base in developing countries has never before assumed such critical importance.

Second, these new strategies seek to combine generic technologies, often from distinct disciplines, using networks as a means to obtain access to knowledge resources from as wide a range of disciplines and geographic areas as possible. In contrast with earlier assumptions concerning the importance of firm size for R&D, critical mass can thus be conceived quite differently today, more in terms of the size of the "system" needed to acquire knowledge than the size of the firm itself. This applies to activities all along the value chain from conception to the market. Such considerations, combined with the need for flexibility, have led a number of firms to decentralize R&D to overseas subsidiaries and to engage in a growing number of strategic partnerships in R&D, linking firms to each other and to research institutions. Subsidiaries in developing countries have been able to benefit from this trend where the scientific and engineering infrastructure exists. Some MNCs have decentralized research and especially product development arrangements to subsidiaries in developing countries and have entered into collaborative activities with research institutions and universities there.[2] These changes in firms' strategies have opened new windows of opportunity for innovation in developing countries and are laying the basis for the kinds of North–South linkages that could complement South–South ties.

Third, MNCs have been turning their subsidiaries into independent profit centres, in both advanced and developing countries. This encourages local firms to specialize, to secure inputs from least-cost suppliers and to export, thus reversing the incentives that had shaped their behaviour in the 1960s and 70s. In addition, new forms of international subcontracting that enable a subcontractor to produce an entire component or product — particularly of the original equipment manufacturer variety, where the product is marketed under the brand of the principal firm — has led to more effective transfers of production and management technology to local firms, thus strengthening their ability to innovate. Because of balance-of-payments constraints and a shortage of foreign exchange, there are also greater pressures on local firms to absorb new technology to reduce costs, identify local sources, and export. In many cases, local firms are better equipped to innovate or adjust to changes in competitive conditions than they were in the 1960s, having acquired new capabilities through previous licensing agreements or subcontracting activities. This is particularly notable in Asia and in a number of Latin American countries (see Frishtak 1990; Mytelka 1991a; Ernst and O'Connor 1992; Perez n.d.; Warhurst forthcoming). For such firms,

---

[2] For example, computer companies such as Wang Laboratories (USA) and Nixdorf (Germany) have established research laboratories in Singapore; Hewlett Packard has located all of the research on the colour-injection system used in its laser printers in Singapore; Texas Instruments has located a software design facility in Bangalore, India, where researchers are using computers to design VLSI circuits; and IBM has established a software development company in Shenzhen, China. Strategic partnerships in R&D are also emerging. Sim Darby (Malaysia), for example, has created the ASEAN Biotechnology Corporation jointly with International Plant Research (USA) to carry out biotechnology research in Malaysia; Agroceres (Brazil) has formed an R&D partnerships with Noragro (USA); and Analogic Scientific Inc. (USA), an electronics firms, has formed an R&D partnerships with China's Kejian Company, which specializes in superconductive magnet technology to develop medical diagnostic equipment.

trade liberation within a region now plays a more positive role than protectionism as a means of achieving competitiveness through innovation.

Such changes provide the basis of a quite different approach to
South–South cooperation that moves away from regional trade as a simple mechanism for overcoming the small size of domestic markets in the
search for specialization and economies of scale, toward a more dynamic
perspective in which knowledge, networks, and flexible structures are
fundamental building blocks. Unlike earlier models of regional integration, this new approach to South–South cooperation can best be
described as "innovation" driven, where innovation implies the introduction of a product or a process that is new to that firm or that country
— regardless of whether it is new to the world — and where it is understood to be a key element in the competitiveness of firms and nations. In
the present conjuncture, the value of regional integration among developing countries and South-South cooperation more broadly thus
increases the more it contributes to the launching of a virtuous circle of
learning and technological change.

In innovation driven models of South–South cooperation, trade is
not an end in itself. It results from, and stimulates in turn, a process of
continuous innovation. The focus in innovation-driven models of
South–South cooperation is thus:

- less on specific firms and products and more on building the
  underlying knowledge and capacity required to find imaginative
  solutions to bottlenecks in production or distribution;

- less on scale economies and more on opportunities for the flexible
  combination of knowledge assets and the development of economies of scope in production, wherever networking is feasible;

- less on allocative efficiency and more on learning, x-efficiency,
  and other means of increasing returns under conditions of
  dynamic uncertainty.

The new role for intraregional trade envisaged in innovation-driven
models of South–South cooperation enhances the potential for change by
generating the kind of competitive environment in which mastery of
imported technology is stimulated and problem-solving leads to innovation in quality and design and cost reduction. Innovation-driven models
of South–South cooperation imply a reconceptualization of development
viewed in terms of diversification from agriculture and raw materials
production into manufacturing; the new approach stresses the application of knowledge in all sectors. This opens opportunities for building on

the natural resource base and points to the importance of strengthening the human resource component of the development process to be able to innovate by adapting technology to new uses.

A user-oriented approach to South–South cooperation is likely to prove more effective than earlier top-down models involving governments as initiators, negotiators, and signatories. Bringing key parties into the planning process early on ensures that the design of cooperative projects will correspond more closely to the needs of those who must carry them out. It thus creates a commitment to South–South cooperation that was missing from traditional models. It is also a more flexible process for quickly spotting new opportunities and translating them into action.

Institution-building in an innovation-driven model thus consists of creating coordinating structures which, through scanning and networking, build knowledge about knowledge assets, facilitate international technology brokerage functions, provide financing for technology acquisition and trade and ensure channels for participation, reflection, consensus building and the mobilisation of support.

COMPLEMENTING THIRD WORLD INITIATIVES

A NEW ROLE FOR DONORS

South–South cooperation of this sort will require the maintenance and in some instances, the strengthening, of North–South ties, because much of the technology basic to the innovation process will come from the North. South-South cooperation is itself likely to be more profitable when the firms involved have access to a wide range of technological choices. This requires that there be increased attention to "the learning and dissemination of internationally available know-how; a possibility which has not been sufficiently exploited... in the past" (ECLAC 1990). It is here that government and nongovernmental institutions have a critical role to play in stimulating demand for innovation and catalyzing new linkages between users and suppliers of technology, locally, regionally, and internationally. However, the ability of developing countries to promote innovation and growth through South–South cooperation depends in no small measure on the willingness of donors and international financial institutions to support such initiatives.

LATIN AMERICA

A brief look at two Latin American programs and their interrelations provides an example of the many different roles that donor countries can play in promoting innovation-driven models of South–South cooperation. The Centro de Gestión Tecnológica e Informática Industrial (CEGESTI) in Costa Rica — funded by UNDP and UNIDO — is designed to provide training, technical information, and management consulting to stimulate small and medium-sized enterprises (SMEs) to think strategically and incorporate innovation into their growth strategies. This is particularly important where the historical practice of firms has not been geared to problem identification and problem-solving. The CEGESTI model is already being diffused to other Latin American and Caribbean countries.

CEGESTI's training program teaches firms to initiate changes via the creation of small experimental laboratories. As part of a program to foster innovative behaviour in SMEs, nine local firms were chosen from various sectors (chemicals, pharmaceuticals, metalworking, and software). CEGESTI trained a nucleus of two people from each firm, mainly industrial engineers trained in technology management, who worked as advisors to the managing director. In the year and a half since the training period, all but one nucleus has successfully developed preinvestment projects. In addition to identifying potential innovation projects within the firm, the trained people are responsible for establishing links with local universities and managing the ensuing R&D projects. According to the directors of the participating firms, the impact of this program has already been felt in the following areas:

◆ increased sales;

◆ productivity gains;

◆ development of new products and services or new markets;

◆ development of innovation projects, five of which had been approved for funding by the Costa Rican government; and

◆ an interest in hiring the trainees at the end of the contract period.

CEGESTI's program induces firms to innovate and lays the groundwork for strategic partnering among these firms and associated research institutions in both the domestic and wider Latin American environments.

The second example, the Bolivar Programme, is an 18-country initiative modeled after the European EUREKA program. Costa Rica is one of its members. Its two main objectives are: to promote innovation in the region by stimulating greater interaction between local research institutions and the enterprise sector in the member countries; and to promote regional integration by facilitating the establishment of partnerships between enterprises and research institutes in two or more countries of the region.

Establishment of the Bolivar Programme has given impetus to the creation of R&D partnerships across the continent. By April 1993, 110 projects in a wide range of productive sectors had been submitted to the Bolivar Programme for support, which includes the financing of feasibility studies as well as assistance in finding partners, technologies, markets, and financing.

In March 1992, the program was given further encouragement when the Inter-American Development Bank made $4.2 million in technical cooperation grants available to it. An additional $3 million was contributed by the member governments. The $7.2 million budget is expected to cover the set-up and operating costs of a regional network of national coordinating committees and a lightly staffed secretariat in Caracas over the next 2 years.

Financial support is not the only form of assistance that donors are giving to this program. General Directorate 12 (DG 12) of the European Communities, working with the current EUREKA presidency, is supporting a training program for national coordinators who will be the principal agents for partner identification, project evaluation, and funding in the Bolivar Programme. The Canadian government is supporting initiatives to involve Canadian R&D consortia and firms in joint projects with the program. North–South partnership will thus be a complement to South–South initiatives undertaken within the Bolivar Programme.

AFRICA

Technological accumulation involving public-sector institutions, universities, and a few private enterprises is also taking place in Africa, although at a much slower pace. A notable example of this is the evolution of the informal sector which expanded as devaluations and a shortage of foreign exchange made imports of spare parts for industry and transportation more difficult.

The Suame Magazine, a grouping of some 5,000 craftsmen in small garages and workshops making spare parts and repairing vehicles in Kumasi, Ghana is a case in point. Of particular interest in the Suame Magazine case is that "the government has supported these indigenous engineers through technology services, training, and credit" (World Bank 1989, p. 121). This includes government funding for the Intermediate Technology Training Unit of the Technology Consultancy Centre at the University of Science and Technology in Kumasi and an extension of the training unit concept throughout the country via the Ghana Regional Appropriate Technology Industrial Services Institutes under the Transport Rehabilitation Project supported by the International Development Association. The government is providing training to upgrade the technical skills of informal-sector mechanics and teach them basic accounting and management methods. It has also helped to establish a pilot program to provide credit to small operators: for example, a mechanics' cooperative in need of lathes and crankshaft grinders (World Bank 1989, p. 121).

Other technological capabilities are accumulating in public research institutions supported by local governments and donors. These include any number of agricultural research institutes, along with the African Regional Centre for Technology (ARCT), the Institut de Technologie Alimentaire in Dakar, the Centre Regional d'Énergie Solaire in Bamako, and the newly established International Institute for Scientific Research for the Development of Africa in Côte d'Ivoire. However, few links have been established between such research activities and production, and the contribution of research to applied innovation has thus remained limited (Vitta 1992).

Further initiatives to stimulate problem-solving in African industry are required. This is particularly important because the need to stimulate firms in Africa to solve restructuring problems and innovate in the course of rehabilitation is critical to the sustainability of development on that continent. Given current financial constraints, the transfer of technology from abroad, although vital, cannot fulfil all of Africa's needs. Technology transfer is, moreover, a costly process that generally requires recurrent expenditures for the import of capital and intermediate goods, management skills, maintenance services, and technical know-how, which Africa can ill afford at this time. It has thus become imperative for the enterprise sector in Africa to strengthen its ability to solve its own problems and to overcome bottlenecks in production.

To engage in problem-solving innovation in an environment where firms rarely think strategically or incorporate innovation into their growth strategies requires an outside stimulus of the sort illustrated by the CEGESTI example. This cannot be done without access to financial and technological resources. These resources can and must come through collaborative R&D involving other domestic actors including supplier firms, university faculties, engineering consultancy firms, and research institutions. Regional networking can play an important role in this, because African countries, other perhaps than Nigeria, South Africa, and Zimbabwe, do not have the critical mass required to launch this sort of initiative.

African governments have acknowledged the need for new approaches to training, that promote innovation. They are also attempting to establish a policy environment that is more conducive to innovation. To complement these initiatives, a mechanism is needed to encourage innovation at the firm level and marshall local resources in support of it. In view of Africa's limited financial resources, one could imagine a "Fund for Innovation and Development" in Africa that would have an important financial role to play in underwriting the costs and risks of innovation.

Adapting principles derived from other innovation-driven regional collaboration schemes to the African context, such a fund would function through a locally-based and networked institutional structure and perform the following functions:

- It would focus on the process of technological innovation rather than on scientific research.

- It would involve users in the initiation, design, and R&D phases of all projects, thereby ensuring concordance with users' needs, user commitment to the process, and rapid acceptance of the projects' outputs.

- It would stimulate the formation of consortia within and across national borders in Africa, thus reducing costs and creating the critical mass and cross-disciplinarity needed for the innovation process to succeed.

- It would foster a culture of innovation in African enterprises.

- It would build competitiveness in African industry as one element in the movement toward regional integration and cooperation.

To ensure its financial and managerial independence and access to technological resources outside the continent, such a fund could be launched on the basis of an endowment, of which 50% could be solicited from the world's largest and most innovative companies. The remaining 50% could be made up of grants from institutions that have traditionally funded research in developing countries, the bilateral donor community, the United Nations system, African governments and African institutions.

Although many funds for "research" have been created in the past, their commercial impact has generally been meagre. Any new initiative along these lines should distinguish itself in three ways:

- abandonment of a supply-driven approach to research and adaption of a bottom-up approach to project identification and selection;

- creation of a partnership involving the private and public sectors along with the donor community; and

- a networked institutional structure.

REFERENCES

Berg, E. 1988. Applied development economics, regionalism and economic development in sub-Saharan Africa. Vol. 1: Regional co-operation in Africa. United States Agency for International Development, Washington, DC, USA.

Brusco, S. 1982. The Emilian Model: productive decentralisation and social integration. Cambridge Journal of Economics, 6 (2), 167–184.

Caves, R. 1982. Multinational enterprise and economic analysis. Cambridge University Press, Cambridge, UK.

Dell, S. 1966. A Latin American common market? Oxford University Press, London, UK.

ECLAC (United Nations Economic Commission for Latin America and the Caribbean). 1990. Changing production patterns with social equity. ECLAC, Santiago, Chile, p. 158.

Ernst, D.; O'Connor, D. 1992. Competing in the electronics industry the experience of newly industrialising economies. OECD Development Centre, Paris, France.

Frischtak, C.R. 1990. Specialization, technical change and competitiveness in the Brazilian electronics industry. OECD Development Centre, Paris, France. Technical paper 27.

INTAL (Instituto para la Integración de America Latina). 1990. El proceso de integración en America Latina en 1989. BID, INTAL, Buenos Aires, Argentina.

Mansoor, A.; Inotai, A. 1990. Integration efforts in sub-Saharan Africa: failures, results and prospects: a suggested strategy for achieving efficient integration. Presented at the African economic issues conference, 5–7 June, Nairobi, Kenya.

Myrdal, G. 1957. Economic theory and underdeveloped regions. Duckworth, London, UK.

Mytelka, L.K. 1973a. The salience of gains in Third World integrative systems. World Politics, 25 (2), 236–250.

———— 1973b. Foreign aid and regional integration: the UDEAC case. Journal of Common Market Studies, 12 (2), 138–158.

———— 1979. Regional development in a global economy: multinational corporations, technology and Andean integration. Yale University Press, New Haven, CT, USA.

————— 1984. Competition, conflict and decline in the Union Douanière et Économique de l'Afrique Centrale. *In* Mazzeo, D. (ed.). African regional organisations. Cambridge University Press, Cambridge, UK.

————— 1987. Changements technologiques et nouvelles formes de la concurrence dans l'industrie textile et de l'habillement. Economie Prospective Internationale, Revue du CEPII, 31, 5–28.

————— 1991a. New modes of competition in the textile and clothing: some consequences for Third World exporters. *In* Niosi, J. (ed.). Technology and national competitiveness. McGill-Queen's University Press, Montreal. Pp. 225–246.

————— 1991b. Crisis, technological change and the strategic alliance. *In* Mytelka, L.K. (ed.). Strategic partnerships: states, firms and international competition. Pinter Publishers, pp. 7–34.

————— 1993. Regional co-operation and the new logic of international competition. *In* Mytelka, L.K. (ed.). South–South cooperation in a global perspective. OECD Development Centre, Paris, France.

OECD (Organization for Economic Co-operation and Development). 1992. Technology and the economy: the key relationships. OECD, Paris, France.

Oman, C. 1990. Trends in global FDI and Latin America. Prepared for the Inter-American Dialogue meeting, 18–20 December, Washington.

Perez, C. n.d. Electronics and development in Venezuela: a user-oriented strategy and its policy implications. OECD, Paris, France. Technical paper 25.

Piore, M.; Sabel, C. 1984. The second industrial divide: possibilities for prosperity. Basic Books, New York.

Robson, P. 1983. Integration, development and equity: economic integration in West Africa. Routledge, New York, NY, USA.

UNCTAD (United Nations Conference of Trade and Development). 1973. The distribution of benefits and costs in integration among developing countries. *In* Lizano, E. Current problems of economic integration. United Nations, New York, NY, USA. Doc. TD/B/394.

————— 1989. Debt and structural adjustment policies of developing countries: impact on economic integration. UNCTAD Secretariat, Geneva, Switzerland. Doc. TD/B/C.7/AC.3/5.

Vaitsos, C. 1978. Crisis in regional economic co-operation, (integration) among developing countries: a survey. World Development, 6, 719–769.

Vitta, P. 1992. Utility of research in sub-Saharan Africa: beyond the leap of faith. Science and Public Policy, 19 (4).

Warhurst, A. 1985. Biotechnology for metals extraction: the potential of an emerging technology, the Andean Pact copper project and some implications. Development and Change, 16, January.

————— forthcoming. South-South cooperation: opportunities in minerals development. South-South cooperation in a global perspective. OECD Development Centre, Paris, France.

World Bank. 1989. World development report. World Bank, Washington, DC, USA.

PART II

ECONOMIC PERSPECTIVES

CHAPTER 8

NATIONAL POLICIES AS IMPEDIMENTS TO REGIONAL ECONOMIC INTEGRATION

– Ousmane Badiane –

Badiane identifies two important omissions from past negotiations on regional integration: macroeconomic policies and sectoral policies in the areas of marketing and transport. He joins other authors in this volume in calling for greater attention to macroeconomic policy at the national level as a precondition for successful regional integration. In his view, it is illusory and incompatible to pursue regional integration based on preferential trading arrangements while domestic policy remains inward-looking in orientation. Experience has shown the political incompatibility of such a combination, as well as its economic incompatibility, due to the depressive effects of inward-looking strategies on export competitiveness and import demand. Marketing costs are a major component of the price of goods and constitute a major constraint to intraregional trade in West Africa, where roads and communications are probably the most underdeveloped in the world. The marketing and transport sectors in West Africa are overregulated and overtaxed, and there is a need for policies more favourable to the these sectors, including easier conditions of access to legal status and greater availability of financing, simplification of unnecessary regulations, elimination of road blocks, and lower levels of taxation. Badiane thus identifies two requirements for increasing regional trade: a general shift to an outward-oriented development strategy; and the promotion of efficient and competitive marketing and transport sectors.

AS SEVERAL AUTHORS in this volume have shown, a renewal of interest in regional economic integration has emerged in discussions of development strategy at the continental and subregional levels in Africa, despite the lack of impact of existing regional trade and integration schemes on participating economies. Past economic integration efforts in West Africa have relied overwhelmingly on institutional mechanisms, ranging from negotiated tariff concessions and compensation schemes to the establishment of joint institutions for research, training, and transportation. These arrangements can contribute to the integration of national economies, but cannot do so in the absence of supporting and coherent macroeconomic and sectoral policies at the individual country level that ultimately determine the ability of individual countries to trade with each other. Accordingly, the real challenge is to create national economic environments that would raise the level and efficiency of intercountry trade and ensure that the effects of increased trade ramify throughout the economy.

This chapter analyses the implications of macroeconomic and sector policies for regional integration from three perspectives, in terms of countries' demand for imports from regional markets, countries' capacity to raise and sustain export performance, and the cost of trading on local and transborder markets. It is divided into two main parts — one on the implications of macroeconomic policies and one on the obstacles to trade arising from high marketing costs.

National development strategies and regional trade

Trade policy has figured prominently in the development and industrialization strategies of West African and other developing countries, and has conditioned the macroeconomic and sector policies adopted in those countries. It follows that the choice of overall development strategy has shaped trading relations between domestic economies and the rest of the world, while having a specific bearing on these countries' propensity to trade on regional markets. A significant amount of empirical work has demonstrated the close relation between country-level macroeconomic and trade policies, on one hand, and the effect of those policies on overall trade and growth performance, on the other (Oyejide 1986; Avillez et al. 1988; Jansen 1988; Krueger et al. 1988; Mundlak et al. 1989; Stryker 1990; Dollar 1992). The pursuit of regional integration implies recognition of the importance of international trade in the development process.

However, regional integration as conventionally applied in West Africa has gone hand in hand with inward-looking economic strategies based on import-substituting industrialization. One study of trade policy in 95 developing countries by Dollar (1992) found 10 out of 16 West African countries to be among the most inward-looking developing countries, and the four biggest trading partners in West Africa (Côte d'Ivoire, Ghana, Nigeria, and Senegal) to be in the most or second-most inward-looking group. As practical experience has shown, anti-trade-biased country strategies offer limited scope for sustained intercountry trade expansion through mutual tariff concessions and other (institutional) arrangements, because national governments relying on protectionist strategies to promote domestic manufacturing are unlikely to encourage unrestricted trade with neighbouring countries (Mytelka, this volume).

This tendency is exemplified in the design and operation of the Taxe de Coopération Régionale (TCR) of the now defunct CEAO, which clearly reflected the conflict between national industrialization and fiscal objectives and economic integrationBecause trade regimes at the country level were primarily driven by considerations of fiscal balance and protectionism, the regime allowed for the TCR rates applied by each CEAO member country to be a function of its own extraregional tariffs. Moreover, the adopted rates varied by product and for any given product, according to the exporting member country. Consequently, the rate applied by the importing member country on a given product tended to be a function of the perceived level of relative development of the exporting country and the importance of the product or sector to the importing country's industrialization objectives (Robson, 1983; Ouali 1982). Such an arrangement, which failed to encourage economic restructuring, was obviously not well suited to promoting efficient trade among participating countries — *even if* the system had worked properly.

In reality, its application was also inadequate. Indeed, only 2 years after its inception in 1976, preferential TCR rates applied by individual members to intracommunity imports were raised substantially (Badiane 1988, pp. 75–76). The above move, the periodic confrontations over tariff issues and nontariff barriers that subsequently erupted between members, and the eventual dissolution of CEAO in March 1994 show that the lowering of regional tariff rates in the context of inward-oriented trade regimes has not been a workable option.

Figure 1 shows an analytical framework for studying the links between country-level macroeconomic policies and regional integration through increased intercountry trade. Monetary, fiscal, trade, and exchange-rate policies affect intercountry imports and exports through two principal channels: first, through the impact on the exchange rate and the induced effects of this on sectoral output levels and aggregate incomes; and second, through taxes and other direct measures affecting the cost of regional imports and exports. These two effects combined determine the demand for imports from regional sources and affect the country's capacity to export competitively.

It is now widely accepted that inward-looking macroeconomic and trade policies have a negative impact on incentives and competitiveness

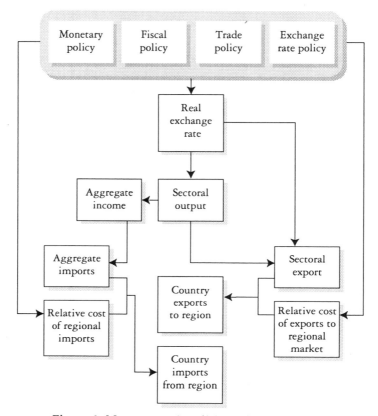

Figure 1. Macroeconomic policies and regional trade.

in the export sector through their impact on the real exchange rate (Dornbusch 1974; Clements and Sjaastad 1984; Krueger et al. 1988; Edwards 1989). Table 1 illustrates this relationship, through several estimates of "shift parameters," a quantification of the extent to which some degree of import-protection is shifted onto exporters in the form of reduced real prices for their products. A shift parameter of 0.5 means that a 10% increase in import protection would lead to a reduction equal to half that much (5%) in the real price paid to producers of exportables.

Estimates presented in Table 1 show that 82% of protection to industry in Côte d'Ivoire fell as a tax on agricultural exports from 1970 to 1984. The corresponding figure for nonagricultural exports was 43%. In Nigeria, the proportion of import protection shifted onto exports was

Table 1. Impact of country-level macroeconomic policies on real prices paid to producers of exportables during the 1970s and 80s. (shift parameters).

Country	All exports	Agricultural exports	Nonagricultural exports
Benin	-0.72a	—	—
Burkina Faso	-0.79[a]	—	—
Côte d'Ivoire	—	-0.82[b]	-0.43[b]
Ghana	-0.12[a]	-0.30 to -0.70[c]	—
Nigeria	-0.55 to -0.90[c]	-0.83[c]	—

Note: Numbers represent the percentage impact on export prices of a 1% increase in import protection.

[a] Simulation results assuming 10% reduction of import duties (DeRosa 1992).

[b] Implicit taxation resulting from trade regimes (World Bank 1987, p. 80).

[c] Implicit taxation resulting from trade regimes (Oyejide 1986).

83% for agriculture and 55% to 90% for the export sector as a whole, depending upon the time period. Corresponding figures for Benin, Burkina Faso, and Ghana at the end of the 1980s, were estimated at 72%, 79%, and 12%, respectively. Although similar figures are not available for other West African countries, it is likely that their export sectors have suffered to a similar extent from domestic protectionism. Other studies have estimated the implicit taxation being imposed on exports through overvaluation of the real exchange rate due to overall economic and trade policies in the 1980s: Stryker (1990) found rates of overvaluation of 30% to 70% in Ghana; Salinger and Stryker (1991) found rates of 51% to 64% in Senegal. These numbers indicate an implicit tax of like amount on both agricultural and nonagricultural exports. The level of taxation implied by these estimates has inevitably retarded the expansion of intraregional trade by reducing the competitiveness of regional export sectors.

Country strategies that discriminate against trade often rebound against the expansion of regional trade for several other reasons. First, they encourage high-cost production structures. Second, they induce a shortage of foreign exchange, through the appreciation of the real exchange rate and the resulting disincentive to produce for export. In most cases, countries respond to the foreign exchange crisis by resorting to various mechanisms of foreign exchange controls, such as import bans, licensing, and foreign exchange rationing. These measures unavoidably disrupt trade with neighbouring countries.

THE BIAS AGAINST AGRICULTURE

Another basic characteristic of post-independence trading regimes and development strategies in West Africa has been their bias against agriculture, through the protection of import-competing industries combined with taxation of agricultural exportables and relatively low levels of import protection for agricultural products. The taxation of export crops is unlikely to have depressed regional exports in a direct way, because these products are traded primarily on the world market. However, it must have affected regional trade indirectly, as revenues from these exports have traditionally fueled demand for exports, particularly in coastal countries. Numerous empirical studies have revealed the depressive effect that heavy direct and indirect taxation on agriculture can have on overall economic expansion (Balassa 1978; World Bank 1982; Bautista 1988; Ahluwalia and Rangarajan 1989; Hwa 1989; Lächler 1989; Panchamukhi et al. 1989). Hwa's (1989) results, based on data for 60 developing and developed countries, show that a 1% increase in agricultural growth raises industrial output by more than 0.5%. Similar results were obtained in a study of 49 African countries, including almost all West African countries (Badiane 1991). In general, these studies suggest that agricultural growth and overall economic expansion are closely interrelated. It follows that one would expect import-substitution strategies that discriminate against the agricultural sector to reduce long-term demand, including demand for regional imports, thus slowing the pace of market integration.

TRANSACTION COSTS IN LOCAL AND TRANSBORDER MARKETS

Efficiently operating markets are as important as the macroeconomic and trading environment for economic integration. Although investments in regional infrastructure, such as roads and telecommunications, have helped to reduce costs, these efforts have been concentrated on a limited number of connecting routes and networks. National policies relating to the commercial sector have paid little attention to regional trade. They have focused on the major export crops or the satisfaction of domestic food needs. Although reforms to liberalize domestic marketing in the agricultural sector are currently under way in most West African countries, some aspects have received inadequate attention, notably the provision of credit for commercial-sector activities and the regulation and taxation of the transport sector. Reforms have focused on the privatization, deregulation, and direct taxation of marketing activities, but such activities continue to be hampered by many preliberalization regulations as well as by some of the new measures accompanying the reform process itself.

Two recent studies from Côte d'Ivoire and Senegal give some idea of the constraints surrounding the operation of local and transborder agricultural markets (Gaye et al. 1991; Camara 1992). Results from Senegal (Table 2) are of particular interest, because Senegal was one of the first countries to launch domestic marketing reforms in the 1980s. This study asked a sample of 142 traders in the most commercialized agricultural region of the country to summarize their perception of the five most important obstacles to expanding their activities. Each trader was asked to identify and rank the three most severe constraints they faced. The severity of each constraint was then assessed by constructing a composite index, P, which is a weighted sum of the number of times the constraint is ranked first (N1), second (N2), or third (N3). Financing was most frequently identified, with 92% of respondents placing it among the top three constraints to their operations and 77% of those respondents considering it the most severe constraint they faced. This is followed by taxes and regulations, transportation, and "market operation" (organization of and access to local markets, which operate primarily on a weekly basis).

Table 3 shows similar results for Côte d'Ivoire, as obtained by Camara (1992). Although the same method was used, the results are presented a little differently. Camara provides a simple count of the frequency with which each constraint was identified, along with a finer breakdown of these constraints. The results are similar to those for Senegal, with regard to financing in particular, which ranks first among the constraints cited and accounts for about 26% of all the responses

Table 2. Constraints to increased marketing activities
in the Senegalese peanut basin.

Constraints	Value of P^a	Frequency of ranking (%)			% of responses
		N1	N2	N3	
Financing	356	77	20	3	92
Taxes and regulations	93	42	32	26	30
Transportation	85	11	59	30	33
Market operation	83	31	51	18	27
Storage facilities	17	24	62	13	6

Source: Gaye et al. (1991).

[a] N1, N2 and N3 indicate the distribution of responses for each constraint. P is a weighted index of these percentages equal to 3N1 + 2N2 + N3.

Table 3. Constraints to increased marketing activities
in northern border areas of Côte d'Ivoire.

Constraints	Number of responses identifying constraint (%)	% of total responses
1. Financing	25.9	25.9
2. Road controls	13.1	39.0
3. Market infrastructure	11.3	50.3
4. Road infrastructure	10.1	60.4
5. Information access	9.5	69.9
6. Transportation	8.8	78.7
7. Taxation	8.2	86.9
8. Storage facilities	7.6	4.5
9. Others	3.1	7.6
10. No constraints	2.4	100.0
Total	100.0	—

Source: Camara (1992).

received. Infrastructural constraints come across more clearly in this study, because a large number of traders mention market infrastructure and road infrastructure as constraints. Often neglected, access to information also appears as a constraint. However the most remarkable constraint identified here is road controls, which are considered more important than infrastructural constraints by Ivoirian traders.

The classification of constraints by traders suggests three areas for improvement: financing, taxes and regulations, and infrastructure development. Taxes and regulations are second in importance in the Senegal study as well as in Côte d'Ivoire, where they take the form of road controls.

The importance that traders attribute to financing as a constraint has a lot to do with prevailing marketing policies, regulations, and institutional arrangements, which impede traders from obtaining the formal legal status they require to obtain access to credit. The experience in Senegal shows that institutional regulations in the marketing sector still severely restrict the entry of traders into the formal sector, despite several years of liberalization and reforms. Nearly half the traders in the survey were operating illegally and 35% of those operating legally acquired their legal status only after the liberalization reforms had been introduced (Gaye et al. 1991). The most important reason mentioned by traders for not possessing legal documents was a lack of financial

Table 4. Selected components of marketing costs
in local agricultural markets (%).

	Côte d'Ivoire	Senegal	Mali
Transport	46–72	53–77	72
Fees and taxes	6–30	16–37	6–21
Handling	6–23	6–23	8

Sources: Gaye et al. (1991); Camara (1992); Gabre-Madhin (1991).

resources to cover the costs associated with the acquisition of the various documents. By choosing to stay out of the formal trading systems, private traders are unlikely to acquire the resources necessary to expand trade in local and border markets.

The importance of transport policies is demonstrated by the structure of marketing costs in local agricultural markets in many West African countries, where transportation costs account for half to three-quarters of total marketing costs (Table 4). The predominance of these costs has traditionally been explained by the low density and quality of the road network. However, the costs shown as "Transport" in Table 4 also include fuel taxes (which are considerable everywhere outside Nigeria), other taxes related to the acquisition and operation of transport vehicles, and various controls and regulatory measures that indirectly raise the costs of transport services.

Studies of the transport sector in West Africa suggest that fiscal policies have a substantial impact on domestic marketing costs. Estimates performed by the Laboratoire d'Économie des Transports of the Institut National de Recherche sur les Transports et leur Sécurité, (INRETS-LET) show that the level of taxes on the purchase of new and used trucks of different sizes in Côte d'Ivoire and Mali can be as high as 60% (INRETS-LET 1989a,b). In addition, registration fees are levied annually. Such taxes vary significantly from country to country, but are especially high in Côte d'Ivoire and Senegal. Fiscal measures such as these have a direct impact on transport costs. They also raise barriers to entry into the transport sector, thus reducing the supply of transport services and reducing competition.

Other policies, such as road controls and other regulatory measures also raise transport costs. Such measures affect the supply of transport services and create rent situations that ultimately raise user prices in the sector. Estimates of the costs of road blocks for various market routes between Côte d'Ivoire and the Sahel in 1989 ranged from 9.4 to 100 CFA francs per kilometre (USD 0.033–0.357) (Table 5).[1] On average the cost of road blocks appeared to be about 49 CFA francs (USD 0.175) per kilometre. Whether these costs consist of fiscal fees or amounts extorted illegally by control agents is irrelevant in terms of their implications for the domestic costs of marketing, but fees collected by the state at least have the potential of being reinvested in long-term infrastructure programs. The relative importance of such costs in disrupting trade in local and border markets can be appreciated by comparing them with transport prices charged for similar distances. According to recent calculations (INRETS-LET 1989b; Gersovitz 1992), the cost of transport per tonne-kilometre for similar distances is substantially less than 100 CFA francs

Table 5. Costs of road blocks on routes in Côte d'Ivoire or linking Côte d'Ivoire with the Sahel.

Route	Distance (km)	Cost of road blocks (CFA francs)	Average cost per km (CFA francs)
Abidjan–Niamey	1 480	45 000	30.4
Abidjan–Bobo Dioulasso	831	25 000	30.1
Abidjan–Bamako	1 130	15 000	13.3
Abidjan–Ferkessédougou (near Burkina border on road to Bobo)	534	5 000	9.4
Bouna (near intersection of Burkina and Ghana borders)–Abidjan	537	50 000	93.1
Bouaké (central Côte d'Ivoire) –Abidjan	372	20 000	53.8
Daloa (central Côte d'Ivoire) –Abidjan	357	30 000	84.0
Daloa–Bamako	1 000	100 000	100.0
Arithmetic average			49.3

Source: INRETS-LET 1989b.

---

[1] There are some oddities in these data. Why should Abidjan–Bamako be the least-cost destination and Daloa–Bamako the highest cost when there is little difference between these two routes and Daloa is not far from Abidjan? Why should internal routes such as Daloa–Abidjan or Bouna–Abidjan cost so much more than international routes such as Abidjan–Niamey or Abidjan–Ouagadougou? However, the general trends are of more interest here than any specific figures. The arbitrariness involved in extracting such "taxes" might explain some of the variations observed, while differences in the values of good transported along different roads leads to variability in the total values that are taxable on each axis.

per kilometre on most of the routes that have been studied. The average road "tax" of 49.3 CFA francs per kilometre, which is shown for illustrative purposes in Table 5, is not directly comparable (as the cost per tonne will depend on the average tonnage of vehicles travelling each route), but is obviously important.

Domestic policies in the marketing and transport sectors can have a significant impact on the capacity to expand trade in local and transborder markets. Whether they restrict entry to the formal system of marketing, raise the cost of acquisition and operation of transport vehicles, or directly tax the movement of vehicles and commodities, the net effect of current policies is to boost domestic unit costs of trading, thus cutting into the potential for increased regional trade. The results presented in this section point to the need for public-sector policies that minimize marketing and transport costs, which have been much neglected as a possible impediment to intraregional trade despite the many reform programs launched in recent years.

CONCLUSIONS

Our analysis underlines the importance of macroeconomic and sectoral policies for the expansion of intercountry trade and the promotion of regional market integration. Our general conclusion on the macroeconomic side is that higher levels of regional trade and integration require national policies generally favourable to international trade. Strongly inward-oriented policies adopted in pursuit of domestic objectives are difficult to reconcile with those of regional integration schemes and create an environment for production and trade that is incompatible with the integration of regional markets. Distorted macroeconomic and trade policies are likely to bring about the failure of regional integration for three reasons:

- ◆ They weaken domestic export sectors, leading to a loss of competitiveness and the stagnation or decline of country exports on regional markets.

- ◆ They impede economic growth, thus contributing to the stagnation or decline of demand for regional imports.

- ◆ They ultimately result in foreign exchange shortages, inducing national governments to adopt licensing and other control measures disruptive of regional trade.

Sector policies bearing on domestic trade and transport also have significant implications for regional market integration. Marketing policies retard the process of regional integration if they severely limit trader entry into the marketing system, raise the costs of operating legally, or restrict the movement of commodities. Transport policies such as heavy taxation, restriction of entry in the transport sector, and road blocks, similarly increase transborder transfer costs.

The creation of intergovernmental organizations and the establishment of trade preference schemes, such as have been attempted so far, are no substitute for eliminating the protectionist bias of macroeconomic policies at the national level or improving market and transport policies. Instead of focusing exclusively on tariff preferences and other similar institutional arrangements, future negotiations on regional trade and integration should be extended to include greater attention to macroeconomic, marketing, and other sector policies in participating member countries.

REFERENCES

Ahluwalia, U.J.; Rangarajan, C. 1989. A study of linkages between agriculture and industry: the Indian experience. In Williamson, J.G.; Panchamukhi, V.R. (ed.). The balance between industry and agriculture in economic development. Vol. 2: Sector proportions. MacMillan, London, UK. Pp. 305–319.

Avillez, F.; Finan, T.J.; Josling, T. 1988. Trade, exchange rates, and agricultural pricing policy in Portugal. In The political economy of agricultural pricing policy. World Bank, Washington, DC, USA.

Badiane, O. 1988. National food security and regional integration in West Africa. Wissenschaftsverlag Vauk, Kiel, Germany.

———— 1991. Regional agricultural markets and development strategies in West Africa. Quarterly Journal of International Agriculture, 3 (1), 37–50.

Balassa, B. 1978. Exports and economic growth: further evidence. Journal of Development Economics, 5.

Bautista, R. 1988. Agriculture-based development strategy: issues and policy framework. Presented at the Development policy seminar, 20 July, at the East-West Centre's Resources Systems Institute. East-West Centre, Honolulu, HA, USA.

Camara, A. 1992. Les coûts de commercialisation des produits vivriers en Côte d'Ivoire. Centre ivoirien de recherches économiques et sociales, Abidjan, Côte d'Ivoire. Unpublished project report.

Clements, K.W.; Sjaastad, L.A. 1984. How protection taxes exporters. Trade Policy Centre, London, UK. Thames essay 39.

DeRosa, D. 1992. Protection and export performance in sub-Saharan Africa. Weltwirtschoftliches Bechiv (Review of World Economies), 128 (1).

Dollar, D. 1992. Outward-oriented developing economies really do grow more rapidly: evidence from 95 LDCs, 1976–1985. In Economic development and cultural change. University of Chicago Press, Chicago, IL, USA.

Dornbusch, R.M. 1974. Tariffs and non-traded goods. Journal of International Economics, 4 (2), 177–185.

Edwards, S. 1989. Real exchange rates, devaluation, and adjustment: exchange rate policy in developing countries. MIT Press, Cambridge, MA, USA.

Gabre-Madhin, E.Z. 1991. Transfer costs of cereals marketing in Mali: implications for Mali's regional trade in West Africa. Michigan State University, East Lansing, MI, USA. Master's thesis.

Gaye, M.; Badiane, O.; Delgado, C. 1991. L'intervention des opérateurs privés dans le marché des produits agricoles au Sénégal : réalités actuelles et implications sur la filière commerciale. International Food Policy Research Institute, Washington, DC, USA.

Gersovitz, M. 1992. Transportation policy and panterritorial pricing in Africa. The World Bank Economic Review, World Bank, Washington, DC, USA.

Hwa, E. 1989. The contribution of agriculture to economic growth: some empirical evidence. In Williamson, J.G.; Panchamukhi, V.R. (ed.). The balance between industry and agriculture in economic development. Vol. 2: Sector proportions. MacMillan, London, UK. Pp. 106–126.

Institut National de Recherche sur les Transports et leur Sécurité, Laboratoire d'Économie des Transports. 1989a. Politiques de réduction des coûts du camionnage en Afrique sub-saharienne : cas du Mali. INRETS-LET, Lyons, France.

—— 1989b. Politiques de réduction des coûts du camionnage en Afrique sub-saharienne : cas de la Côte d'Ivoire. INRETS-LET, Lyons, France.

Jansen, D. 1988. Trade, exchange rate, and agricultural pricing policies in Zambia. In The political economy of agricultural pricing policy. World Bank, Washington, DC, USA.

Krueger, A.O.; Schiff, M.; Valdes, A. 1988. Agricultural incentives in developing countries: measuring the effects of sectoral and economy wide policies. World Bank Economic Review, 3 (2), 225–271.

Lächler, U. 1989. Regional integration and economic development. Industry and Energy Department, World Bank, Washington, DC, USA. Industry series 4.

Mundlak, Y.; Cavallo, D.; Domenech, R. 1989. Agriculture and economic growth in Argentina, 1913–84. International Food Policy Research Institute, Washington, DC, USA. Research report 76.

Ouali, K. 1982. Intégration africaine: le cas de la CEAO. Economica, Paris, France.

Oyejide, T.A. 1986. The effects of trade and exchange rate policies on agriculture in Nigeria. International Food Policy Research Institute, Washington, DC, USA. Research report 55.

Panchamukhi, V.R.; Nambiar, R.G.; Mehia, R. 1989. Structural change and economic growth in developing countries. In Williamson, J.G.; Panchamukhi, V.R. (ed.). The balance between industry and agriculture in economic development. Vol. 2: Sector proportions. MacMillan, London, UK.

Robson, P. 1983. Integration, development and equity: economic integration in West Africa. Routledge, New York, NY, USA.

Salinger, B.L.; Stryker, J.D. 1991. Exchange rate policy and implications for agricultural market INTEGRATION in West Africa. Associates for International Resources and Development, Cambridge, MA, USA. Unpublished project report.

Stryker, J.D. 1990. Trade, exchange rate, and agricultural pricing policies in Ghana. In The political economy of agricultural pricing policy. World Bank, Washington, DC, USA.

World Bank 1982. World development report. World Bank, Washington, DC, USA.

—— 1987. World development report. World Bank, Washington, DC, USA.

CHAPTER 9

INFORMAL INTEGRATION OR ECONOMIC SUBVERSION? PARALLEL TRADE IN WEST AFRICA

— Kate Meagher —

Meagher criticizes the frequently held view of parallel trade as a possible answer to some of the obstacles to trade mentioned elsewhere in this volume. Based on a review of the literature, she describes the organization of parallel trade as a circuitous flow in which illegal exports generate the foreign exchange needed to engage in the illegal import of other goods. Most parallel trade involves the exchange of smuggled primary export commodities and goods imported from outside the sub-region. These products are traded to take advantage of price differences due to divergent economic policies in neighbouring countries.

Private fortunes and public privileges are based on such trade and are defended through coalitions of powerful commercial and political interests. These interest groups are opposed to genuine regional integration, which would put an end to the opportunities for arbitrage that sustain their fortunes. Politically, the existence of parallel trade thus tends to work against regional integration rather than for it. Economically, it contributes little to the exchange of regionally produced goods.

THE ISSUE OF African integration has been toyed with for decades and attempted in various regional forms with, at best, limited success. With the formation of large regional trading blocs in Europe, North America, and Asia, the issue of economic integration in Africa has resurfaced over the past few years with much greater urgency. Earlier integration initiatives were handicapped by the existence of preferential trading links with the European Economic Community (EEC) enshrined in the Lomé Convention. Such preferential arrangements undermined the commitment of African countries to integration, as individual countries pursued their more immediate interests through the perpetuation of import–export relations with their former colonial masters. These preferential trade arrangements are now threatened by the exigencies of European integration and the liberalization of international trade negotiated under the Uruguay round of the GATT (Martin 1985, p. 10; Oyejide 1990, p. 431; Essien 1991, p. 44). Meanwhile, the collapse of the Soviet Union has eliminated an alternative source of aid and led to increased competitition for EEC aid and export markets, forcing African countries to look increasingly in the direction of self-reliance (Griffin and Khan 1992). African countries are thus faced with the poor record of official integration schemes over the past two decades and confront the prospect of contending with formidable First World trading blocs in a context of declining access to aid, without the benefit of preferential agreements.

This has stimulated interest in the performance of informal trading networks, which appear to have succeeded where official initiatives have failed. Although the volume of official intra-African trade stands at only 6% of estimated total trade for the region (World Bank 1989, p. 158), unofficial intra-African trade in the 1980s is estimated to have comprised as much as 30–50% of export crop production in a range of African countries, as well as millions of dollars annually in food crops, minerals, and consumer goods (Green 1981, 1989; MacGaffey 1987; Amselle and Grégoire 1988; Chazan 1988; Lambert 1989). In addition to moving a substantial volume of goods, this unofficial trade is conducted with much greater efficiency, speed, and responsiveness than official trade, despite the obstacles attributable to its illegal status.

The question now being raised is whether these parallel trading channels can serve as a basis for effective and development-oriented economic integration in Sub-Saharan Africa, by promoting trade liberalization and gradually becoming incorporated into the formal sector. The consensus among many prominent African scholars appears to favour such a view. Parallel trade is increasingly being portrayed as the expression of an overwhelming indigenous bid for economic liberalization and integration, as well as a form of popular resistance to the economic inefficiency and corruption of official national economies (MacGaffey 1987; Chazan 1988; Diamond et al. 1988; Igué and Soulé 1992). One World Bank report portrays parallel trade as not only efficient and welfare enhancing, but as rooted in the history and traditional organization of African societies (World Bank 1989, p. 158).

Those who are concerned with the developmental objectives of integration should be wary of such views. The currently favourable attitude of the World Bank toward parallel trade requires closer scrutiny, if only because it represents a significant reversal of its position and that of other market-oriented thinkers in the early 1980s (World Bank 1981). In addition, current notions of parallel trade are based largely on vague, theoretical notions of how parallel activities actually operate. To seriously assess the developmental potential of parallel trade requires more systematic consideration to its development, structure, and impact on popular welfare as well as on national and regional development objectives.

This chapter begins with a discussion of the populist view of parallel trade that currently dominates the literature. A critique is presented of the central theme of the populist perspective according to which parallel trade is a reassertion of the ethnic solidarity and popular economic initiative which were repressed by the imposition of arbitrary colonial borders and elitist economic policies. The derivative notions that parallel trade is essentially redistributive and gender positive and provides a source of authentic class formation independent of the state, are also challenged.

The next section presents an empirical analysis of parallel trade since the 1970s in West Africa, and examines the structure and composition of parallel trading circuits. An analysis of the characteristic structural features of this trade is used to question the adequacy of the orthodox economic perspective, which argues that parallel trade is reducible to price distortions at the national level and can be eliminated through the internal liberalization of prices, trade, and exchange rates. Fuller explanations are sought at the regional level, in terms of the strategic role of zones of convertible currency and liberal import policy within wider complexes of states. The role of the state in the expansion of parallel activity is also examined.

The final section considers the implications of parallel trade for West African integration, with particular reference to the current context of structural adjustment. The ideological influences motivating the favourable reassessment of parallel trade as an agent of integration rather than a symptom of economic distortion are also examined.

Before proceeding, it is important to clarify the meaning of the term "parallel trade," in view of the ambiguity with which the term has been used. "Parallel trade" and "parallel economy" have been used rather loosely to denote a whole range of unofficial economic activities, including informal-sector activities and illegal activities such as prostitution or drug trafficking (MacGaffey 1987; Chazan 1988). The convention in economic literature, however, is to reserve the term "parallel" to refer to the movement of legal goods through illegal or unofficial channels, thus distinguishing it from "informal" productive and small-scale service activities, on one hand, and criminal or "underground" activities, on the other (Lindauer 1989, p. 1874). It is in this sense that "parallel" is used here. Although this definition includes both illegal cross-border trade and illegal channels of trade operating inside a given country, only the international dimension of parallel trade is considered in this chapter.

HISTORICAL APPROACH
AND POPULIST MYTHS

In the late 1970s and early 1980s, studies of parallel trade in the anglophone world were largely the domain of economists and political scientists. The dominant perspective on parallel trade was that it developed as a result of excessive regulation, price distortions, and the corruption of post-independence African governments and would be eliminated once these distortions were corrected.

During the same period, an alternative interpretation of the origins of parallel trade was put forward by the more historically and empirically oriented studies of economic historians, anthropologists, and francophone geographers. These studies emphasize its precolonial origins, which are seen to be rooted in the traditions of ethnic solidarity of precolonial Africa and in the extensive long-distance trading networks that operated across vast areas of the continent for centuries before the creation of colonial national boundaries. Parallel trade is seen as a form of indigenous resistance to the imposition of colonial borders and metropolitan economic regulations on traditional African economic and social formations (Asiwaju 1976; Igué 1977, 1985; MacGaffey 1987).

Significantly, parallel activities have flourished in areas where precolonial long-distance trade was most highly developed, notably in East and West Africa. This contrasts with the situation in Southern Africa, where indigenous systems of long-distance trade were poorly developed in the precolonial period (Hodder 1965). This helps to explain the subsequent lack of significant levels of parallel activity in the post-independence period. With the exception of countries bordering on East and central Africa, such as Zambia, Mozambique, and Angola, the main smuggling networks in southern Africa have, until recently, involved essentially underworld circuits organized around stolen cars, soft drugs, and gem stones (Schissel 1989, p. 46; field observations). The high level of conflict and the accompanying movement of refugees in the region has increased the level of parallel activity, but this trade does not compare with that of East and West Africa either in volume or in the extensiveness of traditional trading infrastructure to support the movement of goods.

The historical approach to parallel trade has generated a wealth of detailed information on the relationship between precolonial and modern parallel trading activities and has contributed significantly to the recent shift in perspective on parallel trade expressed in market-oriented political and economic literature. However, the analysis used in the majority of these historically oriented studies tends to suffer from a rather romantic representation of parallel trade as a more democratic and authentically African form of economic organization. This idealization tends to gloss over the existence of ethnic, political, and socioeconomic divisions in precolonial African societies, and obscures the ways in which colonial and post-colonial official economies fundamentally altered the operation and social impact of precolonial trading patterns. In the interest of a more critical understanding of parallel trade, we examine four common populist myths concerning the nature of parallel activity:

- that parallel trade represents the reassertion of African solidarity in the face of colonial distortions;
- that it is essentially redistributive;
- that it is independent of the official economy;
- that it is gender positive.

THE MYTH OF AFRICAN SOLIDARITY

It is one of the ironies of the historical–empirical literature on parallel trade that the ideology of African solidarity places the analysis within an ahistorical framework. The prevailing vision of precolonial economic society tends to ignore important political and socioeconomic divisions that structured precolonial long-distance trade. Borders between precolonial kingdoms, feudal systems of tolls and taxes, and the general insecurity that forced trading caravans to move as fully armed regiments are largely ignored in the genealogies of parallel trade (Thom 1975; Baier 1980; Falola 1989). The far-reaching changes that took place in the organization of inter-African trade with the advent of colonialism are also subjected to a slanted interpretation. These changes are seen as means of evading colonial attempts at regulation or of profiting from colonial innovations, such as the railways and colonial currencies. There is little or no recognition of how these adjustments may have fundamentally altered the supposed autonomy and popular orientation of inter-African trade.

The notion that parallel trade arose in response to the artificial separation of solidary ethnic groups by colonial borders is also misleading in some ways. Even in precolonial times, ethnic boundaries could be cross-cut by political boundaries (Mafeje 1991). The division of ethnic groups by colonial borders was therefore not a new phenomenon, nor did it necessarily violate prior forms of sociopolitical organization. For example, the Hausa population inhabiting both sides of the Nigeria–Niger border — still one of the more active parallel trade zones in West Africa — was not a unified political entity before the border was delineated in 1906. The colonial border was drawn along a preexisting political boundary between the Sokoto Caliphate to the south and the kingdoms of the Habe (prejihadist Hausa aristocracy) to the north (Thom 1975). Furthermore, it was not the colonial borders themselves, but the differential economic policies of the colonial regimes on either side of them that most decisively affected inter-African trade (Igué 1977; Asiwaju 1976).

Although the historical–empirical literature documents the changes in inter-African trade resulting from such policy differentials, it fails to analyze fully the implications of these changes, presenting them as evidence of the responsiveness and tenacity of indigenous trading formations that are assumed to have maintained their authentically African economic orientation in the process. A closer look reveals rather more profound shifts in the structure of inter-African trade. The two most decisive changes precipitated by colonialism were in the types of goods handled and in the direction of trade. Although foreign consumer goods had been an element even in precolonial long-distance trade, its major staples were African primary products and local manufactures traded on the basis of ecological specialization (Mamdani 1976; Baier 1980). In West Africa, the Sahel, savanna, forest, and coastal regions exchanged such primary products as salt, dried fish, livestock, kola, and gold, as well as local manufactures, such as cotton cloth, iron implements, mortars, and leather goods, to name only a few (Meillassoux 1971, p. 77; Igué 1977, p. 11; Baier 1980, p. 157). With the advent of colonialism, these traditional West African circuits became dwarfed by the more profitable parallel opportunities created by contraband trade between British and French colonies. Trading staples were no longer determined by ecological specialization or local manufacturing skills, but by the fiscal and legal discrepancies of cash-cropping and import regimes in French and British colonies. Inter-African trade in primary products became dominated by export-crop smuggling, and the trade in consumer goods shifted decisively from local manufactures to foreign industrial imports. Cheap industrial textiles and other foreign consumer goods, which enjoyed tariff-free import into British colonies but were heavily taxed in French colonies, became major parallel staples, in return for alcohol and cigarettes, which were heavily taxed in British but not in French colonies (Igué 1977; Asiwaju 1976).

Differential currencies in conjunction with differential fiscal policies between French and British colonies resulted in currency zones replacing ecological zones in the orientation of parallel trading circuits. The development of active parallel exchange markets by the 1920s turned these discrepancies from an obstacle to inter-African trade into a transaction that not only facilitated but accelerated trade (Asiwaju 1976, p. 176; Baier 1980, p. 113). However, the trade flows resulting from this process became increasingly detached from the economic base of the region, as determined by the comparative advantage of each economy. Access to foreign imports, as mediated through the parallel value of currencies, became, and remains, the central regulating mechanism of parallel inter-African trade.

THE MYTH OF COMMUNAL REDISTRIBUTION

Another populist myth about parallel trade is that it has few barriers to entry and is fundamentally redistributive, contrary to the official economy. Parallel trade is said to redistribute resources toward the rural and border areas neglected by the official economy and to offer an alternative to proletarianization (Igué 1985, p. 97ff; MacGaffey 1987, p. 112).

Ironically, this redistributive character may have been truer of early parallel trade under colonialism than it was of precolonial long-distance trade, which was dominated, at least in West Africa, by well-established merchants. The major shifts in trade routes and profitable goods as a result of colonialism ruined many of the established precolonial merchants and, along with the *pax Britannica*, increased opportunities for the entry of small-scale, rural-based traders into long-distance and cross-border trade (Hopkins 1973; Baier 1980).

However, the opening for small-scale traders was soon closed off. As border regulations became stricter and a new class of parallel merchants better established, participation by small-scale traders became more difficult. Contrary to the assumption of microeconomic analyses, parallel trade enjoys economies of scale for those who can pay the necessary bribes (Devarajan et al. 1989, p. 1883; Puetz and von Braun 1990, p. 230).

Already by the 1950s, small-scale traders on the Nigeria–Niger border were finding themselves unable to compete with large-scale, urban-based traders, who had the capital to pay the required bribes and to smuggle goods across the border in lorries (Baier 1980, p. 164). Recent studies in the Gambia, Nigeria, and Zaire indicate that transaction costs and the low capital base of small-scale traders make it difficult for them to participate profitably in parallel trade, and prevent poor farmers from participating in parallel trade at all (Russell 1989; Puetz and von Braun 1990; Meagher 1991).

In the same vein, attention has recently been focused on the fact that African parallel trading operations tend to be organized in networks (Igué 1985; MacGaffey 1987; Lambert 1989). Some authors have emphasized the redistributive potential of this form of organization, while tending to ignore its potential for concentration and exploitation (Weiss 1987; Portes et al. 1989, p. 305ff). Important lines of parallel activity tend to be controlled by small groups of large traders, particularly in West Africa. Flour and rice smuggling in Mauritania, Mali, the Gambia, Guinea, Guinea-Bissau, and Benin have been found to be controlled by three to ten large traders in each country (Igué 1985, p. 57; Lambert 1989, p. 12; Coste et al. 1991, p. 148). Similarly, parallel trade between Nigeria and Niger has been found to be concentrated in the hands of wealthy Alhazai (Amselle and Grégoire 1988).

Nor does the evidence support the assumption that parallel trade enhances welfare to any substantial extent for indirect participants such as farmers (MacGaffey 1987; Devarajan et al. 1989, p. 1892). Small farmers participate in the parallel economy out of desperation under terms of trade that are less favourable than those offered in the official economy (Lambert 1989, pp. 29–32; Wuyts 1989, p. 144; Gibbon et al., 1992, p. 78). The problem is not a lack of competition among traders, but the resource constraints of small farmers, which make them susceptible to cut-rate marketing in the parallel economy; they cannot afford the transportation costs and delays in payment involved in marketing goods in the official economy nor the transaction costs of engaging directly in parallel trade. Evidence from Uganda, Nigeria, and Senegal indicates that, rather than passing on high parallel prices to the farmer in such situations, parallel traders are as efficient in exploiting the economic pressures faced by small farmers as they are in exploiting the price distortions of national economies. Communal or ethnic ties between parallel trade and small farmers do not appear to protect farmers from this market logic (Igué 1985; Russell 1989).

The myth of independence from the state

One of the most entrenched beliefs is that parallel activity provides opportunities for accumulation of wealth independent of the state and may be giving rise to the development of an authentic indigenous bourgeoisie (Leys 1978, p. 253; Igué 1985; MacGaffey 1987). However, empirical evidence concerning the parallel bourgeoisie indicates that successful accumulation through parallel channels is largely dependent on connections and collaboration with state officials (Kasfir 1984; Lambert 1989; Russell 1989; Meagher 1991). In most cases, it was through their involvement in the official economy, rather than their independence from it, that many large-scale parallel traders got their start. The massive scale at which parallel magnates operate in modern times has only been possible through official complicity and access to official resources, which reaches the highest levels.

As to the degree of productive investment based on parallel accumulation — without which parallel accumulators cannot qualify as a bourgeoisie of any kind — there is little evidence that it goes beyond fronts for laundering funds or gaining privileged access to subsidies or foreign exchange through the official economy. Evidence suggests that this group's investments centre on commerce, real estate, and other speculative activities (Igué 1985; Amselle and Grégoire 1988; MacGaffey 1987, 1988).

Gender positive myth

It has become increasingly popular to represent parallel trade as a sphere of activity that opens up economic opportunities for women (MacGaffey 1988; Sow 1991; Igué and Soulé 1992). Parallel and informal activities provide the bulk of female employment in Sub-Saharan Africa, and, under conditions of economic crisis and rising male unemployment in the official economy, an increasing number of women are entering the parallel economy to support their households. The parallel economy is seen as an avenue for evading the patriarchal structures that limit women's opportunities in the official economy and as a means for women to reassert their economic importance in times of crisis. However, closer scrutiny reveals that the vast majority of women involved in informal and parallel activities are confined to low-income activities with little opportunity for accumulation of wealth. Furthermore, these activities are among the hardest hit by crisis in the official economy (Beneria 1991; Meagher and Yunusa 1993). The few women who are able to accumulate are those who acquire privileged access to resources or licences through personal or official connections to the state. In neither case can one speak of increased economic autonomy or forms of accumulation independent of the official economy.

PARALLEL TRADE IN THE 1970S AND 1980S

In spite of its populist leanings, the historical–empirical literature on parallel trade has contributed greatly to our understanding of the long history and structural complexity of parallel activity in Africa. Against this background, the pricist explanations that are normally used to account for the explosion of parallel activity in the 1970s appear inadequate. The attempt to reduce the complexities of parallel trade to product-specific price distortions blinds most economic analyses to some fundamental aspects of the structure of parallel trade.

Analyses in terms of product-specific price distortions divide parallel activity into a series of independent flows of goods. However, parallel trade is now widely known to be organized, not in independent flows, but in circuits based on illegal exports to procure foreign exchange for illegal imports (May 1985; Singh 1986; Azam and Besley 1989). The profitability of parallel trade in a given commodity is determined by the operation of the entire circuit, as mediated through the parallel exchange rate.

Because pricing policy is set by individual governments, the focus on product price distortions produces a nation-centred understanding of parallel trade that obscures the wider regional dynamics at work. Similar price distortions and problems of currency overvaluation are characteristic of most countries in Sub-Saharan Africa, yet specific regional and sub-regional patterns of parallel trade relations have emerged in which various national economies play distinct roles.

We now move from a discussion of what parallel trade is *not*, to grappling with what it *is*. This will provide a sounder basis for evaluating its concrete potential as a basis for African integration. The following analysis is an attempt to sketch the regional dynamics of parallel trade that have developed in the post-independence period. Quantitative data have been included where available, but, as in most studies of this sort, they should be taken as rough and often unstable indications of magnitude.[1]

---

[1] Given the nation-centred and often fragmentary approach of many parallel trade studies, an analysis of the regional dynamics of the trade has necessitated the use of a wide variety of empirical sources, including articles from journals that may be considered "unacademic." Care has been taken, however, to avoid the danger of analysis giving way to journalism. Material from questionable sources was included only where it was corroborated by evidence from other sources or fit into a well-established pattern.

GENERAL FEATURES OF PARALLEL CIRCUITS

Before turning to the analysis of specific circuits, an attempt will be made to model some of the general features common to parallel trading circuits to highlight similarities as well as regional contrasts in the empirical studies that follow. The ideal parallel trading circuit is predicated upon the existence of three conditions in a pair or group of neighbouring countries. On one side, will be a foreign-exchange-controlled economy, with a parallel foreign-exchange market. On the other, will be one or more economies with internationally convertible currencies and liberal import policies. In practice, the last two characteristics are frequently combined in a single economy. The essence of parallel trading circuits is the procurement of illegal supplies of convertible currencies to address the foreign-exchange constraint of the foreign-exchange-controlled economy for the purchase and illegal import of foreign goods. Access to internationally convertible currencies for traders from foreign-exchange-controlled economies is obtained largely through export smuggling, which involves two main categories of goods: either agricultural and other primary commodities, such as mineral resources; or subsidized goods, primarily sugar, petrol, foodstuffs, and agricultural inputs, depending on the subsidies provided in a given country. Convertible currencies so acquired are used to bring in foreign imports, such as cigarettes, textiles, secondhand clothing, and electronics, as well as imported rice and wheat flour, which are imported through the liberal-importing convertible-currency economy and smuggled back into the first country. This pattern of parallel exports and imports is fairly consistent across both East and West Africa.

One of the most useful contributions of historical–empirical theories of parallel trade has been to shift the focus from product prices to currency matters. Igué (1977) explains the movement of parallel trade in post-colonial West Africa with reference to the uneven distribution of zones of convertible and inconvertible currencies. Convertible currency zones include the franc-zone countries and, until fairly recently, Liberia (whose currency was convertible to the US dollar until the late 1980s). In the context of foreign-exchange scarcity, convertible currency zones attract smuggled agricultural and other export commodities from neighbouring (largely anglophone) countries with inconvertible currencies, as described above. The attraction that convertible currencies exert on primary commodities is translated into price incentives through the parallel exchange rate. The high demand for convertible currencies on the parallel market increases their value relative to nonconvertible currencies, and creates opportunities to profit from the sale of goods in exchange for such currencies. Naudet (1993) refers to a "transactional advantage" that biases relative prices in favour of convertible currency zones, through a sort of convertibility premium. A similar premium applies to the currencies of countries with particularly liberal import policies (Asiwaju 1976; Igué 1985).

Two other important features of parallel trade that are not immediately evident at the national level are reexport trade and transit trade. Reexport trade refers to the importation of foreign goods by one country for onward export to neighbouring countries in which the official import of such goods is controlled or banned (Igué 1977). This practice is a central element in the regional organization of parallel trade in both East and West Africa. Transit trade refers to the transport of goods destined for smuggling through an intermediary country that lies between the country of original importation and the country for which the goods are destined (Amselle and Grégoire 1988; Coste et al. 1991). For example, imports smuggled into Mali or Mauritania from the Gambia are transmitted through Senegal, whereas imports smuggled into Nigeria from Benin may pass through Niger. Transit trade is usually not illegal in the country of transit and is frequently a useful source of tax revenue.

PARALLEL TRADE CIRCUITS IN WEST AFRICA

In West Africa, the intermingling of zones of convertible and nonconvertible currency has divided the region into three subsystems of parallel activity. These are centred around Nigeria, Ghana–Côte d'Ivoire, and Senegambia, and correspond fairly closely to the three "submarkets" identified in the study of cross-border agricultural trade by the Institut de recherches et d'applications des méthodes de développement (IRAM) and the Laboratoire d'analyse régionale et d'expertise sociale (LARES) (Lambert 1989; Egg and Igué 1993; Naudet 1993). In each subsystem, the franc zone provides access to foreign exchange and one country with a traditionally liberal import policy provides the main entry point for imports: Benin, Togo, and the Gambia. Although there are parallel trading circuits at the margins of these subsystems, the bulk of parallel activity is concentrated within them.

The Nigerian subsystem

During the colonial period, when Nigeria was blessed with the liberal import policy of the British Empire and a currency directly convertible with the pound sterling, the country was a magnet for cocoa, grain, cattle, and other primary commodities smuggled from surrounding franc-zone countries in return for imported goods. This situation was reversed in the decade after independence, in the context of growing Nigerian protectionism and the delinking of the Nigerian pound (now the naira) from the pound sterling. The growth of protectionism and various forms of import controls was accompanied by a gradual decline in the parallel value of the Nigerian pound, which stood about 30% above its official parity with the CFA franc in the late 1950s, but had fallen to 6% below its official value by 1967 (Igué 1977). However, it was the loss of international convertibility of Nigeria's currency at that time that had the most profound effect on both parallel currency values and trading circuits. Delinking precipitated the collapse of the parallel value of the Nigerian pound, which fell in a single year from 650 to 400 CFA francs, 42% below its official parity (Table 1). The parallel inflows of cocoa from Benin and grain from Niger, which had continued through the early independence period, were reversed. Instead Nigerian food grains have flowed into Niger since then at the rate of about 200 000 tonnes annually (Igué 1985; Egg and Igué 1993). Nigerian cocoa is estimated to make up one-third or more of Benin's official cocoa exports (Igué 1988; Deutsch, personal communication). Subsidized fertilizer and petrol flow across all of Nigeria's borders, along with locally manufactured goods (Egg and Igué 1993).[2]

The CFA francs obtained through these parallel exports are used to import banned, highly protected, or otherwise scarce consumer goods into Nigeria — principally cigarettes, textiles, used clothing, wheat flour (until it was unbanned in October 1992), rice (unbanned in 1995), and electronics (Igué 1985; Amselle and Grégoire 1988). These goods are imported primarily through the main ports of Benin and Togo, and smuggled into Nigeria directly or via Niger. Smuggling also takes place on the Cameroon and Chad borders. Benin actively promoted its role as a source of smuggled imports by liberalizing its import policy as early as 1973, when many other economies in the region were tightening theirs (Igué 1977). Niger has similarly promoted itself as a transit point. Customs statistics in Niger suggest that the value of parallel imports passing through Niger was as high as 7.1 billion CFA francs in 1986, falling to 4.5 billion in 1987 after the first devaluation of the naira (Amselle and

---

[2] In Cameroon, the state petrol monopoly, "Nationale," faces serious competition from cheap and widely available smuggled Nigerian petrol, affectionately known by Cameroonians as "Fédérale" (BBC Radio report 1991).

Grégoire 1988). Given Benin's proximity to Lagos, parallel imports across the Benin border are likely to have been even greater.

The introduction of Nigeria's structural adjustment program in 1986 and the 99% devaluation of the naira between 1986 and 1995 have not arrested these activities, and some forms of smuggling have increased. Grain smuggling across the Niger border is a case in point: it has increased, rather than diminished, in reaction to the liberalization of marketing and the ongoing devaluation of the naira that have left CFA-denominated grain prices in Niger more attractive than prices in devalued naira. The liberalization of cocoa marketing and rising internal prices in Nigeria have been more successful in stemming parallel exports along the Benin border, but cocoa smuggling continues as a vehicle for speculation and capital flight as business enterprises and private individuals scramble to convert depreciating naira into foreign exchange (Economist Intelligence Unit 1988, p. 20; Mustapha 1990).

The Ghanaian subsystem

A similar parallel exchange history is evident in the case of Ghana, once a magnet for primary commodities from its francophone neighbours. Ghana's delinking from the sterling zone combined with a mounting foreign exchange of import crisis led to the development of a parallel exchange market for the cedi, and by the mid-1970s, the parallel value of the cedi was 60% below its official value with respect to the CFA franc (Igué 1977). Primary commodities in the form of cocoa, gold, diamonds, and locally manufactured goods began to flow from Ghana into Togo and Côte d'Ivoire in return for imported cigarettes, textiles, used cars, and other consumer goods. The imposition of a structural adjustment program in 1983, which has included large successive currency devaluations, did not succeed in eliminating the smuggling trade.

For example, diamonds have remained the object of massive smuggling out of Ghana since the imposition of its structural adjustment programme. The Ghana Diamond Mining Corporation estimated that in 1984 at least USD 14 million in diamonds were smuggled into Togo, and in 1985, up to 70% of diamonds produced in Ghana were said to have been smuggled out of the country (West Africa 1989a). A similar dynamic was evident in Sierra Leone, which witnessed the wholesale smuggling of diamonds and cattle into Liberia in search of convertible Liberian dollars in the 1980s. Some $65 million in diamonds are estimated to have been smuggled out of Sierra Leone in the first half of 1987 (West Africa 1989b).

Togo has promoted itself as the main entrepôt for trade with Ghana and other West African countries, through the adoption of an official policy of reexport in the early 1970s. By cutting tariffs and restrictions on luxury consumer goods, Togo increased its customs receipts to fully 62% of the national budget by 1974 (Igué 1977). Lomé has become not only a portal for imported goods, but a central point for the export of smuggled gold and diamonds to Europe and an important centre of the parallel currency trade in West Africa (Schissel 1989, p. 45; West Africa 1990, p. 1248).

The Senegambian subsystem

The parallel circuits centred around Senegambia are an exception to the pattern of parallel commodity-export trade oriented toward convertible currency zones. Although the Gambia is bordered on three side by Senegal, which is a member of the CFA franc zone, the direction of parallel primary export has been from Senegal and neighbouring countries into the Gambia, despite the nonconvertibility of the Gambian dalasi. The attraction of the Gambian economy has been its extremely liberal import policy. Like Benin and Togo, the Gambia functions as the parallel entrepôt of its subsystem (Igué 1977; Coste et al. 1991). Although its currency was delinked from the sterling zone in the mid-1970s, Gambia has managed to sustain a favourable parallel exchange rate by means of its liberal import policies. Although inconvertible, the dalasi is a source of access to imported goods for its neighbours. This increases its parallel value and converts it into a magnet for primary commodity smuggling.

Senegalese groundnuts, which flowed into the Gambia for most of the period between the late 1960s (with the elimination of French price support) and 1985, are estimated to have increased Gambian foreign exchange earnings by an average of 20% each year until the mid-1970s. Over the same period, it is estimated that as much as 45% of Gambian imports were reexported into Senegal (Igué 1977; Lambert 1989).

Important shifts in some of these patterns occurred after the adoption of the Gambian economic recovery program in 1985. The devaluation of the dalasi in the first year of the program, coupled with an increase in the price of groundnuts in Senegal, reversed the cross-border flow of groundnuts. However, the liberalization of Gambian rice imports in the same year provided Gambian traders with an alternative means of obtaining convertible currency to fund the continued importation of foreign consumer goods, especially electronics, for reexport to neighbouring countries. In a country where annual rice consumption is estimated at

55 000 tonnes, Gambian rice imports rose from about 50 000 tonnes per year in the early 1980s to over 100 000 tonnes per year in the last half of the decade, more than half of which was reexported into Senegal, Mali, and Guinea–Bissau (Lambert 1989; Schissel 1989; Coste et al. 1991).

This parallel strategy is highly sensitive to events in Senegal. The reduction of the price of rice in Senegal in 1988 as a result of social pressure was estimated to have wiped out as much as 80% of the Gambian reexport market for imported rice (Lambert 1989, p. 13). Increased competition in the parallel electronics market from Senegalese Mouride traders has also cut into Gambian intermediation. Since January 1994, the massive devaluation of the CFA franc and accompanying changes in Senegalese pricing and tariff policy have introduced further changes in the smuggling trade.

Official policy and reexport strategies

A close examination of parallel trade reveals that it is intimately bound to the official economy, not simply through the corruption of government agents, but as part of the official policy of certain countries that have come to recognize the fiscal advantages of acting as conduits for parallel goods. This has contributed to what Igué refers to as the "semi-official" character of parallel trade, by which he means that it is frequently illegal on only one side of the border and an important contributor to the official economy on the other (Igué 1985, p. 58; IGADD 1989, p. iv).

A number of studies in West Africa have noted the involvement of official agencies as agents of parallel trade, particularly in reexport-oriented, or entrepôt, economies such as Togo, Benin, and the Gambia. In Benin, the cocoa-marketing parastatal, Société Nationale pour la Promotion Agricole (SONAPRA), is the final buyer of smuggled Nigerian cocoa, the export of which is a state monopoly (Igué 1985, p. 58). The Togolese government derives tax revenue from exporting smuggled gold and diamonds. The Gambian government derives as much as 71% of its tax revenues from imports destined largely for reexport to neighbouring countries (Schissel 1989, p. 44; Coste et al. 1991, p. 77).

Similarly, the government of Niger derives considerable fiscal advantage from its participation in parallel import and export circuits with Nigeria. Parallel grain exports from Nigeria have become an important source of cheap supply for the Office des produits vivriers du Niger (OPVN), Niger's grain parastatal (Amselle and Grégoire 1988, pp. 8–9).

Meanwhile, parallel imports passing through Niger to Nigeria provide a source of tax revenue to the government, but approximately 80% of this transit trade is actually handled by the Niger parastatal NITRA, which was created in 1974 to manage and capitalize on the rising level of parallel trade with Nigeria (Amselle and Grégoire 1988, pp. 33–36).

An examination of official import and export statistics in these economies reveals the curious phenomenon of countries that export what they do not produce and import what they cannot consume. For example, in the last few years of the 1980s, Togo, a country without mines, is said to have officially exported $150 million in gold and $40 million in diamonds (West Africa 1989a, p. 1248). Liberia, also a non-diamond-producing country, had 24 diamond buying stations until the 1989 devaluation of the leone, when the number of stations was reduced to 16 (West Africa 1989b, p. 1048). A similar phenomenon occurs in the case of export crops. After the liberalization of the Nigerian cocoa trade in 1986, Niger, a Sahelian country, began to export cocoa through the parastatal NITRA (Amselle and Grégoire 1988, p. 36). A much more common phenomenon involves countries that export far more of a commodity than they produce, including Benin and Togo in the case of cocoa and the Gambia in the case of groundnuts (at least until 1985).

The other side of this phenomenon involves the importation of goods in quantities far beyond the consumption capacity of a given country's inhabitants. This is particularly noticeable in the case of small entrepôt economies, such as Togo, Benin, and the Gambia. According to official statistics, Togo reexported 71% of its consumer imports in the 1970s (Igué 1977, p. 48), a figure estimated to have reached over 90% in the 1980s. Imports of rice into Benin, Guinea, and the Gambia similarly far exceed the consumption capacity of their populations (Igué 1985, p. 60; Coste et al. 1991, p. 54). The Gambia is said to import annually twice as many radios as it has inhabitants (Schissel 1989, p. 45).

It is clear from the extensive and systematic nature of these "anomalies" that they are not isolated instances of government opportunism. They represent an official policy of reexport and part of an explicit national development strategy in a number of African economies, particularly those too small or poorly endowed to industrialize or prosper on their own. This type of policy stance has played a vital role in the development of parallel trade on the scale witnessed since the mid-1970s, by providing the cover and the institutional facilities of legitimate trade afforded by reexport oriented economies.

PARALLEL TRADE AND
REGIONAL INTEGRATION

The official status of reexport strategies in countries like Togo, Benin, and the Gambia poses serious and obvious questions about the future of regional integration. As we have seen, parallel trade is not simply an unofficial mechanism for integrating otherwise disjointed official economies, but a struggle for advantage in which the official development strategies of countries within the same region are pitted against each other, and vested interests are intrinsically opposed to economic rationalization.

The case of the Gambia and Senegal illustrates the difficulties of achieving economic integration under such circumstances. Although the Gambia's liberal import policies are highly profitable for the Gambian elite, thanks to the reexport trade, they were reported to have cost Senegal 20 billion CFA francs annually in revenues lost due to extensive import smuggling (*West Africa* 1989c, 11–17 September 1989). The fundamental conflict of interest that this represents has led to considerable foot dragging on the part of the Gambian government in attempts to achieve confederation and economic integration with Senegal and ultimately led to the collapse of the confederation project in 1989 (Schissel 1989, p. 45; *West Africa* 1989d, p. 1454; Coste et al. 1991, p. 85). One can legitimately question what the future holds for regional integration in West Africa, when neighbours as closely related as Senegal and Gambia are unable to come to terms.

Some of the more sanguine attitudes toward the potential contribution of parallel trade to regional integration in West Africa are best understood keeping in mind the commitment of a number of international institutions to a vision of integration based on the liberalization of factor and product markets. There is an increasing tendency to shroud this liberal economic agenda in the legitimacy of popular initiatives and pan-Africanist sentiment by reference to the integrationist drive of parallel activity. Parallel trade is presented as a bid by the African people for market-led integration, which is pointedly contrasted with the state-led strategies of official integration schemes, characterized by their interventionism and a fixation with grandiose industrialization projects (World Bank 1989, p. 158).

While emphasizing the importance of enlarging markets, the World Bank and other international organizations leave out the question of where the goods for those markets will come from (Beckman 1992). Our examination of the regional structure of parallel trade shows that the products promoted by this trade consist mainly of primary product exports or smuggled imports of manufactures. Far from representing a more authentic and developmental alternative to official economic organization, parallel trade seems to involve a reassertion of the commodity-export dependence established during the colonial period. A number of studies show that parallel trade has undermined the development of industry and agriculture throughout the region (Egg and Igué 1993; Meagher 1993; Olukoshi and Obi 1993). This is not only true of economies characterized by foreign-exchange and import restrictions, but also of the more liberal entrepôt economies, where parallel inflows of food and export crops from neighbouring countries and liberal imports of rice and wheat combine to undermine the profitability of local agriculture, while liberal import policies for consumer manufactures choke off the development of local industry (Igué 1985; Coste et al. 1991).

Although there is general recognition that the grandiose state-led initiatives of past integration efforts have been failures, the preoccupation with local production remains a legitimate area of concern. The trade policy agenda for Africa being promoted by international development organizations is, in general, quite different from what would be necessary to encourage the development and restructuring of local production and could benefit First World exporters and transnational investors more than indigenous African industrial and agricultural producers.

More appropriate and better coordinated development policies are clearly required to promote regional production and trade in the face of the new world order. Unfortunately, the formulation and implementation of such policies will run up against structural adjustment programmes, with their strict adherence to liberal principles, as well as the vested interests of the elite fractions and well-connected commercial groups who have made the parallel economy a central element in their accumulation strategies. Contrary to the presumption of market-oriented thinkers, a constituency for developmental integration is unlikely to be found among parallel market entrepreneurs and liberalizing elites. It can only emerge from those social groups who have suffered under the impact of parallel trade — groups such as small-scale food crop producers and local manufacturers, for whom the developmental objectives of integration increasingly represent an economic necessity rather than a lucrative opportunity for subversion.

REFERENCES

Amselle, J.L.; Grégoire, E. 1988. Politiques nationales et réseaux marchands transnationaux — les cas du Mali et du Niger–Nord Nigeria. Échanges régionaux, commerce frontalier et sécurité alimentaire en Afrique de l'Ouest. Institut national de recherche agronomique/Université nationale du Bénin/Institut de recherches et d'applications des méthodes de développement, Paris, France.

Asiwaju, A.I. 1976. Western Yorubaland under European rule 1889–1945. Longman, London, UK.

Azam, J.P.; Besley, T. 1989. General equilibrium with parallel markets for goods and foreign exchange: theory and application to Ghana. World Development, 17 (12), 1921–1930.

Baier, S. 1980. An economic history of central Niger. Clarendon Press, Oxford, UK.

Beckman, B. 1992. Empowerment or repression? The World Bank and the politics of African adjustment. In Gibbon, P. et al. (ed.). Authoritarianism, democracy and adjustment: the politics of economic reform in Africa. Scandinavian Institute of African Studies, Uppsala, Sweden. Seminar proceedings.

Beneria, L. 1991. Structural adjustment, the labour market and the household, the case of Mexico. In Standing, G.; Tokman, V. (ed.). Toward social adjustment. International Labour Organization, Geneva, Switzerland.

Chazan, N. 1988. Ghana: problems of governance and the emergence of civil society. In Diamond, L.; Linz, J.J.; Lipset, S.M. (ed.). Democracy in developing countries. Vol. 2: Africa. Lynne Rienner, Boulder, CO, USA.

Coste, J. et al. (ed.). 1991. Échanges céréaliers et politiques agricoles dans le sous-espace ouest (Gambie, Guinée, Bissau, Mali, Mauritanie, Sénégal) : quelle dynamique régionale : rapport de Synthèse. Permanent Interstate Committee for Drought Control in the Sahel, Organisation for Economic Co-operation and Development, Paris, France.

Devarajan, S. et al. 1989. Markets under price controls in partial and general equilibrium. World Development, 17 (2), 1881–1893.

Diamond, L.; Linz, J.J.; Lipset, S.M. (ed.). 1988. Democracy in developing countries. Vol. 2: Africa. Lynne Rienner, Boulder, CO, USA.

Economist Intelligence Unit. 1988. Nigeria country report n° 1.

Egg, J.; Igué, J. 1993. Market driven integration in the eastern subregion: Nigeria's impact on its neighbours. Institut national de recherche agronomique/Institut de recherches et d'applications des méthodes de développement/Université nationale du Bénin, Paris, France. Synthesis report.

Essien, O.E. 1991. The implications of full European integration in 1992 for the Nigerian economy. Central Bank of Nigeria Economic and Financial Review, 29 (1), 35–49.

Falola, T. 1989. The Yoruba toll system: its operation and abolition. Journal of African History, 30, 69–88.

Gibbon, P. et al. 1992. A blighted harvest? The World Bank and African Agriculture in the 1980s. Unpublished manuscript.

Green, R.H. 1981. Magendo in the political economy of Uganda: pathology, parallel system or dominant sub-mode of production? Institute of Development Studies, University of Sussex, Sussex,England. Discussion paper 64.

——— 1989. Articulating stabilisation programmes and structural adjustment: Sub-Saharan Africa. In Commander, S. (ed.). Structural adjustment and agriculture: theory and practice in Africa and Latin America. Oversease Development Institute, London, UK.

Griffin, K.; Khan, A.R. 1992. Globalization and the developing world: an essay on the international dimensions of development in the post-Cold War era. United Nations Research Institute for Social Development, Geneva, Switzerland. Report 92.3.

Hodder, B.W. 1965. Traditional markets in Africa south of the Sahara. Transactions of the Institute of British Geographers, 36 (June), 97–105.

Hopkins, A.G. 1973. An economic history of West Africa. Longman, London, UK.

IGADD (Intergovernmental Authority on Drought and Development). 1989. Study of the potential for intra-regional trade in cereals in the IGADD region (final draft report, vol. 1). Oxford.

Igué, J.O. 1977. Le commerce de contrebande et les problèmes monétaires en Afrique occidentale. CEFAP, Université Nationale du Bénin, Cotonou, Bénin.

———— 1985. Rente pétrolière et commerce des produits agricoles à la périphérie du Nigéria : le cas du Bénin et du Niger. Institut national de recherche agronomique, Centre international des hautes études agronomiques méditerranéennes/Institut agronomique méditerranéen de Montpellier, Montpellier, France.

Igué, J.O.; Soulé, B. 1992. L'état-entrepôt au Bénin : commerce informel ou solution à la crise? Karthala, Paris, France.

IMF (International Monetary Fund). 1976. International statistics, 29 (12). IMF, Washington, DC, USA.

———— 1984. International statistics, 37 (2). IMF, Washington, DC, USA.

———— 1989. International statistics, 42 (1). IMF, Washington, DC, USA.

———— 1991. International statistics, 44 (6). IMF, Washington, DC, USA.

IMF (International Monetary Fund)/World Bank. 19??. Direction of trade, 3, 1961–65. IMF and World Bank, Washington, DC, USA.

———— 19??. Direction of trade, 8, 1968–72. IMF and World Bank, Washington, DC, USA.

Kasfir, N. 1984. State, magendo, and class formation in Uganda. In Kasfir, N. (ed.). State and class in Africa. Frank Cass, London, UK. Pp. 84–103.

Lambert, A. 1989. Espaces et réseaux marchands au Sénégal : les échanges céréaliers avec la Gambie et la Mauritanie. In Échanges régionaux, commerce frontalier et sécurité alimentaire en Afrique de l'Ouest. Institut national de recherche agronomique/Université nationale du Bénin/Institut de recherches et d'applications des méthodes de développement, Paris, France.

Leys, C. 1978. Capital accumulation, class formation and dependency: the significance of the Kenya case. In Miliband, R.; Saville, J. (ed.). The socialist register. Merlin Press, London, UK.

Lindauer, D.L. 1989. Parallel, fragmented or black: defining market structure in developing economies. World Development, 17 (12), 1871–1880.

MacGaffey, J. 1983. How to survive and become rich amidst devastation: the second economy in Zaire. African Affairs, 82, 351–366.

———— 1987. Entrepreneurs and parasites: the struggle for indigenous capitalism in Zaire. Cambridge University Press, Cambridge, UK.

———— 1988. Evading male control: women in the second economy in Zaire. In Stichter, S.; Parpart, J. (ed.). Patriarchy and class. Westview Press, Boulder, CO, USA.

Mafeje, A. 1991. The theory and ethnography of African social formations: the case of the interlacustrine kingdoms. Council for the Development of Economic and Social Research in Africa. Book series.

Mamdani, M. 1976. Politics and class formation in Uganda. Monthly Review Press, London, UK.

Martin, G. 1985. Regional integration in West Africa: the role of ECOWAS. Prepared for the Seminar on peace, development and regional security in Africa, January, Addis Ababa, Ethiopia. United Nations University.

May, E. 1985. Exchange controls and parallel market economies in Sub-Saharan Africa: focus on Ghana. World Bank, Washington, DC, USA. Staff working paper 711.

Meagher, K. 1991. Priced out of the market: the effect of market liberalization and parallel trade on smallholder incomes in northern Nigeria. MacNamara Fellowship Report.

———— 1993. Regional complementarities or policy disparities? Cross-border trade and food security among Nigeria and her Sahelian and coastal neighbours. Presented at the Conference on West African economic integration, Nigerian policy perspectives for the 1990s, 26–27 October. Nigerian Institute of International Affairs, Lagos, Nigeria.

Meagher, K.; Yunusa, M.B. 1993. Informalization and its discontents: coping with structural adjustment in the Nigerian urban informal sector. United Nations Research Institute for Social Development, Geneva, Switzerland.

Meillassoux, C. (ed.). 1971. The development of indigenous trade and markets in West Africa. Oxford University Press, London, UK.

Mustapha, A.R. 1990. From boom to bust? Structural adjustment and the cocoa industry in Nigeria. Presented at the Conference on crisis, adjustment and social change, Lagos. United Nations Research Institute for Social Development, Geneva, Switzerland.

Naudet, D. 1993. L'impact des échanges nigéro-nigérians sur les équilibres macro-économiques du Niger. In Egg, J. (ed.). L'économie agricole et alimentaire du Niger : vers une intégration au marché du Nigéria? Institut national de recherche agronomique/Université nationale du Bénin/Institut de recherches et d'applications des méthodes de développement, Paris, France.

Olukoshi, A.; Obi, C. 1993. The state of Nigeria's trade relations with its neighbours: issues and problems. Presented at the Conference on West African economic integration, Nigerian policy perspectives for the 1990s, 26–27 October. Nigerian Institute of International Affairs, Lagos, Nigeria.

Oyejide, T.A. 1990. The participation of developing countries in the Uruguay round, an African perspective. World Economy 13 (3).

Portes, A. et al. (ed.). 1989. The informal economy. John Hopkins University Press, Baltimore, MD, USA.

Puetz, D.; von Braun, J. 1990. Parallel markets for agriculture in a West African setting: origins and distributional effects. Journal of International Agricultural Literature, 29 (3), 216–235.

Russell, D. 1989. The struggle for the rice trade after "liberalization" in Zaire. Séminaire d'économie rurale des régions chaudes, Montpellier, France.

Schissel, H. 1989. Africa's underground economy. Africa Report, 34 (1), 43–46.

Singh, A. 1986. The IMF-World Bank policy programme in Africa: a commentary. In Lawrence, P. (ed.). World recesion and the food crisis in Africa. James Currey, London, UK.

Sow, F. 1991. Les initiatives féminines au Sénégal, une réponse à la crise. Presented at the Conference on État et société au Sénégal, crises et dynamiques sociales, 22–25 October, Bordeaux, France. Centre d'études d'Afrique noire and Institut fondamental d'Afrique noire–Cheikh Anta Diop, Bordeaux, France.

Thom, D.J. 1975. The Niger–Nigeria boundary 1890–1906: a study of ethnic frontiers and a colonial boundary. Center for International Studies, Ohio University, Athens, OH, USA. Papers in international studies: Africa series 23.

Weiss, L. 1987. Explaining the underground economy: state and social structure." Journal of British Sociology, 38 (2), 216–234.

West Africa. 1989a. 31 July to 6 August.

———— 1989b. 26 June to 2 July.

———— 1989c. 11–17 September.

———— 1989d. 4–10 September.

———— 1990. 31 July to 6 August.

World Bank. 1981. Accelerated development in Sub-Saharan Africa: an agenda for action. World Bank, Washington, DC, USA.

———— 1989. Sub-Saharan Africa: from crisis to sustainable growth. World Bank, Washington, DC, USA.

Wuyts, M. 1989. Money and planning for socialist transition. The Mozambican experience. Gower/ISS, UK.

CHAPTER 10

A REGIONAL STRATEGY FOR TRADE AND GROWTH IN WEST AFRICA[1]

– J. Dirck Stryker, Jeffrey C. Metzel and B. Lynn Salinger –

Although the stimulation of regional trade has been the primary objective of regional integration schemes in West Africa, there has been remarkably little strategic thinking on the need for export promotion. Stryker, Metzel, and Salinger help to rectify this gap by reviewing the many obstacles to the growth of exports in West Africa and the wide range of existing opportunities in different sectors and geographical settings. Export promotion is seen as the centrepiece of a growth strategy for West Africa. Although the policy reforms of the last decade have reduced many of the obstacles to export growth, the authors identify a number of areas requiring further policy reform and investment. The proposed strategy is not confined exclusively to regional markets. However the importance of regional markets is clearly visible in the authors' analysis of the agricultural and livestock sectors or of basic manufactures. Many of the measures proposed by the authors are of special importance for stimulating regional trade, including measures for the promotion of nontraditional exports, and negotiations for the reduction of intraregional trade barriers.

MOST COUNTRIES IN West Africa have experienced little or no economic growth over the past two decades. Although external factors have played a role in this poor performance, deliberate policy choices on the part of governments have severely handicapped growth by reducing incentives for producers to look outward and encouraging inefficient production for the domestic market. The limited size of domestic markets has constrained growth, in turn, by inhibiting competition and reducing the possibilities for exploitation of economies of scale. The result has

---

[1] This paper is adapted from a larger study by Associates for International Resources and Development (AIRD), funded by USAID (Stryker et al. 1994). The views and interpretations are those of the authors and should not be attributed to USAID.

been economic stagnation and continued impoverishment of a large part of the population.

Some of the worst of these policy distortions have recently been corrected, partly as a result of structural adjustment programs undertaken everywhere in the region, including liberalization measures adopted immediately after the devaluation of the CFA franc in January 1994 (Stryker et al. 1994, p. 11). Although much remains to be done, these reforms are opening up opportunities for renewed economic growth and the reduction of poverty. Some of this growth is likely to come from traditional exports, which have been penalized for many years by an unfavourable policy environment. However, there are important constraints on both the demand and supply of these exports. Sustained economic growth will have to rely increasingly on nontraditional exports, such as horticultural, marine, and other primary products, handicrafts, and manufactured goods.

Both traditional and nontraditional exports can be marketed overseas or in neighbouring countries. Although traditional exports to overseas markets are likely to decline in relative importance because of limitations on both demand and supply, the same does not hold for nontraditional exports, which have been growing quite rapidly for some African countries. These exports constitute only a small share of total foreign exchange earnings, but they are likely to become more important as this sector takes the lead in stimulating economic growth.

Although all countries can benefit from the expansion of nontraditional exports to overseas markets, this type of growth is likely to be concentrated, in the first instance, in countries such as Côte d'Ivoire, Ghana, Nigeria, and Senegal, which have a budding supply of trained labour, transportation and telecommunications infrastructure, contacts with overseas importers, and the institutional base required to support overseas trading operations. As their exports expand and per capita incomes increase, these countries will become growth poles, drawing imports from neighbouring West African countries, assuming the absence of major barriers to trade.

The next section of this chapter assesses some of the factors contributing to the poor performance of trade and growth in Africa. We then examine the potential for export growth in various sectors of economic activity, with particular attention to regional trade. Finally, we propose an action program for trade and growth in West Africa with attention to the possibilities for action in different regional settings.

TRADE AND ECONOMIC GROWTH
IN SUB-SAHARAN AFRICA

The colonial powers in Africa viewed their colonies primarily as a source of primary products to be exchanged for manufactured goods produced in Europe. Emphasis was on bulk commodities such as groundnuts, cotton, coffee, cocoa, sisal, rubber, oil palm, sugar, and various minerals. These were subject to little, if any, local processing. No effort was made to promote the production of food crops, and industrial enterprises were usually established only if this led to large savings in transportation costs.

With independence came a change of policy favouring accelerated industrialization through import-substitution. The initial result of this policy was rapid growth in the manufacturing sectors of many countries. In Sub-Saharan Africa, manufacturing value added measured in domestic prices grew by more than 8% per year during the 1960s. This was almost twice the rate of growth of GDP. By 1973, manufacturing accounted for 15% or more of GDP in 18 countries. Although consumer goods predominated, intermediate goods constituted 40% of total value added in the manufacturing sector by the end of the 1970s (World Bank 1989).

However, import competing industries remained heavily dependent on imports of intermediate goods, spare parts, and capital equipment. This made them highly vulnerable to shortages of foreign exchange. Further none, industrial growth was possible only because high trade barriers protected inefficient manufacturing firms from outside competition, raising domestic compared with world market prices. Had value added been measured in world rather than domestic prices, growth would have been much lower. Although growth continued for a time, the small size of most domestic markets meant that import substitution was ultimately self-limiting.

The pace of industrial growth slackened considerably during the 1970s and 1980s, despite heavy public investment in the industrial sector. By the mid-1980s, industry in Sub-Saharan Africa had fallen to only 10% of GDP — only slightly more than the 1965 level. The industrial sector in most countries was characterized by excess capacity, high costs of production, weak links with the rest of the economy, and lack of incentives to increase productivity (World Bank 1989).

Efforts to increase food production in Africa have also met with limited success. About one-quarter of the population of Sub-Saharan Africa subsists on less than 80% of its calorie needs. Severe food shortages, which were exceptional in the early 1960s, are now widespread. Overall, agricultural production in Africa has been rising by only about 2% per year, well below annual population growth, which is about 3.1%. Agricultural exports have declined, and food imports have increased at an annual rate of about 7% (World Bank 1989, pp. 72, 89).

There are numerous reasons for this state of affairs. Many irrigation projects, which absorbed a large share of total investment, have been disasters. Among the problems encountered have been low yields, poor water delivery, high capital and recurrent costs, inadequate maintenance and repair of irrigation systems and equipment, lack of motivation to grow a dry season crop, and siltation of dams and irrigation canals. Yet the heavy investment in irrigation and river-basin management has resulted in inordinate efforts to make these projects work at the expense of more effective activities to promote economic growth (Stryker et al. 1981).

Efforts to improve rain-fed cultivation in marginal areas have failed just as badly but have encouraged people to remain in these areas, damaging vegetation and soils, when a more effective policy would have been to induce emigration to more productive areas or to encourage diversification into new lines of endeavour that are less stressful to the environment. Projects in marginal areas have been expensive in relation to the benefits achieved, due to the absence of commercial activities to sustain recurrent costs, the riskiness associated with drought, the lack of viable technical packages, and the high cost of maintaining project personnel and administration in inaccessible areas.

The failure of efforts to promote food self-sufficiency is illustrated in the Sahel by the changes in the food self-sufficiency ratio (local production/total availability) from 1965–67 to 1986–88. In no Sahelian country did this ratio increase. In many, especially those for which rice imports are an important component of food supply, it fell markedly: from 83% to 47% in the Gambia, from 69% to 39% in Mauritania, from 80% to 58% in Senegal. In other countries that consume mostly coarse grains, the self-sufficiency ratio for total cereals fell much less, but that for rice declined to a similar degree (Stryker 1993, p. 2).

Greater success was achieved in cotton production in certain countries. In Burkina Faso, cotton lint production increased from 3000 tonnes in 1965 to 71 000 tonnes in 1990. Mali similarly increased production from 8500 tonnes in 1965 to 111 000 tonnes in 1990. This had a favorable impact on farm incomes, government revenues, and foreign exchange earnings. It also helped to increase cereals production by providing the capital and cash income that farmers required to purchase intermediate inputs such as fertilizers (Stryker 1993, pp. 2–3).

Despite gains such as these, the real value of Sub-Saharan Africa's agricultural exports declined substantially during the three decades following independence. Although some of this decline was due to falling terms of trade, Africa also lost over half its market share of world agricultural exports, suggesting that supply-side factors were more important than those on the demand side (Koester et al. 1990, p. 41). The decrease in market share was especially severe for cocoa and oilseeds. Detailed analyses of a number of country case studies suggest that export taxes, overvalued currencies, and low real producer prices were among the most important causes of this poor performance (Lele 1991).

POLICY REFORM AND OPPORTUNITIES FOR TRADE AND GROWTH IN WEST AFRICA

RECENT POLICY REFORM

This lacklustre economic performance has led a number of countries in Sub-Saharan Africa to undertake key policy reforms to adjust the structure of their economies over the past decade. A major goal of these reforms has been to reduce the bias against exports resulting from export taxation, trade protection for import-competing activities, and an overvalued domestic currency. Also important have been the freeing up of markets and the reduced relative importance of the public sector in the economy. The World Bank and IMF have had a major influence in defining the policy reforms undertaken by these countries. In addition to macroeconomic stabilization measures, these reforms have comprised some combination of:

- devaluation,
- movement toward a more flexible exchange rate,
- reduction or elimination of export taxes,
- easing or elimination of import controls,
- reduction in the magnitude and variability of import tariffs,
- privatization or reform of parastatals,
- elimination of price controls and restrictions on the involvement of the private sector in marketing activities, and
- reduction in public-sector employment.

Altogether, these reforms have altered the structure of incentives in favour of greater openness to international trade, while giving greater importance to the private compared with the public sector.

Whether these reforms have been successful in expanding exports and increasing economic growth is less clear, due to the clouding effect of other variables. Many of the countries undertaking major reform programs have also experienced a severe deterioration in their terms of trade. On the other hand, they have benefitted from debt relief and increased flows of foreign aid, which has helped to sustain investment at a time when public budgets have been severely reduced (World Bank and UNDP 1989, pp. 27–29).

CURRENT POLICY ENVIRONMENT FOR TRADE AND GROWTH

The current policy environment in most African countries is much more conducive to trade and growth than it was a few years ago. Exchange rates in most countries, now including those in the CFA franc zone, are close to their long-term equilibrium levels. Export taxes are lower or nonexistent, and marketing boards and stabilization funds have been replaced in some countries by liberalized export regimes. Quantitative restrictions on imports have been substantially reduced or eliminated in most countries, and some progress has been made in lowering the level and variability of import tariff rates. Price controls have also been reduced or eliminated.

Substantial impediments to trade remain, nevertheless. For example, franc zone countries have erected numerous barriers to free trade over the years to prevent these countries being flooded with imports due to the overvaluation of the CFA franc. Many of these barriers take the form of quantitative restrictions that are administrative rather than legislative in nature, and thus are often difficult to identify and eliminate. It is illuminating, in this respect, to consider the results of a recent survey of foreign companies operating in Africa that found greater concern for nontariff than for tariff barrier to trade (Blakey 1993, pp. 6–7).

Another impediment to trade is lack of adequate infrastructure to support export-oriented activity. After years of neglect, countries like Ghana and Guinea need to rebuild, expand, and modernize their roads, ports, airports, telecommunications equipment, and power-generating facilities. This is especially important for the export trade because of the need for quality control, timeliness, and flexibility in responding to overseas demand.

Investment in knowledge, technology, and marketing is also essential. The development of horticultural exports in Kenya depended on investment in research, training, and extension, yet too many countries have allowed their agricultural research and extension capabilities to deteriorate. Nural Islam (1990), who describes how horticultural exports have served as a natural bridge for the development of nontraditional export capacity in manufactured goods, highlights the importance of market information, quality control, processing and storage facilities, and agricultural research. Countries such as Mauritius, that have been successful in exporting manufactured goods, have had to acquire knowledge of foreign market opportunities, develop linkages with foreign partners, pay close attention to quality control, and develop a pool of competitively-priced semiskilled labour. Foreign firms can play an important catalytic role in this, by providing access to world markets, capacity to package exports, and technical, marketing, and management know-how (World Bank and USAID 1991).

Attention should also be paid to "institutional" matters such as the ease or difficulty of complying with administrative procedures, access to credit, mechanisms for contract enforcement, access to information about export markets, factors affecting the timing of purchases and deliveries, and mechanisms for quality control. Inadequacies at these levels often result from deficiencies in the public sector and how it interacts with private economic agents: although excessive regulation can be blamed for inhibiting the reallocation of resources necessary to adjust the economy in a more outward-oriented direction, there is also a dearth of appropriate public or quasi-public institutions to help overcome market deficiencies and promote export growth. Examples of the kinds of support institutions that are required might include organizations to assist potential exporters in exploring overseas markets or mechanisms for pooling risk in order to facilitate access to credit by exporters with little history of formal banking relations.

Many of the major constraints on trade and growth are specific to various sectors of the economy. The following outlines some of the more important of these constraints in the context of likely opportunities for increased exports in the region.

Agriculture and livestock

Recent research on regional economic integration in agriculture in West Africa has identified clear areas of economic potential for increased trade on regional markets (Salinger and Stryker 1994). In an undistorted policy environment, for example, rice and coarse grain cereals would flow from upper Guinea and the middle and upper Senegal River Valley into eastern Mali and Mauritania and from southern Mali into northern Côte d'Ivoire. Malian groundnut production would flow to Senegal for processing. Economic analysis also suggests a strong comparative advantage for Sahelian livestock production in competition with world markets for meat exports to coastal West Africa. (Metzel and Cook 1994).

Substantial excess demand for vegetable oils and meat already exists that the Sahelian countries should be able to supply profitably in competition with imports, now that the CFA franc has been devalued. Should growth in the coastal markets be restored to levels that existed during the 1960s, and to a lesser extent the 1970s, there would be a substantial increase in demand for coarse grain cereals, vegetable oils, cotton, and meat and other livestock products. These are products in which the Sahelian countries will have an increasing comparative advantage as the coastal countries specialize in tree crops, forest and marine products, and manufactured goods. There is also excess demand for rice, but the ability to compete with imports in the coastal markets is restricted to nearby producing regions because of the low world price of rice and the high cost of transportation within the region.

Unfortunately, the actual structure of production and trade within the region does not follow this pattern of comparative advantage. Uncoordinated trade, exchange rate, and agricultural pricing policies have accumulated to create a distorted incentive structure that has encouraged the inefficient allocation of productive resources and wasteful activities such as smuggling and other forms of rent-seeking behaviour.

The most important of these distortions, the overvaluation of the CFA franc, has now been removed. However, this leaves behind numerous other policy distortions. Within the agricultural sector, these include quantitative restrictions on food imports, wide variation in producer prices between countries, high rates of effective import taxation, various forms of subsidy, and a host of other measures. For example, prices paid to cocoa, cotton, and groundnut producers vary markedly between countries, giving rise to intraregional flows in spite of official bans on such trade. Policy with regard to the pricing and importation of rice also varies a great deal between countries (Salinger and Stryker 1994, pp. 22–24).

Policy distortions in the livestock sector consist of taxes on exports and imports of livestock products, a combination of minor subsidies on productive inputs, and taxation of livestock marketing. Taxes on transport and marketing have the most important impact on livestock-sector costs, some of this "tax" taking the form of illegal extortion to obtain right-of-way for live animals being transported within West Africa. Due to its links with other French-speaking countries, Côte d'Ivoire has been willing to allow relatively unrestricted import of livestock products from within West Africa, while Ghana and Nigeria have shown much less interest in promoting intraregional trade. The current health quarantine policy for live animals being imported into Ghana effectively prohibits official trade. These restrictions have not caused much tension until recently because the overvaluation of the CFA franc rendered imports from the Sahelian countries unprofitable, but the restrictions assume greater importance following the January 1994 devaluation (Metzel and Cook 1994, p. vi).

The distortions that inhibit trade between West African countries and protect domestic production also result in a substantial bias against exports to markets outside the region. Yet such exports hold considerable potential. Studies recently completed or currently under way indicate the degree to which some West African countries have a comparative advantage in exporting agricultural and livestock products outside the region. For example, Ghana has a comparative advantage in the overseas export of pineapples, mangoes, yams, and frozen seafood (Stryker and Shaw 1994); the World Bank is studying the potential for horticultural exports in Mali, Niger, and Senegal; and Côte d'Ivoire and Guinea have demonstrated their comparative advantage in the export of pineapples, bananas, and other tropical fruits.

The traditional agricultural tree crop exports from West Africa — cocoa, coffee, rubber, oil, and coconut palm — also have potential for steady growth in the long run, although low world market prices combined with stagnation of production of these crops within the region have frustrated efforts to increase export growth. The weakness of world markets has been due to the rapid growth of production among West Africa's competitors in South Asia (especially Malaysia and Indonesia) and Latin America (especially Brazil), where concerted plantings in the last decade before prices fell, as well as substantial advances in productivity, have assured surpluses on world markets through most of the 1990s. In contrast, ill-conceived parastatal marketing boards, heavy taxation of exports, and weak research structures in coastal West African economies through most of the 1980s stifled producer initiatives and resulted in an aging tree stock for most of these crops with few new plantings to replace it. In the long run, however, steady growth in world demand for these commodities will catch up with the South Asian expansions of the 1980s, while rising incomes and pressure on resources will reduce comparative advantage and incentives to produce in Asia. In this context, Africa should begin now to lay the groundwork for rebuilding its share of these traditional markets. This should include reducing marketing inefficiencies to allow a greater share of world prices to be passed through to producers, and introducing new advances in production technologies to producers.

Industry

West Africa has a long tradition of industrial activity. The historical literature for the region cites numerous examples of artisanal and medium-scale manufacturing and agroindustrial processing, including milling, edible oil extraction and refining, brewing, tanning, soap-making, metallurgy, furniture construction, cotton spinning and weaving, and the production or assembly of such goods as matches, pots and pans, clothing, agricultural machinery, and personal vehicles. In some countries, such as Nigeria, Côte d'Ivoire, Senegal, and Ghana, these activities predate the era of import-substituting industrialization (1960s and 1970s), and in some instances the colonial era.

Many activities that were initiated during the colonial period were designed to satisfy demand in the broader colonial market, and the financial viability of these activities was undermined by the parceling of markets after independence. For example, many of the industrial investments made by France in Senegal in the 1950s were rendered uncompetitive by the dismantling of the colonial customs union, Afrique Occidentale Française, which drastically narrowed the scope of the "domestic" market for Senegalese industrial output (Horton 1976).

In other countries, such as Mali, Burkina Faso, and Niger, "modern industry" was almost nonexistent before independence (Shepherd 1975), following which the governments of those countries established medium- and large-scale public enterprises in the 1960s and early 1970s. These enterprises were primarily engaged in processing locally produced commodities for domestic consumption (cigarettes, canned tomatoes and fruit, matches), but some export capacity was also developed (textiles, groundnut oil, leather). Other activities initiated during the 1960s and 70s in West Africa focused on the processing of imported semi-finished products. In Côte d'Ivoire, industries processing imported semi-finished goods grew at a much faster rate than industries using mainly local raw materials until the early 1970s; these trends were then reversed as import-substitution industries began to exhaust the small domestic market (den Tuinder 1978, p. 227).

Growth of industry in West Africa was thus based on a combination of resource-based industrialization and import substitution. Resource-based industrialization sought to build on a country's comparative advantage in the export of primary products — mining, agriculture, forestry, and tourism — by intensifying, expanding or diversifying those activities. Import-substitution was fostered primarily via tariff protection, which allowed domestic industries to compete against relatively more efficient external sources. There has been very little outward-looking industrial activity to date, i.e., manufacturing for the world market, although entrepreneurial pockets along these lines are beginning to form.[2]

As elsewhere in the world, the resulting policy mix was often costly. Levels of protection were high and uneven and set without concern for any particular long-term strategic imperative. There was little awareness of the negative impact of this protection on other sectors of activity. This is confirmed by a series of recent and ongoing studies of incentive structures and comparative advantage in francophone Africa, which is being supported by CODESRIA's Réseau sur les Politiques Industrielles. Studies of West African countries such as Senegal (Fall et al. 1993), Burkina Faso (Kaboré and Kouanda 1993), Mali (Coulibaly 1993), Niger (Abdo Hassan et al. 1993), Togo (Baninganti and Lawson-Body 1993), and Côte d'Ivoire (Bouabré and Kouassy 1992) show effective rates of protection ranging from negative to infinity, with prices for domestic value added often two or three times the corresponding world market values. Many industries produce negative international value added, which is to say that the cost of imported inputs exceeds what it would cost to import the final product. Aside from imposing substantial costs on consumers, such industries usually have few prospects for becoming competitive, and little potential for increasing productivity over time within the confines of narrow, uncompetitive domestic markets.

The economic profitability or comparative advantage of industrial production is traditionally a function of resource availability, productivity, and the economic costs of production. However, global economic interdependence has made some international industries indifferent to certain types of resource availability. For example, the international

---

[2] The classification used here is borrowed from Roemer (1993), who distinguishes three alternative strategies of industrialization: resource-based industrialization, import substitution, and outward-looking industrialization.

garment industry is less concerned today with the existence of a domestic cotton industry than it is with the ease of exporting from a particular base, the existence of quotas in consumer markets for a particular country's exports, the relative cost of labour, and the flexibility of a country's labour codes. The combination of relatively inexpensive labour in Ghana, Zimbabwe, and Kenya — even relative to Mauritius — and West Africa's relative proximity to European and American markets suggests that this region may become increasingly attractive to garment manufacturers. To the extent that devaluation of the CFA franc is successful in bringing down the relative cost of labour in Côte d'Ivoire and Senegal, these countries, with their reasonably modern infrastructure, may begin to elicit renewed interest from international investors. However, according to Van Leeuwen (1994), excessive regulation of port and transport facilities, rigid labour codes, and persistent constraints in the banking sector continue to plague industrial expansion in West Africa.

The experience of manufacturers in Ghana, one of the "early adjusters" in Sub-Saharan Africa, is instructive (World Bank 1990). After a decade of decline, industrial production has revived, thanks partly to improved access to imported inputs. Established, medium to large-scale import-competing firms that have lost their protected, often monopolistic market niche have had to adjust to shifts in relative prices to survive through increased capacity utilization, improved quality, and changes in product lines. Manufacturers of wood-based products, processed foods, beer, and worked metal, many of whom had relatively up-to-date technology and adequate economies of scale, seem to have survived the transition through the Economic Recovery Program, manufacturing not only for the domestic but also for regional markets. On the other hand, enterprises with no real comparative advantage (e.g., electric light bulb assembly) have had difficulty competing with imports. Small-scale enterprises are emerging as important industrial actors, contributing one-quarter of Ghana's manufacturing value added and providing employment for an estimated 85% of the sector. This subsector comprises everything from artisanal, subsistence-oriented producers to modern sector enterprises. Among the more dynamic elements of this subsector are manufacturers of low-cost domestic alternatives to more expensive imports (knives made from used band saw blades; low-quality pottery and kitchen utensils; locally mixed paints produced using ground, local oyster shells as a base; simple agricultural tools; low-cost appliances such as freezers and water coolers). More recent analysis in Mali suggests that a wider range of products can be produced competitively there as well, from soap and animal feed to milk, agro-chemicals, shoes, medicines, bicycles and mopeds, and roofing materials (Coulibaly 1993).

Substantial growth potential also exists in the mining sector, given the existence of valuable deposits of gold, diamonds, iron, phosphates, zinc, and magnesium, and the prospects that world markets for these minerals will continue to expand at a steady rate. Moreover, this oppor-tunity is spread among most of the countries of the region, although Ghana, Guinea, Liberia, and Mali share the most attractive and diverse mineral resources. Burkina Faso, Niger, and Côte d'Ivoire also have sub-stantial but unexploited mineral reserves. The World Bank has called for a substantial increase in exploration in West Africa to better capture this potential. There is also a need for large investments in capital-intensive technology. Investment codes for mining need to be rewritten to provide adequate incentives to attract the necessary investments to develop these resources. The exploitation of opportunities in the mining sector could yield important dividends in terms of foreign exchange earnings and tax revenues even extractive industries do not typically create substantial linkages to other segments of the regional economy.[3]

ACTION PROGRAM

The examples of obstacles to trade cited earlier are merely illustrative and do not begin to exhaust the actual distortions and other barriers that are impeding trade and growth in West Africa. These can only be fully iden-tified through case-by-case study of the sectors and countries involved. The outline of an action program for the expansion of nontraditional exports in West Africa can, nonetheless, be established.

STRATEGIC ORIENTATIONS

What follows is based on the premise that African nations can derive important benefits from expanded international trade. The evidence con-tinues to mount from other parts of the world, as well as from a few African countries, that economic growth is closely interlinked with for-eign trade (see references cited by Badiane, this volume). Aside from the usual economic arguments associated with efficiency of resource alloca-tion due to the exploitation of comparative advantage and economies of

---

[3] Mineral processing industries do create these links, but do not generally appear very profitable for the region.

scale, there are a number of other ways in which trade is seen to contribute to economic growth. These include using trade and associated
investment as a conduit for technology transfer, increasing the efficiency
of enterprises forced to compete on foreign markets, expanding the commercial and managerial competence of entrepreneurs, augmenting the
skills of the work force, creating a market for labour in the face of growing population pressure, increasing foreign exchange earnings that can be
used to import capital equipment, and a host of other factors.

Assuming that trade is desirable, do the benefits from trade accrue
equally regardless of whether exports, especially nontraditional exports,
are directed at overseas markets or to neighbouring countries? Overseas
markets present several advantages: their demand for nontraditional
exports from Africa is relatively elastic, their contribution to the transfer
of technology and managerial know-how is potentially great, and the
range of goods that may be exported is virtually infinite. On the other
hand, transportation costs can be considerable, standards of quality and
timeliness of delivery are high, and contracts may be difficult for African
exporters to enforce. There is thus an argument for trying to penetrate
regional markets first, before attacking overseas markets, even though
regional markets may offer fewer opportunities for growth in the longer
run.

There are many opportunities for expanded regional as well as overseas trade in the products of agriculture, livestock, fishing, and industry.
For some countries, especially the landlocked countries of the interior,
regional trade is the major avenue for escaping the limited size of the
domestic market. Their comparative advantage in livestock, cereals, and
other primary products can play a key role in allowing them to benefit
from the growth of coastal markets. There is also substantial potential for
regional trade in processed foods and other agricultural and livestock
products, as well as a broader range of manufactured goods. Even within
the same industry there may be opportunities for the exchange of goods
satisfying various standards of quality and taste.

There are dangers in excessive reliance on the regional market, however, especially if this implies high levels of preferential tariff protection.
First are the classic arguments: 1) that trade preferences are likely to
result in trade diversion to a much greater extent than trade creation and
2) there is limited potential for economies of scale (de Melo and Panagariya 1992). Beyond this, there is evidence that intraregional trade in
nontraditional exports tends to be a secondary activity undertaken by
larger firms originally established to supply highly protected domestic

markets, whereas firms that export overseas tend to be established specifically for that purpose. This ensures that they are reasonably efficient and competitive. Finally, much of the effort to promote intraregional trade has focused on the direct allocation of investment to exploit economies of scale, while fostering economic complementarity. This effort has generally been a failure because most countries want to produce as wide a range of products as they can. It also ignores the difficulty of picking the winners in advance and the possibilities for countries to export similar products to each other on an intra-industry in response to consumer demand for product variety.

Assuming that the basic economic reforms necessary for export-led economic growth have been undertaken in most West African countries, one must ask what the export base is likely to resemble. Some export growth can occur through the expansion of traditional primary product exports to overseas markets, as African nations recapture some of the market shares that they have lost over the past 20 years. However, most of the expansion of exports will have to occur through the growth of nontraditional exports and intraregional trade based on the principle of comparative advantage. Although it is impossible to predict with complete accuracy the comparative advantage of each country in each specific product, it is possible to describe the general conditions that are likely to contribute to that advantage in different areas and the problems impeding the exploitation of that advantage.

ARID, SEMI-ARID, AND SUBHUMID REGIONS

The major area of comparative advantage in the arid, semi-arid, and subhumid regions of West Africa is in livestock production, both for the regional market and possibly also for export overseas. The regional market is already growing, and this growth can be expected to accelerate as a function of economic growth along the coast. As truck transportation has replaced trekking to coastal markets, the comparative advantage of the interior countries has increased in competition with imports.

Although there are limits to the capacity of the arid and semi-arid regions of West Africa to expand ruminant production based on use of pasture and crop residues alone, these limits have not yet been reached except in years of extreme drought. Economic analysis suggests that more intensive schemes involving fattening on crop by-products, feed grains, and cultivated forage are also profitable, and there is considerable potential for closer links between agriculture and livestock production. There is also some possibility of exporting red meat beyond the traditional coastal markets. This will require lowering the cost of air transport to more distant markets, increasing the value of the product sold, and meeting health and sanitation restrictions in world markets (Metzel and Cook 1994, p. v).

Many of the existing constraints to livestock production and marketing can feasibly be dealt with. Some of the measures which might be considered include the following:

- development of a common trade policy throughout the region to counter the dumping of livestock products on the world market by the European Union and other international exporters;

- measures to reduce taxes on the trade of livestock, simplify administrative procedures, and discourage the illegal collection of fees by public officials;

- development of market infrastructure to accommodate the special needs of trucked animals;

- elimination of policies that slow trucking transit times;

- identification of ways to promote the better use of railways as a competitive transportation alternative;

- support for research on the intensification of animal production, through optimal use of crop by-products and other feeds, cost-effective control of trypanosomiasis, and management options to address labour and land conflicts between livestock and agriculture;

- investigation of opportunities in overseas markets and exploitation of those opportunities through measures to supply and promote products of appropriate quality in these markets; this should create opportunities for new value-added activities, including the canning, drying, and freezing of meat and the manufacture of milk derivatives.

The arid and semi-arid regions of West Africa are also particularly suitable for growing horticultural crops under irrigated conditions. For years, Senegal has produced a variety of fruits and vegetables for domestic use and export to the European market; Mali and Burkina Faso have had some success in exporting horticultural products; and Niger has found a market for its onions as far away as Abidjan. With the devaluation of the CFA franc, exports of these and similar products should become much more profitable. The major constraints include the need for localized research on these crops and problems of quality control, packaging, storage, transportation, and timing of delivery.

The subhumid and semi-arid zones have a strong comparative advantage in a wide range of annual crops, such as sorghum, maize, cotton, groundnuts, and cowpeas. Notable successes have been achieved over the past few decades in increasing production of maize, cotton, and cowpeas. This is also the area of greatest potential for integrating livestock with agriculture. Unlike the semi-arid zone of West Africa, which is densely populated in relation to the resource base, the subhumid zone's population density is generally low. As diseases such as river blindness are overcome, this zone is increasingly able to act as a safety valve for excess population elsewhere. Constraints impeding its fuller development include the numerous trade barriers imposed in compensation for the overvaluation of the CFA franc, the lack of infrastructure (e.g., roads, schools, health facilities), the continued prevalence of trypanosomiasis, inadequate marketing networks for agricultural products and inputs, and poorly developed financial institutions to promote savings and investment.

HUMID REGIONS

The humid regions of West Africa have rich potential for growing and exporting a range of cash crops, including coffee, cocoa, rubber, oil palm, bananas, pineapples, and other tropical fruit. Some room for expansion still exists for timber production as well, although these possibilities are rapidly being exhausted. Marine products constitute another important area in which the coastal countries have a comparative advantage. The major constraint in the humid regions is the increasing shortage of good land to support there cash crops, as a result of their past expansion and increasing demographic pressure on the land. Limited demand on world markets is also an important constraint for cocoa and, to a lesser extent, for coffee.

The agricultural potential of humid regions could also be tapped of nearby urban markets. One of the most important opportunities is in rice production. In the past, the CFA countries have found it difficult to produce rice profitably in competition with imports because of the overvalued CFA franc. Following the devaluation, production areas located sufficiently close to urban markets should now be able to compete. Other agricultural products for which the humid regions have a comparative advantage in nearby urban markets are poultry, pig meat, dairy products, roots and tubers, and fruits and vegetables. Major constraints include marketing, storage, plant disease control, and animal health.

URBAN AND INDUSTRIAL CENTRES

Although population densities in West Africa are relatively low, demographic growth rates are among the highest in the world. Urban areas have grown rapidly, as migrants from rural areas have flooded into the cities, driven by overpopulation in rural areas in relation to the natural resource base under current farming practices. This urban migration has created a large unemployed or underemployed work force willing to work at relatively low wages in whatever alternative opportunities may exist.[4] A significant proportion of this labour force is literate, consisting of school graduates who have been unable to find work and former civil servants displaced as a result of structural adjustment. This work force provides an attractive basis for establishing low-cost, labour-intensive production of manufactured goods able to compete in global export markets.

Industrial-export competitiveness is likely to develop over time in centres capable of providing the required range of labour services at competitive cost, along with the infrastructure, utilities, and commercial and financial services required for export operations to succeed. Policies designed to increase the free flow of labour and capital in the region would make it easier to mobilize the necessary resources in one place, and help raise the competitiveness of the region as a whole. Coastal countries such as Côte d'Ivoire, Ghana, Nigeria, and Senegal are fortunate in having industrial centres upon which to build up their manufacturing sectors. These centres possess the infrastructure (ports, roads, railways, telecommunications), public utilities (electricity and water), and financial and commercial services that can serve as a basis for further growth.

Numerous problems stand in the way of such growth, however. Most industrial-sector enterprises in West Africa are relatively capital-intensive and highly dependent on imported equipment and intermediate inputs, the prices of which have risen steeply as a result of currency devaluations throughout the region. These firms have been strongly protected and oriented toward the domestic market, and a major effort will be required to refocus these firms toward export opportunities in Africa and overseas. Weaning industry from over-dependence on import protection will require further reductions in protectionist measures, and the

---

[4] The effects of land scarcity on the labour market have been observed in many countries. Taking an example from another part of Africa, people who have customarily been involved in the highly labour-intensive cultivation of rice in the highlands of Madagascar are said by employers to be among the best industrial workers in the world. The same is often said of the Burkinabè or the Bamileke in Cameroon.

establishment of incentives to aid nontraditional exporters through duty-free admission of imported equipment and intermediate inputs, tax incentives linked to export performance, and assured access to credit.

Basic infrastructure in the sub-region is presently inadequate for supporting an expanding industrial export sector, especially in the non-CFA countries. Telecommunication systems are inadequate, port facilities need to be improved, roads are in poor condition, electrical power failures are frequent, and water supplies are often unsatisfactory. Shipment of exports is problematic because of insufficient air and sea freight capacity and the high cost of freight resulting from low volumes and monopoly pricing.

Institutional constraints also impede manufactured exports. Administrative procedures are often cumbersome and subject to abuse and need to be simplified. They need to be subjected to thorough scrutiny and private-sector lobbying to elicit the required public-sector response. Access to both pre- and post-shipment working capital must be improved, along with access to capital for fixed investments, especially for smaller firms. Contacts with overseas markets and importers should be facilitated, and legal systems for contract enforcement and loan recovery need to be strengthened.[5]

COMPONENTS OF AN ACTION PROGRAM

A viable action program for the promotion of exports in West Africa should include a number of components. Some are already in place in some countries. Others may be financed by the donor community. Each is essential for the revitalization of trade and economic growth.

Import liberalization and tariff reduction

A vital element for raising export competitiveness and increasing the volume of trade is a reduction in the protection offered to import-competing sectors of the economy. This calls for the reduction or elimination of quantitative restrictions on imports, lower import tariffs, and some harmonization of the tariff structure. Exchange controls should likewise be either abandoned or substantially liberalized.

---

[5] AIRD has quantified the importance of a number of these institutional constraints in its study of the costs and benefits of eliminating institutional constraints on the expansion of non-traditional exports. See Stryker et al. 1994.

Producer prices of traditional exports

While the CFA franc was overvalued, it was extremely difficult for CFA countries to tax traditional exports while also paying producers an adequate price. Producer prices have even had to be subsidized in some years, when world prices were particularly low. The devaluation of the CFA franc has allowed governments to raise producer prices as well as taxes on these exports. It is urgent that governments raise producer prices sufficiently to recapture some of the shares lost on world markets.

Nontraditional export promotion projects

Nontraditional export promotion projects have been developed in a number of reforming countries, such as Ghana and Guinea in West Africa. These projects usually involve:

- simplification of export procedures;
- elimination of export taxes;
- freer access to foreign exchange controls for exporters;
- technical assistance to exporting firms;
- mechanisms and institutions for the financing of trade;
- promotion of contacts between exporters and overseas importers;
- improved facilities for the storage and transport of exported products;
- mechanisms for duty-free importation of equipment and intermediate products by exporting firms; and
- export incentives.

Reduction of barriers to intraregional trade

Barriers to trade between West African countries remain very high, impeding the spread of growth from the coast to the interior, and sharply reducing the potential for intra-regional trade. Reducing these barriers requires that they be thoroughly catalogued and subjected to a process of policy dialogue and reform. This requires that studies be undertaken and communicated to policymakers, business interests, professionals, and the public at large. This should followed by negotiations between the various interested parties, including representatives of neighbouring countries, and policy action to reduce or eliminate the barriers so identified.

This will often require negotiations between countries on a bilateral or multilateral basis. Although more comprehensive in formal terms, multilateral trade agreements in Africa have been relatively unsuccessful in actual practice. This suggests the need for greater recourse to bilateral negotiations between major actual or potential trading partners, such as those currently being undertaken in West Africa in conjunction with the Livestock Action Plan financed by USAID. These negotiations might be based on the concepts of reciprocity and most-favoured-nation status that were the forerunner to GATT in the industrial world. This approach has two components: concessions would first be negotiated bilaterally on a reciprocal basis by the parties most concerned with a particular set of trade barriers; then, these concessions would be extended unilaterally to third countries less affected by the concessions.

Agricultural research

As the pattern of demand for exports changes, there will be an urgent need for agricultural research on products where demand is growing most rapidly, such as horticultural crops, livestock and dairy products, and marine products. The virtually total absence of research on horticulture, including research on postharvest and preharvest technology, is particularly remarkable at the present time.

Infrastructure in support of exports

Adequate infrastructure is critical for the expansion of nontraditional exports and must be reinforced on a priority basis wherever there are major gaps in the areas of transportation and communications, power generation, and water delivery.

Training

Although the level of skills required in labour-intensive export industries is not high, there is a need to educate and train high- and middle-level managers and supervisors, as well as the technicians necessary to keep industrial machinery and other equipment running and to assure adequate quality control. This training should be provided in close coordination with professionals in each subsector to ensure maximum relevance to their needs.

Building support for policy reform

Policy reform ideally requires that a constituency of professional, business and public support be built up for such measures. However, over the past decade, many of the trade and exchange rate policy reforms instituted in Africa have been the object of relatively closed discussions between donors and host-country governments. Often these reforms have been imposed as conditions for the receipt of foreign aid. Despite the importance of these reforms, the atmosphere in which they have been undertaken has not tended to engender widespread public support. The reforms have nonetheless been tolerated as possible solutions to falling standards of living in severely distorted economies.

It is unclear whether this approach will continue to succeed after the worst cases of economic malaise have been attended to. Although the need for further reform is widely evident, there are signs that reforms are becoming increasingly difficult to implement under the combined influence of special interests, public resistance, and bureaucratic inertia. In the absence of strong public pressure to pursue the reform process, governments may be content to muddle along and avoid alienating important constituencies. The result would be continued economic stagnation.

What is needed to accelerate trade and growth in Africa is for Africans themselves to engage in problem identification, research, and analysis, while working to reduce or eliminate the problems so identified through public disclosure, creation of public pressure, and dialogue among competing interest groups, to arrive at decisions for policy reform. This process is beginning in some countries, especially where there has been a move toward democratization and public discussion of major economic issues.

CONCLUSION

This review of export growth potential in West Africa has identified numerous areas of opportunity in various subsectors of agriculture and industry. These opportunities have previously been masked by policies undermining profitability for producers and entrepreneurs who might have exploited them. However, most West African countries have now emerged from a decade of policy reform intended to liberate markets and improve the structure of incentives for production, consumption, and trade. The resulting economic climate places West Africa in a position to realize substantial growth in sectors of traditional comparative advantage, while exploring new areas whose attractiveness has been enhanced by changes in world markets and changes in Africa itself, including a rapidly growing work force and a more highly developed economic infrastructure.

An action program to stimulate exports in West Africa should include a number of policy components:

- import liberalization;

- increased producer prices for traditional exports;

- the promotion of nontraditional exports;

- reduced barriers to intraregional trade;

- agricultural research;

- improved infrastructure in support of trade;

- specialized training programs; and

- the promotion of professional and public support for policy reform.

REFERENCES

Abdo Hassan, M.; Lama, J.; Woba, A. Analyse des politiques de protection et d'incitation industrielles au Niger (research report). Réseau sur les politiques industrielles, Council for the Development of Economic and Social Research in Africa, Dakar, Senegal, and Faculté des sciences économiques et juridiques, Université Abdou Moumouni, Niamey, Niger, November.

Baninganti, K.; Lawson-Body, K. 1993. La politique industrielle et le système de protection et d'incitation de l'industrie manufacturière au Togo (temporary final research report). Réseau sur les politiques industrielles, Council for the Development of Economic and Social Research in Africa, Dakar, Senegal, and Faculté des sciences économiques et de gestion, Université du Bénin, Lomé, Togo.

Blakey, M.G. 1993. Economic integration in Sub-Saharan Africa: the implications for direct private investment. Presented at the International conference on regional integration in West Africa, 11–15 January, Dakar. Economic Commission for Africa, Addis Ababa, Ethiopia. Document E/ECA/CM.17/2.

Bouabré, B.; Kouassi, O. 1992. La performance des entreprises industrielles en Côte d'Ivoire : analyse des impacts des incitations le long des filières agro-industrielles. Council for the Development of Economic and Social Research in Africa, Dakar, Senegal, and Faculté des sciences économiques, Université Nationale de Côte d'Ivoire, Abidjan, Côte d'Ivoire.

Coulibaly, M. 1993. L'efficacité des incitations à l'industrie au Mali (research report). Réseau sur les politiques industrielles, Council for the Development of Economic and Social Research in Africa, Dakar, Senegal, and École nationale d'administration, Bamako, Mali.

de Melo, J.; Panagariya, A. 1992. The new regionalism in trade policy. World Bank and Centre for Economic Policy Research, Washington, DC, USA.

den Tuinder, B.A. 1978. Ivory Coast: the challenge of success. Johns Hopkins University Press, Baltimore, MD, USA.

Fall, B.; Lom, A.D.; Touré, A.C.; El Bachir Wade, M. 1993. Système de protection et d'incitations industrielles sous la Nouvelle politique industrielle du Sénégal (research report). Réseau sur les politiques industrielles, Council for the Development of Economic and Social Research in Africa, and Ministère de l'Économie des Finances et du Plan, Dakar, Senegal.

Horton, B. 1976. Incentives and resource costs in Senegalese industry. Western Africa Regional Project, World Bank, Washington, DC, USA.

Islam, N. 1990. Horticultural exports of developing countries: past performances, future prospects, and policy issues. International Food Policy Research Institute, Washington, DC, USA. Research report 80.

Kaboré, F.; Kouanda, M. 1993. Evaluation des politiques de protection et d'incitation de l'industrie manufacturière au Burkina Faso (intermediate report). Réseau sur les politiques industrielles, Council for the Development of Economic and Social Research in Africa, Dakar, Senegal and Université de Ouagadougou, Ouagadougou, Burkina Faso.

Koester, U.; Schafe, H.; Valdes, A. 1990. Demand-side constraints and structural adjustment in Sub-Saharan African countries. International Food Policy Research Institute, Washington, DC, USA.

Lele, U. 1991. Aid to African agriculture: lessons from two decades of donors' experience. Johns Hopkins University Press, Baltimore, MD, USA.

Metzel, J.; Cook, A. 1994. Economic comparative advantage and incentives in livestock production and trade in West Africa's central corridor. Associates for International Resources and Development, Cambridge, MA, USA.

Roemer, M. 1993. Strategies for industrialization: lessons for the Gambia. Harvard Institute for International Development, Cambridge, MA, USA. CAER discussion paper 16.

Salinger, L.; Stryker, D. 1994. Regional economic integration in West Africa: potential for agricultural trade as an engine of growth in the western subregion. Harvard Institute for International Development, Cambridge , MA, USA. CAER discussion paper 21.

Shepherd, G. 1975. Incentives and industrial performance in Mali. Western Africa Regional Project, World Bank, Washington, DC, USA.

Stryker, J.D. 1993. Economic growth and food security in the Sahel: the role of economic integration. Associates for International Resources and Development, Cambridge, MA, USA.

Stryker, J.D. et al. 1981. Investments in large scale infrastructure: irrigation and river management in the Sahel. Fletcher School of Law and Diplomacy, Tufts University, and Food Research Institute, Stanford University.

Stryker, J.D.; Salinger, B.L.; Metzel, J.C. 1994. A regional strategy for trade and growth in West Africa: sectoral analyses and action plan. Associates for International Resources and Development, Cambridge, MA, USA.

Stryker, J.D.; Shaw, C.L. 1994. Costs and benefits of eliminating institutional constraints on the expansion of nontraditional exports. Associates for International Resources and Development, Cambridge, MA, USA.

Van Leeuwen, J.H. 1994. L'Afrique peut être compétitive! Une étude de cas sur la compétivité de fabrication des vêtements dans cinq pays sub-sahariens : Zimbabwe, Kenya, Sénégal, Côte d'Ivoire, Ghana. Presented at the seminar, Le Sénégal peut s'en sortir : les voies de la relance économique, organized by the

Confédération nationale des employeurs du Sénégal, Dakar, 20–21 January. World Bank, Washington, DC, USA.

World Bank. 1989. Sub-Saharan Africa: from crisis to sustainable growth. A long-term perspective study. World Bank, Washington, DC, USA.

———— 1990. Ghana: towards a dynamic investment response. World Bank, Washington, DC, USA. Report 8911-GH.

World Bank; UNDP (United Nations Development Programme). 1989. Africa's adjustment and growth in the 1980s. World Bank, Washington, DC, USA.

World Bank; USAID (United States Agency for International Development). 1991. Building a competitive edge in Sub-Saharan countries: the catalytic role of foreign and domestic enterprise collaboration in export activities. World Bank, Washington, DC, USA.

CHAPTER 11

LESSONS FROM UMOA[1]

— Rohinton Medhora —

Medhora reviews the experience of the West African Monetary Union (UMOA), which became the West African Economic and Monetary Union (UEMOA) in January 1994. A review of the literature shows the economic performance of UMOA countries to have been relatively good in comparison to that of other Sub-Saharan African countries, particularly in terms of the low rates of inflation which have been observed. This may be attributed to various factors, including the discipline imposed by the fixed exchange rate, the existence of a relatively independent, supranational bank, and the French guarantee of convertibility for the CFA franc. However, the author also discusses some of the problems UMOA has had to contend with. He seeks to draw lessons from this experience for other groups of developing countries that are contemplating monetary integration in West Africa or elsewhere. A monetary union is more likely to be successful if the supranational central bank is empowered to override national authorities in major areas of money and finance. In exchange for giving up sovereignty over monetary matters, members gain the advantage of stable, noninflationary monetary policies insulated from political interference. Risk and transactions costs are reduced, and this could help stimulate investment and growth, while encouraging greater economic integration among the member states.

THE WEST AFRICAN Monetary Union (UMOA), which became the West African Economic and Monetary Union (UEMOA) on 10 January 1994 is one of the world's most far-reaching examples of monetary integration. The Union's monetary arrangements, which remain unchanged by the expansion of UMOA's functions into the economic sphere under UEMOA, make it a "complete" monetary union in the sense that its members share a fully convertible common currency issued by a supranational central bank that oversees the operations of an external reserve pool. There are seven member countries: Benin, Burkina Faso, Côte d'Ivoire, Mali, Niger, Senegal, and Togo. The common currency is the CFA franc, issued by the Banque Centrale des États de l'Afrique de

[1] Although I retain sole responsibility for the final contents, I wish to thank Youssouf Dembélé, Abdoulaye Diagne, Henri Josserand, Sams Dine Sy, Ousmane Badiane, Jean Coussy, Mohammed Mah'Moud, and Diery Seck for their comments on an earlier version of this paper.

l'Ouest (BCEAO), based in Dakar. Despite statutory and other limitations on action by individual governments, UMOA member countries
retained some leeway — too much leeway, perhaps — in fiscal, trade, and
monetary matters, and the need for greater harmonization of economic
policies was one of the principal reason for the transformation of UMOA
into UEMOA.

The Union's monetary arrangements have obvious appeal. They
include the use of a fully convertible currency backed by a G-7 country,
risk-free investment within the franc zone, economies of scale resulting
from the issue of a common currency, and the existence of an apolitical
central bank that can pursue consistent policies. The cost to member
countries has been the loss of the exchange rate as an instrument of
macroeconomic policy. Although Cobham and Robson (this volume)
consider this cost to be of secondary importance, UMOA's inability even
jointly to devalue the CFA franc was the subject of much debate as those
countries struggled to adjust without devaluation, through the dreadful
1980s and early 1990s. Having now succeeded in devaluating the CFA
franc in January 1994, and having managed the process as well as could
be hoped so far, UMOA now appears better equipped than in the past to
meet the challenges of adjustment.

The OAU's "Abuja Declaration" of 1991 and numerous statements
by West African institutions seem to suggest a strong desire to enhance
monetary integration, and UMOA's nearly two decades of experience since
it last went through major institutional changes provides fertile ground
to address such issues. This chapter presents a review and analysis of
UMOA's experience to date. Its future prospects are examined, and lessons
for generalizing this model to other countries in the region are considered.

INSTITUTIONAL FRAMEWORK AND
ECONOMIC PERFORMANCE

UMOA's institutional arrangements have received attention elsewhere
and will only be discussed here briefly.[2] The Union is headed by the Conference of the Heads of State, and the BCEAO is headed by a Council of

---

[2] The standard reference for a critical analysis of the economic arrangements of the franc
zone remains Guillaumont and Guillaumont (1984). This book takes a decidedly optimistic
view of UMOA, which continues to inspire the authors in later work (Guillaumont et al. 1988,
for instance). Other works include that of Julienne (1988), which provides a more descriptive
and anecdotal account of the early years of the BCEAO (1955-75), and more critical, but still
positive overviews (Vinay 1980; Bhatia 1985; Neurrisse 1987; Vallée 1989; Medhora 1992a).
Sacerdoti (1991) presents a recent description of events and arrangements in the region. The formal statutes governing the UMOA and BCEAO may be found in UMOA (1962, 1973, 1989).

Ministers, comprising the finance minister of each member country. Each member country has input into the BCEAO's decision-making process, and, nominally, all members including France have one "vote" each. In practice, decisions are made by consensus. However, the era of structural adjustment has brought considerable influence from abroad, and it is apparent that *de facto*, some members are more equal than others.

The BCEAO conducts an annual programming exercise to estimate credit requirements, both Union-wide as well as by member country, before it makes its credit allocation decisions. By statute, government borrowing from the BCEAO is limited to 20% of the government's previous year's fiscal receipts. Governments are free to borrow at home and abroad and are required only to inform the central bank of their actions.

In normal circumstances, each member is required to contribute 65% of its external reserves to an operations account run by the BCEAO and maintained with the French Treasury in Paris. Any serious payments imbalance of one member is covered by the external assets of the others. If the account as a whole runs low, the remaining 35% of the reserves may be called in. If this, too, is inadequate, a vaguely defined "crisis management" scheme takes over, but, more importantly, the French Treasury stands ready to augment the account, in an unlimited and unconditional manner. This, in practice, is how the French guarantee of full convertibility of the CFA franc is established. This system allowed the exchange rate to remain unchanged at 50 CFA francs to 1 French franc from 1948 until January 1994, when it was changed, overnight, to 100 CFA francs to 1 French franc.

The advantages and disadvantages of the UMOA system have been the subject of a growing body of literature regarding the impact of UMOA membership on various indicators of economic performance. For a long time, the obvious stability and well-being of UMOA countries was contrasted with the "learning by doing" pratfalls of the nonfrancophone African countries, and a positive association developed between UMOA-type arrangements and development. A permanently fixed and externally guaranteed exchange rate coupled with a supranational central bank was expected to breed low inflation and encourage savings, investment, possibly exports, and, ultimately, a higher rate of growth. However, fixed exchange rates increasingly fell into disrepute in the 1970s and 1980s, specifically in the case of UMOA, as it struggled with problems of structural adjustment and increased loss of competitiveness on world markets.

Devarajan and de Melo (1987) examined the impact of UMOA by comparing growth in GNP in the franc zone with 11 sets of other countries, variously defined, during the period 1960–82. Using a variance-components model, they find that for the entire period, growth in the CFA countries was higher than that in other Sub-Saharan African countries, but lower, or not significantly different, than that of other groups. However, stronger results were obtained for the CFA group relative to comparable groups when the sample period was divided into 1960–73 and 1973–82. With the CFA group of countries improving its performance from one period to the other, the authors concluded that "the discipline imposed by monetary union participation was helpful for adjustment during the period of generalized floating and supply shocks" of the more turbulent latter period (Devarajan and de Melo 1987, p. 493).

This somewhat crude test was supplemented by Guillaumont et al. (1988) who specified a growth equation and ran econometric tests to compare actual growth with "predicted" growth for a sample of CFA and non-CFA countries. Here, the CFA group compared favourably with others. During the subperiod 1970–81, the "unexplained" component of growth attributable to institutional or other causes was superior to that of other Sub-Saharan African countries as well as non-African developing countries. However, the result is conditioned by the strong performance of the larger countries (Côte d'Ivoire and Cameroon). The Central African Republic, Chad, Gabon, Senegal, and Togo fared relatively poorly compared with the non-African group of developing countries. This hints at the possibility that not every member may benefit, or benefit equally, from the arrangements of the franc zone and suggests the need for further research on this topic.

Elbadawi and Majd's (1992) more recent findings are more pessimistic. A modified-control-group approach, which controls for initial conditions and changes in the internal, external, and policy environment, was used to measure the marginal impact of membership in the franc zone relative to a group of Sub-Saharan African and a group of low-income countries. This study yielded very different results for the 1970s and 1980s. In the 1970s, zone membership had a largely positive effect on all variables (the sole exception was growth compared with the low-income developing countries). However, during the 1980s, zone membership had a negative effect on growth, exports, investment, and savings compared with both comparison groups. These results echo Devarajan and de Melo's (1990) previous work using a similar method.

The conclusion may be drawn that the arrangements of the franc zone may have "worked" over the long haul, but were unable to prevent or sustain the shocks of the past decade. What was ominous for the long term was that overvaluation of the currency during this latter period was fought with expenditure reductions that fell largely on investment spending, thus boding ill for future productive capacity and growth in the region. One bright spot emerges: no matter what time frame and what comparison group, inflation was unambiguously lower in the franc zone.

Linkage of the CFA franc to the French franc is expected to have a stabilizing influence on the economies of the franc zone for various theoretical and institutional reasons. Whether this transpires empirically depends on the extent to which inflation in the CFA countries is found to track French inflation. It also depends on the stability of the French franc relative to other world currencies. Evidence regarding the correlation between inflation in the franc zone and French inflation suggests an imperfect relationship. De Macedo (1986) found inflation in UMOA to have been largely insulated from that in France between 1958 and 1982. If anything, there was a *negative* correlation. However, later work, by Honohan (1990a) did find the expected tendency for inflation rates to converge, between 1964 and 1987.

Other studies have directly addressed the issue of real exchange-rate stability in the franc zone relative to other regions. Paraire (1988) and Honohan (1983) found lower or statistically indistinct nominal and real exchange-rate variability in the CFA countries relative to other developing countries. Elbadawi's (1991) results were similar through to 1988, but he found differences in exchange-rate variability between the CFA countries, as a result of differing rates of inflation from country to country. Exchange rate variability in the franc zone increased in the late 1980s, but remained low by developing country standards.

A few broad conclusions may be derived from this literature. Historically, UMOA countries have enjoyed favourable growth rates compared with other Sub-Saharan African countries. Arguably, given the potential for omitted variables and specific regional circumstances, this is the only valid comparison group, and unfavourable comparisons with Asian and other developing countries should be taken less seriously. However, the stronger growth rate of UMOA countries has been slipping, even with respect to this narrow group. This can, at least partly, be attributed to the inability of the central bank to control inflation in the late 1970s and early 1980s and the overvaluation of the currency resulting at least in part from such inflation. The poor performance of savings and investment is probably linked to the ongoing financial-sector crisis in the region and capital flight due to the overvalued CFA franc. Overvaluation of the CFA franc also offers an obvious explanation for the region's weak export performance. Still, the arrangements have produced lower inflation and more stable real exchange rates, thanks to the common central bank and convergence to French indicators.

THE BCEAO

As the institution in charge of monetary policy in seven countries, the BCEAO has an onerous responsibility, for which it is only partly equipped. We consider here a number of features conditioning BCEAO's ability to deliver sound monetary policy:

- its relatively high degree of independence;
- a *de facto* bias toward its larger member countries, as revealed by the pattern of seigniorage flows;
- its inability to prevent a financial sector crisis in some countries;
- its inability to manage the level of macroeconomic activity in some countries; and
- its inability to prevent overvaluation of the CFA franc.

CENTRAL BANK INDEPENDENCE

The importance of central bank independence can be appreciated in the context of Kydland and Prescott's (1977) notion of "time consistent" and "time inconsistent" policies, that so changed the tone of the "rules versus discretion" debate in monetary policy. In that view, an announced "rule" will not be credible (i.e., time consistent) if it is merely announced and not underpinned by forces that make it irrevocable. On the other hand, policy announcements may still be time consistent, despite the lack of an explicitly stated rule, if they are always seen to be enforceable. Such arguments have been used to explain why some central banks that tried switching to strict money rules failed (those of the United States and Canada in the early 1980s), whereas others that have no explicit money rules have been more successful in managing inflation (Germany and Japan). The reason is that credibility cannot be acquired by simply announcing a rule. It has to be earned, either through reputation (which presumably explains the success of the central banks in Germany and

Japan) or through fundamental statutory changes (as in New Zealand, Chile, and possibly Canada).

Monetary announcements are deemed to be credible if they are made by an authoritative source, i.e., an independent, apolitical, technocratic central bank, preferably with a history or statutory commitment to a single, achievable goal, such as low and stable inflation. Grilli et al. (1991) have composed an index of central banks' independence in the OECD countries. Applying the index reveals that: central bank independence may be classified as "political," "economic," or both and that one usually goes with the other; in the post-war era (1950–89), the more independent central banks are associated with lower rates of inflation; and this result does not come with a real cost in terms of output growth. These results may be seen as the empirical application of the Kydland and Prescott (1977) proposal, and the strongest evidence to date in its favour.[3]

The application of this analytical framework to the BCEAO shows it to have an enviable degree of independence and, therefore, credibility. The BCEAO lies above the average for OECD central banks, largely because of its freedom from pressure from any single fiscal authority and the statutory limits on government borrowing (Figure 1).[4] This degree of independence *has* delivered lower inflation, as indicated earlier, independently of whatever else might be said about the performance of UMOA in the late 1980s and early 1990s.

Seigniorage

Seigniorage is the command over real resources that a central bank captures by issuing "high-powered" money. This monetary seigniorage is then used for central bank operating costs, retained, or returned to the public via dividends to the national treasury or via subsidized lending to designated sectors. How the benefits of seigniorage are used is an issue for public and central bank policy.

In UMOA, there is the additional issue of distributing seigniorage rights between the member countries; this is examined in Honohan (1990b) and Medhora (1992b, 1993). Dividends, until they ceased in 1987, were allocated equally among the members of the Union, and thus had a built-in bias toward the smaller (and coincidentally poorer)

---

[3] For a full and recent discussion of the design and practice of central banking, see Downes and Vaez-Zadeh (1991).

[4] See Appendix to this chapter for details on the derivation of the index of central bank independence.

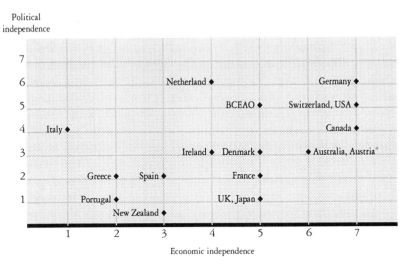

Figure 1. Central Bank independence: OECD and BCEAO.
Source: derived from Grilli et al (1991); see also Appendix I.

members. The alternative of distributing seigniorage via subsidized lending in effect means that the larger members (or, at least, those members with large sectors entitled to the preferred credit) benefit most.

The BCEAO's active role in resolving the financial sector crisis alluded to below resulted in a marked shift in the pattern of seigniorage allocation. For example, comparing the boom years (1976–80) with the bust years (1984–89), subsidized lending and operating costs grew as a proportion of total seigniorage, at the expense of dividends (Figure 2). This had profound implications in the intraregional distribution of seigniorage (Figure 3). Most remarkable is Côte d'Ivoire's share, which is not proportional to any indicator of its relative size within the region, and has grown at the expense of the smaller members' shares. The tighter monetary policy of the late 1980s has also had an effect on the availability of dividends for distribution, leading to an increase in the share of seigniorage benefits being consumed by operating costs (Figure 1).

With the elimination of the "taux d'escompte préférentiel," one source of seigniorage for the members has been removed, but the BCEAO's role in restructuring insolvent banks will ensure a similar pattern of distribution in the foreseeable future. What should be an issue of macroeconomic and central banking policy and intraregional relations has become caught up in the whirl of crisis management. One could

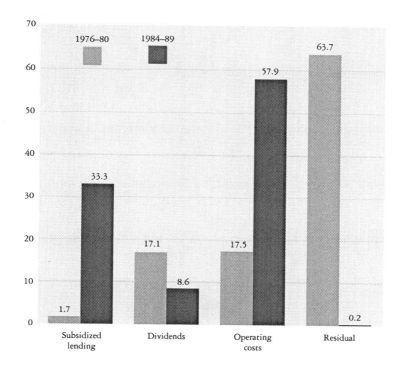

Figure 2. Distribution of seigniorage by use (average annual flows, as %).
Source: Medhora (1992b).

make a valid case for the central bank distributing seigniorage equally among its members, or unequally to favour a target group of countries, but it is more difficult to defend an allocation policy based on compensation for financial mismanagement!

THE FINANCIAL-SECTOR CRISIS

The ongoing financial-sector crisis, primarily in Côte d'Ivoire, Senegal, and Benin, has drained the region of savings and scarce management resources and set back financial development. A combination of a weak external and domestic economic environment, coupled with poor lending practices and inadequate supervision by the authorities are to blame for this situation.[5]

---

[5] For an overview of financial-system management — and mismanagement — in developing countries, see World Bank (1990). For some detail of the African situation see Seck and El Nil (1992) and Callier (1991). Brief descriptions of the UMOA situation may be found in Honohan (1990b) and de Zamaroczy (1992), as well as in recent annual reports of the BCEAO.

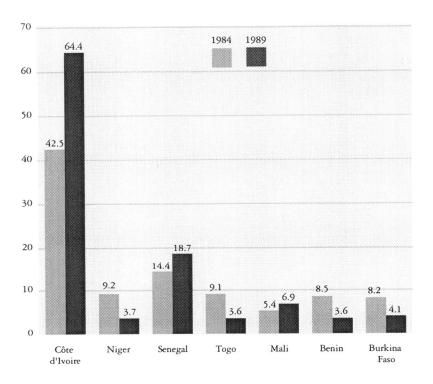

Figure 3. Distribution of seigniorage by country (country shares in total seigniorage, as %). Source: Medhora (1992b).

The designation of some sectors as privileged, entitled to funds at the BCEAO's below-market discount rate led to abuse of the system. Problem institutions were either not identified or not dealt with soon enough. After passively refinancing credit to governments, the agricultural sector, and designated entities for years, the BCEAO found itself dealing with the aftermath of a crisis among lending institutions at the end of the 1980s. The familiar "too big to fail" logic meant that the central bank was also the chief, perhaps only, institution in the region deemed capable of rectifying the situation with minimal damage. The result was that large amounts of assets, both performing and nonperforming, were rediscounted by the central bank.

A strong case can be made that a central bank — particularly that of a monetary union — should not have to deal with financial-sector regulation. If it must do so, it should be given *all* the powers normally associated with domestic financial-sector regulation agencies. Central banks in developing countries have traditionally been given a primary role in financial-sector regulation and development because of the obvious links between credit creation, financial intermediation, and economic development.

However, when compulsory subsidized lending is injected into this equation, the risk of abuse increases, and monetary policy becomes "hostage" to such abuse.

A system of market-based interest rates combined with tighter supervision and an internally financed insurance scheme for the financial sector would, in principle, unlink monetary policy from financial-sector events. The move to a more market-based system and the creation of an autonomous Commission Bancaire at the Union level, as spelled out in UMOA (1989), goes a long way toward addressing the problem. It is not entirely clear how the regulatory powers of the new agency and its monitoring capacity will coincide with those of the BCEAO, but, on pure central banking grounds, the BCEAO could make a strong case for having this aspect given over almost completely to the new agency.[6] In any case, the BCEAO is not rid of the matter entirely, as it will almost certainly continue to be involved in the resolution of financial crises.

Domestic credit creation and external borrowing

The BCEAO's role in macroeconomic management of the franc zone depends upon its willingness and ability to manage levels of credit and economic activity in the member countries. The BCEAO's control over money supply is exercised principally through the 20% rule described earlier. Unfortunately, the 20% rule tends to be viewed more as a right than a ceiling, and credit expansion at such levels may not always be appropriate.

---

[6] This "narrow" view of central banking operations, although popular in some quarters in discussions on the creation of a European central bank, is not universally accepted. Folkerts-Landau and Garber (1992) argue that the separation of responsibilities for price stability and financial-sector supervision could impede the creation of truly regional financial markets, making the central bank no more than a "monetary policy rule." They address the charge that credit allocation abuse may compromise the functioning of a common central bank by arguing that an independent central bank with its own resources at stake is more likely than an independent monitoring agency to assess accurately the solvency of potential borrowers (p. 30). However it may be useful to differentiate between a liquidity crisis and a solvency crisis. The former is very much the responsibility of a central bank; the latter, in UMOA, has been the result of poor lending policies and practices by the BCEAO. A self-contained insurance and regulatory body whose mandate and accounts are transparent is at least as likely to be rigorous in its operations, and possibly more so, than a central bank, except perhaps one that is exceptionally independent.

One assumes a desire to control the expansion of domestic credit on the part of the BCEAO, because the BCEAO is largely free from political influence, and its mandate includes defending the historical parity of the CFA franc with the French franc. However, the *ability* of the BCEAO to control domestic credit is less certain.[7] Its member countries have small open economies characterized by perfect capital mobility and a fixed exchange rate; and the level of economic activity in individual countries will be conditioned by the amount of external borrowing and its positive effect on the national money supply whenever hard currency is exchanged for CFA francs. Such borrowing is likely to reflect the credit-worthiness of the borrowing countries and the degree of international confidence in the CFA franc. Countries in need of funds may also tap into the surplus reserves of other member countries, through access to the BCEAO reserve pool, or into the French Treasury which stands ready to replenish the BCEAO's operations account when necessary. Countries running large fiscal deficits can thus draw upon three sources of credit that are beyond the control of the BCEAO: international financial markets; deficit financing from the BCEAO's reserve pool; and contributions to the operations account by the French Treasury. All this substantially circumscribes the BCEAO's ability to manage the level of economic activity in individual countries as well as the Union as a whole.

This situation underscores the importance of the BCEAO's monitoring role with regard to external borrowing. Unfortunately, even that monitoring role has been handicapped. Although the central bank is supposed to estimate credit demand and supply in each member country annually, the reporting requirements regarding external borrowing by individual governments is weak. It is not at all clear that the BCEAO has been operating with "full information" in this regard, both in terms of the completeness, as well as the speed of reporting. A tightening of the relevant statutes or some definition of a mechanism by which the BCEAO is empowered to oversee credit developments within its region seems in order. Put another way, a supranational central bank cannot behave like a supranational central bank if it does not have the mandate to do so. At the very least, a free and full flow of relevant information seems well within the limits of what such a mandate should entail.

The most obvious reflection of how economic management has varied from country to country is indicated in the different rates of inflation

---

[7] Domestic credit creation in UMOA has been the subject of some discussion in Bhatia (1971, 1985), IMF (1963, 1969), and Medhora (1992a).

which are observed. Between 1977 and 1990, the consumer price index rose by 130% in Côte d'Ivoire, 118% in Senegal, 100% in Burkina Faso, 74% in Togo, and 61% in Niger (similar data for Benin are not available). These differences highlight not so much a failing in monetary policy in the Union, as a lack of coordination between the BCEAO's policies and the fiscal policies of individual members.

Such differences will bear, in turn, on the economic competitiveness of these countries, as reflected in the evolution of the real effective exchange rate (Figure 4). Less obvious is the general loss of international competitiveness of the franc zone through the 1980s and early 1990s. Although this competitiveness depends on the relative level of inflation in the zone as reflected by the real effective exchange rate, it also depends upon the evolution of the terms of trade for traditional exports, the burden of debt service the region is obliged to bear, the zone's ability to develop nontraditional exports, and the exchange rate policy of competing countries (such as Ghana and Nigeria or other developing countries). Evolving trends in all these variables combined to make the parity level of the CFA franc increasingly uncompetitive through the 1980s and early 1990s. The 50% devaluation of the CFA franc in January 1994 was the confirmation of what everyone had come to know about the continued and secular uncompetitiveness of the franc zone at the old parity.

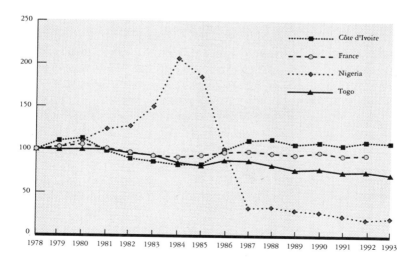

Figure 4. Real effective exchange rates (1978 = 100).
Source: IMF, International Financial Statistics.

ADJUSTMENT WITHOUT DEVALUATION

That the inevitable should have been put off for so long can be explained in many ways, and is not unique to UMOA's case. Individual countries have hobbled along with overvalued exchange rates before. Yet the UMOA case is special for two reasons. One is the illustration it provides of the special difficulty of exchange rate devaluation in a monetary union. The second is the lesson to be derived from its efforts to adjust "without devaluation."

What complicates devaluation in a monetary union, is that the different countries have different needs. It was commonly acknowledged that Côte d'Ivoire and Senegal needed to devalue much more than Niger or Togo at the other extreme, and the data on inflation in these countries bore this out. Coming to agreement on an appropriate rate of devaluation under those circumstances was problematic at best, and it is not surprising that Côte d'Ivoire was in the lead of countries calling for devaluation.

There were also some good reasons to resist devaluation: the fear of destroying confidence in the UMOA system, the fear of spiraling inflation, and fears of repeated, and ineffectual devaluations, as have occurred elsewhere.

The special link of UMOA to France delayed the process for two reasons. One was France's opposition to devaluation, for reasons mentioned above and others of a geopolitical nature. The other was France's readiness to facilitate any attempt to adjust without devaluation.

The upshot was that the UMOA countries attempted to adjust in the classic manner of the gold standard, with France's augmentation of the operations account softening the blow of deflation for member countries. Indeed the franc zone as a whole was a net drain on the French Treasury more or less continuously for some years after 1987, according to the calculations of M'Bet and Niamkey (1990).[8] One may argue that this promise of convertibility — open-ended and unconditional as it has been — only delayed the inevitable. The incentive to remain competitive is weaker in the presence of such a guarantee, and it no doubt introduces a form of "moral hazard," if not in the actions of the BCEAO, then at least in the actions of some of the governments, some of the time.

Of course, it would be quite wrong to characterize the past decade as one where adjustment was merely postponed. It could be argued, as Collier and Gunning (1992) do, that the guarantee of convertibility

---

[8] Interestingly, this is a recent phenomenon, encountered previously only in 1983, and then in a minor way.

allows UMOA governments to pursue policies (such as trade liberalization or industrial diversification) that have long-term payoffs but short-term costs, as these countries are not bound, to the usual extent, by immediate foreign-exchange constraints. This is a luxury that most developing countries cannot claim to have. UMOA countries have, with varying degrees of success, initiated adjustment policies.

However, exchange-rate adjustment without devaluation ("artificial" devaluation) requires direct — therefore visible and contentious — pressure on wages, costs, prices, and the public-sector deficit. A nominal devaluation can achieve the same result less transparently and more quickly. It, too, needs to be accompanied by other austerity measures, but presumably these are more severe in the absence of an accompanying nominal devaluation. In a survey of artificial devaluations, Laker (1981) considers them to be second-best solutions to a nominal devaluation. Judging by the theoretical literature as well as UMOA countries' experience of the last decade or so, countries that attempt this approach to correct a disequilibrium of major proportions should expect one or more of the following:

- some public resistance as wage and cost controls and higher tariffs on imports are announced;
- allocative inefficiencies, because the reach of such a plan would never be as universal as that of a nominal devaluation;
- capital flight due to uncertainty about the success of the operation;
- a proliferation of administrative costs and corruption, as a system of increased import tariffs and export subsidies is put into place;
- an imbalance in the structure of economic incentives due to limitations on the ability to subsidize exports in the face of fiscal pressures; and
- the risk that after all the time and pain, a competitor may achieve the same result by simply devaluing.

UMOA's experience of the 1980s and early 1990s, culminating in the devaluation of the CFA franc after 10 years of procrastination, suggests the need for a degree of flexibility in the formula for pegging the Union's common currency. It remains to be seen whether future adjustments in UMOA may be easier now that the barrier of devaluation has been breached.

LESSONS FOR OTHERS

The UMOA experience is replete with lessons regarding the advantages and costs of monetary integration, the limits which should be imposed on the role of the central bank, and exchange rate management.

A "first principles" approach to monetary union must necessarily find its way through the literature on optimum currency areas, initiated by Mundell (1961) and surveyed by Ishiyama (1975). However, using a single criterion to determine the "optimum" area, as some of the early theorists did, is of limited practical use. Ishiyama concluded his survey of the issue by proposing a more flexible cost–benefit approach. To Canzoneri and Rogers (1990), this means exploring the trade-off between the loss of sovereignty over monetary policy (and with it control over the use of seigniorage as a form of tax revenue), and the savings in transaction costs inherent in a single-currency system. The feasibility and desirability of monetary integration also depends on historical, regional, and political considerations. For a small country overwhelmed by regional events, there may well be no choice at all. In all cases, only rough and ready "calculations" can be made about joining, because the counterfactual is itself purely hypothetical. What matters is not the optimality of the solution, but its practicality.

The adjustment problems that UMOA has had to face in the past decade should not blind us to the benefits of membership in a monetary union of this sort, nor lead us to overestimate the benefits of sovereignty in matters of monetary policy. However, we should be aware that at least some of the desirable features of UEMOA (such as the French guarantee of convertibility) will not accrue to other regional groupings, or an expanded "franc zone."

Furthermore, membership in a monetary union largely involves "buying into a package," involving substantial changes in the way individual countries conduct their affairs in some areas of policy. Monetary union has strong fiscal overtones. There is no *a priori* reason why a common currency area should also have uniform intraregional trade and taxation policies; for obvious examples, consider the creative array of trade impediments and tax regimes *within* the United States, Canada, and the "united" Europe.[9] However, the creation of a common central bank

---

[9] There is a large body of literature on the links between monetary union and fiscal coordination. Bhatia (1985) contains a brief survey, and Allen (1976) and Robson (1971) deal with the nuts and bolts of the issue. For recent discussions on the subject in the European and US contexts, see de Cecco and Giovannini (1989) and Eichengreen (1990), respectively. Although a monetary union can function, at a certain level, in the absence of fiscal and trade policy harmonization and factor mobility, it will do so more efficiently in a more economically integrated setting. UMOA has an ongoing history of attempts at enhanced integration in nonmonetary areas and will be pursuing such efforts more aggressively under the new UEMOA Treaty.

means that individual governments have little discretion in the use of the inflation tax. On the assumption that the common central bank will choose a policy geared to inflation at the low end of the regional spectrum (or lower still), members with historically high rates of inflation will face a larger adjustment than those with inflation rates close to those sought for the union as a whole.[10]

A common central bank that has a few, well defined, goals is far more likely to be successful than one burdened with many tasks. This is arguably true of national central banks, and particularly true of a supranational one, as the BCEAO's experience demonstrates. Tasks such as financial-sector regulation and deposit insurance are best left to separate agencies.

Regional imbalances within a nation-state are often corrected by the existence of stabilizing tax and transfer payment flows, as Eichengreen (1990) shows for the United States. The mechanics of this form of "fiscal federalism" is at the heart of the debate over monetary integration in Europe. However, it is probably unrealistic to expect intermember equalization payments of the type seen in the United States and Canada and envisaged in Europe in a monetary union of developing countries. The lack of such fiscal federalism will mean the persistence of pockets of both chronically poor and perennially gifted regions, as experience proves all over the world. As Youssouf Dembélé pointed out in his comments to me on this paper, a regional development bank that is adequately capitalized and has an explicit mandate to fund projects with regional overtones may go some way toward complementing a common central bank in the spirit of economic integration. The West African Development Bank (BOAD: Banque ouest-africaine de développement) has not been an outstanding success in this regard, but a more effective regional development bank could clearly play a useful role in promoting intraregional trade and a better balanced process of industrialization.

Care should be taken in any equalization formula to respect certain principles of separation and transparency. Separation implies that central banking decisions be made independent of political pressures, through the separation of central-banking and development-banking functions. Transparency means that the common central bank's seigniorage allocation policy should be clear, open, and statutorily unalterable. Because this policy would be agreed upon by the members, there is no reason why it might not have an equalizing bias of some sort.

---

[10] Among the ECOWAS countries during the 1980s, annual inflation ranged from an average of 5–7% in UMOA and Liberia, to 17% in the Gambia, 21% in Nigeria, 48% in Ghana, and 63% in Sierra Leone.

Management of the exchange rate (or management of the average inflation rate union-wide) is a valid task for a common central bank, but there is no reason why the external value of the currency has to be immutably fixed. Indeed, it is highly unlikely that any future monetary union of developing countries would gain the type of guarantee that the CFA franc has historically enjoyed from the French Treasury. The choice of exchange rate regime should be a matter specific to the economic and institutional features of each particular monetary union. The possibility of an expanded or transformed franc zone linked to the ECU is an interesting option, discussed at length in Cobham and Robson (this volume). These authors join Guillaumont and Guillaumont (1989) and Collier (1992) in suggesting that an integrated Europe might extend some form of guarantee of convertibility to a larger African monetary grouping, perhaps through "associate status" in the European monetary union. Even if this were to happen, the guarantee would undoubtedly be far more restrictive than the current one, and the job of the common (African) central bank would include some management of the nominal external value of the common currency.[11]

The need for a monetary union to manage the nominal external value of a common currency raises new issues in the management of the union's reserve pool. Reserve pooling is an integral part of any monetary union, and in its various forms has been a successful half-step toward closer monetary coordination in many parts of the world.[12] In UMOA, the system has worked automatically — surplus countries have covered the deficits of the others, and the French Treasury has covered the deficit of the franc zone account as a whole. When surpluses accrue, franc zone deposits in Paris earn a market rate of interest, in favour of the member countries. In a monetary union with no immutably fixed external parity, the coverage of deficits by certain countries is no longer automatic. Rules are needed to define when and how much to devalue and what conditions to impose on deficit countries, if the reserve pool is to operate effectively and without charges of bias.

---

[11] There is, of course, some question about the viability of UMOA itself when the European monetary system is transformed into a full monetary union. In principle, the parity value of the CFA could be reattached to the ECU, and there is no reason why France could not maintain its guarantee of convertibility of the CFA franc, if it wished. Some rethinking of the UMOA arrangement would seem the most likely option, however.

[12] See Kaplan and Schleiminger (1989), who detail the ultimately successful efforts to bring Europe from the constrictive bilateralism of the post-war years to full convertibility a decade later. Medhora (1992c) and M'Bet and Niamkey (1990) quantify the gains from the reserve pools in the UMOA and BEAC regions, respectively.

CONCLUSION

This overview of the UMOA experience testifies to a number of advantages of monetary unification. Under the proper conditions, a monetary union will minimize conversion, valuation, and transactions costs; substantially reduce intraregional risk; and provide an independent, apolitical monetary regime that should breed low inflation. There will be some saving of international reserves, and other economies of scale will be realized in areas of high fixed cost. Harmonization of some regulations and laws will further reduce costs, thus helping to promote regional trade.

The UMOA experience is also instructive of some of the conditions for successful monetary integration. In matters of money and finance, such as the degree of external borrowing or control over the exchange rate, members should be subservient to the common central bank, or at the very least face more onerous reporting requirements than has been the case in UMOA. UMOA experience suggests that the 20% rule that governs credit to national governments by the BCEAO is insufficient and should be buttressed by controls over foreign borrowing. A more comprehensive rule is thus needed if the common central bank is to have real control of the macroeconomic situation in the member states.

Over a wide range of "normal" conditions, i.e., from 1963 to the early 1980s, the Union functioned well. Hindsight tells us that it was not equipped to deal with deliberate or accidental overborrowing, overlending, overspending, and fraud in the decade that followed. The Union will not be able to prevent macroeconomic imbalance if it is not allowed to function in the proper spirit and it could constitute an impediment to economic adjustment if it is excessively inflexible, too long, as UMOA seems to have been regarding the parity of the exchange rate. A properly designed monetary union will promote good policy and ensure the materialization of all potential benefits from the union.

APPENDIX I:
MEASURING THE INDEPENDENCE OF CENTRAL BANKS

Grilli et al. (1991) divide central banks' independence into political independence (defined as "the capacity to choose the *final goal* of monetary policy"), and economic independence (defined as "the capacity to choose *the instruments* with which to pursue [the] goals"). The authors construct two indices of central bank independence by awarding one point for each of the following attributes.

POLITICAL INDEPENDENCE

1. Governor *not* appointed by government.

2. Governor appointed for more than 5 years.

3. All the board *not* appointed by government.

4. Board appointed for more than 5 years.

5. No mandatory participation of government in the board.

6. No governmental approval of monetary policy formulation required.

7. Statutory requirement that central bank pursues monetary stability among its goals.

8. Legal provisions that strengthen the central bank's position in conflicts with the government.

ECONOMIC INDEPENDENCE

1. Government access to direct credit facility of the central bank not automatic.

2. Direct credit facility available at market rate of interest.

3. Direct credit facility explicitly temporary.

4. Direct credit facility limits amounts loaned.

5. Central bank does not participate in primary market for public debt.

6. Discount rate set by central bank.

7. Banking supervision *not* entrusted to central bank (two points) or not entrusted to central bank alone (one point).

For its political independence, the BCEAO gets three points for the first three criteria (because no *individual* government controls such decisions), and one half point for the fourth (because its board comprises ministers of finance, some of whom have better tenure and credibility than others). No points are given for criteria 5, 6, and 8, but a point is given for 7, as the bank has a statutry obligation to maintain the internal and external value of the CFA franc. The total here is four and a half.

For its economic independence, the rules governing the BCEAO's direct credit facility are such that points are given for criteria 2, 3, and 4, but not for 1 and 5. The discount rate is set by the bank and, since 1989, a separate agency has been established to oversee the financial system in the union; thus, one point is given for each of criteria 6 and 7. The total here is five.

No doubt, such an index conceals the subtleties of the monetary pol-icymaking process in countries, and there is also the issue of whether the existence of a statute necessarily means that its intent is carried out in practice. This would particularly be the case if such an index were con-structed for some developing countries. In our case, this framework rep-resents well the position of the BCEAO in such matters — slightly above the OECD norm and probably well above the norm for developing countries.

REFERENCES

Allen, P.R. 1976. Organization and administration of a monetary union. Princeton University, Princeton, NJ, USA. Studies in international finance 38.

Bhatia, R.J. 1971. Factors influencing money supply in BCEAO countries. IMF Staff Papers, 18, 389–398.

———— 1985. The West African Monetary Union, an analytical review. Interna-tional Monetary Fund, Washington, DC, USA. Occasional paper 35.

Callier, P. (ed.). 1991. Financial systems and development in Africa. World Bank/Economic Development Institute, Washington, DC, USA.

Canzoneri, B.M.; Rogers, C.A. 1990. Is the European Community an optimal cur-rency area? American Economic Review, 80 (3), 419–433.

Collier, P. 1992. European monetary union and "1992": opportunities for Africa. The World Economy, 15 (5), 633–643.

Collier, P.; Gunning, J.W. 1992. Aid and exchange rate adjustment in African trade liberalizations. Economic Journal, 102 (413), 925–939.

de Cecco, M.; Giovannini, A. (ed.). 1989. A European central bank? Cambridge Uni-versity Press, New York, NY, USA.

De Macedo, J.B. 1986. Collective pegging to a single currency: the West African Monetary Union. In Edwards, S.; Ahamed, L. (ed.). Economic adjustment and exchange rates in developing countries. University of Chicago Press, Chicago, IL, USA.

Devarajan, S.; de Melo, J. 1987. Evaluating participation in African monetary unions: a statistical analysis of the CFA zones. World Development, 15 (4), 483–496.

———— 1990. Membership in the CFA zone: odyssean fourney or Trojan horse? World Bank, Washington, DC, USA. Policy Research Working Paper WPS 482.

de Zamaróczy, M. 1992. The reform of Senegal's banking system. Finance and Devel-opment, 29 (1), 14–15.

Downes, P.; Vaez-Zadeh, R. (ed.). 1991. The evolving role of central banks. Interna-tional Monetary Fund, Washington DC, USA.

Eichengreen, B. 1990. One money for Europe? Lessons from the U.S. currency union. Economic Policy, 10, 117–188.

Elbadawi, I. 1991. Macroeconomic stability and real exchange rate and price conver-gence in the CFA zone. World Bank, Washington, DC, USA.

Elbadawi, I.; Majd, N. 1992. Fixed parity of the exchange rate and economic perfor-mance in the CFA zone. World Bank, Washington, DC, USA. Policy Research Working Paper WPS 830.

Folkerts-Landau, D.; Garber, P.M. 1992. The European central bank: a bank or a monetary policy rule. National Bureau for Economic Research, Boston, MA, USA. Working paper 4016.

Grilli, V.; Masciandaro, D.; Tabellini, G. 1991. Political and monetary institutions and public financial policies in the industrial countries. Economic Policy, 13, 341–392.

Guillaumont, P.; Guillaumont, S. 1984. Zone franc et développement africain. Economica, Paris, France.

———— 1989. The implications of European monetary union for African countries. Journal of Common Market Studies, 28 (2), 139–154.

Guillaumont, P.; Guillaumont, S.; Plane, P. 1988. Participating in African monetary unions: an alternative evaluation. World Development, 16 (5), 569–576.

Honohan, P. 1983. Measures of exchange rate variability for one hundred countries. Applied Economics, 15, 583–602.

———— 1990a. Price and monetary convergence in currency unions. World Bank, Washington, DC, USA. PRE working papers WPS 390.

———— 1990b. Monetary cooperation in the CFA zone. World Bank, Washington, DC, USA. PRE working papers WPS 389.

IMF (International Monetary Fund). 1963. The CFA franc system. IMF Staff Papers, 10, 345–396.

———— 1969. Financial arrangements of countries using the CFA franc. IMF Staff Papers, 16, 289–389.

Ishiyama, Y. 1975. The theory of optimum currency areas: a survey. IMF Staff Papers, 22, 344–383.

Julienne, R. 1988. Vingt ans d'institutions monétaires ouest-africaines. Harmattan, Paris, France.

Kaplan, J.J.; Schleiminger, G. 1989. The European payments union. Oxford University Press, New York, NY, USA.

Kydland, F.E.; Prescott, E.C. 1977. Rules rather than discretion: the inconsistency of optimal plans. Journal of Political Economy, 85, 473–491.

Laker, J.F. 1981. Fiscal proxies for devaluation: a general review. IMF Staff Papers, 28, 118–143.

M'bet, A.; Niamkey, A. 1990. European economic integration and the franc zone. Centre Ivoirien de Recherches Économiques et Sociales, Abidjan, Côte d'Ivoire.

Medhora, R. 1992a. The West African Monetary Union: institutional arrangements and the link with France. Canadian Journal of Development Studies, 12 (2), 151–180.

———— 1992b. Seigniorage flows in the West African Monetary Union, 1976–89. Weltwirtschaftliches Archiv, 128, 513–526.

———— 1992c. Reserve pooling in the West African Monetary Union. Economia Internazionale, 45 (2), 209–222.

———— 1993. The allocation of seigniorage in the franc zone: the BEAC and BCEAO regions compared. International Development Research Centre, Ottawa, Canada.

Mundell, R.A. 1961. A theory of optimum currency areas. American Economic Review, 51, 657–665.

Neurrisse, A. 1987. Le franc CFA. Librairie Générale de Droit et de Jurisprudence, Paris, France.

Paraire, J. 1988. L'instabilité des taux de change. In Guillaumont, P.; Guillaumont, S. (ed.). Stratégies de développement comparées zone franc et hors zone franc. Economica, Paris, France.

Robson, P. 1971. Current problems of economic integration. United Nations Conference on Trade and Development, Geneva, Switzerland.

Sacerdoti, E. 1991. Central bank operations and independence in a monetary union: BCEAO and BEAC. *In* Downes, P.; Vaez-Zadeh, R. (ed.). The evolving role of central banks. International Monetary Fund, Washington DC, USA.

Seck, D.; El Nil, Y. 1992. The experience of African countries with financial liberalization (vol. 1 and 2). African Centre For Monetary Studies, Dakar, Senegal.

UMOA (Union Monétaire Ouest-Africaine). 1962. Traité du 12 mai 1962 : accords de coopération; statuts de la Banque Centrale; convention de compte d'opérations. BCEAO, Dakar, Senegal.

———— 1973. Traité constituant l'Union monétaire ouest africaine. BCEAO, Dakar, Senegal.

———— 1989. La nouvelle politique de la monnaie et du crédit de la Banque Centrale des États de l'Afrique de l'Ouest. BCEAO, Dakar, Senegal.

Vallée, O. 1989. Le prix de l'argent CFA : heurs et malheurs de la zone franc. Karthala, Paris, France.

Vinay, B. 1980. Zone franc et coopération monétaire. Ministère de la Coopération, Paris, France.

CHAPTER 12

MONETARY INTEGRATION IN THE LIGHT OF THE EUROPEAN DEBATE[1]

– David Cobham and Peter Robson –

Cobham and Robson look at broad strategies for monetary integration at the subregional level in Africa, drawing lessons from the European experience, while stressing the specifics of the African situation. Recent literature on this subject justifies monetary integration with reference principally to the macroeconomic stability it can induce. The experience of the franc zone reinforces this view in the light of the relative economic stability observed in member countries compared with the high inflation and exchange rate instability in most other West and central African countries. The authors assess the benefits and costs of various forms of monetary integration and argue in favour of full monetary union, similar to what currently exists in the franc zone. In the authors' view, this could be achieved in West Africa through the institution of an "ECU" zone, in place of the franc zone. Anchoring the African currency to the ECU would offer a number of advantages for West African countries. It would impose monetary discipline, reduce the need for the usual macroeconomic convergence period as a condition for establishing the monetary union and could include the provision of external support of the kind currently being provided by France in the franc zone. Anchoring to an external currency would also help neutralize the danger of domination by Nigeria in monetary matters, thus attenuating a concern of other member countries.

IN THE LAST few years considerable interest has been expressed in the idea of further monetary integration in Africa on a subregional basis. Some monetary unions already exist in Africa, and others have recently been proposed (e.g. for the Eastern and Southern African Preferential Trade Area, for the Economic Community of West African States, and for the the Maghreb area). At the pan-African level, the Abuja Declaration of June 1991 envisaged the establishment of a single African central bank and a single African currency during the last 5 years of its 34-year program to create an African economic community.

---

[1] The authors are grateful to Ousmane Badiane, Jean Coussy, Mohammed Mahmoud and Rohinton Medhora for comments on earlier drafts, but retain full responsibility for the final version.

Most of the analytical literature on monetary integration has focused on the European Union (EU), for obvious reasons. The African context is very different, however, and it is important to beware of transposing arguments without appropriate qualifications. The key differences between the African and European situations can be summarized as follows:

- There is a much lower level of economic integration among African than European countries, with respect not only to trade, but also to financial and other factor flows (even if allowance is made for unrecorded intra-African trade).

- Greater disparities exist between African countries at the macroeconomic level, for example in monetary growth rates, budget deficits, exchange-rate regimes, inflation rates, and balance of payments deficits, although the structural adjustment programs now in place should lead to greater convergence if they are successful.

- African countries and subregions are small relative to European ones, in terms of indicators such as GDP, trade flows, and money supply.

- There are very few organized financial markets in African countries, and nearly all financial flows pass through intermediaries such as banks (or their informal equivalents).

This paper discusses broad strategies for monetary integration in Africa at the subregional level, in the light of these structural differences. We draw explicitly on research on European monetary integration, but bring out the significance for African economic policy of the specifics of the African situation. We begin by assessing the relative costs and benefits of general types of monetary integration and go on to examine the arrangements of existing African monetary unions. We then consider alternative strategies by which subregional monetary integration in Africa could be achieved. We conclude with a broader look at the external arrangements appropriate for monetary integration in Africa in the light of some explicit African–European comparisons and the possible role of external support.

ALTERNATIVE FORMS OF MONETARY UNION

All types of monetary integration entail both fixed exchange rates and full convertibility among national currencies, but a distinction must be made between the informal exchange-rate union, the formal exchange-rate union, and full monetary union (Table 1, first three columns). The

Table 1. Characteristics of different types of monetary integration.

Characteristics	Informal exchange-rate union	Formal exchange-rate union	Full monetary union	Franc zone
Between members				
Current account convertible	Yes	Yes	Yes	Yes
Capital market integrated	Yes	Yes	Yes	Yes
Exchange rate fixed	Yes (within margins)	Yes (narrower or zero margins)	Yes (zero margins)	Yes (zero margins)
Ex ante credibility of parities	No	No	Yes	Yes
Currencies	Separate	Separate	Single	Common
Central banks	Multiple, independent	Multiple, strongly coordinated	Single	Single
Reserve pooling	No	Yes	Yes	Yes, but individual accounts
Foreign-exchange market interventions	Separately	By single agency	By single agency	By single agency

Source: ACMS 1991.

crucial difference between the first two of these is that the formal exchange-rate union has a central agency coordinating the national central banks; whereas the crucial difference between the second and third is that the full monetary union has a single currency and a single central bank.[2]

The relative costs and benefits of these different forms of monetary integration can be analyzed using Table 2, which reflects the African context but was inspired by comparable exercises for Europe (Gros 1989; CEC 1990). We argue below that any African monetary union should adopt an external peg that will ensure a low inflation rate over the medium term, and we assume such a policy to have been adopted in each of the cases considered in Table 2.[3] The table shows that "higher" forms of monetary integration are more desirable. The main costs — the loss of the exchange rate as an instrument of adjustment between member countries, the initial disinflation required to enter a union, and the loss of seigniorage and inflation tax revenue — are the same for each form of monetary integration. However, the benefits tend to be greater for the "higher" forms. Improvements in domestic and international resource allocation will be larger if the integration is closer and irreversible (advantages 1–3). Any consequent dynamic gains (7) will also be greater. At the same time, full monetary union yields greater benefits in terms of the reduction in interest rates on government debt (4) and in terms of the resource savings from the pooling of foreign-exchange reserves (5) and the centralization of monetary policy (6). If countries want some form of monetary integration, they should opt for full monetary union rather than either form of exchange-rate union as the costs of each form are identical, but the benefits differ.

This conclusion is essentially the same as that reached by Gros (1989), who compared three types of monetary union,[4] and by the CEC (1990), which compared stage I of the Delors report (CEC 1989) with stage IIIa (European Monetary Union with multiple currencies) and stage IIIb (single currency). Cobham and Robson's (1994) comparison of these

---

[2] In terms of Corden's (1972) distinctions, the informal exchange-rate union suffers from inadequate coordination of policy, and in this sense is only a pseudo-union; the formal exchange-rate union has adequate coordination, and the full monetary union includes a centralization of policy.

[3] In a union whose exchange rate is not so pegged, the members would incur lower costs from the loss of the exchange rate as a policy instrument, but they would also obtain smaller benefits from monetary integration.

[4] These were the "ex post macro" union, in which exchange rates are in principle adjustable but do not, in fact, change, the "ex ante macro" union, in which exchange rates are understood to be irrevocably fixed, and the "micro" union, in which there is a single currency.

Table 2. Costs and benefits of different forms of monetary integration.

	Informal exchange rate union	Formal exchange exchange rate union	Full monetary union
Costs			
1) loss of exchange rate as instrument vis-à-vis other members	yes	yes	yes
2) initial disinflation where necessary	yes	yes	yes
3) loss of seigniorage and inflation-tax revenue, due to lower inflation	yes	yes	yes
Advantages			
1) improved price stability (actual and expected) leading to better resource allocation	partially	yes	yes
2) reduced exchange rate variability (actual and expected) leading to increased trade and investment flows within the union	partially	partially	yes
3) reduced transactions costs and improved price transparency leading to increased trade and investment within the union	—	partially (if zero margins)	yes
4) interest savings on government debt from lower nominal interest rates and reduced exchange-rate risk premium	partially	partially	yes
5) resource saving from pooling of foreign-exchange reserves	—	partially	yes
6) resource saving from centralisation of monetary policy	—	partially	yes
7) dynamic gains	—	partially	yes

Source : African Centre for Monetary Studies (1991).

two studies and that of the African Centre for Monetary Studies (ACMS 1991) summarized in Table 2 confirms the superior benefits of a full monetary union in the African context. Under traditional criteria for identifying optimum currency areas, African subregions appear to be much less suitable candidates for monetary integration than the existing European Union (EU) countries, because of the much lower level of economic integration in Africa than in Europe (Aigbokhan 1993). There is, moreover, little prospect of reaching the European level of integration in the near future. However, monetary integration can be evaluated according to broader criteria, and it is instructive to look at the benefits from the existing African monetary unions in the franc zones of West and central Africa, namely the West African Monetary Union (UMOA which has now become the West African Economic and Monetary Union, UEMOA) and the Bank of Central African States (BEAC which has become the Central African Economic and Monetary Union, CEMAC).

EXISTING MONETARY UNIONS IN WEST AND CENTRAL AFRICA

The salient arrangements governing the franc zone unions are summarized in the last column of Table 1. Comparison with alternative arrangements in the Table makes it clear that the existing African monetary unions are a variant on full monetary union. There is a common currency and a single central bank, and foreign exchange reserves are pooled and managed by a single agency. On the other hand, the note issues are separately identifiable, and on the basis of this and other information, separate balance-of-payments accounts are estimated and separate reserve positions identified. The change in a country's reserves is then used as an input into the fixing of the country-specific lending ceilings in the subsequent period. The exchange rate is pegged to the French franc, and the convertibility of the currency (the CFA franc) is guaranteed by the French Treasury by means of an "operations account."

What is the rationale for these arrangements? From an historical point of view, these unions were not set up as the result of any process of monetary integration. At no stage, for example, were there separate central banks, that were merged into or superseded by a single institution. Instead, the unions are the direct descendants of arrangements instituted by the colonial power. They have been modified only partly by certain reforms in the early 1970s (which brought about a process of Africanization and a weakening of France's direct control over monetary policy).

At the same time, the African unions operate in a context of relatively low economic integration between the member countries (although intra-bloc trade in UEMOA is more extensive than among most other African countries) and their scope is not coterminous with natural geographic blocs.

Rather, these African monetary unions have been from the outset (and continue to be, despite the 1970 changes) geared primarily toward producing macroeconomic stability. In this regard, they have been relatively successful. Member countries have experienced relatively low monetary growth, relatively strict budgetary discipline, and hence consistently lower inflation rates than most other African countries (Devarajan and de Melo 1987; Guillaumont et al. 1988). During the 1960s and 1970s, this stability was accompanied by generally better growth performance for the area as a whole. Relative performance in the 1980s has been more difficult to evaluate and remains a controversial issue.[5] It seems likely that the unions have also made a contribution to promoting economic integration among their members in the form of expanded trade and cross-border investment flows (Medhora 1990).

The significance of any economic policy constraints due to the operation of these unions should be evaluated in the context of the modern case for monetary integration as presented, for example, by De Grauwe (1992). First, there is more scepticism today about the usefulness of devaluation as a frequently used tool of macroeconomic policy, on the basis of results from the monetary approach to the balance of payments or from Keynesian models of devaluation in which wages respond to increases in import prices. A devaluation can, in certain circumstances and if it is accompanied by an appropriate package of other policies, galvanize or "kick-start" the economy. However, the effects of devaluations on competitiveness and the balance of payments are often eliminated within a short period by increases in domestic prices and costs, particularly if governments repeatedly resort to them.[6]

Second, the time-consistency literature initiated by Kydland and Prescott (1977), developed by Barro and Gordon (1983), and applied to the open economies of the European context by Giavazzi and Pagano (1988), has emphasized the importance of credibility and reputation in monetary policy. The argument is a rational expectations one. If the monetary authority is tempted to raise inflation in the short run to reduce unemployment or boost income, the private sector perceives this temptation and adjusts its expectations of inflation accordingly. The economy therefore ends up in a long-run equilibrium with high inflation, which is unequivocally a worse outcome than other possible equilibria from the point of view of both the authorities and the private sector. This poor

---

[5] See, for example, Devarajan and de Melo (1991) for a negative view of franc zone membership in the 1980s. We do not intend, or need, to reach here a considered judgement on this issue. Medhora (this volume) and Boughton (1993) provide up-to-date discussions of the literature. The latter takes a more positive general view. Medhora stresses the point that weaker performance in the 1980s may be attributable in part to poor lending practices and inadequate supervision, and notes that benefits of belonging to the union may have varied significantly between member countries. See also van de Walle (1991) and Plane (1988, 1990).

[6] Considerations such as these underlie the criticism of excessive recourse to devaluation in structural adjustment programs made by authors such as Guillaumont Jeanneney (1988) and Killick (1993).

outcome can be avoided if the monetary authority can acquire a reputation for being tough on inflation (for example, by announcing strict monetary targets and attaining them on a regular basis, or by pegging its currency to that of a central bank with greater credibility). It could also be avoided through some form of monetary integration in which control of monetary policy is transferred to a different or new authority that is perceived to be better insulated from political pressure.

If the above is true, then the loss of the exchange rate as a policy instrument within the existing African monetary unions (or, more exactly, its permanent assignment to the control of inflation via the peg to the French franc) is less significant than might at first appear. At the same time, the assignment of monetary policy to a supranational central bank has clear advantages in terms of reputation and credibility. This is clearly the case for the BCEAO, whose independence is estimated by Medhora (this volume) to be "slightly above the OECD norm, and probably well above the norm for developing countries."

A crucial aspect of arrangements in the franc zone is the country-specific lending ceilings backed up by the separate note issues and separate reserve accounts. Cobham and Robson (1994) have argued that these ceilings as they operate in the existing West African monetary unions are a sensible, although rough, means of ensuring the allocation of credit between countries. As simple and transparent allocational devices, they also ensure and demonstrate that no one country "gains" from a union at the expense of other members.

STRATEGIES FOR MONETARY UNIFICATION

If full monetary union in the variant represented by the existing African unions is preferred, how should countries belonging to a coherent subregion aim to achieve it? In what follows, the question is addressed first for the case of countries committed to monetary union, then for the case where governments are attracted to monetary integration but are unwilling to commit themselves (as has predominantly been the case in the context of European debates on this subject).

Where countries are sure of the goal, monetary unification requires two stages: a preparatory period during which inflation rates would be brought together, exchange rates stabilized and convertibility introduced; and a subsequent transitional period during which the old currencies would be phased out and the new one phased in. The preparatory period would also be used for the establishment of the new union-level central bank and the transformation of the existing national central banks into subordinate agencies.

National monetary agencies would retain important policy roles, notably in the management of national clearing systems, in the prudential supervision of banks, and in the operation of the country-specific elements of union-level monetary and credit policy. However, they would have less autonomy than at present. For its part, the new union-level central bank would presumably draw heavily on the existing national central banks for its personnel and expertise.

If the objective of monetary integration in Africa is to provide a framework of macroeconomic stability, the new union-level central bank would need to be given a specific policy mandate to pursue price stability or support the exchange rate. It would also need a managerial structure that would insulate it as much as possible from political pressures (this is probably more easily achieved in a monetary union, where pressures from different governments may offset and neutralize each other, than at the national level).

The preparatory period evidently involves important processes and decisions, but in the light of current experience with structural adjustment programs, a period of 5 years (or less, perhaps, for the countries in the subregion not confronting significant adjustment problems) might be an appropriate time scale. Once a decision on monetary unification has been taken, there are obvious advantages to implementing it without delay. The subsequent transition period to a new currency would call for extensive prior publicity and information, but is not difficult in principle, and should not require more than 6 months.

Within the context of such an approach, a country with a high initial rate of inflation might prefer to introduce the new currency directly, in the form of a currency reform, rather than go through a painful preparatory period of deflation. The choice should hinge on factors such as the costs of currency reform — the difficulties of controlling overall monetary growth and the costs to price-setters of having to set prices in both currencies, when one currency is depreciating strongly against the other — as against the unemployment costs of disinflating within the standard approach.

The main alternative strategies that have been discussed within the European context are the currency competition strategy and the parallel currency strategy (Cobham 1989, 1991; Gros and Thygesen 1990; Vaubel 1990). The first of these involves allowing the free circulation of each national currency in each member country until one becomes dominant; the second involves the creation of a new currency, which is allowed to compete with and eventually dominate each of the national currencies. These strategies would suffer from a number of drawbacks in any circumstances, but seem particularly inappropriate in the African context, where trade and financial flows between countries are limited so that intensive competition seems unlikely (although there is some de facto informal currency competition in border areas, based on the CFA franc, in particular). One standard objection is that both, but particularly the competition strategy, would exacerbate national rivalries. Another is that they entail the circulation of a greater number of currencies, or a higher degree of substitutability of currencies, in each country, which would create considerable difficulties for the various monetary authorities in controlling overall monetary growth and inflation.

A further argument is that because of the public goods characteristics and externalities associated with money, it is far from obvious that the free choices of economic agents would result in a single currency becoming dominant if either of these strategies was pursued. Transactors choose what currencies to hold and use in light of the choices made by others, because those choices will affect transaction costs. There are economies of scale in currency holdings, and there is, therefore, a strong gravitational pull toward the existing established currency. Only a major shock in the form of a substantial divergence in inflation rates can be expected to cause transactors to shift into a different currency.

For countries that are not committed to the goal of monetary integration, but are interested in moving at least some distance toward it, two policies can be suggested: first, they should peg their currencies to the same external anchor; and, second, they should make current and capital account transactions convertible. Such policies can be expected to bring about a considerable convergence in terms of macroeconomic policies and inflation rates, and place the countries concerned in a position from which they could decide to embark on the basic strategy outlined above.

MONETARY INTEGRATION AND EXTERNAL ARRANGEMENTS

In this section, we offer a comparative view of monetary integration issues in Europe and Africa and consider strategies for dealing with them. We discuss the advantages which might accrue from an external "anchor" in the African case. An understanding of the issues and strategic options requires an awareness of the motives or impulses behind monetary integration in Europe and Africa, and we will start by recalling these.

The first motive or incentive in either case is the desire for further integration of the "real" economies of the region through increased trade and investment. In Europe, this reflects primarily a political preference for greater unification, coupled with the belief that further integration will improve economic growth (CEC 1990). In Africa the primacy of politics is less clear-cut, and the concern with faster growth may be the dominant motivation.

The second incentive for monetary integration comes from the hope that it would contribute to macroeconomic stability. In Europe, Germany's partners in the Exchange Rate Mechanism of the European Monetary System (EMS) wished to import credibility from the German Bundesbank by tying their currencies to the mark. The European Monetary Union (EMU) is also widely seen as a way of removing monetary policy from the hands of national politicians and constructing a more explicit disciplinary framework than that which previously existed in most EU member countries other than Germany. In Africa, no national central bank has anything approaching either the independence or the reputation of the Bundesbank — indeed most central banks (apart from the BCEAO and BEAC) have a lack of independence comparable to that of the central banks of the United Kingdom, France (before 1994), or even of Soviet-type economic systems. However, there is a hope and a possibility that greater independence and credibility might be obtained in the framework of a monetary union, within which the influences of individual national governments would tend to neutralize each other. An extra-African involvement could play an important role in bolstering the independence and credibility of such a mechanism.

The third incentive in both Europe and Africa is conjunctural. In the European case, the prospect of the single European market, with its implied abolition of capital controls, prompted officials and governments to fear for the continued viability of monetary arrangements that, many were convinced, relied heavily on the existence of capital controls.[7] In Africa, the possible absorption of the French franc into the ECU has made clear that certain institutional changes are called for in the operation of the franc zone. In that connection, Guillaumont and Guillaumont (1989) have discussed the possibility of at least a partial generalization of the franc zone arrangements to certain other African countries through

---

[7] The most elegant exposition of this case is that of Padoa-Schioppa (1988), who argued that the "inconsistent quartet" of free trade, capital mobility, fixed exchange rates, and national autonomy of monetary policy could not coexist; in previous periods, it was capital mobility that had been sacrificed, but, in the context of the single market, national monetary sovereignty should be abandoned.

the creation of an ECU zone; Collier (1991) has drawn attention to the opportunities for the creation of other currency unions elsewhere in Africa (with appropriate once-and-for-all currency realignments at the same time).

The incentives for monetary integration in Europe and Africa thus display certain differences of emphasis, but the basic similarities are striking. An examination of the main problems that have been encountered in Europe provides a background to a discussion of ways to resolve them in the African context.

First, the discussion of monetary integration in Europe has long been bound up with the division between those who want exchange rates to be fixed as a first step (the "monetarists," notably the French authorities) and those who want to see a prior convergence of economic policies and economies (the "economists," notably the German authorities). This division was responsible for the Werner (1970) committee's inability to suggest a path by which the EC countries could proceed from its first phase to the final objective of monetary union; this divergence of view is still pervasive in the most recent debates.

Second, the European discussion has paid great attention to imbalances of power or asymmetries in the burdens of adjustment between member countries. Since the Snake, which was the EU's first attempt to fix exchange rates between member countries, was widely regarded as having degenerated into a deutschmark zone by the end of the 1970s, the establishment of the EMS involved lengthy discussions about the problem of the asymmetry of the pressures for adjustment for countries with balance-of-payments deficits compared with those with surpluses. In the event, member countries chose to use the system in an asymmetric way as part of their counterinflation policies. They accepted that the burden of adjustment should fall mainly on countries with higher inflation rates. These countries were under pressure to reduce their inflation rates and could use the peg to the deutschmark to help them do so (without Germany coming under pressure to increase its inflation). More recent concerns about the dominance of the German economy and German monetary policy have been expressed both by those who see a move to full integration as a means of diluting German dominance and by those who resist any integration at all.

Third, there have been long discussions in Europe on the status and objectives of the proposed European central bank. By 1990–91, views were converging on the need for the bank to be given full independence and a mandate to pursue price stability, and both of these were incorporated in the Maastricht Treaty that was signed in March 1992 (CEC 1992).

Fourth, the problem of fiscal coordination has been a major focus of debate in Europe. The solution recommended in the Delors report (CEC 1989) was to set limits on budget deficits, but this evoked fierce opposition in some quarters. Controversy has centred on why any coordination of national budgetary policies should be needed and how that coordination should be implemented. A further aspect of the discussion has to do with issues of "fiscal federalism." The MacDougall Committee (CEC 1977) initiated a debate on the role of the EU budget in cushioning short-term and cyclical fluctuations or redistributing incomes. These issues have been reexamined more recently in the context of the Maastricht Treaty. Goodhart (1990), for instance, has argued for a larger Community budget to facilitate automatic transfers between regions to aid adjustment to differential shocks; the EU has produced a study (CEC 1993) of the public finance implications of the monetary union aspects of the Maastricht Treaty.

What solutions to these problems can be offered within the African context? Note that the first and the second problems mentioned above arise only because European currencies have no suitable anchor currency (since the final demise of the Bretton Woods system in early 1973). In contrast, African subregions can readily find an external anchor that is both strong enough not to be affected by developments or policies in Africa itself and, at the same time, is appropriate to the structure of their trade flows. The ECU is such an anchor.

If and when the franc–mark exchange rate is consolidated in the ECU along with the lira and the pound sterling,[8] the ECU is likely to be a more or less optimal peg for most if not all African countries, whose trade with Europe is much greater than that with the United States or Japan, the only other countries with currencies significant enough to serve as anchors.[9] Moreover, under an independent European central bank

---

[8] The EMS was shaken by a series of currency upheavals between September 1992 and July 1993 that led to two currencies, the lira and sterling, leaving the system and the official parity margins being widened from 2.25% to 15%. Since then, however, the EMS has settled down again, with most other currencies near the (unchanged) parities. Although the objective of EMU may be harder to reach, and may have to be reached by a somewhat different route from that laid down at Maastricht, it remains likely that EMU will be attained by the end of the century, with the adoption of the ECU as the sole currency with a wider domain than any other existing currency. For further information on the causes and consequences of the crises of 1992–93, see Cobham (1994).

[9] Guillaumont Jeanneney and Paraire (1991) found, using 1975–89 data, that the French franc was the optimal peg for the franc zone countries, the dollar was not the best for some of the countries pegging to it, and the basket peg chosen by others was optimal for them. The various EC currencies typically make up the major part of such baskets.

with a price stability mandate as prescribed in the Maastricht Treaty, the ECU could be expected to exhibit low inflation over the medium term. Finally, pegging to the ECU would carry advantages in terms of simplicity and transparency, and possible EU support, which could be expected to more than compensate for any deviation from optimality that might be implied for a few individual countries. The current ECU, which is simply a basket of currencies that are themselves no longer pegged to each other, would be less desirable as an anchor, but it would still be preferable to any existing alternative.

If African countries peg their currencies to the ECU (initially their separate and later their common currencies), they can avoid any problems of asymmetries and inequalities, because the anchor will be strong enough to ensure that no individual African country would be able to pull other countries in a direction in which they did not want to go. In the case of West Africa, in particular, an external anchor would go some way at least toward preventing the enormous weight of Nigeria causing problems for its smaller neighbours. In addition, pegging to a common external anchor currency would provide, for those not yet committed to monetary integration, a clear and straightforward initial measure that sidesteps the question of whether convergence or intramember exchange-rate fixity should take precedence in the process of transition.

The political significance of pegging to the ECU requires some comment. Using an external anchor is a way of controlling inflation and reducing external shocks, and Africa's trade patterns imply that the ECU is the best available peg for most African countries for these purposes. From a West African perspective, a peg to the ECU, rather than the French franc, might also help to overcome some of the divisions resulting from the different colonial heritages of francophone and anglophone countries. Any benefit to the EU as a whole from African countries pegging to the ECU would be negligible (because of the small share of trade with Africa in overall European trade and the low level of African foreign-exchange reserves). Finally, any African monetary union that adopted an ECU peg would reserve the right to change the parity between its currency and the ECU in exceptional circumstances. In short, pegging to the ECU would represent not a subordination of African monetary policy to European decision-making, but a means chosen by African countries themselves of attaining their own policy objectives.

As far as the status and objectives of an African subregional central bank are concerned, which is the third problem listed above, both an adequate degree of independence and an appropriately clear mandate for the bank could be provided through what would amount to a generalization of the franc zone. The new African central bank(s) would issue a new currency with an ECU peg underpinned by a guarantee of external convertibility provided by the European central bank in return for an institutionalized European central bank influence on African monetary policy. The latter may be seen as a form of protection of the African central bank(s) from governments that might be tempted to print money to cover their own expenditures. The package as a whole can be seen as offering a framework for macroeconomic discipline through membership in what Collier (1991) refers to as "participatory supranational agencies of restraint." However, the arrangements should involve the establishment of new institutions (rather than the simple extension of the franc zone institutions themselves) so that all countries can feel like equal partners in their creation.

The fourth problem — fiscal policy coordination — is obviously more difficult to resolve in Africa because the machinery for the setting and implementation of common economic policy is not well developed in existing economic communities and blocs. However, because the macroeconomic spill-over effects in the African context are generally much smaller (because intra-African trade flows are smaller), there is less danger of the overall fiscal–monetary policy mix being severely suboptimal when it is determined by independent national fiscal decisions and the union-level central bank's monetary decisions. What is important is to set coarse limits that are defensible and viable rather than to attempt to fine-tune fiscal management at the community level. The UEMO limit of 20% of the previous year's tax revenues on borrowing from the BCEAO provides an appropriate mechanism for doing this, although experience suggests the need to preclude evasions of the limit via external borrowing or directed bank lending (Plane 1990; Medhora, this volume).

As to the issue addressed by the fiscal-federalist arguments regarding the need for intra-union budgetary transfers to offset differential shocks to member countries, both the political and institutional obstacles to any such action and the variations in country-specific shocks are even greater in an African context than in the EU. In Africa the only alternative would be to address the problem through external aid. Already, by way of the STABEX arrangements of the Lomé convention, all sub-Saharan countries except South Africa are eligible to receive grants to cover shortfalls in earnings from agricultural exports to the EU that are attributable to price or output fluctuations (ECU 1500 million is provided for this purpose under Lomé IV). SYSMIN (for which ECU 480 million is available) assists mineral exporters in a similar way. Development and modification of such stabilization assistance might be envisaged, with the aim of underpinning regional monetary cooperation and integration initiatives, and such a course of action has in fact been recommended in a recent study undertaken on behalf of the EU (Cerruti and Hugon 1993).

CONCLUSION

Our argument can be summarized in terms of the justification for monetary integration in Africa and the means for achieving it. In our view, any further move to monetary integration in Africa, at the subregional level or in still smaller areas, would be justified primarily by the prospect that it holds out of greatly improved macroeconomic stability, although there may also be some limited stimulus to economic integration. On both counts economic growth should be increased. An assessment of costs and benefits associated with various forms of monetary integration suggests that full monetary union, as currently exemplified in the franc zone, would be superior to less complete forms of integration.

If governments are fully committed to monetary union, the path to be taken is straightforward. It involves a preparatory period of macroeconomic stabilization and convergence, the move to convertibility, and the introduction of a regional currency. Some obviously useful steps can also be taken by countries not committed to full and irrevocable monetary union, notably the adoption of a common external peg.

The existence of a suitable external anchor currency in the form of the ECU offers African countries the possibility of sidestepping or resolving most of the contentious problems faced in Europe. The EU would, in principle, be well placed to offer support for such arrangements in a way that could be attractive to individual African countries, while greatly facilitating the process of monetary integration in Africa.[10] Such assistance would be consistent with the support for regional economic integration that is envisaged under Lomé IV (although that agreement lacks a specific reference to monetary cooperation), and would not impose an unacceptable financial burden on the EU. It would also provide an

---

[10] In this context the problem of African countries' external debt and its implications for future harmonization of fiscal policy would have to be addressed. An EC package might include the partial remission or rescheduling of such debts for countries willing to enter monetary unions along the lines envisaged.

important practical manifestation of the leading role in promoting economic cooperation and integration in Africa that the EU has assumed, in line with the consensus reached at the Maastricht conference on Africa of July 1990.

REFERENCES

ACMS (African Centre for Monetary Studies). 1991. Towards monetary integration in Africa: options and issues. ACMS, Dakar, Senegal. Mimeo.

Aigbokhan, B.E. 1993. Optimum currency areas and monetary integration in West Africa: lessons from the European Community. Presented at the International conference on regional integration in West Africa, 11–15 January, Dakar. International Development Research Centre, Dakar, Senegal.

Barro, R.; Gordon, D. 1983. Rules, discretion and reputation in a model of monetary policy. Journal of Monetary Economics, 12 (1), 101–122.

Boughton, J.M. 1993. The CFA franc zone: currency union and monetary standard. In Courakis, A.; Tavlas, G. (ed.). Monetary integration. Cambridge University Press, Cambridge, UK.

CEC (Commission of the European Communities). 1977. The role of public finance in the European Communities (MacDougall report). Office for Official Publications of the European Communities, Luxembourg.

———— 1989. Report on economic and monetary union in the European Community (Delors report). Office for Official Publications of the European Communities, Luxembourg.

———— 1990. One market, one money. European Economy, 44.

———— 1992. Treaty on European union. Office for Official Publications of the European Communities, Luxembourg.

———— 1993. Stable money — sound finances: community public finance in the perspective of EMU. European Economy, 53.

Cerruti, P.; Hugon, P. 1993. La coopération monétaire et l'ajustement structurel en Afrique sub-saharienne. Laboratoire de Recherche en économie appliquée, Université de Paris X, Paris, France.

Cobham, D. 1989. Strategies for monetary integration revisited. Journal of Common Market Studies, 28 (3), 203–218.

———— 1991. European monetary integration: a survey of recent literature. Journal of Common Market Studies, 29 (4), 363–383.

———— 1994. European monetary upheavals. Manchester University Press, Manchester, UK.

Cobham, D.; Robson, P. 1994. Monetary integration in Africa: a deliberately European perspective. World Development, 22 (3), 285–299.

Collier, P. 1991. Africa's external economic relations: 1960–90. African Affairs, 90 (360), 339–356.

Corden, W.M. 1972. Monetary integration. Essays in international finance 98. Princeton University, New Jersey, NJ.

De Grauwe, P. 1992. The economics of monetary integration. Oxford University Press, Oxford, UK.

Devarajan, S.; de Melo, J. 1987. Evaluating participation in African monetary unions: a statistical analysis of the CFA zones. World Development, 15 (4), 483–496.

———— 1991. Membership in the CFA zone: odyssean journey or Trojan horse? *In* Chibber, A.; Fischer, S. (ed.). Economic reform in sub-Saharan Africa. World Bank, Washington, DC, USA.

Giavazzi, F.; Pagano, M. 1988. The advantage of tying one's hands: EMS discipline and central bank credibility. European Economic Review, 32 (5), 1055–1082.

Goodhart, C.A.E. 1990. Fiscal policy and EMU. *In* Dornbusch, R.; Goodhart, C.; Layard, R. (ed.). Britain and EMU. Centre for Economic Performance, London School of Economics, London, UK. Pp. 81–95.

Gros, D. 1989. Paradigms for the monetary union of Europe. Journal of Common Market Studies, 27 (3), 219–230.

Gros, D.; Thygesen, N. 1990. The institutional approach to monetary union in Europe. Economic Journal, 100 (402), 925–935.

Guillaumont, P.; Guillaumont, S. 1989. The implications of European monetary union for African countries. Journal of Common Market Studies, 28 (2), 139–153.

Guillaumont, P.; Guillaumont, S.; Plane, P. 1988. Participating in African monetary unions: an alternative evaluation. World Development, 16 (5), 569–576.

Guillaumont Jeanneney, S. 1988. Dévaluer en Afrique? Revue de l'OFCE, 25.

Guillaumont Jeanneney, S.; Paraire, J.L. 1991. La variabilité des taux de change et le rattachement optimal des monnaies des pays en voie de développement. Revue d'Economie politique, 101 (3), 438–462.

Killick, T. 1993. The adaptive economy: adjustment policies in small, low-income countries. Economic Development Institute, World Bank, Washington, DC, USA.

Kydland, F.E.; Prescott, E.C. 1977. Rules rather than discretion: the inconsistency of optimal plans. Journal of Political Economy, 85 (3), 473–492.

Medhora, R. 1990. The effect of exchange rate variability on trade: the case of the West African Monetary Union. World Development, 18 (2), 313–324.

Padoa-Schioppa, T. 1988. The European monetary system: a long-term view. *In* Giavazzi, F.; Micossi, S.; Miller, M. (ed.). The European monetary system. Cambridge University Press, Cambridge, MA, USA. Pp. 369–384.

Plane, P. 1988. Les facteurs de déséquilibre des paiements courants en union monétaire ouest africaine (1970–83). Revue d'économie politique, 98 (1), 111–126.

———— 1990. La génèse de la crise financière extérieure de l'Union monétaire ouest africaine (1970–85). Politique africaine, 35 (1), 105–119.

Van de Walle, N. 1991. The decline of the franc zone: monetary politics in francophone Africa. African Affairs, 90 (360), 383–405.

Vaubel, R. 1990. Currency competition and European monetary integration. Economic Journal, 100 (402), 936–946.

Werner, P. 1970. Report to the council and the commission on the realisation by stages of economic and monetary union in the community. Bulletin of the European Communities, 3 (11; suppl.).

PART III

POLITICAL DIMENSIONS

CHAPTER 13

HUMAN RIGHTS AND INTEGRATION[1]

– *E.K. Quashigah* –

E.K. Quashigah would like to see regional institutions reinforced in their ability to support the cause of human rights in Africa as a whole, and in West Africa, more specifically. Human rights are increasingly seen as a matter of international concern, and there is greater acceptance of the notion of limited state sovereignty in areas such as the protection of human rights. Quashigah looks at the possibilities for building on some of the existing charters and treaties established by the Heads of State, including the African Charter on Human and People's Rights, the OAU Treaty to create the African Economic Community, the Declaration of Political Principles approved by the ECOWAS Heads of States, and the ECOWAS Revised Treaty. He argues that regional and subregional parliaments and courts should be instruments for the collective promotion of human rights and establishes some of the conditions necessary to make this work. Humanitarian intervention should also be envisaged to end dramatic cases of abuse and education by nongovernmental and human-rights organizations should be reinforced, as further instruments for the promotion of human rights. The relation between regional integration and human rights is likely to be bipolar. Regional institutions can help further the cause of human rights, while the pursuit of respect for human rights can help nurture the regional sense of community and purpose that has proven to be elusive so far, but is indispensable to the pursuit of regional integration in West Africa and Africa as a whole.

THE DECLARATION OF political principles by the Authority of Heads of State and Government of ECOWAS in Abuja on 6 June 1991 (ECOWAS 1991) was a manifestation of the growing belief of West Africans that it is not only through coordinated economic strategies and policies that regional integration and cooperation can contribute to a better life for all, but also through subregional peace, political stability, and shared political beliefs. The declaration is a powerful statement in

---

[1] This article is adapted from *Protection of Human Rights in the Changing Domestic and International Scenes: Prospects in Sub-Saharan Africa,* produced in 1992 while the author was at the University of Wisconsin (Madison) as a Social Science Research Council McArthur Foundation Visiting Scholar.

support of democratic principles and human rights. The following excerpts, from the preamble and Articles 4 to 6 are relevant in this regard:

> Determined to concert our efforts to promote democracy in the sub-region on the basis of political pluralism and respect for fundamental human rights as embodied in universally recognized international instruments on human rights and in the African Charter on Human and Peoples Rights.
>
> We will respect human rights and fundamental freedoms in all their plenitude including in particular freedom of thought, conscience, association, religion or belief for all peoples without distinction as to race, sex, language or creed.
>
> We will promote and encourage the full enjoyment of all our peoples of their fundamental human rights, especially their political, economic, social, cultural and other rights inherent in the dignity of the human person and essential to his free and progressive development.
>
> We believe in the liberty of the individual and his inalienable right to participate by means of free and democratic processes in the framing of the society in which he lives. We will therefore strive to encourage and promote in each of our countries, political pluralism and those representative institutions and guarantees for personal safety and freedom under the law that are our common heritage.

Since then, the principles adhered to in the declaration have been incorporated into the ECOWAS Revised Treaty, adopted by the Heads of State in July 1993, in Article 4(j), which calls for the promotion and consolidation of a democratic system of government in each member state as foreseen in the Declaration of Political Principles adopted in Abuja.

The treaty giving birth to the African Economic Community (AEC), signed in Abuja on 3 July 1991, similarly provides that the contracting parties solemnly affirm and declare their adherence to the principles of "accountability, economic justice and popular participation in development" [Article 3(h)].[2]

Such principles also reflect a certain evolution in ways of thinking about national sovereignty, in Africa as elsewhere. In its modern context, the concept of sovereignty is traceable to the peace of Westphalia in 1648 when the emerging nation-states of Europe, weary of war, agreed to live in peace with one another on the basis of sovereign equality and non-interference in each other's affairs (Gyandoh 1990). This concept of sovereignty has since become the basis on which governments, even those

---

[2] The AEC Treaty was signed by the OAU Heads of State and Government on 3 June 1991, in Abuja. Article 101 stipulates that the treaty shall enter into force 30 days after the deposit of the instrument of ratification by two-thirds of the member states of the OAU. This condition was satisfied in May 1993.

lacking the moral authority, continue to stave off intervention from other countries. It is a political principle that has been recognized in customary international law and international treaties, such as the United Nations and OAU charters [Articles 2 (4) and III (2), respectively].

However, contemporary thought and state practice have been attempting to steer understanding of the concept of sovereignty away from its absolutist notion of the erstwhile monarchical era toward a notion more in tune with the humanitarian duty of all to protect human rights even in foreign nations. The need for this change in conception, as it relates to the protection of human rights, was expressed by the former Secretary-General of the United Nations, Javier Perez de Cuellar as follows:

> The time has come for the international community to undertake a contemporary reassessment of the implications of the world system of sovereignty... international security will be enhanced only when human security is enhanced. Both require democracy and popular participation, the rule of law and respect for human rights and fundamental freedoms. [Bilder 1992, p. 13]

Even though the current international system based on sovereign states is likely to be with us for a long time to come, the way we think about the national state and national sovereignty appears to be gradually changing. Sovereignty no longer implies absolute government authority, because sovereignty refers only to that competence of states conferred by international law (Lillich 1979, p. 616). Political theory is replete with ideas about the purpose of government and the basis for its legitimacy. The gist of these is that governments are the instruments of people to enhance the welfare of the citizenry, and no government can retain its legitimacy and hence its claim to sovereignty if its activities erode the dignity of the people and destroy human life with impunity. As Gyandoh (1990, p. 172) points out,

> The history of the world, both ancient and modern has shown and continues to show that individual nation-states, left to themselves, cannot be trusted to protect their citizens and other residents against arbitrary, discriminatory and other repressive acts and decisions of state officials acting in the name of the State.

It follows that aspirations for a world where the promotion and respect for human rights is a general concern can no longer be submitted to the sacred and inviolable principle of territorial sovereignty. The domestic jurisdiction issue thus becomes a relative question, the balance of which is determined by the character of prevailing international aspirations. This view was expressed in much those terms in a celebrated opinion of the Permanent Court of International Justice: "The question whether a certain matter is not solely within domestic jurisdiction of a State is an essentially relative question; it depends upon the development of international relations" (quoted in Bernhardt 1986, p. 205).

In a comment on this view, Bernhardt believes that the scope of matters falling within the domestic jurisdiction of states will continue to shrink as the number of norms considered necessary for civilized society continues to increase in the international community. In his view, the protection of human rights has been elevated into an international issue in view of the immense efforts of the United Nations and the international community in the protection and promotion of human rights and can no longer be seen as a matter falling exclusively within the domestic jurisdiction of states (Bernhardt 1986, p. 206).

Declarations such as those embodied in the AEC and ECOWAS Revised treaties give some hope to the cause of human rights in Africa, despite the legendary habit of African leaders of not honouring their own declarations. In this chapter, we examine the possibility of harnessing the political commitments of the AEC and the ECOWAS Revised treaties to institutionalize certain instruments and approaches for the defence of human rights in Africa. I begin by reviewing the impact of the African Charter on Human and People's Rights (ACHPR), before considering three possible instruments: the proposed regional and subregional parliaments; the proposed regional and subregional courts; and humanitarian interventions. The chapter closes with a consideration of roles for nongovernmental organizations (NGOs) and human rights education.

THE AFRICAN CHARTER ON HUMAN AND PEOPLES' RIGHTS

The adoption of the ACHPR in 1981, at a time when despotism reigned supreme in Africa, was a major event that has been the subject of substantial discussion (Tucker 1983, p. 1351; Eze 1984; Okere 1984, p. 141). Like its predecessors, the United Nations' Covenant on Civil and Political Rights and the European Convention on Human Rights (ECHR), the ACHPR provides for traditional or first-generation rights, which guarantee the right to life and respect for same, equality before the law, etc. In addition, the ACHPR contains second-generation rights — mainly social, economic, and cultural — and third-generation rights. This last category refers to rights that are rather inchoate, including the right to development (Article 22), the right to benefit from the common heritage of mankind (Article 22), the right to national and international peace and security (Article 23), environmental rights (Article 24), and even the right to be different (Article 19). A great deal of criticism has been leveled at these third-generation rights, especially with regard to their imprecise and vague nature (Alston 1982/83).

A peculiarity of the ACHPR is its extensive reference to "peoples' rights" (Kiwanuka 1988, p. 80). As explained by Peter Onu, the secretary-general of OAU when the ACHPR was drafted, the concept "peoples" was introduced to suggest that the individual in Africa is part and parcel of the group, meaning that "individual rights could be explained and justified only by the rights of the community" (Onu 1985). The concept also involves a compromise between the ideological leanings of the capitalist and socialist-minded governments of the time.

Because absolute rights are rare, derogations from such guarantees are generally permitted. However, the peculiarity of the ACHPR resides in the far-reaching nature of its derogation clauses, which extensively erode the potency of the charter's provisions compared with other conventions. Consider Article 6 of the ACHPR, which affords the right to liberty and security, "*except for reasons and conditions previously laid down by law*" (emphasis added). This is referred to as a "clawback" clause that allows domestic legislation to define the circumstances under which preventive detention may be allowed (Higgins 1976/77, p. 281; D'Sa 1985, p. 75). Unlike other international conventions on human rights, which provide for special occasions when fundamental rights can be suspended, the ACHPR permits such derogations in everyday circumstances (D'Sa 1985, p. 75). The clawback clauses give African governments the flexibility to derogate from the fundamental rights, provided it is done through the law.

Unlike the ECHR and the Inter-American Convention, the ACHPR did not provide for a court system. It was similar in this regard to the United Nations' Covenant on Civil and Political Rights and made provision only for the African Commission on Human Rights (the Commission). The understandable fear of the justice ministers of the member states of the OAU who drafted the ACHPR was that political realities would scare many leaders away from any form of court system.

As it turned out, the powers conferred on the Commission were themselves quite limited. The Commission does have a degree of independence. Even though its members are elected by the OAU Assembly of Heads of State and Government, the ACHPR attempted to secure their independence by providing that members serve in their personal capacity (Article 31). Furthermore, the Commission has the mandate to receive and consider briefs from both states and individuals or groups of individuals. However, Article 59 greatly limits the possible influence of the Commission; it stipulates that all measures taken by the Commission, including all findings of human rights abuse, shall remain confidential until such time as the Assembly of Heads of State and Government shall otherwise decide. In other words, no report of the Commission's activities shall be published unless authorized by the Assembly of Heads of State and Government. As Leckie (1988) has observed, any human rights organization or treaty so dependent upon the actions of the governments for the implementation and enforcement of human rights would seem doomed to failure from the start (see also Ojo and Sesay 1986, p. 89).

Another shortcoming of the ACHPR, and for that matter the OAU charter itself, is the lack of any mechanism of collective sanctioning by the Assembly of Heads of State and Government. All told, the enforcement machinery under the ACHPR is remarkably weak, and of little consequence to the ordinary citizen.

The African Commission has been described as nothing more than a "note-taking" organ, compared with its more effective European and Inter-American counterparts (Okere 1984, p. 141; Weston and Ors 1987, p. 613). In a political environment where African leaders treat the OAU as a sort of trade union of heads of state (Africa Now, Dec. 1983, p. 118) and where there appears to be a shared conspiracy of silence on issues of human rights abuse, nothing beneficial can be expected from the work of the Commission. It is, therefore, not surprising that the impact of the ACHPR on the promotion and protection of human rights in Africa has hardly been felt since it came into force, several years after its adoption, on 21 October 1986. The African Commission on Human Rights, as its powers and functions currently stand, is incapable of making any impact on the promotion and protection of human rights in Africa.

THE PAN-AFRICAN AND ECOWAS PARLIAMENTS

The AEC Treaty and the ECOWAS Revised Treaty make provision for pan-African and West African parliaments, in the pursuit of greater popular involvement in regional development and integration. Individual participation in the governance of political institutions is high on the list of liberal values inherent in the defense of human rights, and a truly pluralistic parliament could help safeguard governmental respect for other basic rights.

No protocols spelling out the powers of the Pan-African Parliament and the ECOWAS Parliament have as yet been drawn up. When this is done, it would be desirable to confer on these parliaments not only advisory powers but also powers to censure the Assembly of Heads of State and Government of the OAU and the Authority of the Heads of State and Government of ECOWAS, respectively. The creation of these regional parliaments was inspired by the European parliament, but their powers should not be limited in the same way as those of the European parliament, which is mainly advisory; although the EEC treaty requires that parliament be consulted, its opinions are not binding. Perhaps its only compelling powers are its budgetary powers and the power to force the resignation of the Commission of the European Communities (Hartley 1988). Such powers would be insufficient for the regional parliaments to act as the vanguard of human rights that we hope they can become.

Preferably, the parliaments should possess some legal powers to censure erring governments. By way of suggestion, these parliaments should have the power to order international investigations into reported or suspected abuses of human rights; based on the results, they should be empowered to request prosecution of officials implicated in such abuses before the AEC Court of Justice or the ECOWAS Court of Justice, as the case might be. They should have the power to compel the Assembly of Heads of State and Government of the OAU or the Authority of Heads of State and Government of ECOWAS to undertake humanitarian intervention when necessary. Such powers would enable the regional parliaments to supervise the promotion of respect for human rights in member countries on a regular basis and ensure prompt intervention when abuse of human rights becomes intolerable.

However even weak regional parliaments would be of value, through their ability to influence public opinion. Bernhardt (1986) lists a number of occasions when the European parliament adopted resolutions calling on governments, including even ones that were not members of the Council of Europe, to take appropriate steps to correct certain lapses in their respect of human rights. Viable regional parliaments could perform similar monitoring functions.

The election of members of regional parliaments on the basis of universal suffrage could provide additional long-term benefits in furthering a culture of respect for pluralism in the political systems of individual countries. As noted by Professor Gambari (1992, p. 7):

> It would be unusual, although not inconceivable, for a government that itself is not a product of the democratic process to allow democratic elections for members of the Community Parliament. The logic would therefore seem to suggest a certain degree of symmetry between the democratic basis of the major organs of the AEC and the principal organs which constitute the governments of the member states.

The question is how this required symmetry in democratic processes at the national and regional levels will be achieved in practice when some countries are less advanced than others on the road to democracy. It will certainly be more difficult to launch the democratization process at the regional level under those conditions. However, one might hope for regional practice to emulate democratic values as practised in the more-advanced states. Should this occur, the institutionalization of democratic processes at the community level could be expected to seep into the political fabric of all member states, by reinforcing a general culture of respect for these principles.

THE NEW REGIONAL COURTS AND HUMAN RIGHTS

Two institutions that have the potential to promote and protect human rights in Africa are the proposed African Court of Justice (African Court) and the ECOWAS Court of Justice (ECOWAS Court), as foreseen in Article 18 of the AEC Treaty and Article 15 of the ECOWAS Revised Treaty. Both courts are integral parts of their respective organizations.

Although Article 20 of the AEC Treaty provides that a protocol would be concluded by the Assembly of Heads of State and Government setting out the membership, procedures, and other relevant matters pertaining to the African Court, this protocol has yet to be prepared. The protocol relating to the ECOWAS Court *has*, however, been signed (ECOWAS Protocol A/P.1/7/91). In the absence of the protocol relative to the African Court, one can only conjecture that its terms will not differ much from that of the ECOWAS Court. This assumption allows us to examine the possible impact of the two courts on human rights in Sub-Saharan Africa, using the experience of the European Court of Justice as a reference point.

If these courts are to be of any value in the promotion of human rights, the nature of their jurisdiction and the efficacy of their decisions matter even more than their creation. At issue are the subject matter that comes within their scope of authority, the category of people who have lawful access to the courts, and the choice of enforcement mechanisms.

SUBJECT MATTER

The treaties of the EU contain no explicit general reference to human rights in their provisions (McBride and Brown 1981, p. 167), although they guarantee some rights such as free movement of workers and equal pay for equal work. This gap notwithstanding, the European Court of Justice has on occasions come close to giving direct effect to the ECHR.[3] Mendelsen (1981) has also made some suggestions for subsuming the provisions of the ECHR under the adjudicatory powers of the European Court of Justice, through either the "guidelines approach" whereby the provisions of the ECHR would be taken by the European Court of Justice as the best combination of the fundamental rights of the member states; or the "substitution approach" based on Article 234 of the EEC treaty, which binds the member states to relevant treaties relating to the community (Mendelsen 1981, p. 125; Foster 1987, p. 245).

The AEC and the ECOWAS treaties do not suffer the same lack of explicit reference to the provisions of the ACHPR. Article 18(2) of the AEC Treaty calls for the African Court to ensure the adherence to law in the interpretation of the treaty and to decide on disputes pursuant to the treaty. Article 18(3)(a) further provides that the court:

> Decide on actions brought by a Member State or Assembly on grounds of the violation of the provisions of this Treaty, or of a decision or a regulation or on grounds of lack of competence or abuse of powers by an organ, an authority or a Member State.

Among the matters in Article 3 of the AEC Treaty, which sets out the basic principles to which the high contracting parties solemnly affirmed and declared their adherence, is paragraph (g) which reaffirms their commitment to the

> Recognition, promotion and protection of human and peoples' rights in accordance with the provisions of the African Charter on Human and Peoples' Rights.

---

[3]See the case of Rutili described in Brown and Jacobs 1983, p. 272). The Commission of the European Communities had considered the options of adopting a Community Bill of Rights or acceding directly to the European Convention on Human Rights as ways of ensuring clarity on the issue of fundamental rights as it relates to the European Court of Justice; however, neither of these options was pursued (see McBride and Brown 1981, p. 168; Brown and Jacobs 1983, p. 274).

The remaining portions of the treaty make no mention of the ACHPR and its provisions. However, the jurisdiction of the African Court, as described in Article 18(3)(a), to include actions brought on grounds of the violation of the provisions of the treaty, extends to the provisions of the ACHPR, as a function of Article 3(g). The provisions of the ACHPR have, by implication, been incorporated into the provisions of the AEC Treaty, and the court should therefore have jurisdiction over it.

The ECOWAS Revised Treaty accords similar recognition to the ACHPR, since Article 4(g) of the ECOWAS Revised Treaty is a carbon copy of Article 3(g) of the AEC Treaty. The argument advanced for the African Court's jurisdiction on matters of relevance to the ACHPR thus applies to the ECOWAS Court as well.

Should the above argument be controverted, Article 18(4) of the AEC Treaty contains an overriding clause that permits the Assembly of Heads of State and Government to "confer on the Court of Justice the power to assume jurisdiction by virtue of this Treaty over *any dispute*, other than those referred to in paragraph 3(a) [of Article 18]" (emphasis added). By virtue of this provision, the Assembly could easily incorporate the subject matter covered by the ACHPR into the scope of jurisdiction of the African Court. A similar argument can be made for the ECOWAS Court.

The scope of jurisdiction of the two African courts thus appears wide enough to cover the human rights issues of the continent as provided for under the ACHPR.

Access to the Courts

Human rights violations are more often than not the result of government action toward its citizens or those of other countries. It follows that concerns to redress human rights abuses will more often be the preoccupation of individuals, or groups of individuals, rather than the state. Any machinery for the enforcement of human rights that is not easily accessible to ordinary people is, therefore, inappropriate from the start.

Unfortunately, the two African courts suffer from precisely such a defect. According to Articles 3 and 4 of the AEC Treaty and Article 9 of the ECOWAS Treaty, only a member state or the Assembly of Heads of State and Government can seize the court. This lack of access is exacerbated by the absence of an independent commission (such as the Commission of the European Communities) capable of acting as an intermediary for individuals or groups in seizing the courts. Such commissions, if created, could join the regional and subregional parliaments as human rights monitors on the continent or in West Africa.

In comparison, the European system affords people other than member states greater opportunity. The European Court of Human Rights, established under the ECHR, did not accord direct access to individuals, either. However, the EEC treaty did permit access of individuals to the European Court of Justice to review the legality of actions by the Council of the European Communities or the Commission of the European Communities.[4] Infringements by member states are shielded from direct individual complaint procedures by Articles 169 to 171 of the EEC treaty (Wyatt and Dashwood 1987, p. 74), and only the Commission or a member state can initiate actions against a member state that fails to honour its obligations under the treaty. However, individuals can act by lodging a complaint with the Commission, which might then proceed, in accordance with Article 169, to the European Court of Justice. The individual may also institute action against a member state in that state's own court and, where appropriate, request that a reference be made to the European Court for a preliminary ruling on the interpretation of the community provision under dispute (Wyatt and Dashwood 1987).

The importance attached to direct individual access to the courts in Europe is further reflected in Article 11 of the 1986 *Single Europe Act*, which added a new section to the EEC Treaty (section 168A). This new section envisaged the attachment to the Court of Justice of a court of first instances with jurisdiction to hear and determine (subject to a right of appeal to the Court of Justice on points of law) a certain class of actions or proceedings brought by natural or legal persons. Such a Court of First Instances has since been established and charged with certain matters brought by firms concerning the special community "tax," production controls, price regulations or antitrust matters, and damages arising from improper acts of community institutions (for a brief comment on this, see Wyatt and Dashwood 1987, p. 83; also Suit and Herzog 1992, vol. 4).

---

[4] This has been labeled an action for annulment (Articles 173, 174, and 176 of the EEC treaty). Article 173 of the EEC treaty limits access to individuals with some "direct" interest in any act other than recommendations or opinions of the Council of the European Communities or the Commission of the European Communities (Wyatt and Dashwood 1987, p. 75). However, the court has been liberal in its construction of that provision (Suit and Herzog 1992, vol. 5, p. 363 et seq). Of equal importance is Article 175 which permits any natural or legal person to complain to the Court of Justice that an institution of the community has failed to address to that person any act other than a recommendation or an opinion.

ENFORCEMENT PROVISIONS

A human rights regulating mechanism that lacks the force of compulsion to ensure compliance with the decisions of the adjudicatory authorities is of little value to an aggrieved individual, especially in the African context where public opinion and outrage at human rights abuses normally have had little effect on African leaders. Even the African commission created under the ACHPR can only make its reports public if so authorized by the Assembly of Heads of State and Government. Apart from this possibility of publication, nothing is said under the ACHPR about the steps that should be taken by the defaulting government to redress any grievances. Everything is left to the discretion of the defaulting state.

Article 3 of the AEC Treaty and Article 5 of the ECOWAS Revised Treaty have now introduced some seriousness into the decisions that might be reached by the Assembly and Authority of Heads of State and Government, respectively. Article 3 of the AEC Treaty is very clear on this issue. It states:

> Any Member State which persistently fails to honour its general undertakings under this Treaty or fails to abide by the decisions or regulations of the Community may be subjected to sanctions by the Assembly upon the recommendation of the Council. Such sanctions may include the suspension of the rights and privileges of membership and may be lifted by the Assembly upon the recommendation of the Council.

The recognition of sanctions in these treaties makes it possible, at least in principle, for African leaders to take positive steps to ensure respect for their decisions. Vigorously applied, such a mechanism would enable African leaders to prevail upon their colleagues to respect basic human rights or face diplomatic and economic boycotts or suspension of their rights and privileges of membership in the community.

HUMANITARIAN INTERVENTION

The third mechanism of potential importance is humanitarian intervention. The doctrine of humanitarian intervention relates to the forceful intervention by one country in the affairs of another to prevent further gross and persistent violation of the rights of citizens in that country. A number of commentators have cast doubts on the existence of any such right to intervene for humanitarian purposes in customary international law; others grant the doctrine limited legality; and still others claim that it is recognized as an integral part of the Law of Nations (US Institute of

Peace n.d.). However an interesting feature of most humanitarian interventions has been the lack of condemnation by the international community, or tacit approval.

The obvious fear of those who have persistently denied the doctrine the character of legality is the possibility of its abuse against the sovereign rights of nations, but as we saw in the introduction, the concept of absolute sovereignty of states is being eroded, and theorists have supported intervention in defence of human rights on the grounds that the rights of states themselves derive from human rights (Teson 1988). Of course the magnitude of the human rights violations cannot be ignored. According to Teson (1988, p. 243), intervention is warranted for violations that are shocking to the conscience of mankind because they are so widespread or persistent, or because the are so manifestly "disrespectful" of human values. The doctrine or notion of *national margin of appreciation* which has developed in the jurisprudence of the European Court of Human Rights cautions that "certain evaluations and value judgements in the human rights field must be left to the competent state organs and cannot be substituted by evaluations and judgements of the Commission of the European Communities or the European Court" (Bernhardt 1986, p. 213). However, it is the international organ, i.e., the court, that has the competence to decide where to set the limits.

There has been some debate on the adequacy of the accumulated experience of humanitarian intervention for establishing the legal basis of the doctrine (Lillich 1979, p. 598 et seq), but recent experiences in Somalia, Liberia, Bosnia, and Rwanda are providing new cases for the establishment of customary rules.

The ECOWAS intervention in the Liberian imbroglio established a precedent for the future use of humanitarian intervention in West Africa. Although difficult to justify on the basis of the 1975 ECOWAS Treaty, the decision to send the ECOWAS Monitoring Group into Liberia was clearly determined by humanitarian considerations. According to President Babangida, it would have been "morally reprehensible and politically indefensible to stand by and watch while the citizens of that country decimate themselves" (West Africa 1991, p. 213). From the ECOWAS perspective, it was a humanitarian intervention.

An analysis of the ECOWAS Revised Treaty reveals an opening for this sort of intervention. Under it, all member states of ECOWAS commit themselves to regional security, the establishment of a "regional peace and security observation system and... peace-keeping forces where appropriate" (Article 58). If one takes gross violations of human rights as a threat to regional peace and security, and taking together the letter and the spirit of the ECOWAS Revised Treaty and the Declaration of Political Principles, the conclusion is obvious that the concept of absolute sovereignty is no longer considered acceptable. This evolution of international principles includes an implicit acceptance by the countries of the subregion of the legality of humanitarian intervention.

Evolving views such as these stand in contrast to the traditionally conservative view of the OAU on the subject of noninterference, as expressed in Article III(2) of the OAU Charter, which prohibits interference in the internal affairs of member states, even in pursuit of the purposes of the OAU. However, the OAU's position has also begun to change. According to its secretary-general, in an interview with *West Africa* magazine, the 1990 declaration of the OAU Summit on the Political and Socio-Economic Situation in Africa and the Foundational Changes Taking Place in the World was path-breaking in its reflection of a broadening consensus among member states on the need to revisit the noninterference principle. In his words, this change signaled "acceptance by member states that the OAU could concern itself not only with interstate conflicts but with internal ones as well" (West Africa 1992, p. 1524).

The follow-up to this came at the 28th ordinary session of the assembly (19 June to 1 July 1992) when the assembly expressed its grave concerns over the proliferation of conflicts in Africa, the accompanying suffering, and the adverse security and socioeconomic implications. This led the assembly to agree on the establishment, within the framework of the OAU, of a mechanism for the prevention, management, and resolution of conflicts in Africa. The resolution then called upon the secretary-general of the OAU to "undertake an in-depth study on all aspects relating to such a mechanism including institutional and operational details as well as its financing" (OAU 1992). The impact of these resolutions on the principle of noninterference and the issue of humanitarian intervention was clearly explained by the secretary-general as follows:

> Within the context of general international law as well as humanitarian law, Africa should take the lead in *developing the notion that sovereignty can legally be transcended by the "intervention" of "outside forces,"* in their will to facilitate prevention and/or resolution, particularly on humanitarian grounds. In other words, given that every African is his brother's keeper, and that our borders are at best artificial, we in Africa need to use our own cultural and social relationships to interpret the principle of non-interference in such a way that we are enabled to apply

it to our own advantage in conflict prevention and resolution. [West Africa 1992; emphasis added]

The will to carry out multilateral humanitarian intervention on the continent has clearly evolved, and is gradually being reflected in international legal structures.

BEYOND THE STATE: THE ROLE OF NGOS

Although the emphasis of this chapter has been on the legal and political instruments on the horizon for the defense of human rights at the regional level, such instruments do not operate in a social vacuum. As US Justice Hand eloquently expressed it, "liberty lies in the hearts of men and women; when it dies there, no constitution, no law, no court can even do much to help it" (quoted in Proehl 1970, p. 1).

It is the whole culture of respect for human rights that must be reinforced in Africa. Human rights must be taken for granted, not only by heads of state or human rights activists, but also by every citizen. The first step in achieving this would be by educating all citizens on their basic rights and how to protect them. One is reminded of the Universal Declaration of Human Rights that, since 1948, has exhorted that, "every individual and every organ of society... shall strive by teaching and education to promote respect for these rights..." and much remains to be done in this regard.

Many NGOs devoted to the promotion and protection of human rights have recently emerged in Africa. The importance of these organizations cannot be overemphasized because the individuals who fall victim to human rights abuses at the hands of the government do not usually have the resources to defend themselves unaided.

Recourse to the courts by NGOs constitutes one means for putting pressure on errant governments. In this, it bears repeating that the AEC Treaty and the ECOWAS Treaty should have gone a step further to confer legal capacity upon both individuals and NGOs to seize the respective regional courts, thus enhancing the seriousness with which human rights abuses can be challenged.

According to Welch (1992), the dearth of NGOs in Africa has been one of the factors contributing to the ineffectiveness of the African Commission on Human Rights. In his view, the Commission lacks the independent, Africa-based sources of information about human rights abuses and the domestic advocacy groups for its activities that NGOs could provide and will continue to suffer in that capacity "until and unless a substantial number of human rights organizations are founded south of the Sahara" (Welch 1992, p. 60).

Of late, the expanding political consciousness of the people of the Sub-Saharan region and their strong motivation to defend fundamental rights have led to an increase in the number of NGOs in many countries of the region. Examples are the Ghana Committee for Human and Peoples' Rights, the Civil Liberties Organization of Nigeria, the Constitutional Rights Project and others of Nigeria, the Cameroon Human Rights Organization, the National Commission of Human Rights in Togo, the Chadian League of Human Rights, and many others (see Wiseberg and Reiner 1988/89). As of April 1991, the African Commission on Human Rights had granted observer status to 37 human rights NGOs, including some from outside the continent (Welch 1992, p. 60).

The effectiveness of these and emerging NGOs in tackling politically delicate operations could be increased through better cooperation at the subregional level, around one or more networks of national and international human rights groups, in cooperation with organizations such as Amnesty International. Such cooperation would permit a pooling of efforts and resources and a degree of international publicity otherwise unavailable to mobilize public opinion, marshall political pressure, and apply legal pressure to ensure respect for the basic rights of individuals, while preventing intimidation of NGOs themselves by irate governments. One organization currently doing this is the Union interafricaine des droits de l'homme (UIDH). This new organization, based in Burkina Faso, aims to link human rights organizations of African countries into a single network. Its current activities are more strongly felt in the French-speaking nations of West Africa, but this is the sort of activity that is needed region-wide.

The danger of harassment of NGOs and human rights activists is currently very real, and Wiseberg and Reiner (1988/89) provide a useful review of some of the protective measures that can be used. These include constant public exposure of any persecution of NGOs and activists; diplomatic pressure on defaulting governments to release detained human rights activists; and expressions of international solidarity and recognition. Wiseberg and Reiner suggest the need for an association of human rights activists, charged with maintaining links between NGOs and monitoring their situations and those of individual activists. They also recommend the appointment of a high commissioner or ombudsman for human rights, and greater access to international organizations by human rights NGOs.

Conclusion

There are reasons to hope that the next 10 years will see substantial progress in the area of human rights in Africa: democratization has taken hold in most countries, in one form or another; human rights NGOs are flourishing; and heads of states are themselves seeking to advance the principles of human rights, through regional and subregional institutions and the recognition that responsibility for the respect of human rights extends beyond national borders.

In this chapter, I have attempted to show the potential contribution of regional institutions and regional collaboration in the furtherance of human rights, through the regional and subregional parliaments and courts of justice and, when necessary, through humanitarian intervention. The materialization of these suggestions will take time, but the realization that human rights is not a strictly internal matter is already a substantial achievement.

The relationship between human rights and regional integration is a bipolar one. Regional institutions can help further the cause of human rights; but a concentration of political energy around common political values can also help further the process of regional integration. The pursuit of respect for human rights can help nurture that sense of community that religion, ideology, and ethnicity have so far failed to provide, but that is essential to the pursuit of regional integration in West Africa and Africa as a whole. The defense of human rights by regional institutions would greatly reinforce the legitimacy of those institutions, and efforts to marshal resources in defense of human rights could help develop the solidarity of people from different nationalities, through a system in which people of all origins can protest before the courts about the human rights abuses suffered by others.

References

Alston, P. 1982/83. A third generation of solidarity rights: progressive development or obfuscation of international rights law? Netherlands International Law Review, 29, 307-322.

Bernhardt, R. 1986. Domestic jurisdiction of states and international organizations. Human Rights Laws Journal, 7, 205-216.

Bilder, R. 1992. International law in the new world orders: some preliminary reflections. Florida State University Journal of Transnational Law and Policy, 1 (1).

Brown, L.N. and Jacobs. 1983. The court of justice of the European communities (2nd ed). Sweet and Maxwell, London, UK.

D'Sa, Rose M. 1985. Human and peoples' rights: distinctive features of the African charter. Journal of African Law, 29 (1), 72-81.

ECOWAS (Economic Community of West African States). 1991. Declaration of political principles. ECOWAS, Lagos, Nigeria.

———— 1993. Economic Community of West African States Revised Treaty. ECOWAS Secretariat, Lagos, Nigeria.

Eze, O.C. 1984. Human rights in Africa: some selected problems. Nigerian Institute of International Affairs, Macmillan Nigerian Publishers, Lagos, Nigeria.

Foster, N. 1987. The European court of justice and the European convention for the protection of human rights. Human Rights Law Journal, 9, 245-272.

Gambari, I. 1992. The political implications of the African economic community. Presented at the International conference on the African economic community treaty, 27–30 January. Nigerian Institute of Advanced Legal Studies, Lagos, Nigeria.

Gyandoh, S.O. Jr. 1990. Human rights and the acquisition of national sovereignty. In Berting, J. et al. (ed.). Human rights in a pluralist world. Greenwood, Westport, CT, USA.

Hartley, T.C. 1988. The foundations of European community law. Clarendon Press, Oxford, UK.

Higgins, R. 1976/77. Derogations under human rights treaties. British Year Book of International Law, 47, 281-320.

Kiwanuka, R.N. 1988. The meaning of people in the African charter on human and peoples' rights. American Journal of International Law, 82 (1), 80-101.

Leckie, S. 1988. The inter-state complaint procedure in international human rights law: hopeful prospector or wishful thinking? Human Rights Quarterly, 10, 249–250.

Lillich, R.B. 1979. International human rights: problems of law, policy and practice (2nd ed). Little Brown, London, UK.

McBride, J.; Brown, L.N. 1981. The United Kingdom, the European Community and the European Convention on Human Rights. Year Book of European Law. Oxford University Press, Oxford, England, 167-205.

Mendelsen, M.H. 1981. The European court of justice and human rights. Year Book of European Law. Oxford University Press, Oxford, England, 125-165.

OAU (Organization of African Unity). 1991. Treaty of the African Economic Community (AEC). OAU, Addis Ababa, Ethiopia.

———— 1992. Decision on a mechanism for conflict prevention, management and resolution. OAU, Addis Ababa, Ethopia.

Ojo, O.; Sesay, A. 1986. The OAU and human rights: prospects for the 1980s and beyond. Human Rights Quarterly, 8.

Okere, B.O. 1984. The protection of human rights in Africa and the African charter on human and peoples' rights: a comparative analysis with the European and American systems. Human Rights Quarterly, 6 (2).

Onu, P. 1985. The concept of peoples' rights in the "Banjul" charter. Presented at the International conference on human rights education in rural environment, 26–29 November, 1985. Nigeria Institute of Advanced Legal Studies, University of Lagos, Nigeria.

Proehl, P.D. 1970. Fundamental rights under the Nigerian constitution, 1960–1965. African Studies Centre, University of California, Los Angeles, CA, USA.

Suit, H.; Herzog, P. 1992. The law of the European Economic Community. Matthew Bender, New York.

Teson, F.R. 1988. Humanitarian intervention: an inquiry into law morality. Transnational Publishers, Dobbs Ferry, NY, USA.

Tucker, C.M. 1983. Regional human rights models in Europe and Africa: a comparison. Syracuse Journal of International Law and Commerce, 10, 135-168.

United States Institute for Peace. n.d. The three views on the issue of humanitarian intervention. US Institute for Peace, University of Hawaii, Honolulu, HI, USA. Mimeo.

Welch, C.E. Jr. 1992. African Commission on Human and Peoples' Rights: a five year report on assessment. Human Rights Quarterly, 14 (1), 43–61.

West Africa. 1991. A ticklish question. West Africa, 18-24 February, p. 213.

West Africa. 1992. Salim on security: the OAU Secretary-General Salim Ahmed talks to editor-in-chief Kaye Whiteman on his ideas for a security mechanism for Africa. West Africa, 7-13 Septembre, p. 1525.

Weston, B.H. 1987. Regional human rights regimes: a comparison and appraisal. Vanderbilt Journal of Transnational Law, 20 (4), 585-637.

Wiseberg, L.S.; Reiner, L. (ed). 1988/89. Africa: human rights directory and bibliography. Human Rights Internet Reporter, 1 (4).

Wyatt, D.; Dashwood, A. 1987. The substantive law of the EEC. Sweet and Maxwell, London, UK.

CHAPTER 14

THE REGIONAL DIMENSION OF ENVIRONMENTAL MANAGEMENT

*– Guy Debailleul, Éric Grenon,
Muimana-Muende Kalala,
and André Vuillet –*

The authors of this chapter take a geopolitical approach that combines geo-physical, institutional, and sociopolitical aspects of how to promote sustainable development in the subregion. Desertification is one of the most urgent environmental challenges in West Africa, and the authors have targeted it as a way off illustrating their approach. They review the causes of desertification, focusing on the impact of human actions, and go on to highlight the wide range of remedial measures that have been attempted, and the lack of coordination among them.

The impact of desertification is primarily felt in the Sahelian and sub-Sahelian regions, but also in coastal areas. The effect on coastal areas includes the indirect impact of migration from northern areas to the coast as people are obliged to abandon their degraded lands in search of new livelihoods. The causes of desertification also appear to have a regional dimension, due to bioclimatic links whereby the destruction of the vegetative cover in one zone (deforestation along the coast, for example) leads to a reduction in rainfall in adjoining areas.

The authors propose the use of remote sensing as one tool for studying these phenomena while monitoring the progress of remedial action on the ground, but point to the political challenges involved in making effective use of this technology. The costs of desertification control will have to be widely shared at all levels of intervention, from that of the international agencies covering the cost of satellite images all the way down to the villages or individual farmers taking on reforestation or dike-building projects.

NUMEROUS AFRICAN STATES and external aid agencies have adopted sustainable development and regional integration as systematic points of reference. It is, therefore, surprising to find how little recognition has been given to the interplay between these two issue areas, and how reluctant the major international bodies are to address them in an integrated fashion. However, the interdependence of environmental and socioeconomic issues and the need for harmonization of efforts at the regional level are becoming increasingly clear.

Environmental problems affect most West African countries, which share the same ecosystems and are subject to similar phenomena: the extension of agriculture to new lands, reduced fallowing, demographic pressures, migration, water management problems, conflicts between farmers and pastoralists, etc. Arresting the degradation of renewable resources has become an important goal in redefining agricultural and rural development policies and designing rural development projects and programs. However, the effectiveness of such efforts is severely handicapped by the narrowness of the national framework within which they are being applied.

To the extent that regional harmonization of environmental action is desirable, the challenge is to define the kinds of regional integration and cooperation best suited to the promotion of effective responses to the environmental problems facing West Africa, with regard to the types and levels of cooperation and the resources to be invested.

As defined by the Brundtland Report (1989), sustainable development involves the satisfaction of basic human needs and the opportunity for everyone to aspire to a better life. It must therefore meet the needs of today without compromising the ability of future generations to meet their own needs. This involves avoiding certain types of debt capable of foreclosing the prospects of future generations. Such "debts" can take several forms, including:

- *financial* debts, resulting from the build-up of long-term borrowing, abroad or at home;

- *social* debts, incurred by failure to invest in human development;

- *demographic* debts, arising from the effects of uncontrolled population growth; and

- *ecological* debts, resulting from the overexploitation of natural resources or pollution of the soil, water, and atmosphere.

The concept of sustainable development argues in favour of greater integration of both economic and environmental policies at the national level and that of ecological zones, irrespective of political boundaries.

It seems to us important, in dealing with regional aspects of the environmental challenge in West Africa, to highlight a few of the relations between the environment and development, the economy, demographics, human behaviour, and political structures, across the dimensions of space and time, from the local to the international level, and linking past actions to their future implications over the long term.

The political dimension is of special importance, because geographic and political areas seldom correspond to ecological ones. Yet all activity involving regional integration or cooperation runs into obstacles of a technical, financial, or human sort, stemming from competing political interests. The integration process is thus marked by conflict and contradiction, due to the multiplicity of players, the range of relationships involved, and the overlapping of spatial jurisdictions (Hugon 1990, p. 13). To apply the frequently used notion of political will to issues of environmental integration thus requires that we understand the motivations of a whole range of actors, at the subregional and international levels, acting in concert with national leaders, all of whom have a role to play in restoring and protecting the environment. This calls for an understanding of the constraints faced by these various actors, and an appreciation of sociopolitical realities in West African countries.

We seek to illustrate the regional nature of some of West Africa's environmental problems and argue for the incorporation of environmental issues in current efforts at West African integration and cooperation. For illustrative purposes, we focus on the issue of desertification, which represents a major environmental challenge of regional scope, in terms of breadth, cause, and consequence, and critically review international, national, and local initiatives taken in response to desertification in the Sahel.

We then propose an analytical framework in aid of current reflection and practice regarding integrated regional action on the environment. Environmental initiatives have suffered in a serious way from lack of regional coordination, and this leads us to propose a geopolitical model intended to lend a degree of coherence to the many facets of environmental degradation in West Africa. We illustrate the applicability of the geopolitical model to environmental issues on a regional scale through a discussion of remote sensing, which we highlight as an ideal instrument for demonstrating the many layers involved in an understanding of the desertification issue.

DESERTIFICATION: A MAJOR ENVIRONMENTAL CHALLENGE FOR WEST AFRICA

West Africa faces numerous environmental problems, each of which would seem to demand absolute priority from decision-makers and external agencies in the elaboration of their strategies for sustainable development. These environmental challenges are most clearly apparent at the strictly biophysical level, where they show up as major ecological problems such as deforestation and the degeneration of arid lands. However, they also take on a human dimension, as a result of demographic pressures on the environment or the impact of poverty on the degradation of the natural resource base.

The desertification phenomenon in Sahelian and sub-Sahelian regions has attracted substantial attention from the international community since the great droughts of the 1970s and, more generally, in light of the decline in rainfall in the Sahel in the 1970s and 1980s compared with levels of the 1950s and 60s (often used as a yardstick of good rainfall). The vegetative cover of the Sahel has been receding for the last several decades, and time-series imaging from satellites, aerial photographs, and vegetation studies clearly show the process of desertification at work (Stroosnijder 1992, p. 78).

It is nonetheless important to differentiate the impact of declining rainfall on the environment from that of human intervention. A report of the United Nations Sudano-Sahelian Office (UNSO) (UNDP 1992), thus makes a distinction between three major ecological problems in the Sahel:

- unpredictable and often severe *droughts* that may last for 2 years or more, when rainfall is substantially below average;

- *desiccation*, characterized by increased aridity of the soil after several decades of dry weather; and

- *arid-land degradation* resulting from improper exploitation of the land in an already precarious environment.

Whereas drought is a natural climatic phenomenon entailing a serious water deficit that temporarily restricts agricultural production, desertification results from a complex phenomenon of human interaction with the environment leading to the "irreversible" degradation of the soil and ground cover. Desertification can occur not only in drought-prone areas, such as the Sahel, but also in places relatively distant from the desert. Pockets of desert can thus form even in the midst of semihumid or humid zones.

Desertification occurs throughout the Sahel wherever the physical or chemical deterioration of the soil induced by human intervention has deprived the ecosystem of the vitality it needs to recuperate from short or long periods of drought or overexploitation. Three human activities are conventionally cited as main causes of desertification, although the nature of their interaction is not fully understood. These are agricultural overexploitation (stemming jointly from population growth and the development of cash crops), overgrazing, and deforestation (Mathieu 1991).

According to Tabutin and Thilgès (1992, p. 288), desertification is a complex process conditioned by three types of factors:

♦ the *structural characteristics* of production systems, whether of a physical (soil, climate), socioeconomic, or cultural nature;

♦ *behavioural strategies*, involving either individuals (such as subsistence farmers and pastoralists) or collectives (such as governments or funding agencies);

♦ *major secular trends*, such as population growth, the spread of the monetary economy, or the reduced role of the community in natural resource management.

The human problems that have an impact on the environment in West Africa have to do with the perverse effects of several factors: *demographic growth*; *migration* from rural to urban areas, or from countries of the Sahel to those of the coast; particular forms of *land tenure*; and *poverty*, which is both a cause and effect of environmental degradation.

According to Engelhard and Ben Abdallah (1992, p. 73), there is a causal relationship in Africa, as there was in certain parts of Europe before the agricultural revolution, between growing demographic pressure, ecological degradation, and decreasing agricultural output per capita. In this analysis, population density is interpreted relative to the "natural" carrying capacity of the environment as determined by the fragility of natural resources and the harshness of the climate (Stroosnijder 1992, p. 79). Regional disparities mirror the destabilizing effects of demographic pressure and are translated into migratory flows toward the towns or more privileged regions (Engelhard and Ben Abdallah 1992, p. 74).

Streeten (1992) points to poverty as the greatest enemy of sustainable development, but adds that environmental degradation only makes poverty worse. Projects aimed at restoring ecosystems and giving people a greater sense of responsibility for managing their environment are thus doomed to failure unless basic human needs can be satisfied. One can hardly blame rural people for seeking to satisfy their immediate food requirements before worrying about the environment. Rural communities are, in most cases, fully aware that they are contributing to the deterioration of their own lands, but have little choice in the matter when their short-term survival is at stake.

African officials and the various funding agencies are well aware of the degradation of the natural environment due to drought, desertification, and deforestation. Many strategies have been developed to conserve, maintain, and exploit the natural resource base, and this has led to the implementation of numerous action plans and programs. These initiatives can be grouped into those of an international, regional, or subregional character, and those that are of a purely national or local nature (Figures 1 to 3).

INTERNATIONAL AND REGIONAL CONFERENCES AND FRAMEWORK AGREEMENTS

As Falloux and Talbot (1992, pp. 19–20) have pointed out, international conservation strategies date back to the colonial period, through such initiatives as:

- the Convention for the Preservation of Wild Animals, Birds and Fish, signed by the colonial authorities in London in 1900, which committed the signatories to better management of African wildlife and the protection of natural resources in their respective colonies;

- the creation in 1903 of the Imperial Wildlife Preservation Society, which later became the Flora and Fauna Preservation Society, and remains today one of the most active NGOs in this field;

- the Convention on the Preservation of Flora and Fauna in their Natural State, which resulted from the London conference on the protection of African flora and fauna organized by the British government in 1933. This agreement was intended not only to strengthen the protection of wildlife but also to promote the establishment of national parks and the adoption of new conservation measures for wildlife and natural ecosystems;

- the 1961 Arusha conference, jointly sponsored by FAO, Unesco and the Commission for Technical Cooperation in Africa of the

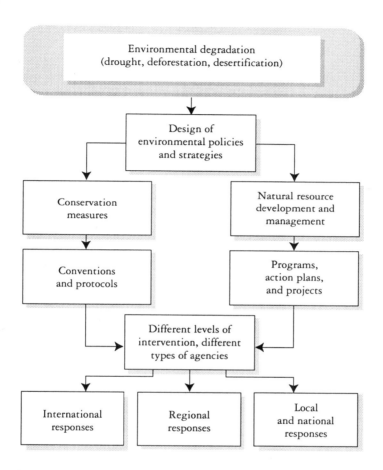

Figure 1. A Global View of Responses to Environmental Degradation.
Source: Developed from information in CILSS, 1991 and UNDP, 1992.

Scientific Council for Africa (CTCA/SCA), to which the newly
independent African countries were invited by the International
Union for the Conservation of Nature and Natural Resources
(IUCN), with the aim of introducing conservation into the planning and development process of these new states. This was the
first time such a conference went beyond questions of parks and
reserves, to address the broader issue of the environment writ
large, in an attempt to place development in an ecological and
cultural perspective.

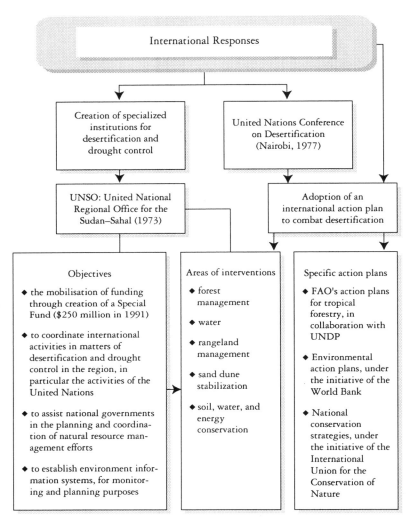

Figure 2. International Responses.
Source: Developed from information in CILSS, 1991 and UNDP, 1992.

The Arusha conference was the precursor of growing international awareness of the ecological dimensions of development. The strong links between development and environment were increasingly recognized and confirmed by a series of international events: first the United Nations Conference on the Human Environment (Stockholm 1972), the IUCN's World Conservation Strategy, and finally the creation of the World

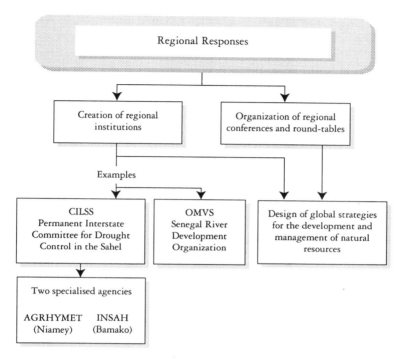

Figure 3. Examples of Regional and Sub-regional Actions.
Source: Developed from information in CILSS, 1991 and UNDP, 1992.

Commission on the Environment and Development, which produced the Brundtland Report (*Our Common Future*) in 1989.

Faced with continued destruction of Africa's natural resources, the United Nations Environment Programme (UNEP) accepted the proposal of African members at its 11th session in 1983 to promote the organization of a ministerial conference on the environment. The aim was to examine priorities for the continent, identify issues of common interest, and prepare a regional action program. This led to the creation of the African Ministerial Conference on the Environment (AMCE). Its first meeting was held in Cairo in December 1985, and resulted in an ambitious document known as the *Cairo Program*, which took the rehabilitation and improvement of the environment as the indispensable starting point for sustainable development.

Four commissions (on deserts and arid lands, river and lake basins, the oceans, and forests and wooded areas) were set up to translate the program's proposals into action, along with eight networks aimed at promoting institutional cooperation, information gathering and distribution, research, and the sharing of expertise (on the subjects of environmental monitoring, climate, water, soils and fertilizers, energy, environmental education and training, genetic resources, and science and technology).

REGIONAL INSTITUTIONS

These conferences and framework agreements have led to the establishment of institutions and agencies for regional and subregional coordination. As a result, there now exist in Africa, especially in West Africa, a great number of regional and subregional organizations with a wide range of mandates. In the area of natural resource development, notably that of watershed management, there are: the Niger Basin Authority (ABN); the Organization for the Management and Development of the Kagera River Basin (OBK); the Gambia River Basin Development Organization (OMVG); the Senegal River Development Organization (OMVS); and the Liptako Gourma Integrated Development Authority (ADILG) (Belaouane-Gherari and Gherari 1988). To these can be added certain United Nations institutions, certain NGOs, and various bilateral or multilateral financial and technical assistance institutions.

In the area of environment and natural resource management, three agencies stand out in particular: the Permanent Inter-State Committee on Drought Control in the Sahel (CILSS), the Club du Sahel, and the UNSO. CILSS was founded in September 1973, in the wake of the great drought that gripped a large part of West Africa from 1968 to 1973. Its mandate and goals make CILSS a unique organization in West Africa in matters of drought and desertification control. Its dual mandate is to coordinate international assistance to Sahelian countries, while promoting the adoption of sound strategies and policies (CILSS 1991, p. 55). It is supported by the Club du Sahel, made up of over 20 funding agencies, under the aegis of the OECD.

UNSO is attached to the United Nations Development Programme (UNDP) and was established at virtually the same time as CILSS, in October 1973, by the United Nations' General Assembly. Its mandate is to respond to requests for assistance from CILSS and member governments, while providing aid in UNEP's name to the nine CILSS countries, the six countries of the Intergovernmental Authority on Drought and Development (IGADD), and other Sudano-Sahelian countries. Among its activities is included the provision of support to various countries and regional institutions in the planning and design of projects and programs in the area of drought and desertification control. An effort has been made to refocus UNSO's activities over the last 3 years, with CILSS and UNSO increasingly operating in tandem. UNSO has also encouraged greater collaboration between CILSS and IGADD.

Difficulties encountered by most regional agencies in fulfilling their roles point to a wide gap between declarations of good intentions, or the signature of general policy agreements, and their actual implementation. Any regional initiative will depend for its success on how well it manages the "national–regional" divide; as Club du Sahel experts have underlined, one of the major constraints in trying to promote a regional approach is that national leaders seem unwilling to accept any regional arrangement that might prove costly to their own countries, even when long-term benefits might be expected (Club du Sahel 1992).

OVERLAPPING PROGRAMS AT THE NATIONAL AND LOCAL LEVELS

If it is to be credible and effective, any regional initiative should be the fruit of sustained dialogue among participating countries with regard to the program's goals and objectives, strategy of action, and resource requirements. However, this presupposes a degree of internal policy coherence at the level of each country, which is rarely achieved. One can question the prospects for effective dialogue on regional actions in view of the discord that can be observed in natural resource management plans and programs at the national and local levels.

There are serious problems even with the harmonization of data and the standardization of measures in the area of natural resource management at the country level. In her study on setting up an environmental monitoring network in Niger, Hecht (1994, pp. 26–27) found that currently available data were virtually unusable for setting up a unified geographic information system, because they are so heterogeneous. In fact, more than 15 institutions and development projects were found to be producing information on natural resource management in Niger in January 1994. The lack of coordination between these various agencies makes it impossible to set standard units and measurement scales for the information that is collected on natural resource management. This means starting over again with new data-gathering exercises every time a new development project is undertaken. Such inconsistency takes on truly alarming proportions when we extrapolate it to the West African scene as a whole.

National strategies have been developed for drought and desertification control, natural resource management, and environmental management. However, these strategies have yielded a host of uncoordinated plans, programs, and initiatives, suffering from duplication, overlap, competition, and lack of coordination. A good illustration of this problem can be found in the case of Burkina Faso, where there exist a multitude of programs, only weakly linked to each other, including the following:

- the Drought Control and Development Strategy proposed by CILSS;

- the Desertification Control Strategy emanating from the above;

- the National Conservation Strategy of the International Union for the Conservation of Nature;

- the National Plan for Desertification Control;

- the National Environmental Action Plan;

- the Tropical Forestry Action Plan;

- the National Plan for the Management of Village Lands; and

- the Economic and Social Development Plan (CILSS 1991; UNDP 1992).

Much also remains to be done between countries, despite the numerous coordination efforts currently being attempted, because these efforts continue to be frustrated by a plethora of national initiatives that are often working at cross purposes as a result of competition for funds. International funding agencies are quite probably as responsible as any for waste of their own funds. However, the worst outcome may be the tremendous waste of national and local resources.

It is, therefore, indispensable to promote effective dialogue between the various players in the region so that environmental strategies and programs can be harmonized at the local and national levels, as well as regionally. This process requires that we address a number of questions. What monitoring systems might be used to create common points of reference and avoid the proliferation of isolated initiatives? What are the underlying motives and interests of actual plans and programs: are some programs largely the efforts of cash-strapped countries to marshall additional funds from the aid community, for example? What reluctance can one identify for certain partners to collaborate in certain programs, and for what reasons? What forms of coordination and dialogue should be of highest priority?

In the next section (inspired by Bernier and Vuillet 1992), we sketch the elements of an analytical framework addressing the environmental challenges of West Africa, in an attempt to capture the complexity of the political stakes around these issues, in space and time. Such an analysis might contribute to our understanding of the obstacles to increased coordination of environmental plans and programs in the region, and help us identify alternative approaches.

A GEOPOLITICAL APPROACH

Several observations can be highlighted from the preceding sections:

- the regional dimension of the desertification problem in West Africa;

- the numerous institutional initiatives at the international, regional, and national levels dedicated to the promotion of regional environmental management; and

- the need for the greater coordination of efforts, at the national level in particular.

Questions of "political will" regularly come to the surface in discussions of these issues, regarding for example: the will of countries to collaborate in an effective fashion in regional programs; the will of various actors to coordinate their efforts; and the true commitment of participating actors to the success of certain action programs. Problems of political will are systematically invoked as the magic wand of success or failure, by researchers and decision-makers alike, from the moment a new initiative is launched. Lack of political will serves as the perfect excuse for the failure of projects, the economic good sense of which seemed unquestionable at their inception.

The importance assigned to the concept of political will and the tremendous complexity of integrated environmental action suggest the need for appropriate analytical tools for finding one's way through the maze of players and levels of action involved in any effort to coordinate environmental action at the regional level.

An approach that lends itself well to this is that of geopolitics, a discipline that marries geography, history, and politics and seems made to order for our purposes. The geopolitical approach helps us to organize time and space in such as way as to highlight the interplay between political and geographic factors (Foucher 1991, p. 13). However, note that politics, in this approach, is not limited to affairs of the state. The notion of space, likewise, extends beyond that of political boundaries. The range of spacial scales explored under the geopolitical approach brings into play political rivalries between territories that are more confined or more extensive than those corresponding to national borders, depending on the level at which social interaction effectively takes place (Lacoste 1990, p. 1025).

An "interscalar" approach allows us to confront reality according to different analytical levels and spacial groupings (Figure 4). The horizontal scale represents a synoptic approach involving the study of all observable phenomena on a single scale; on the vertical axis are shown the various geographic scales (Foucher 1991, p. 35). This diagrammatic arrangement, borrowed from Lacoste (1990), allows us to visualize the problem as a three dimensional puzzle. Four scales are represented. At the first level are indicated the intersecting surfaces A, B, and C, corresponding to areas measured in tens of thousands of kilometers. These are areas measured on a planetary scale. At the other extreme (level 4), are those surfaces measured in tens of kilometers. As Lacoste puts it, "the geographic characteristics of a specific place or the interaction of phenomena that must be taken into account in acting upon this place can only be established with reference to the intersections of analytical levels" (Lacoste 1985, p. 72). Figure 4 provides a conceptual framework for mapping these intersecting spaces, and each level of the figure intersects the levels above and below it. Consider level three, for example, where the inner rectangle represents level 4, in reduced scale, while the heavy line F represents a part of surface F in level 2.

In West Africa, this kind of exercise allows us to superimpose various dimensions of reality across geoclimatic zones; major communications lines; regions of "traditional" or "informal" trading activity; the principal ecological, administrative, and political zones; areas corresponding to religious, linguistic, and ethnic groups; etc. Geopolitics also takes into account the dynamics of international cooperation.

GEOPOLITICS AND DESERTIFICATION

The geopolitical approach is also suggestive of the inadequacy of geographically bound analytical frameworks in approaching questions of the environment or of sustainable development, such as desertification in the Sahel. We pointed earlier to the regional scope of natural resource degradation through drought, desertification, and deforestation in West Africa. These phenomena are interrelated in important, if imperfectly understood, ways that are currently the object of research under the

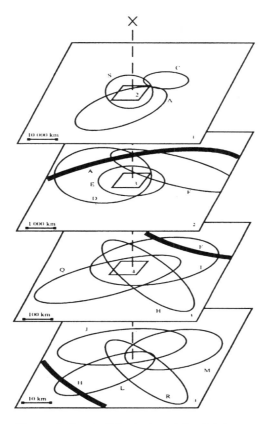

Figure 4. Level of Analysis and Spatial Areas.
Source: Lacoste, 1985:72.

Hydrological and Atmospheric Pilot Experiment in the Sahel being carried out by the Hapex-Sahel team. This is a study of the full range of
parameters affecting the interaction of the continental landmass and the
atmosphere, over an area of some 12 000 km^2 in the dry tropics. The
team's working hypothesis is that there exist fundamental interdependencies between the climate, the effects of the atmosphere on continental land surfaces through solar radiation, rain, and wind, and the variable
features of these land surfaces themselves (Lebel et al. 1993).

    Such exchanges between the atmosphere and the continental land
mass show little respect for political borders. Nor are they limited to the
Sahelian and sub-Sahelian regions. In his article on the use of remote
sensing for drought and desertification control in West Africa, Grégoire

(1990, p. 98) points out how environmental conditions of the Sahelian, sub-Sahelian, and coastal regions interact with each other:

It is now widely recognized that the thick belt of humid forest surrounding the Gulf of Guinea returns a major portion of its rainfall back into the atmosphere; this water vapour may account for up to 30% of the rain that eventually falls in the drier areas further north, between the 12th and 16th parallels, whenever the intertropical front extends to these latitudes. We should therefore be protecting this forest, the area of which is rapidly disappearing under the hoe, with little heed for proper forest management, and with apparent disregard for the future, in exploiting the forest.

Such interrelations cannot be properly diagnosed or addressed at the local level. The bioclimatic and ecological interdependence of the entire region must be taken into account. Neither can we ignore the human dimension of the problem, which adds a further element of interdependence in the form of migratory flows from one ecological zone to another, as people are forced to flee the degraded lands of Sahelian and sub-Sahelian areas to seek a better life in the cities or coastal areas.

REMOTE SENSING AS AN INSTRUMENT OF CHOICE

Remote sensing is an extremely valuable instrument of environmental analysis that allows for the collection of data in a systematic, continuous and comprehensive manner at various levels of the spatial scale. The term "remote sensing" applies to the use of various data gathering techniques, including aerial photography and satellite imagery, as a function of the scale to be explored (Figure 5).

Remote sensing thus provides a global perspective that allows us to monitor more systematically the way degradation of the Sahelian and coastal environments is evolving. Its use can provide information on climate, biomass, animal populations, soils, water, and human activity. We can track the evolution, across time and space, of such variables as the albedo of the land surface (the amount of light reflected), surface temperatures, the vegetative cover, and the productivity of the soil. An appreciation can thus be gained of the extent of environmental degradation, which can be analyzed in terms of both geomorphologic data and the constraints imposed by land-management systems.

Remote sensing offers a splendid example of the need for international and regional cooperation in environmental management. Compartmentalization and duplication of effort have no place in remote-sensing work, given the nature of the phenomena to be observed and the

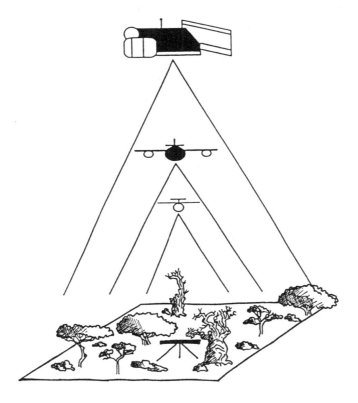

Figure 5. Different Remote-sensing Platforms.
Source: Lafrance and Dubois, 1990:66.

high cost of the technology. Attempts to apply this kind of high technology run the risk of failure or of engendering ambitious but ineffectual
research programs, unless funding is strictly focused on the most urgent
needs, and unless data are regularly compiled and transmitted in easily
accessible and comparable formats.

By providing global, regional, subregional and local perspectives of
a comprehensive nature, remote sensing encourages the adoption of a sys-
temic and strategic approach at all levels. Observations provided by
remote sensing can thus help to reform current field practice, while providing guidance on future approaches and priorities in the control of
environmental degradation. For example, site selection and monitoring
could both be improved, under initiatives such as:

◆ sand-dune stabilization;

- erosion control through planting of hedges;
- planting of windbreaks;
- construction of filtration dikes and half-moons;
- the demarcation and management of water sources and grazing areas, etc.

As with remote sensing itself, activities of this kind require major investments at both the local and regional level, and their efficiency requires that they be strictly prioritized and coordinated in response to a strategic approach focusing resources on human and ecological targets likely to produce maximum leverage. As Grégoire (1990, p. 98) sees it, such leverage can only be achieved by concentrating efforts so that:

> they are focused on ecological areas which retain a certain agricultural potential for human exploitation, with the maximum possible spillover effects on neighbouring regions, in order to embrace as much as possible of the area afflicted by drought. A certain "critical mass" is necessary, else the weight of human activity and unfavourable ecological factors overwhelm any action we might undertake.

Environmental priorities at the regional and national levels thus have to be clearly defined; and sources of actual and potential resistance will have to be identified and overcome.

The problem is not just one of coordination and priority-setting. People involved in any initiative must see an interest in it for themselves and feel fully involved in the decision-making process. Even the most legitimate priorities, based on the most convincing economic arguments and the best diagnosis of the situation, using the most sophisticated analytical tools cannot guarantee the success of any environmental strategy. Whatever policies are adopted will make their full impact felt on the protection of West Africa's ecosystems only if the people most directly concerned are effectively integrated into the equation and can feel themselves to be part of the solutions proposed.

To promote vertical integration and to maximize the effects of interventions on the ground, we must ensure that strategic information of the sort made available by remote sensing reaches the greatest number of people. The same logic applies to the need for new forms of dialogue between the people at large and various levels of public administration in each collectivity. New forms of local initiative are required, because adequate financial means are not available at central levels of government. Decentralization thus becomes a *sine qua non* of success.

POLITICAL WILL REVISITED

The effective participation of a wide range of actors, from the farmer to the politician or funding agency, is a precondition for the success of any integrated campaign (Grégoire 1990, p. 98). Viewed in this light, the concept of political will takes on a new meaning. It involves both decision-makers and people at the grass-roots level, and manifests itself in actual political practice as the product of the coordination and interplay of international and national policies (as part of a top-down or "deductive" approach to integration) and popular initiatives (as part of a bottom-up, "spontaneous" or "inductive" approach). Thus, for the notion of political will to have any meaning requires careful identification of the actors involved, examination of what motivates them, and an understanding of the constraints they face. The chance of effective political will emerging can be seen to depend on the interplay of power relations between players and groups of players and their perceptions of the issues at stake.

Effective reflection and action are rarely the affair of a small group of government officials or individual rulers, however authoritarian most African regimes might be. To understand the extent of "political will" with respect to any particular environmental initiative requires a thorough appreciation of how state authorities operate and how they relate to other components of society.

The geopolitical approach should be useful in finding our way through the profusion of players and the history of attempts at West African regional integration. By systematically tracing the "interscalar" paths of integrated environmental policies through the local, national, and regional levels, it may be possible to identify the majors blockages impeding progress or the major catalysts promoting it.

Specialized researchers could usefully examine a relatively limited number of policies that are representative or most revealing of actual practice. This would involve, as a first step, the identification of the main factors having shaped the initial policy statement, followed by research to track each policy step-by-step through the administrative process and observe how it was handled and applied by each responsibility centre. Research organized on a regional level could yield particularly interesting results of a comparative nature regarding the overall structure of environmental policies and the way regulations are applied.

CONCLUSION

THE CHALLENGE

The general lesson that emerges from this overview is that the promotion of sustainable development requires a spatial perspective of variable scale, depending on the ecological dimensions of any specific problem. This has obvious consequences for the way in which regional integration and cooperation are conceived.

This paper supports the view that environmental degradation cannot be controlled efficiently from the confines of national borders as inherited from the colonial era. Such a proposition can be defended with regard to the limited means available to individual countries or the economies of scale and improved management to be derived from collaboration. But beyond that is the need to think regionally because of the environmental interdependence of different regions. With environmental issues transcending political borders, the dynamics of the desertification phenomenon are best understood on a regional scale. Meanwhile, the solution, in terms of desertification control, is to be found at all levels, starting on individual plots of land. The upshot, as the time-worn phrase would have it, is the need to *think globally to act locally*.

RESEARCH AND INFORMATION

Thinking globally requires that choices be made at the highest level, in terms of targets and the means for achieving them, which calls for the coordination of research in support of such strategic thinking. A comprehensive view of environmental problems and trends is becoming increasingly possible, thanks to better management of existing environmental information and its articulation with discoveries regularly being made as a result of remote sensing and other techniques.

Duplication of existing information must be avoided, as substantial environmental information already exists in the form of maps and geographically referenced data on natural resources, or in the many lessons learned from previous projects. In many cases, the problem is the low level of utilization or usability of these data. Most are dispersed in any number of national or even foreign institutions and have not been processed or organized in any coherent or systematic way. The priority should, therefore, be to rescue existing data from oblivion, by cataloguing what exists and organizing it in usable form.

This suggests the need for research itself to be better coordinated, with less regard for territoriality and self-interest. An effort should be made to understand the reasons for the current lack of coherence in research efforts to identify new formulas capable of short-circuiting these problems. Research-funding institutions may be able to effect a change by tying research grants to work of a regional and interdisciplinary character, while encouraging the growth of research networks.

Priorities for regional action

The priority in terms of environmental action should be to arrange a better match between the global diagnosis and strategic choices that are made and the role to be played at each level of intervention, from the higher echelons of the government apparatus to the most distant plot of land. In this, the interscalar analysis of past experience would be extremely useful in identifying the stakes at play and understanding the structures of influence among the various groups of actors; and separating areas requiring collective action from those in which the simple coordination of efforts might suffice, to support the initiatives that are most likely to contribute to broader goals.

There tends to be some confusion between what does and does not require an integrative approach, and one of the priorities for research should be to identify the environmental problems most in need of a regional approach. Everything that is being done at a given level need not be coordinated, and decisions can often be made most efficiently at the point of application, as the subsidiarity principle suggests.

The role of agents at higher levels in improving cohesion and efficiency can best be ensured in this context through the provision of better information and technical support to actors at each level, rather than centralizing decision-making in ever more numerous regional institutions and bureaucratic monsters. A sufficient number of coordinating agencies already exists; they must be rendered more effective, while reinforcing their links to reality in the field. A major objective should be redefining the relationship between the state and civil society, by decentralizing responsibilities and providing appropriate recognition and support for public and private groups with a stake in the major environmental challenges of the region.

REFERENCES

Belaouane-Gherari, S.; Gherari, H. 1988. Les organisations régionales africaines. Recueil de textes et documents. Ministère de la coopération et du développement, Paris, France.

Bernier, J.; Vuillet, A. 1992. Géopolitique de l'intégration régionale en Afrique de l'Ouest. Cadre d'analyse et thèmes de réflexion. Presented at the seminar L'intégration économique en Afrique de l'Ouest, 15–19 June. Centre ivoirien de recherches économiques et sociales, Université nationale de Côte d'Ivoire, Abidjan, Côte d'Ivoire.

Brundtland, G.H. (chairperson, World Commission on Environment and Development). 1989. Our common future. Oxford University Press, New York, NY, USA.

CILSS (Permanent Interstate Committee for Drought Control in the Sahel). 1991. Analyse des stratégies et plans de lutte contre la désertification : gestion des ressources naturelles dans les pays membres du CILSS. Presented at the Symposium international sur l'intégration et l'évaluation des actions de lutte contre la désertification/gestion des ressources naturelles, 14–18 October, Niamey, Niger. CILSS, Ouagadougou, Burkina Faso.

Club du Sahel. 1992. Compte-rendu des discussions du Groupe de réflexion interdonateurs du Club du Sahel, Bruxelles du 4 au 6 décembre 1991. Organisation for Economic Co-operation and Development, Paris, France. SAH/CR(92)73.

Engelhard, P.; Ben Abdellah, T. 1992. Environnement, développement et pauvreté. Le Courrier, 133, 73–77.

Falloux, F.; Talbot, L. 1992. Crise et opportunité : environnement et développement en Afrique. L'expérience des plans nationaux d'action pour l'environnement. Maisonneuve and Larose, Agence de coopération culturelle et technique, Paris, France.

Foucher, M. 1991. Un tour du monde géopolitique (rev.). Fayard, Paris, France.

Grégoire, R. 1990. L'expérience communautaire en matière d'utilisation de la télédétection dans la lutte contre la sécheresse et la désertification en Afrique de l'Ouest. In Lafrance, P.; Dubois, J.M. (ed.). Apports de la télédétection à la lutte contre la sécheresse, Journées scientifiques de Thiès, nov. 21–24, 1989. John Libbey Eurotext, Paris, France. Pp. 95–109.

Hecht, E.J. 1994. Mise en place d'un réseau environnemental au Niger : rapport de mission à Niamey du 30 janvier au 26 février 1994 : I, rapport et annexes. Projet de subvention au développement du secteur agricole : Phase II. USAID, Niamey, Niger.

Hugon, P. 1990. Les différentes formes d'intégration régionale en Afrique sub-saharienne et les programmes d'ajustement structurel. Laboratoire de Recherche en économie appliquée, Université de Paris X, Paris, France.

Lacoste, Y. 1985. La géographie, ça sert d'abord à faire la guerre. La Découverte, Paris.

———— 1990. Géopolitique. In Encyclopedia universalis : symposium. Encycopedia Universalis, Paris, France pp. 1024–1030.

Lafrance, P.; Dubois, J.M. 1990. Apports de la télédétection à la lutte contre la sécheresse. Report of Journées scientifiques de Thiès, 21–24 November, 1989. John Libbey Eurotext, Paris, France.

Lebel, T.; Monteny, B.; Tinga, A. 1993. Hapex-Sahel vers une meilleure compréhension des mécanismes du climat. ORSTOM Actualités, 39, 7–12.

Mathieu, P. 1991. La désertification: un processus irréversible? Quelques réflexions à partir du cas du Sahel. *In* Chaumont, J.M.; Van Paris, P. (ed.). Les limites de l'inéluctable : penser la liberté au seuil du troisième millénaire. Boeck-Wesmael, Brussels, Belgium. Pp. 40–59.

Streeten, P. 1992. Des institutions pour un développement durable. Revue Tiers-Monde, 130, 455–470.

Stroosnijder, L. 1992. La désertification en Afrique sahélienne. Le Courrier, 133, 78–81.

Tabutin, D.; Thilges, E. 1992. Relations entre croissance démographique et environnement. Revue Tiers-Monde, 33 (130), 273–294.

UNDP (United Nations Development Programme). 1992. Évaluation de la désertification et de la sécheresse dans la région soudano-sahélienne 1985–1991. UNDP, New York, NY, USA.

CHAPTER 15

INSTITUTIONAL SIMILARITIES AND DIFFERENCES: ECOWAS, ECCAS, AND PTA

– Luaba Lumu Ntumba –

Ntumba Luaba Lumu examines the institutional and decision-making struc-
tures underlying regional integration in Africa. Taking the European expe-
rience as a point of comparison, he studies the political framework,
organizational structures, and legal mechanisms of the major economic inte-
gration schemes in Sub-Saharan Africa: the Economic Community of West
African States (ECOWAS), the Economic Community of Central African
States (ECCAS), and the Preferential Trade Area (PTA) for Eastern and
Southern African states (now COMESA, the Common Market for East and
Southern Africa, since 1994).

His conclusions are similar to those of Adam Malam-Kandine (1993)
regarding the West African Economic Community (CEAO) and ECOWAS.
Both authors view the institutions they studied as incapable of meeting the
challenge of regional integration in any meaningful sense, because of the way
national interests hold sway over all decision-making bodies. This "inter-
state" approach is manifested in several ways: through the preeminence of the
Authority of Heads of State and Government in decision-making; through
national representation in the Council of Ministers and the intergovernmen-
tal technical committees; through rule by consensus; in the limited resources
and responsibilities of the secretariats; and in the limited jurisdiction of the
regional courts.

This approach differs from the European model, which provided from
the outset for the creation of institutions capable of representing the commu-
nity as a whole, through specific institutional formulas, including: the role of
the Commission of the European Communities as guardian of the common
interest; decision-making by qualified majority vote within the Council of
Ministers, as opposed to rule by consensus; the independence of the European
parliament vis-à-vis national governments; and the relatively high profile
and independence of the European Court of Justice.

THE PHENOMENON OF regional integration can be examined from
various angles. Adopting a legal–institutional approach, this chapter
concentrates on the institutional similarities and differences characteristic of the Economic Community of West African States (ECOWAS), the

Preferential Trade Area (PTA) for Eastern and Southern African states, and the Economic Community of Central African States (ECCAS). A comparative review of these three communities suggests itself because of the parallels between them which derive from the order in which these projects emerged and the way they successively inspired one another. As the first community to be created, in January 1975, ECOWAS exerted a great deal of influence on the design and institutional setup of the PTA, which was established in December 1981. Even the numbering and wording of the articles of agreement of these two unions display similarities. In a similar way, there are also more similarities than differences of a normative and institutional nature between these two organizations and ECCAS, whose treaty was signed in October 1983.

In a study for the United Nation Conference on Trade and Development (UNCTAD), Sidjanski (1973, p. 1) criticized the emphasis of most comparative studies on the economic content of regional integration, with little more than passing reference to institutional phenomena. Yet the potential impact of institutional structures on the effectiveness and success of any integration scheme should not be overlooked. The institutional structure must not only be able to meet the short-term objectives that may have inspired the economic grouping in the first place, but also exert a leadership role in stimulating movement toward the fulfilment of the group's long-term goals. Institutional structures are called upon to provide support, guidance, and leadership, and may constitute either a bottleneck or a driving force on the road to regional integration.

Soldatos (1989, p. 185) suggests that the choice of institutional mechanisms should bear "a direct and proportional relationship to the nature, breadth and scope of what is to be integrated." Just as a strong institutional framework relative to the goals being pursued can act as the locomotive or leavening agent of the process, so too will a weak and minimal or modest decision-making structure have difficulty maintaining the momentum for integration.

The effectiveness of any given institutional arrangement will vary depending on whether we are dealing with a free-trade zone, a customs union, a common market, an economic and monetary union, or full-fledged integration. For every stage or degree of regional integration, there should, in principle, be an appropriate institutional and decision-making structure. A fairly rudimentary institutional endowment might suffice in the "negative" phase of integration, involving the removal of tariff and non-tariff barriers to trade, but be totally inadequate in the "positive" stage (agreement on a coordinated or common trade policy;

free movement of people, services, and capital; freedom of establishment; adoption of common, harmonized, or coordinated policies in various fields; joint monetary policy and adoption of a common currency),[1] which requires a complex institutional and decision-making system with a strong supranational character.

This study of institutional and decision-making arrangements in ECOWAS, PTA, and ECCAS revolves around three basic features of these organizations: the predominance of an "interstate" approach, the embryonic nature of integrated mechanisms, and the persistent lack of democracy.

AN INTERSTATE APPROACH TO REGIONAL INTEGRATION

We use the term "interstate" to describe an approach based on the maintenance of national sovereignty and the dominance of member states over the workings of regional institutions. First and foremost, this signifies that national governments retain a direct role in decision-making — what we call "intergovernmentalism." The interstate approach also makes itself felt in the form of rule by consensus, in the process of developing and adopting community decisions, which ensures the primacy of national sovereignty over the general community interest. We find it, finally, in the limited reach and significance of regional decisions.

THE PRIMACY OF INTERGOVERNMENTALISM

Intergovernmentalism results from the position occupied at the apex of the institutional hierarchy by bodies made up of government representatives — the Authority of Heads of State and Government and the Council of Ministers — that dominate the system.

Constituted as the "principal institution" of ECOWAS, and the "supreme body" of the PTA and ECCAS, the Authority of Heads of State and Government is regarded as the sovereign institution in which is concentrated all real power within the regional economic grouping. Sitting on top of the institutional pyramid, the Authority represents the only policymaking unit worthy of the name. It is responsible for governing the community, for defining overall policy directions and approaches, and examining broad policy issues. It is charged with the overriding

---

[1] On the concepts of "negative"and "positive" integration, see Pinder (1968, pp. 90–91).

planning, guidance, and control functions.[2] The Authority makes all decision, acts as the court of last appeal, gives orders to all institutions under it, and oversees operations in the community.

Intergovernmentalism is further accentuated by the fact that the second-ranking community body, the Council of Ministers, is also made up of government figures. The principal mandate of the Council of Ministers is to supervise the operations and evolution of the community.[3] The Council of Ministers gives instructions to other community institutions under its authority,[4] and in this way directs the Secretariat's activities, along with those of the technical and specialized committees. It also directly exercises all powers and functions assigned to it by the corresponding treaty or delegated to it by the Authority.[5]

The Council of Ministers is subordinate to the Authority. Although it may make recommendations on general matters of policy, these must be submitted for the consideration and approval of the Authority.[6] The bylaws and regulations of the Council of Ministers must be elaborated according to the prior directives of the Authority (ECOWAS, PTA) or be approved by the Authority once the Council of Ministers has drafted them (ECCAS).[7]

The Authority also determines the composition, powers, statutes, and all other aspects of the regional tribunals: the ECOWAS and PTA Tribunals, and the ECCAS Court of Justice.[8] Finally, only the Authority has the power to establish any new subsidiary entities it deems necessary,

---

[2] Article 5, ss. 1 and 2 of the ECOWAS Treaty; Article 6, s. 2 of the PTA Treaty; Article 8, s. 2 and Article 9, s. 2a of the ECCAS Treaty.

[3] ECOWAS Treaty, Article 6, s. 2a; ECCAS Treaty, Article 13, s. 1; and PTA Treaty, Article 7, s. 2a, which adds that the Council of Ministers is responsible for constant monitoring of progress.

[4] ECOWAS Treaty, Article 6, s. 2c; PTA Treaty, Article 7, s. 2c; and ECCAS Treaty, Article 12, s. 2b.

[5] ECOWAS Treaty, Article 6, s. 2d; PTA Treaty, Article 7, s. 2d; and ECCAS Treaty, Article 13, ss. 2e and 2f. The delegation of powers to the Council of Ministers from the conference is explicitly authorized in the ECOWAS and PTA treaties; the ECCAS Treaty does not make any explicit reference to delegation, but does not exclude it either.

[6] ECOWAS Treaty, Article 6, s. 2; PTA Treaty, Article 7, s. 2b; and ECCAS Treaty, Article 13, s. 2a.

[7] This includes, the rules for convening council meetings and those governing its deliberations and debates, the performance of other tasks assigned to it, and rotation of the chairperson position among the members. See ECOWAS Treaty, Article 6, s. 5; PTA Treaty, Article 7, s. 5; and ECCAS Treaty, Article 13, s. 2e. Article 14, s. 2 provides that the council chairperson shall be a minister of the country whose head of state chairs the conference.

[8] ECOWAS Treaty, Article 11, s. 2; PTA Treaty, Article 10, s. 2; and ECCAS Treaty, Article 16.

in particular the technical and specialized commissions in ECOWAS and the specialized technical committees in ECCAS and PTA.[9]

Appointments to the most senior posts and duties are also in the hands of the Authority. This applies to the appointment of the executive secretaries of ECOWAS and PTA, and the general secretary of ECCAS. In the case of ECOWAS, the Authority also appoints the accounts commissioner. The powers of the Authority of Heads of State and Government vary from one institution to the next with regard to other nominations. Its powers are most extensive in the case of ECCAS. Here, the Authority approves the organizational structure of the General Secretariat and names the assistant secretaries general, the college of accounts commissioners, the financial comptroller, and the chief accountant. In the other two regional economic groups, some of these powers are exercised instead by the Council of Ministers: nomination of assistant secretaries general, designation of members of the committees of accounts commissioners, and appointment of any other member of the Secretariat for which the council wishes to create a position. In the case of ECOWAS, the Authority names the accounts commissioner. In all three cases, the Council of Ministers sets the rules governing the terms and conditions of employment for the executive secretary or secretary general, and other Secretariat officials.[10]

The assignment of authority over budgetary matters varies from case to case. In ECCAS, it lies in the hands of the Authority of Heads of State and Government, which approves the community budget and fixes each member state's annual contribution, on the recommendation of the Council of Ministers. In ECOWAS and PTA, the Council of Ministers approves the annual expenditure budget, member states' contributions, and any other sources of budgetary revenue.[11]

The dominant role played by the Authority of Heads of State and Government stands out clearly in all of this. Nothing is done without the Authority's explicit approval. This illustrates the phenomenon of "pan-African presidentialism" enshrined in the charter of the Organization of African Unity (OAU), adopted in May 1963, and reconfirmed by the treaty establishing the African Economic Community (AEC) at Abuja on 3 June 1991.[12] According to Kouassi (1987, p. 167), this is a key feature.

---

[9] ECOWAS Treaty, Article 5, s. 2 and Article 9, s. 2; PTA Treaty, Article 6, s. 2 and Article 11, s. 2; and ECCAS Treaty, Article 26, s. 1.

[10] ECCAS Treaty, Article 8, ss. 2e and 2g; PTA Treaty, Article 8, s. 5, Article 9, ss. 3 and 4, and Article 38, s. 2; and ECOWAS Treaty, Article 8, ss. and 6.

[11] ECCAS Treaty, Article 9, s. 2h; ECOWAS Treaty, Article 53, ss. 2 and 3; and PTA Treaty, Article 36, ss. 2 and 3.

[12] See Article 8 of the Charter of Addis Ababa, and Article 8 of the Treaty of Abuja.

Because it is the heads of state and government who hold real power at the national level, the Charter of Addis Ababa and the Treaty of Abuja have simply transplanted this power relationship into the OAU. African international organizations have, in effect, reproduced the pyramidal power structure prevailing at the national level, the only difference being that the governing bodies of the international organizations consist of groups of heads of state who manage things collectively (Gonidec 1987, p. 123).

The system is thus one of direct rule by the heads of state and government over the regional communities (Buchman 1957, p. 20). National rulers are responsible for their own country's interests and that of their regional grouping, combining both policymaking and executive functions with regard to regional integration. This presents a fundamental problem, as it is not a natural tendency for government delegates to subordinate their national preoccupations to the community interest in the resolution of specific issues.

As the World Bank (1989, p. 152) has noted, the existence of two plenary deliberating bodies (the Authority and the Council) makes the structure top-heavy and hard to manage. The problem is exacerbated by the infrequency of meetings. The Authority of Heads of State and Government normally meets only once a year, the Council of Ministers only twice a year, including one meeting just preceding the annual session of the Authority.[13] By way of comparison, the European Council, made up of Europe's heads of state or government, meets at least three times each year, and the Council of Ministers of the European Union (EU) has 50 or 60 sessions a year, involving either ministers of foreign affairs or ministers with specialized portfolios.

The gap between sessions of the Authority and Council tends to engender inertia and procrastination and slows implementation of the communities' decisions. It may take up to 6 months before decisions of the Council of Ministers are approved by the Authority and put into effect.

The lack of decision-making authority on the part of the Council of Ministers constitutes an institutional sword of Damocles. Because the Council runs the risk of seeing its decisions amended or overturned by

---

[13] Under the Treaty, regular summits of the authority are held at least once a year, and meetings of the Council of Ministers at least twice a year in the case of ECCAS. The authority and council may also be convened in special session.

the Authority, the Council of Ministers has a natural propensity to avoid new or daring initiatives (Kouassi 1987, p. 326).

The Council of Ministers also suffers from the way it is composed, at the whim of the states, because the treaty's provisions call for the membership of the Council of Ministers to vary depending on the nature and degree of technical specialization of the questions on its agenda.[14] The Council may be composed of foreign affairs ministers, or it may comprise ministers with more technical portfolios such as industry, finance, planning, transportation, social affairs, culture, or justice. This lack of continuity and consistency in the make-up of the Council leads to confusion and misunderstanding in decision-making.

RULE BY CONSENSUS

One of the chief institutional drawbacks of the treaties establishing the PTA and ECCAS — in the spirit of the interstate approach — is the enshrining of rule by consensus in every area of decision-making by the Authority or by the Council of Ministers.[15] Similar norms have been established as a matter of actual practice in ECOWAS.

Rule by consensus, like unanimity, is intended to ensure full respect for the sovereignty of member states, as no obligation can be imposed on a member state without its acquiescence or expressed consent. However, there is a difference between consensus and unanimity. Plantey (1980, p. 360) explains that consensus is often accompanied by explanations, abstentions, or reservations. A country may agree to a measure, but not agree to be legally bound by it. It may even disagree altogether, provided it directly expresses this disagreement. Consensus implies only that the conclusion reached is acceptable, in the sense that no country is sufficiently opposed to cast a negative vote.

The advantage of consensus is that it allows member countries to circumvent certain difficulties and avoid the kind of open splits and conflicts that emerge when difficult issues are taken to a vote (Dreyfus 1987, p. 228). However, there are drawbacks to this approach. Negotiations are often difficult and time-consuming, and usually end up in compromise;

---

[14] Under ECOWAS Treaty, Article 6, s. 1, the Council of Ministers comprises two representatives from each member state, with no specifications as to their portfolios. The PTA Treaty simply states that the council shall include ministers designated by the member states (Article 7, s. 1). In ECCAS, ministers of economic development are to be the regular members of the Council of Ministers, but member states are free to send any minister they choose (Article 12, s. 2).

[15] PTA Treaty, Article 6, s. 5 and Article 7, s. 6; for ECCAS, except as provided otherwise by the treaty.

the facade of unanimity that is preserved often hides a coalition of discontented parties. Often, consensus becomes a formula for allowing countries to agree to disagree (Quoc Dinh et al. 1987, pp. 514 and 560).

Rule by consensus is thus little more than a safety measure guaranteeing that any act of the community will be subordinated to national sovereignty. This places a severe limit on the ability of anyone to show leadership and innovation at the community level. It also slows decision-making, because any objection by a member state can block the process.[16] The likely outcome is a kind of "soft" community law incapable of sustaining the momentum toward regional integration. As Dreyfus (1987, p. 228) puts it, "By trying too hard to please everyone, we sometimes end up with decisions devoid of any significant content."

THE LIMITED WRIT OF REGIONAL DECISIONS

The final characteristic of the interstate approach is that decisions made at the regional level have little currency. This is best appreciated in contrast with the EU, whose Council and Commission boast a remarkably wide range of legal instruments to call upon in pursuing their missions. These instruments include a range of options, adapted to different needs and circumstances. They consist of regulations, directives, decisions, and recommendations, as defined in Article 189 of the Treaty of Rome.

The EU regulation is a quasi-legislative act equivalent to domestic law. It is of general and impersonal applicability, and represents the key instrument for the implementation of common policies. As Isaac (1989, p. 116) describes it, it is "mandatory in all respects" and "directly applicable in any member state." In other words, "it has legal effect, on its own and automatically, without any intervention on the part of national authorities, in the internal affairs of member states, and must be implemented within their territories."

Directives are binding on member states only regarding their results, and do not impose any obligation as to the means used to attain those results. Member states can freely choose the legal instrument best suited to give effect to the directive (law, decree, order, edict, regulation, etc.), and enjoy full discretion in the choice of domestic institutional arrangements for applying it. In principle, a directive is not directly applicable. It represents a preferred means for coordinating and harmonizing member states' economic policies and national legislation.

---

[16] ECOWAS Treaty, Article 7; and PTA Treaty, Article 7, s. 7.

EU *decisions* are mandatory in all respects for a target group. This instrument differs from a regulation in that it does not have general legal effect, and concerns only those to whom it is addressed. In contrast to a directive, a decision is binding with respect both to its results and the means employed to achieve them. An intermediate measure, it has a wide range of application in the community.

Recommendations and *opinions* are non-binding, i.e., they have no constraining force and do not, strictly speaking, impose any legal obligation. They are nonetheless useful in providing administrative and legislative guidance (Isaac 1989, p. 119).

ECOWAS, PTA, and ECCAS do not have such a range of well defined instruments at their disposal. They operate through *decisions* and *directives*,[17] without any clear distinction between these instruments as to their force and content. In ECOWAS and PTA, the Authority itself determines the rules for proclaiming, implementing, and applying its decisions and directives and those of the Council of Ministers. Only in the case of ECCAS does the treaty establish any distinction between decisions and directives concerning those directly affected: whereas decisions are equally applicable to member states and community institutions (other than the Court of Justice, which enjoys a degree of independence), directives concern only the community's own institutions (again, other than the Court).[18]

The ECOWAS, PTA, and ECCAS treaties also refer to *recommendations*, which may be addressed to the Authority by the Council of Ministers. These include recommendations that technical and specialized commissions and committees may make to the Council of Ministers. However, these recommendations are really no more than proposals submitted to the Authority for approval.

In principle, the Tribunal and the Community Court also have the power to issue non-binding *opinions* on any legal question, at the request of either the Council of Ministers or the Authority.[19]

Generally, the Authority's decisions and directives are applicable only to the community's own institutions.[20] Directives of the Council of Ministers are subordinate to those of the Authority and affect only the community institutions within the Council's competence, i.e., the

---

[17] This is equally true for the Authority of Heads of State and Government and the Council of Ministers, except for ECCAS's Council of Ministers, which relies on regulations. See ECOWAS Treaty, Article 5, s. 3; ECCAS Treaty, Article 11; and PTA Treaty, Article 6, s. 3.

[18] ECOWAS Treaty, Article 7; PTA Treaty, Article 8; and ECCAS Treaty, Article 11.

[19] See, in particular, ECCAS Treaty, Article 16, s. 3d.

[20] PTA Treaty, Article 6, s. 2; ECCAS Treaty, Article 11, ss. 2 and 3.

secretariats and the technical and specialized committees.[21] Neither the Authority nor the Council of Ministers has power to impose any legal obligations on member countries under the ECOWAS and PTA treaties. In other words, their decisions have a direct binding effect only within the institutional structure of the community itself, and not in the national territory of the member states (Gonidec 1987, p. 184). The legal jurisdiction of these communities is, therefore, quite weak and dependent upon the good will of member states to make it effective.

Only ECCAS allows the community to impose legal obligations on its member states. By virtue of Articles 11 and 15 of its treaty, the Authority's decisions and the Council's regulations have binding force not only on the community's own institutions (except for the Court of Justice), but also on member states. These decisions and regulations become applicable with the full force of law in member states, 30 days after they are officially published by the community.[22]

The other regional institutions would do well to follow this example, as regional integration will not make much progress until community decisions are given direct force of law over businesses and individuals operating in the member states.

The embryonic nature of integrated institutions

Adopting a wide range of community decisions is of course of little consequence if member states do not implement them. This raises the issue of monitoring the implementation of community decisions, in particular through the community's own integrated bodies, i.e., permanent agencies staffed by international officials with independent status from national governments. However, integrated institutions in Africa are still at an embryonic stage. Only two types of entities could be considered "integrated" in African international organizations: the secretariats and the tribunals or courts of justice. These agencies are, furthermore, handicapped by severe institutional weaknesses.

---

[21] ECOWAS Treaty, Article 6, s. 23 and Article 7; PTA Treaty, Article 7, ss. 2b and 3; and ECCAS Treaty, Article 6, s. 2b.
[22] ECCAS Treaty, Article 15.

WEAK SECRETARIATS

ECOWAS's Executive Secretariat, ECCAS's General Secretariat and PTA's Secretariat are permanent technical and administrative bodies. Considered as the community's "principal executive officer" under the ECOWAS Treaty, and "principal executive administrator" under the ECCAS and PTA treaties, in each case, the executive or general secretary is the senior official of the community administration.[23] The executive secretary is responsible for the day-to-day administration of the community and all its institutions. He or she is appointed by the Authority of Heads of State and Government for a 4-year term, renewable once, and can only be dismissed by the Authority itself, upon the recommendation of the Council of Ministers. He or she is supported by two assistant executive secretaries (ECOWAS) or assistant secretaries general (ECCAS), and by all the other members of the Secretariat staff.

The Secretariat provides support to the other community institutions by preparing their meetings, offering assistance and services in the performance of their functions, ensuring implementation of the measures they adopt and preparing the program and budget of the organization. The Secretariat is expected to monitor the operations of the community, and keeps the Council of Ministers and the Authority informed through the submission of activity reports at each of their sessions. It conducts studies and produces papers on a range of topics and may draft proposals to promote the smooth and efficient operation and development of the community.[24]

On the whole, the secretariats of all the economic communities serve merely to prepare and execute the decisions of the organizations' intergovernmental bodies. Expected only to ensure the smooth functioning of the community machinery on a day-to-day basis, they are severely handicapped in doing anything else by the lack of any real decision-making power (Adedeji 1991, p. 7).

Although they are the legal embodiment of the communities,[25] the secretariats have seen their prerogatives eroded by the strong presence of the heads of state presiding over the Authority, who have exercised a sort of political trusteeship over their activities.

---

[23] ECOWAS Treaty, Article 8, Article 20, s. 1; ECCAS Treaty, Article 21; and PTA Treaty, Article 9.
[24] ECOWAS Treaty, Article 8, s. 10d; PTA Treaty, Article 9, s. 7c; and ECCAS Treaty, Article 20, s. 2g.
[25] ECOWAS Treaty, Article 60, s. 3; ECCAS Treaty, Article 87, s. 2; and PTA Treaty, Article 44, s. 3.

These problems are exacerbated by the overlap of responsibilities between the secretariats and the intergovernmental committees and commissions,[26] whose powers cut across those of secretariat departments or divisions. This situation leads to misunderstandings as to the division of responsibilities, leading to confusion and duplication, and sometimes to inertia and paralysis.

ECOWAS's Advisory Commission and PTA's Intergovernmental Commission of Experts reporting to their respective councils of ministers represent a virtual duplication of the secretariats of these organizations.[27] ECOWAS's Advisory Commission is expected to review and advise on such issues and projects as are submitted to it by other entities of the community. In PTA, the Intergovernmental Commission of Experts is charged with supervising the application of the treaty, among other duties.

The presence, weight and influence of the member states is such that the various secretariats are reduced to the role of technical and administrative units operating at low levels of responsibility. In an institutional environment so heavily penetrated by intergovernmentalism, the secretariats are incapable of acting as the engine of regional integration and unable to safeguard the integrity of their respective treaties, in the manner of the Commission of the European Communities (CEC) or the Junta of the Andean Pact, which are staffed by independent technocrats.

The significance of the CEC and the Junta of the Andean Pact resides in their ability to act as independent advocates of the common interest vis-à-vis the intergovernmental bodies of the two communities, consisting of the EU's Council of Ministers or the Andean Pact's Ministerial Commission. The CEC has powers of initiative, control, and execution, and represents a counterweight to the Council. Indeed, the Council of Ministers makes decisions only on recommendation of the CEC and cannot amend proposals short of a unanimous decision.[28] The CEC also enjoys regulatory executive powers regarding the EU treaties and decisions of the Council. As a measure of these powers, in 1980 alone, the CEC issued more than 3000 regulations (Isaac 1989, p. 55). It can also make executive decisions of certain types with application to individual member governments or businesses.

---

[26] Called technical and specialized commissions in ECOWAS, specialized technical committees in ECCAS, and technical committees in PTA.

[27] ECCAS Treaty, Articles 23 to 25; and PTA Treaty, Article 11.

[28] Until such time as the Council has taken a decision, the Commission may amend its initial proposal; cf. Article 149 of the EEC Treaty.

In the absence of such an integrated executive body equipped to promote and safeguard the interests of the community, the weight of member governments in African schemes of regional integration tends to frustrate integrationist initiatives and innovations, while perpetuating the intergovernmental approach.

LIMITED LEGAL JURISDICTION

There are also marked differences between the EU and African organizations in their approaches to juridical interpretation and enforcement of treaty provisions and dispute settlement. As Adewoye (this volume) demonstrates, the European Court of Justice has shown itself to be an important factor, and a catalyst, for European integration (see also Lecourt 1976).

The analogous institutions in Africa — the ECOWAS Tribunal, the PTA Tribunal, and the ECCAS Court of Justice — play no such role.[29] Three deficiencies stand out in African communities' legal structures. The first is the limitation of their tribunals' mandates to dealing with disputes between member states[30] and excluding disputes between the community and its member states, among the institutions themselves, and between the community and private parties (an individual or group). It should be possible to allow the Court of Justice and the tribunals to play a more significant, effective role in the development of community law, by endowing them with greater powers and broader jurisdictional mandates.

Second, the ECOWAS, PTA, and ECCAS treaties provide that the Authority shall determine the composition, procedures, and statutes of the tribunals and court and settle any related issues.[31] This provision diminishes the community's legal autonomy, inasmuch as it subjects its statutes to determination and amendment by a political body. Given Africa's tradition of political subjugation of the judiciary, it is vital that

---

[29] See ECOWAS Treaty, Article 11, s. 1; PTA Treaty, Article 10, s. 1; and ECCAS Treaty, Article 16, s. 1.

[30] ECOWAS Treaty, Articles 11 and 56; and PTA Treaty, Articles 10 and 40. The ECCAS Treaty assigns somewhat broader powers to the Court of Justice, which may review the legality of the decisions, directives, and regulations of community institutions, and judge appeals in areas of incompetence, excess of authority, or violation of the treaty's substantive provisions. Even here, complaints must be presented by a member state or by the conference. This treaty, furthermore, provides recourse only against errors of commission by community institutions, and says nothing about omissions (or inertia), along the lines provided for in Article 175 of the Treaty of Rome.

[31] ECOWAS Treaty, Article 11, s. 2; ECCAS Treaty, Article 18; and PTA Treaty, Article 10, s. 2.

the statutes of the court or the tribunal include real guarantees of independence, especially regarding the methods of appointing and dismissing judges and the duration of their tenure.

The third weakness of the dispute settlement mechanisms envisioned under the various treaties is the requirement that any dispute or difference over interpretation or enforcement of community law be settled out of court, by direct agreement among the parties involved, whenever possible. Settlement by diplomatic means thus takes precedence over legal recourse. It is only when the parties are unable to reach a settlement that one or other of them may turn to the Court of Justice or tribunal.[32] This means that disputes sometimes go unsettled because they are never submitted to the judicial body. The effect is to weaken the integrity of the community system, because the prior submission of any dispute over interpretation or enforcement of the community treaty to bilateral diplomatic negotiation introduces the risk of differing interpretations and inconsistent enforcement of the community's basic legal instruments, thus undermining the uniformity of community law. Diplomatic considerations are liable, once again, to work to the detriment of important community interests in this interstate approach.

THE "DEMOCRATIC GAP"

The concept of "democratic gap" has been used by critics of the European Community to highlight three dimensions of its institutional makeup:

- the growing power of the Commission, a technocratic body at once removed from national interests and lacking in political legitimacy because it is not elected and can claim no public mandate;

- the lack of parliamentary oversight and of sufficient controls over the Council, despite its governmental role in the community;

- the weaknesses of the European parliament, which has been elected by direct universal suffrage only since 1979, and still does not rank as the real law-making power in the community (Soldatos 1989, pp. 171–173).

Applying the same concept to Africa's regional economic groupings reveals a democratic gap of substantial proportions. Such is the mistrust of Africa's heads of state and government of the popular will that there is

---

[32] ECOWAS Treaty, Article 56; and PTA Treaty, Article 40.

no parliamentary body nor any council or committee for the representation of popular social and economic concerns within the OAU or the regional economic communities. These groupings have not involved the public at large or the various economic players in the regional integration process, and their governing bodies have no understanding of people's goals, priorities, and expectations for integration. As Kangudi (1990, p. 21) has pointed out, "Africa's experience shows that little if anything has been done to enlist popular enthusiasm and the support of interest groups such as merchants, workers, farmers, tradesmen, etc."

The agreement on the constitution of a pan-African parliament, announced as part of the new AEC, "to ensure full participation by the African people in the development and economic integration of the continent"[33] was not easily arrived at, but constitutes an important step forward in terms of the principle so established. The ECOWAS Revised Treaty similarly includes provision for a West African parliament. This project deserves to be supported and brought to fruition. By providing a forum where representatives of Africa's different social groups can come together to discuss issues of common interest, the various regional parliaments and the continental parliament could help to counter the widely held impression that regional cooperation and integration are topics of concern only for politicians and officials, and of no consequence to ordinary people.

The Abuja treaty instituting the AEC and the ECOWAS Revised Treaty also provide for the creation of economic and social councils. In the case of the AEC, the type of council envisaged is different from the European model, which comprises representatives from different walks of economic and social life, including business people, farmers, workers, merchants, professionals, and others representing the public interest. The Abuja treaty limits itself to the creation of an economic and social committee made up of ministers of development, planning, and economic integration from each member state, assisted if necessary by other ministers.[34] However, the economic and social council envisaged by the ECOWAS Revised Treaty is more conventional in nature in terms of representation from professionals and interest groups (Bundu, this volume).

The "neo-functionalist" approach to regional integration attaches great importance to the role of socioeconomic forces in launching and sustaining the regional integration process (Soldatos 1989, pp. 262 ff). In

---

[33] Article 14, s. 1 of the Treaty of Abuja.
[34] Article 15, s. 2 of the Treaty of Abuja.

Europe, the involvement of social and economic interests in the integration movement has given rise to transnational groups of various categories that are very active in regional affairs: for example, the Committee of Agricultural Organizations (COPA), the Union of Industrial and Employer's Confederations of Europe (UNICE), and the European Confederation of Trade Unions (ETUC). There are more than 500 such integrated groupings at the European level (Soldatos 1989, p. 269).

As was pointed out by Adedeji (1991, p. 7), former deputy secretary general of the United Nations Economic Commission for Africa, the consolidation of Africa's efforts at economic restructuring through economic integration could depend in large measure on support from social, economic, and political groups who believe in the process as a way of promoting their own interests and ideas. Involving such groups in the integration process would thus contribute to the institutional strength of Africa's regional economic communities.

PROPOSALS FOR INSTITUTIONAL CONSOLIDATION

To sum up, the political and institutional model represented by ECOWAS, PTA, and ECCAS is characterized, with minor qualifications, by the dominance of the interstate approach, the embryonic status of integrated bodies, and the persistence of a serious democratic gap. ECOWAS, PTA, and ECCAS have the following elements in common:

- ◆ an authority of heads of state and government and a council of ministers composed of all member states as their deliberative and decision-making bodies;

- ◆ intergovernmental commissions or committees to conduct studies and make recommendations;

- ◆ an administrative secretariat with a purely technical and executive role;

- ◆ decision-making procedures based on unanimity or consensus, yielding decisions whose implementation is left to the member states themselves; and

- ◆ a judicial body with limited powers.

These regional economic groupings are all meant to surpass the free-trade zone and customs union stages of regional integration, to achieve the free movement, not only of traded goods, but also of people, services, and capital. Their goal is to build an economic area that will advance from a common market to a full economic and monetary union. To date, ECOWAS, PTA, and ECCAS have produced only mixed results, and other applications of the same interstate model (the Central African Customs and Economic Union [UDEAC], the Arab Common Market [ACM], CEAO, the Economic Community of the Great Lakes Countries [CEPGL], the Caribbean Community [CARICOM], etc.) have likewise failed in their attempts to generate real momentum for integration, due to the lack of effective institutional structures. The only model to have yielded effective results is one based on a federal or supranational approach, like that of the EU or the Andean Group (Borella 1982, pp. 34–46).

The ECOWAS Revised Treaty, whose features are summarized by Bundu (this volume), moves us in the direction of greater supranationality through the reinforcement of community institutions, the move to qualified but binding majority rule as opposed to unanimity rule, and the creation of a West African parliament and an economic and social council as partial remedies to the democratic gap inherent in the institutional structure.

However, these new directions do not fundamentally challenge the prevailing interstate approach. The two-tier intergovernmental structure at the top, so typical of Africa's international organizations, remains intact and can only encumber the effectiveness of the community. Meanwhile, the ECOWAS Secretariat is still far from being the kind of independent "technostructure" that might lead and promote the integration process, defend the general interests of the community, and be politically accountable to the regional parliament.

In our view, the Authority of Heads of State and Government should intervene only through the issue of directives and general guidelines involving major political commitments. The Council of Ministers could then become the real governing authority of the community, making the appropriate regulatory and executive decisions, and meeting as often as necessary. A vital condition of success would be the creation of an autonomous and technocratic authority along the lines of the EU Commission or the Junta of the Andean Pact that can take decisions on day-to-day management of the community in a timely and effective manner.

What is really needed is a bold recasting of the political and institutional structure of ECOWAS, along truly integrative lines. This would involve substantial transfers of state power to a federal type of community authority responsible for issues fundamental to the economic future and well-being of West African people.

REFERENCES

Adedeji, A. 1991. Programme de développement de l'Afrique pour les années 90 : la restructuration des États et des sociétés en Afrique. Déclaration à la cinquante-quatrième session ordinaire du Conseil des ministres de l'OUA, Abuja, 27–31 mai. Organization of African Unity, Addis Ababa, Ethiopia.

Borella, F. 1982. Modèles européens et organisations économiques internationales. *In* Société française du droit international (ed.). L'Europe dans les relations internationales : unité et diversité. Colloque de Nancy. A. Pedone, Paris, France. Pp. 34–46.

Buchman, J. 1957. À la recherche d'un ordre international. E. Nauwelaerts, Louvain, Belgium. Publications de l'Université Lovanium de Léopoldville.

Dreyfus, S. 1987. Droit des relations internationales (3rd ed.). Cujas, Paris, France.

ECCAS. 1983. Traité portant création de la CEEAC. ECCAS Secretariat, Libreville, 18 October.

ECOWAS. 1975. Traité portant création de la CEDEAO. ECOWAS Secretariat, Lagos, 28 May.

Gonidec, P.F. 1987. Les organisations internationales africaines : étude comparative. Harmattan, Paris, France. Droits et sociétés.

Isaac, G. 1989. Droit communautaire général. Masson, Paris, France.

Kangudi, T.F. 1990. Intégration de l'Organisation de l'unité africaine et de la Communauté économique africaine : examen des scénarios plausibles : études préliminaires des implications d'ordre technique, structurel et institutionnel. Comité de rédaction plénier (2nd session, 13–25 August). Organization of African Unity, Addis Ababa, Ethiopia.

Kouassi, E.K. 1987. Les organisations internationales africaines. Berger Levrault, Paris, France.

Lecourt, R. 1976. *L'Europe des juges.* Bruylant, Brussels, Belgium.

Malam-Kandine, A. 1993. La faiblesse des structures institutionnelles comme frein au processus d'intégration régionale en Afrique de l'Ouest. Presented at the International conference on regional integration in West Africa, 11–15 January, Dakar. IDRC, Dakar, Senegal.

Pinder, J. 1968. Positive and negative integration: some problems of economic union in the EEC. World Today, 3.

Plantey, A. 1980. La négociation internationale : principes et méthodes. Éditions du Centre national de la recherche scientifique, Paris, France.

PTA (1981). Treaty establishing a preferential trade area for Eastern and Southern African states. Lusaka, 21 December.

Quoc Dinh, N.; Daillier, P.; Pellet, A. 1987. Droit international public (3rd ed.). Librairie générale de droit et de jurisprudence, Paris, France.

Sidjanski, D. 1973. Problèmes actuels d'intégration économique : le rôle des institutions dans l'intégration régionale entre pays en voie de développement. United Nations Conference on Trade and Development, New York, NY, USA.

Soldatos, P. 1989. Le système institutionnel et politique des communautés européennes dans un monde en mutation : théorie et pratique. Bruylant, Brussels, Belgium.

World Bank. 1989. Sub-Saharan Africa: from crisis to sustainable growth. World Bank, Washington, DC, USA.

CHAPTER 16

CONSTITUTIONALISM AND ECONOMIC INTEGRATION

– Ominiyi Adewoye –

Adewoye argues that constitutionalism, or the rule of law, is basic to regional integration. The fact that this condition is satisfied in the European case is considered to be one of the important reasons for the success of the European Union. There are several reasons for this relationship. One is that constitutionalist states, accustomed to the separation of powers, more easily accept the transfer of sovereignty to regional institutions. Constitutionalism also ensures the political and social stability necessary to the pursuit of long-term projects such as regional integration. Finally, the rule of law facilitates human interaction among individuals or groups of different nationalities, thanks to the basic freedoms provided and the effective enforcement of contracts. West African states have barely begun instituting constitutionalism as a mode of governance, and it is therefore not surprising that their efforts at economic integration have met with little success. In the author's view, the establishment of a regional tribunal enforcing basic human rights against authoritarian regimes would be a good starting point for the enthronement of constitutionalism and democracy in the subregion.

TODAY THE NATIONS of the world can be divided into two classes: the nations in which the government fears the people, and the nations in which the people fear the government [Amos R.E. Pinchot, cited in Henken 1952, p. 486].

The aim in this chapter is to explore the link between regional integration and constitutionalism. After defining the notion of constitutionalism, we review how its practice and philosophy developed in Europe and its pertinence to the success of the European experience in the area of regional integration. In the second part of the paper, the European experience is contrasted with the African one, with emphasis on the constraints to regional integration resulting from the very different pattern of law and politics observed in Africa.

Constitutionalism denotes a set of principles in the governance of a polity: effective restraints upon the powers of those who govern, the guarantee of individual fundamental rights (ranging from freedom of speech and expression to the right to privacy), the existence of an independent judiciary to enforce these rights, genuine periodic elections by universal suffrage, and the enthronement of the rule of law as reflected in the absence of arbitrariness and the equality of all before the law (de Smith 1964, p. 106; Friedrich 1968; Nwabueze 1973).

In application, constitutionalism penetrates the civic culture and collective consciousness of rulers and ruled alike. It supposes a democratic approach, an attitude of "give-and-take" in public affairs, readiness to accept the limitation of power, a sense of accountability, and readiness to do justice. De Tocqueville wrote that "the spirit of the law which is produced in the schools and courts of justice penetrates beyond their walls into the bosom of society, where it descends to the lowest classes so that at last the whole people contract the habits and tastes of the judicial magistrates" (Westin 1958, p. ii).

CONSTITUTIONALISM IN EUROPE

The philosophy of constitutionalism dates back to the natural law doctrines of the Greek stoics, the medieval church, and the Magna Carta forced on King John of England in 1215. It gained momentum during the 17th century English revolution culminating in the *Bill of Rights* (1689) and the *Act of Settlement* (1701), and was strengthened by the American revolution (1776), the French revolution (1789), and the 1848 revolutions in Europe.

In terms of political practice, there were hints of restraints on governments and an emerging sense of constitutionalism in Western Europe from the 16th century on. Niccolo Machiavelli's picture of political Europe was a land of kings "surrounded by a large number of ancient nobles... [who] have their prerogatives of which the king cannot deprive them without danger to himself" (Machiavelli 1940, pp. 15–16). In his biography of Louis XIV of France, Voltaire (1926, p. 5) said of Europe:

> Already for a long time one could regard Christian Europe (except Russia) as a sort of great *republic* divided into several states, some monarchical, others of a mixed character; the former aristocratic, the latter popular, but all... possessing the same *principles of public and political law* unknown in other parts of the world. [emphasis added]

The same note of an evolving constitutionalist order was sounded by Edmund Burke (1846, p. 119), the 18th century English statesman, in his *Reflections on the Revolution in France*.

The 19th century witnessed remarkable development in constitutionalism in Western Europe. Many countries — Belgium, the Netherlands, the Scandinavian countries, several German kingdoms, Switzerland, Spain, Austria-Hungary, and Italy — fashioned constitutions similar to that of Britain or the United States of America (Friedrich 1968, p. 323). Constitutionalism thus became the battle cry of progressive forces and broadly based popular movements. In the spirit of the age, many European monarchs protected their positions after the 1848 revolutions by "granting constitutions" to their people. Despite their imperfections, such constitutions were checks on arbitrary rule and, to that extent, positive developments in constitutionalism (Friedrich 1968, p. 324).

The egalitarian character of constitutionalism in Europe — the idea that all men should have equal political and social rights — has been a product of social and economic change in the 20th century. This century has witnessed the emergence of universal suffrage, representative government and the rule of law, the development of universal education, the enhancement of the status of the common man before the law, and the enactment of welfare measures of various kinds (Dahrendorf 1964, p. 229).

From the late 19th century on, the institutional autonomy of the legal system was increasingly asserted, the authority of the law applying over that of the state itself.[1] This more liberal perspective on the relationship between law and society in Western Europe was a major step in encouraging meaningful social and political participation. In spite of remaining social differences in many societies, and of national and regional differences, it is fair to say that Western European societies have made tremendous progress in achieving the goal of basic equality of all citizens in the 20th century (Dahrendorf 1964, p. 230).

The rights of citizens have been further buttressed by the unprecedented economic growth in Western Europe since the end of the Second World War. The resulting higher incomes of people have enhanced their independence of outlook as citizens, and, with shorter working hours,

---

[1] This stands in remarkable contrast to the "socialist legality" of the Soviet Union and other socialist countries of Eastern Europe where the legal system was essentially an instrument of state power to give "universal and generally mandatory significance" to the economic, political, and organizational measures carried out in the socialist transformation of society (Alexyev 1990, pp. 12–13). Individuals had rights, but such rights could not override the interests of the state.

more people have been able to participate effectively in the political process.

Ralf Dahrendorf (1964, pp. 232–236) noted four trends in the evolving structure of power in contemporary Europe:

- the institutionalization of political power, with the establishment of limits on the range of discretion of those who govern;

- the establishment of mechanisms to control the exercise of power — these include legislative bodies, periodic elections, a free press, an independent judiciary, and the force of law;

- the separation of roles in the legislation, enforcement, and execution of the law; and

- the growing autonomy of institutions — political parties, economic organizations, churches, professional groupings, women's organizations, trade unions, and the like — all exercising an influence on decision-making processes.

Another trend has been the emergence of what Peter Drucker (1989, ch. 7) has called the "new pluralisms." Since the late 19th century, single-purpose institutions have developed in Western Europe, each with its own mission and considerable autonomy: modern business corporations, the civil service, universities, the professions, and the like. Each of these institutions "perceives its own purpose as central, as an ultimate value, and as the one thing that really matters" (Drucker 1989, p. 84); each has its own language, its own career ladder, and, above all, its own values. Sometimes transcending international boundaries, the new pluralist institutions are veritable power centres, offering citizens the prospects of self-fulfillment even within their limited confines. No longer does "salvation" lie exclusively with the state. These various trends have conditioned the character of constitutionalism in Europe, by diffusing political power to the point that its real location may sometimes be difficult to determine.

CONSTITUTIONALISM AND REGIONAL INTEGRATION IN EUROPE

Constitutionalism has facilitated regional integration in Western Europe by entrenching in each country the notion of a limited state whose will could be subjected to that of a supranational authority in specific areas of activity. This is the fundamental explanation for the success of the European Economic Community (EEC, now the European Union) in establishing and operating its major constituent institutions: the Commission of European Communities, the European Council, the European Parliament, the Court of Justice, and the Court of Auditors. Constitutionalism was so fundamental to the operation of the EEC that Greece, Portugal, and Spain had to throw off the shackles of dictatorship in their domestic politics and rejoin the mainstream of Western European democracy before they could be admitted to membership in the 1980s (EEC 1979).

Constitutionalism or rule of law at the community level manifests itself in various ways and degrees, through *regulations* (which are applied directly throughout the community), *decisions* (which are binding on the member states, companies, or individuals to whom they are addressed), *directives* (which set down compulsory objectives but leave their implementation to the discretion of the member states), or *recommendations and opinions* (which are not binding except where they are equivalent to *directives*) (EEC 1982, p. 7; Ntumba, this volume).

Certain decisions of the European Court of Justice have progressively broadened the jurisprudence underlying the application of community law. Since the 1960s, the court has actively worked to establish an autonomous legal framework for the community distinguishable from the legal orders of the member states, but at the same time prevailing over them (Hurwitz and Lesquesne 1991, p. 45). In the van Gend en Loss case (1963), the court held that the institutions of the EEC were "endowed with sovereign rights" and that the member states have "limited their sovereign rights albeit within limited fields" (Hartley 1986, p. 232). Thus the treaty provisions and all forms of community legislation can give rights directly to the individual without any legislative or executive action by the member states. In the same vein the court has insisted that community law is not foreign law in the member states; "it is valid law of the land and it can directly confer rights on private citizens which must be recognised and enforced by the courts of the member states" (Hartley 1986, p. 232).

The extent to which the European Court of Justice has strengthened the community by its judicial activism is obvious from recent cases. In *Cowan v. Le Trésor public* (1987), the court expanded the scope of article 7 of the Treaty of Rome, which prohibits any discrimination between nationals of the EEC on grounds of nationality (Hurwitz and Lesquesne 1991, p. 51). Ian Cowan, a Briton, was mugged at the exit of a metro station in Paris where he was on vacation. Under French criminal law, victims of assault are entitled to claim compensation before a special judicial commission. The French court held that he was not entitled to state compensation because he neither held a residence permit nor did he come from a country with which France concluded a reciprocity agreement on such matters. Cowan pleaded discrimination before the European court which upheld his submission. The court's reasoning was that Cowan was in France as a tourist receiving services that fell within the ambit of economic activities recognized by the Treaty of Rome. Hence Cowan could invoke article 7 of the treaty to obtain compensation for damage suffered on the same basis as a Frenchman in similar circumstances. Since *Cowan*, it has been said, "anyone receiving a service thereby participates in an economic activity, and can claim Community Law rights (Hurwitz and Lesquesne 1991, p. 52).

Rush Portuguess Limitado v. Office National d'Immigration (ONI) (1990) settled another aspect of economic integration in the EEC — the freedom to provide services across national boundaries. The plaintiff was a construction company engaged in the construction of a railway line in western Paris. The contention arose when, contrary to French labour legislation, the company took its own Portuguese employees to France. The European court ruled in favour of the company on the basis of articles 59 and 60 of the Treaty of Rome. According to the court, the treaty precludes a member state from prohibiting a provider of services established in another member state "from freely travelling within its territory with the whole of its staff or from making the movement of the staff in question subject to restrictive conditions such as a requirement to carry out on-the-spot recruitment or to obtain work permits" (Hurwitz and Lesquesne 1991, p. 55). To impose any restriction on providers of services of other member states would be to discriminate against them in favour of their indigenous competitors in the host country.

Other recent cases adjudicated by the Court of Justice have underscored the importance of article 119 of the Treaty of Rome providing for equal pay without discrimination. In *Rinner Kühn v. FWW Spezial-Gebaüdereinigung GmbH & Co. KG* (1989) the court condemned national rules enabling employers to exclude part-time workers from other member states from enjoying continuity of pay during illness (Hurwitz and Lesquesne 1991, p. 247).

The European court has also developed consistent case law on such issues as protection of human rights, free movement of goods, competition in economic activities, taxation, and the like, even when this has entailed solutions not exactly envisaged in the treaties binding the member states (Hartley 1986, p. 247).

The African situation

The foregoing is a measure of the challenge confronting West Africa in her efforts at economic integration. Constitutionalism is still in its infancy in Sub-Saharan Africa whatever progress may have been made in recent years (Nwabueze 1973; Awolowo 1977). The difficulty of establishing constitutionalism as a mode of governance in black Africa has been compounded by three factors.

First, there is little in African tradition and jurisprudence to reinforce it. Traditionally, African law was intertwined with sociocultural and ethical norms, as a tool of the ruling elite or of those whose duty it was to keep society harmoniously integrated. In general, precolonial Sub-Saharan Africa did not develop what Kiralfy (1958, p. 4) has called a "heritage of legality," not for want of ingenuity, but because the African perception of society was fundamentally different from the European one. Whereas European theories of society tend to emphasize the role of the individual, African societies stress the role of close-knit social formations (Ajayi 1991[2]), and the supremacy of consensus (not law) as the measure for ordering public affairs.

Second, Black Africa's colonial rulers understandably did little to promote constitutionalism. Colonial legislatures in Africa were devoid of any effective voice or responsibility until fairly late in the colonial period, and Africans thus had little opportunity to practice parliamentary democracy. As a case in point, Nigerians had less than a decade of apprenticeship in parliamentary democracy, after approximately 100 years of colonial rule. The same applies to the rest of anglophone Africa, and even more forcibly to francophone areas. Clearly, a decade of participation by Africans in the public affairs of their own countries before achieving political independence could not suffice to develop the collective consciousness of political accountability essential for constitutionalist rule. The rule of law, on which constitutionalism turns, was also not a flourishing legacy at independence. Indeed, the restrictions placed on the practice of the legal profession in anglophone Africa were not removed until toward the close of the colonial era, whereas France positively discouraged the development of a legal elite in her territories. The posture of the colonial judiciary was generally one of self-restraint reflecting a desire to safeguard the interests of the executive — a habit that would persist after independence.

[2] Ajayi, J.F.A. 1991. Tradition in the process of change [unpublished lecture], University of Ibadan.

The third barrier to constitutionalism in Africa was the feeling of urgency about the need for development. Political leaders became victims of their own slogans and promises of the advantages that would follow political autonomy after independence. Africa was suddenly a continent in a hurry. "Development" became the political religion of the ruling elite and a handy excuse for throwing constitutionalism to the winds and stifling the voices of opposition and dissent.

Surveying two decades of political development in Africa in 1982, Jackson and Rosberg (1982, p. 16) wrote that:

> The new African statesman was a personal ruler more than a constitutional and institutional one; he ruled by his ability and skill (as well as the abilities and skills of those he could convince to be his supporters), by his personal power and legitimacy, and not solely by the title granted to him by the office he occupied and the constitution that defined it. Insofar as constitutions remained important features of rule, they were important less as constraints on the abuse of power and more as legal instruments that a personal ruler could amend or rewrite to suit his power needs. In taking such actions the new ruler demonstrated that he regarded himself as being above his office and that the new political system was basically personal and authoritarian.

Few countries in Sub-Saharan Africa were exceptions to authoritarian personal rule. Regimes everywhere were governed less by institutions than by personal manipulation of the ruler and his henchmen, in a system characterized by patron–client ties and by stratagems and conflicts often resolved by expediency, coercion, or violence (Jackson and Rosberg 1982, p. 12).

CONSTITUTIONALISM AND REGIONAL INTEGRATION IN WEST AFRICA

Africa's deficit of constitutionalism has undermined the process of regional integration in several ways. Just as the habit of shared power has facilitated the transition to supranational forms of authority in Europe, so its absence in Africa has undermined that process. The concentration of power in the hands of personal rules in African countries has made the sharing of that power especially difficult, due to the jealousy with which those rulers have guarded their personal fiefdoms.

Politically, a system of governance that is devoid of defined mechanisms and structures of representation or participation undermines the kind of consistent political commitment and long-term legitimacy that regional integration demands, because a change of ruler is sufficient to undermine agreements arrived at by his predecessor. Concentration of power also makes it difficult to promote healthy intergovernmental relations at levels other than the very top. Finally, a system of personal rule precludes the useful role which pressure groups can play in moulding the character and direction of an integration movement, as they did in the development of the European Union (Aziz 1993, pp. 4–5).

Economically, the engine of integration must be the private sector of the national economies — if the experience of Europe is, again, any guide. Peter Drucker's "new pluralisms," referred to earlier, have played no small part in the economic integration of Western Europe. In the form of transnational enterprises, they have been instrumental in knitting Europe's economies together, giving applied meaning to the notions of economic community or of European union. In West Africa, the lack of constitutionalism is impeding the possibility of similar development. The subregion lacks the atmosphere of predictable laws and institutions necessary to the stability and independence of the private sector that explains the success of Europe's transnational enterprises. The absence of predictability and the difficulties associated with contract enforcement, in particular, make regional economic ventures risky. Thus, most indigenous economic institutions and enterprises remain locked within existing national boundaries (Ojo 1993, p. 16), awaiting the day when the subregional atmosphere, in terms of constitutionalist practice, will be conducive to transborder expansion.

The absence of constitutionalist underpinnings also affects the economy in some fairly general ways, with negative consequences for regional integration. Repressive regimes stifle economic, as well as political, initiative. Repression or coercion saps human energy and leads to economic stagnation. Under such conditions, one cannot hope to galvanize the population to productive efforts, or to inspire the citizenry to look beyond the narrow confines of the national state. A constitutionalist framework creates an open society which liberates human energy, enhances creativity, and stimulates competition, to the benefit of the economy. The more developed the economies of a region, the easier it is likely to be for them to integrate, due to the larger number of products and services that can be exchanged, the greater ease of communications and transport, higher levels of education and information, etc. Economic integration thus seems more likely to flourish in the context of economic prosperity such as might be expected to emerge in a constitutionalist environment.

Arbitrary economic policies such as often accompany personal rule discourage the development of long-term economic relations between countries and tend to distort the nature of entrepreneurial activity in favour of rent-seeking behaviour, through smuggling and black market dealings, as both Meagher and Bach show in this volume. Restricted freedoms and arbitrariness at the national level are reflected at the regional level in the form of obstacles to free movement across national borders and regional trade, which are all too often of an arbitrary or extortionary character.

With the tentative wave of democratization and economic liberalization that has spread over much of the region since the late 1980s may come greater progress in the realm of regional integration. The road yet to be traveled is a long one, however, and the political changes we have seen so far are often of limited substance, where they have taken place at all. What is required is not only the trappings of democratic change, but a change of mentality, consistent with constitutional rule, and a better appreciation of the role of the law in modern society.

Two suggestions can be made from a regional perspective. One is to seek a better understanding of the law in different countries and a greater degree of harmonization across linguistic boundaries. West African law schools should consider reinforcing their curriculum through teaching and research of a comparative nature on the legal systems of the subregion. Funding should be mobilized for institutions like the Nigerian Institute of Advanced Legal Studies and similar research centres in the subregion to embark on studies to produce standard laws and practice across linguistic boundaries in specific areas of economic interaction among the peoples of West Africa. Every standardized law on any subject adopted by the states would be a move toward the dream of a virile West African community.

Second, in the struggle for the enthronement of constitutionalism in the subregion, the ECOWAS framework can itself be usefully exploited, through reinforcement of its tribunal. A new kind of tribunal should be set up for the Community, different from the one provided for in article 11 of the 1975 ECOWAS Treaty. Given the rather tentative nature of ECOWAS as fashioned by its founding fathers, no greater function was envisaged for the tribunal than to ensure "the observance of law and justice in the interpretation of the provisions of this Treaty" in settling disputes that may be referred to it by member states (see Ntumba, this volume). Unfortunately, even this limited tribunal has not been established, illustrating the weak commitment of participating governments to any sort of measure capable of undermining national sovereignty.

Given the present precarious state of constitutionalism in West Africa, the sort of tribunal that is required is one that would be empowered to enforce human rights and check abuses of power on the part of governments, in addition to adjudicating issues relating to regional integration. All West African countries are signatories to the African Charter on Human and People's Rights adopted by the 18th Conference of Heads of State and Government of the Organization of African Unity (OAU) in June 1981 in Nairobi. The fact that the Charter has now been given formal recognition in the ECOWAS Revised Treaty (*West Africa*, 19–25 July 1993, p. 1248) is a further step in the right direction.

The next, and more important, step would be to create a tribunal to check on the infringement of the rights so established. The creation of such a tribunal would amount to a partial surrender of sovereignty on the part of participating states and an acceptance of the notion of limited government — the beginning of wisdom in matters of governance. Like the European Court of Justice, the West African tribunal would, in time, develop a stature of its own and contribute substantially to the process of integration in the subregion.

The colonial period offered a precedent for such a tribunal, in Commonwealth West Africa, through the operation of the West Africa Court of Appeal between 1928 and 1954 (Elias 1963, pp. 149–151). In its appellate jurisdiction, it dealt with substantive matters of law, opening up the possibility of the development of West African common law.

Genuine progress can only be made in West Africa in an atmosphere of constitutionalism undergirded by such human values as would promote the full flowering of the human personality. Freedom is basic to development, for it is the key to releasing human energy, whether the goal is building strong national economies or the economic integration of the West African subregion. Constitutionalism was fundamental to the success of regional integration in Europe and will be a necessary ingredient to the success of regional integration in Africa. The current process of democratization and economic liberalization in the subregion moves us in the required direction, and it may be possible to build on that momentum through the creation of a regional tribunal for enforcing basic human rights in the subregion.

REFERENCES

Alexyev, S. 1990. Socialism and law. Progress Publishers, Moscow, Russia.
Aziz, A. 1993. A European view of the opportunities and prospects for regional integration in Africa. Presented at the International conference on regional

integration in West Africa, 11–15 January, Dakar. Economic Commission for Africa, Addis Ababa, Ethiopia. Document E/ECA/CM.17/2.

Awolowo, O. 1977. The problems of Africa. Macmillan, London, UK.

Burke, E. 1846. Works II. Henry G. Bohn, London, UK.

Dahrendorf, R. 1964. Recent changes in the class structure of European societies. Daedalus, Winter.

de Smith, S.A. 1964. The new commonwealth and its constitutions. Stevens & Co., London, UK.

Drucker, P.F. 1989. The new realities. Harper & Row, New York, NY, USA.

EEC (European Economic Community). 1979. The second enlargement of the community. EEC, Brussels, Belgium. Periodical 5(79).

———— 1982. The institutions of the European community. EEC, Brussels, Belgium. European File E, 6(82).

Elias, T.O. 1963. The Nigerian legal system. Routledge & Kegan Paul, London, UK.

Friedrich, C.J. 1968. Constitutions and constitutionalism. In Sills, D.I. (ed.). International encyclopaedia of the social sciences (vol. 3). The Free Press, New York, NY, USA. Pp. 318–325.

Hartley, T.C. 1986. Federalism, courts and the legal systems: the emerging constitution of the European community. American Journal of Comparative Law, 34(2), 229–247.

Hencken, H.L. (ed.). 1952. A new dictionary of quotations. Alfred A. Knopf, New York, NY, USA.

Hurwitz, L.; Lesquesne, C. (ed.). 1991. The state of the European community. Lynne Rienner Publishers, Boulder, CO, USA.

International Commission of Jurists. 1991. Justice in Guinea. The Review, 7 (December), 4–9.

Jackson, R.H.; Rosberg, C.G. 1982. Personal rule in Black Africa. University of Berkeley Press, Berkeley, CA, USA.

Kiralfy, A.R. 1958. Potter's historical introduction to English law and its institutions (4th ed.). Sweet and Maxwell, London, UK.

Legum, C. (ed.). 1970–71, 1972–73, 1974–75, 1975–76. Africa contemporary record. Rex Collings, London, UK.

Machiavelli, N. 1940. The prince and the discourses. The Modern Library, New York, NY, USA.

Nwabueze, B.O. 1973. Constitutionalism in the emergent states. C. Hurst, London, UK. Pp. 1–21.

Ojo, O. 1992. The role of pressure groups in the growth and development of ECOWAS. Presented at the International conference on regional integration in West Africa, 11–15 January, Dakar. Economic Commission for Africa, Addis Ababa, Ethiopia. Document E/ECA/CM.17/2.

Voltaire 1926. The age of Louis XIV (translated by M.P. Pollack). Dent, London, UK.

Welch, C.E. Jr. 1990. Human rights in francophone West Africa. In Naim, A.A.; Deng, F.M. (ed.). Human rights in Africa. Brookings Institute, Washington, DC, USA.

Westin, A.F. 1958. The anatomy of a constitutional law case. Columbia University Press, New York, NY, USA.

LIST OF ACRONYMS

ABN	Niger Basin Authority
ACHPR	African Charter on Human and Peoples' Rights
ACM	Arab Common Market
ACMS	African Centre for Monetary Studies
ACP	Africa, Caribbean and Pacific
ADB	African Development Bank
ADILG	Liptako Gourma Integrated Development Authority
AEC	African Economic Community
AGRHYMET	Regional Centre for Agrometeorology and Operational Hydrology
AIRD	Associates for International Resources and Development
AMCE	African Ministerial Conference on the Environment
AMU	Arab Magreb Union
AOF	Fédération de l'Afrique occidentale française (French West African federation)
ARCT	African Regional Centre for Technology
ASEAN	Association of South East Asian Nations
ASECNA	Agency for the Safety of Aerial Navigation in Africa
BCEAO	Central Bank of West African States
BEAC	Bank of Central African States
CACEU	Central African Customs and Economic Union
CACM	Central American Common Market
CAMES	African and Malagasy Council on Higher Education
CARICOM	Caribbean Community
CARIFTA	Caribbean Free Trade Association
CCCE	Caisse centrale de coopération économique (central fund for economic cooperation)
CEAO	West African Economic Community
CEBV	Communauté économique du bétail et de la viande (economic community for meat and livestock)
CEC	Commission of the European Communities
CEGESTI	Centro de Gestión Technológica e Informática Industrial
CEMAC	Central African Economic and Monetary Union
CEPGL	Economic Community of the Great Lakes Countries
CERPOD	Development Centre for Study and Research on Population
CESAG	Centre africain d'études supérieures en gestion (African centre for management studies)

CFA	African Financial Community
CIDA	Canadian International Development Agency
CIEREA	Conférence des institutions d'enseignement et de recherche économiques et de gestion en Afrique (conference of economics research and training institutions in francophone Africa)
CILSS	Permanent Interstate Committee for Drought Control in the Sahel
CIMA	Conférence interafricaine des marchés d'assurance (inter-African conference on insurance markets)
CIMAO	West African Cement Mill
CINERGIE	Regional Integration Promotion Unit for West and Central Africa
CIPRES	Conférence interafricaine de la prévoyance sociale (inter-African conference on social security)
CIRES	Centre ivoirien de recherches économiques et sociales (Ivoirian centre for social and economic research)
CNRS	Centre national de la recherche scientifique (national centre for scientific research)
CODESRIA	Council for the Development of Economic and Social Research in Africa
COMECON	Council for Mutual Economic Assistance
COMESA	Common Market for East and Southern Africa
COPA	Committee of Agricultural Organizations in the EU
CPA	Common Program of Action
CRES	Regional Centre for Solar Energy
CST	Community Solidarity Tax
CTCA/SCA	Commission for Technical Cooperation in Africa of the Scientific Council for Africa
DAC/OECD	Donor Advisory Committee of the Organization for Economic Cooperation and Development
DFA	Development Fund for Africa
EC	European Community
ECA	United Nations Economic Commission for Africa
ECB	European Central Bank
ECCAS	Economic Community of Central African States (CEEAC)
ECHR	European Convention on Human Rights
ECOWAS	Economic Community of West African States
EEC	European Economic Community
EMS	European Monetary System
EMU	European Monetary Union
ERP	Economic Recovery Plan

ETUC	European Trade Union Confederation
EU	European Union
FCD	Community Development Fund
FDI	Foreign Direct Investment
FOSIDEC	Fonds de solidarité et d'intervention pour le développement de la communauté (solidarity and action fund for the development of the community)
GATT	General Agreement on Tariffs and Trade
GCA	Global Coalition for Africa
IDEP	Institute for Economic Development and Planning
IDRC	International Development Research Centre
IFAN-CAD	Institut fondamental d'Afrique noire-Cheikh Anta Diop (basic research institute of black Africa Cheikh Anta Diop)
IFPRI	International Food Policy Research Institute
IGADD	Intergovernmental Authority on Drought and Development
IGO	Inter-Governmental Organization
IUCN	International Union for the Conservation of Nature and Natural Resources
IM	Institut Marchoux (Marchoux institute)
IMF	International Monetary Fund
INRETS-LET	Institut national de la recherche sur les transports et leur sécurité, laboratoire d'économie des transports (national research institute on transport and safety, transport economics unit)
INSAH	Sahel Institute
IOTA	Institut d'ophtalmologie de l'Afrique de l'Ouest (West African ophthalmology institute)
IRAM	Institut des recherches et d'applications des méthodes de développement (institute for research and application of development methods)
KBO	Organization for the Management and Development of the Kagera River Basin
LAFTA	Latin American Free Trade Association
LARES	Laboratoire d'analyse régionale et d'expertise sociale (centre for regional analysis and social studies)
LAIA	Latin American Integration Association
LCBC	Lake Chad Basin Commission

LPA	Lagos Plan of Action
MERCOSUR	Southern Cone Common Market
MNC	Multinational Corporation
MRU	Mano River Union
NAFTA	North American Free Trade Agreement
NATO	North Atlantic Treaty Organization
NBA	Niger Basin Authority
NGO	Non Governmental Organization
OAU	Organization of African Unity
OCCGE	Coordination and Cooperation Organization for the Control for the Major Endemic Disease
OCLALAV	Organisation commune de lutte anti-acridienne et de lutte anti-aviaire (joint organization for locust and avian pest management)
OECD	Organization for Economic Cooperation and Development
OEM	Original equipment manufacturer
OICMA	Organisation internationale de lutte contre le criquet migrateur africain (international organization for locust control in Africa)
OMVG	Gambia River Development Organization
OMVS	Senegal River Development Organization
PANAFTEL	Pan African Telecommunications Network
PRPB	Benin People's Revolutionary Party
PTA	Preferential Trade Aera for Eastern and Southern African States
PTCI	Programme de troisième cycle interuniversitaire (interuniversity graduate training program in economics for Francophone Africa)
PTZ	Central and East African Preferential Trade Zone
SACU	Southern African Customs Union
SADAOC	Sustainable Food Security in Central West Africa
SADC	Southern African Development Community
SADCC	Southern African Development Coordination Conference
SAP	Structural Adjustment Programme
SELA	Latin American Economic System
SITRASS	Séminaire international sur les transports en Afrique sub-Saharienne (international seminar on transport in Sub-Saharan Africa)
SME	Small and Medium Enterprise

SSA	Sub-Saharan Africa
SYNESCI	Syndicat national des enseignants du secondaire (national union of secondary school teachers)
TCR	Taxe de compensation régionale (regional cooperation tax)
UAM	Union of Africa and Madagascar
UAMCE	Union of Africa and Madagascar for Economic Cooperation
UDEAC	Central African Customs and Economic Union
UDEAO	Union douanière et économique de l'Afrique de l'Ouest
UEMOA	Union économique et monétaire ouest-africaine (West African Monetary and Economic Union)
UIDH	Interafrican Union for Human Rights
UMA	Arab Maghreb Union
UMOA	West African Monetary Union (WAMU)
UNCTAD	United Nation Conference on Trade and Development
UNDP	United Nations Development Program
UNEP	United Nations Environment Program
UNESCO	United Nations Educational Science and Cultural Organization
UNICE	Union of Industrial and Employer's Confederations of Europe
UNIDO	United Nations Industrial Development Organization
UNSO	United Nation Sudano-Sahelian Office
USAID	United States Agency for International Development
UTRAO	Union of West African Road Transporters
WADB	West African Development Bank
WACH	West African Clearing House
WAEA	West African Economics Association
WAEC	West African Examinations Council
WAHC	West African Health Community
WAHO	West African Health Organization
WARDA	West African Rice Development Association
WHO	World Health Organization
WHO-AFRO	World Health Organization – African Regional Office

ABOUT THE AUTHORS

Stanislav Adotevi is Special Advisor to the Executive Director of UNICEF in New York. He has worked for UNICEF since 1981, and was Regional Director in Abidjan between 1988 and 1994. He has a Doctorate in Anthropology, and has held numerous high-level positions in the fields of research and education since 1967. He held positions as Minister of Youth and Information in Benin, Professor of History and Anthropology at the University of Paris, and Visiting Professor in several universities in the US. He is the author of numerous political and literary treatises.

Omoniyi Adewoye is Professor of History, University of Ibadan, Nigeria. He has held positions as Federal Commissioner for Economic Development in Nigeria (1977-1979), first Chairman of the ECOWAS Council of Ministers (1977-1978), and consultant to the United Nations Economic Commission for Africa on economic integration in West Africa (1982-1983). He is the author of books and numerous articles in learned journals on various aspects of law and development in Africa.

Daniel Bach obtained his PhD from St. Anthony's College (Oxford University), and is a researcher with the *Centre national de recherches scientifiques* (CNRS). He is Director of Research and lecturer at the *Centre d'étude d'Afrique noire* of the *Institut d'études politiques* in Bordeaux, and has previously held teaching appointments in Nigeria and Canada. He is currently coordinating a research network on regional integration in Africa. A political scientist, he has published numerous articles on African and African-European international relations. He has a special interest in Nigeria.

Ousmane Badiane is a senior researcher fellow at the International Food Policy Research Institute (IFPRI) and professorial lecturer at the Nitze School of Advanced International Studies (SAIS) of Johns Hopkins University in Washington D.C. He holds a PhD in agricultural economics from the University of Kiel. His main areas of research are regional agricultural trade and domestic marketing in African countries, and he has published a number of articles and books on this subject.

Naceur Bourenane is a staff member of the African Development Bank. He was previously charged with studies and research at the National

Centre for Planning Studies and Analysis in Algeria. He has also been a lecturer and researcher in various institutions of higher learning in Africa, Europe and Latin America. His publications bear mainly on food and agriculture, international cooperation, and regional integration.

Abass Bundu received his D.Phil, specialising in constitutional and international law, from Churchill College, Cambridge. He spent several years with the Commonwealth Secretariat, and was Minister of Agriculture and Natural Resources and Minister of Tourism and Cultural Affairs in Sierra Leone, before serving as Executive Secretary of ECOWAS, from 1989-1993. He became Secretary of State for Foreign Affairs and International Cooperation in Sierra Leone in 1993.

David Cobham is a Senior Lecturer at the Department of Economics in the University of St Andrews. He is a specialist in monetary and macro economics and has published several books in this field.

Cyril Daddieh is Associate Professor of Political Science at Salisbury State University, Maryland. He has published extensively on African subjects, with special emphasis on Ghana and Côte d'Ivoire and foreign policy.

Guy Debailleul is Professor of agricultural economics at Laval University. He is a graduate of the *Institut d'études politiques* in Paris and holds a doctorate in the economics of agricultural development from the *Institut national agronomique de Paris-Grignon*. His main research and teaching interests are in the economics of the environment and sustainable development, with special reference to agriculture and agricultural policy.

Eric Grenon is a professional researcher with Laval University's *Centre Sahel* and Dept. of Agricultural Economics. He holds an MSc in agricultural economics from this same university. He is currently working on the Sahel region, particularly on Burkina Faso and Niger.

Muimana Muende Kalala is a research fellow with the *Centre Sahel* and a lecturer in the Sociology Dept. at Laval University. Agronomist and agricultural economist by training at the MSc level, he also holds a PhD in rural sociology from Laval University. His main research field is natural resource management in the Sahel.

Réal Lavergne is a Senior Program Specialist in the Dakar office of the International Development Research Centre. He holds a PhD in economics from the University of Toronto and has published in the areas of trade and foreign aid policy.

Ntumba Luaba Lumu is Professor of Law at the University of Kinshasa, Zaire. He has a law doctorate from the University of Nancy II, and specializes in regional integration law. His publications include *La Communauté économique européenne et les intégrations régionales des pays en développement*, Brussels: Bruylant, 1990.

Kate Meagher is a Lecturer in Rural Sociology at the Department of Agricultural Economics and Rural Sociology, Ahmadu Bello University, Zaria, Nigeria. She has been conducting field research in Nigeria and Uganda since 1988.

Rohinton Medhora is currently Senior Program Officer with the International Development Research Centre in Ottawa. He has a PhD in economics from the University of Toronto and has published papers on monetary integration and related issues in Africa.

Jeffrey C. Metzel is a Senior Economist with Associates for International Resources and Development (AIRD) in Cambridge Ma. A graduate of The Fletcher School, he has worked extensively on livestock development, irrigation economics, and agricultural production in Senegal, Niger, and the central livestock corridor of West Africa.

Lynn Krieger Mytelka holds a dual appointment as Professor of Political Science at Carleton University in Ottawa and Research Associate at the Université de Paris-X, Nanterre. She has a PhD in international relations and political economy from Johns Hopkins University. She has published widely on industrialization and development, with special attention to technology and political economy.

E.K. Quashigah teaches in the Faculty of Law, University of Nigeria Enugu Campus. His main areas of interest and publication are human rights, constitutional law, jurisprudence, and conflict resolution.

Peter Robson is Professor Emeritus of Economics at the University of St Andrews and is a specialist in development economics and economic integration. His major works include: *Economic integration in Africa* (Allen & Unwin, 1968), *International Economic Integration* (edited, Penguin, 1972), *Integration, Development and Equity: Economic Integration in West Africa* (Allen & Unwin, 1983), and *The Economics of International Integration*, 3rd edition (Allen & Unwin, 1987).

B. Lynn Salinger is a Senior Economist at AIRD, and a graduate of The Fletcher School. Her areas of focus have included agricultural pricing and incentives and international agricultural trade in West and North Africa.

J. Dirck Stryker is President of AIRD. He holds a PhD in Economics from Columbia University and has published widely in the area of trade policy and agricultural development, with particular emphasis on West Africa. He is also Associate Professor of International Economics at The Fletcher School of Law and Diplomacy, at Tufts University.

André Vuillet is a professional researcher with Laval University's *Centre Sahel*, where he is currently working on international migration between the Sahel and the Coast. He is completing his PhD in history and international politics with the *Institut universitaire des hautes études internationales* in Geneva. His areas of special interest include regional integration, migration, and food issues in West Africa.

INDEX